Analyzing Quantitative Data

From Description to Explanation

Analyzing Quantitative Data

From Description to Explanation

Norman Blaikie

SAGE Publications
London • Thousand Oaks • New Delhi

First published 2003

 SAGE Publications Ltd
6 Bonhill Street
London EC2A 4PU

SAGE Publications Inc.
2455 Teller Road
Thousand Oaks, California 91320

SAGE Publications India Pvt Ltd
32, M-Block Market
Greater Kailash – I
New Delhi 110 048

British Library Cataloguing in Publication data

A catalogue record for this book is available from
the British Library

ISBN 0 7619 6758 3
    0 7619 6759 1

Library of Congress Control Number available

Typeset by C&M Digitals (P) Ltd., Chennai, India
Printed in Great Britain The Cromwell Press Ltd, Trowbridge, Wiltshire

In memory of

my father
George Armstrong Blaikie
whose fascination with numbers was infectious

and

my daughter
Shayne Lishman Blaikie
whose logic was impeccable

Contents

Detailed Chapter Contents

List of Figures

List of Tables

Acknowledgements

I am indebted to my early mentors in data analysis, in particular, Charles Gray and Oscar Roberts, for providing this novice researcher with necessary knowledge about which textbooks were usually silent. I am also appreciative of the numerous students who, over many years, have stimulated me to think through the relationship between social science statistics and social research practice.

The data set derived from the sample of residents in the former City of Box Hill, Melbourne, and which has been used to illustrate the data analysis procedures, was produced with the assistance of Malcolm Drysdale, students from the Socio-Environmental Assessment and Policy degree at the RMIT University, and the university's research funding sources. My thanks also go to my wife Catherine for invaluable assistance with the data entry of both of this and the Student sample data set.

Without Chris Rojek's invitation and challenge to write this book, I would never have contemplated committing three years of my life to such a task. I am grateful to Chris, and Kay Bridger at Sage, for their support through the demanding process of its accomplishment. I am particularly indebted to Richard Leigh for not only forcing me to think through some tricky technical issues at the copy-editing stage, but also for computing the statistical tables in Appendix D. The latter enabled me to have accurate tables, in the format that I wanted, and not to have to rely on less suitable existing tables.

Norman Blaikie

Introduction: About the Book

This book is about how to use quantitative data to answer research questions in social research. It is about how to analyze data in the form of a set of variables that have been measured on a collection of individuals or that have been collected about some aspects of social life. This is not a book on statistics, although it covers an array of statistical procedures. It is not a book on research methods, although it deals with some of the methods essential for quantitative social research. It is not a book on how to use statistical software packages, although it refers to such procedures.

Why was it Written?

This is not a book I ever imagined writing. My first reaction when asked to write it was: 'Why do we need another book on statistics or data analysis? Hasn't it all been said already?' Perhaps the reason why so many books continue to be written in this field is that their authors think they can make an improvement to the way students are introduced to a course that most find excruciatingly difficult. This is a worthy aim and was part of my brief. However, the challenge that I was given, and which got me hooked, was to be iconoclastic. I interpreted this to include: challenging unhelpful content and structure that have been taken for granted in successive volumes in the field; being critical of practices that have been perpetuated without having any obvious use to a researcher; and, more particularly, exposing the misuses of certain procedures. Given that I have spent much of my academic career doing just these things in some other areas of my discipline, I could not resist taking up the challenge of putting in writing concerns that I have had about some of the practices in this area of social research.

Like Merton (1968) and Mills (1959), I have been very critical of some forms of mindless empiricism as well as the use of highly sophisticated research techniques that create great gulfs between the researcher and the social reality that is being studied (see, for example, Blaikie, 1977, 1978, 1981). However, in spite of this, I believe that quantitative data analysis is important for certain purposes. But it is not the only form of analysis. There are areas of social research where qualitative methods of data collection and analysis are much more appropriate, if not absolutely essential. The trick is to know which methods to use in which context and for which purpose.

Initially, I set out to cover both quantitative and qualitative data analysis. However, this turned out to be an unmanageable task and a decision was made to concentrate on only quantitative data analysis at this stage.

The key question behind the structure and content of the book has been what students and novice researchers in the social sciences need to know in order to be able to analyze data from group or individual research projects in which they are likely to be involved. In considering what to cover and how to organize it, I decided to abandon tradition in favour of addressing this pragmatic issue. This decision was largely influenced by my experience in teaching a traditional undergraduate course in statistics to students in a degree programme that essentially trained applied social researchers. I kept asking myself what relevance much of the course was likely to have for these students in both the short term and the longer term. What was clearly missing, and had to be covered in other contexts, was practical knowledge about how to actually analyze the results obtained in real research projects.

There was another reason. I had had many unhelpful experiences doing statistics courses when a student. In looking for guidance on how to analyze data, I also found books on statistics extremely unhelpful; books on data analysis were unheard of then. Statistics books seemed to be concerned with issues and procedures that had little to do with the kind of research I was doing. In the end, I had to rely on advice from a few seasoned researchers who had discovered, mainly by trial and error, what was required. So this is the book that I wish had been available when I was a student and novice researcher.

In spite of being competent in basic mathematics, and having earlier earned a living for twelve years in a profession that is based on the use of applied mathematics, I found courses and textbooks on statistics unnecessarily difficult to follow. They used an alienating language, included confusing symbols and covered topics that were largely irrelevant to my needs. I kept asking myself: 'Why am I doing this?'

Courses in statistics are a common requirement in most social science disciplines. Some academics seem to operate on the idea that going through the trauma of doing such a course is a necessary right of passage for each generation of social scientists. If you cannot cope with statistics you are not permitted to call yourself a genuine social scientist. No doubt, an earlier justification for such courses would have been to give social scientific discipline scientific status. This is still true in psychology.

Rather than producing highly trained statisticians, these courses are more likely to produce traumatized and demoralized students. They may also keep potential majors in the disciplines away. Let's face it, programmes in the social sciences usually attract students with limited mathematical ability who are often refugees from high school maths classes. The social sciences are chosen because they are thought to provide a safe haven from the trauma of numbers and symbols. Then a course in statistics appears on the horizon to rekindle the old anxieties. What these students need is to be given confidence that they can do basic analysis, and that they can understand what is required and why. In any case, most of what is learned in these courses is quickly forgotten unless it has direct relevance to real research activities.

There is no point in expecting undergraduates to master what is normally covered in statistics texts if they are unlikely to ever use it. While it might be nice to know the theory behind statistical procedures, such as probability theory and the method of least squares, as well as the intricate details of many complex equations, what most students need is to know what methods to use for analyzing certain kinds of data, and why. Most of their requirements are pretty basic, or can be kept basic by addressing research questions in a manageable way.

In my experience, teachers of courses in statistics fall into two main categories. There are those who treat mathematically challenged students as imbeciles and delight in inflicting great stress and discomfort on them. I have encountered a few of these. On the other hand, there are those who try very hard to make statistics intelligible to students whose mathematical abilities are minimal or who have already convinced themselves that it is just too difficult for them.

I suspect some of my readers will suffer from the common malady of 'symbol phobia'. Presented with a simple equation, such as $a + b = c$, your eyes will glaze over. Or perhaps, like the well-known Indian writer, R.K. Narayan, you suffer from what he called 'figure-blindness'. In his essay on 'Higher mathematics', he argued that it is inappropriate to describe arithmetic as elementary mathematics. In his experience, arithmetic has more terrors than algebra and geometry:

> My mind refuses to work when it encounters numbers. Everything that has anything to do with figures is higher mathematics to me. There is only one sort of mathematics in my view and that is the higher one. To mislead young minds by classifying arithmetic as elementary mathematics has always seemed to me as a base trick. A thing does not become elementary by being called so. ... However elementary we may pretend arithmetic to be, it ever remains puzzling, fatiguing and incalculable. (Narayan, 1988: 11)

Well, this book contains symbols, but only very basic ones, and requires competence in basic arithmetic. However, many of the conventions used in statistics texts are avoided, often by expressing symbols in words. This strategy may upset some of the purists – although even they do not always agree on which symbols to use – but I am prepared to risk this in order to take some of the mystique out of reasonably simple ideas.

Who is it for?

Analyzing Quantitative Data is intended for students in the social sciences. It is designed to meet the needs of average undergraduate and most postgraduate students, and to do this in a way that relates directly to the business of doing social research. The book can be used in courses on quantitative data analysis where such courses complement others on data-gathering techniques. It could be used in a broad-ranging course on research methods when this encompasses methods of both data gathering and data analysis. Where degree programmes have a research practicum, with either individual or group projects, this book should be a useful companion for students doing quantitative research.

The book will also be a useful reference for postgraduate students who are required to undertake a major or minor quantitative research project. For many students, this is the first opportunity to undertake their own research. It usually involves designing a project from scratch (see Blaikie, 2000), collecting data, analyzing it and then writing a thesis or major report. Among many other things, the design stage requires decisions to be made about the methods of data analysis to be used, and then later the analysis will need to be undertaken. When quantitative analysis is involved, based on a set of variables and a substantial sample, this book should help smooth the way.

While I have written the book with sociologists in mind, it will be useful for a range of social science and related disciplines. In fact, it will be useful for anyone who is required to undertake social research. This includes researchers from fields such as political science, social psychology, human geography, urban studies, education, nursing, business studies, management, mass communications, environmental studies and social work. It may also be useful for some kinds of research in economics and other areas of psychology.

Analyzing Quantitative Data will also be useful for novice social researchers anywhere. Academics outside the social sciences, as well as employees in the public and private sectors, may be called on to undertake social research of some kind. Alternatively, they may not be required to actually do any research but may need to commission someone else to do it, to oversee such research, or to evaluate research produced by social scientists. The book will be a useful reference.

What Makes it Different?

There are a number of features of the book that make it different from most if not all books presently available in this field. First, two classification schemes are used to organize the discussion of the many methods of data analysis. One is the type of analysis, and the other is the level of measurement. Types of analysis are classified as *univariate description*, *bivariate description* (association), *explanation* and *inference*. The levels of measurement are divided into two broad categories, *categorical* and *metric*, the former subdivided into *nominal* and *ordinal* levels, the latter into *interval* and *ratio* levels. These categories will be explained in due course. Each of the four key chapters (3–6) deals with one type of analysis, and each chapter is subdivided into sections that deal with the different levels of measurement. The reason for this is that different methods of analysis are appropriate for each type of analysis as well as for the different levels of measurement within each type. Keeping these distinctions clear should make the purpose of the wide array of procedures easier to understand and to select. Surprisingly, this scheme appears to be rather novel.[1]

Second, all the methods of analysis are illustrated and discussed in the context of a real research problem. In many ways, the whole book simulates the kind of considerations and processes social researchers are likely to have to go through in analyzing their data. This approach to statistics, let alone data analysis, is extremely rare.[2] Two data sets from a research programme are used throughout the book. The data sets are typical of those obtained from small to moderate-sized social surveys. Both are from my research programme on environmentalism and cover the same variables. While the research topic is specific, the methods of analysis are universal. They can certainly be generalized to almost any study on the relationship between attitudes (or worldviews) and behaviour.

The data sets will be explained in Chapter 2, analyses of certain variables will be used as examples in Chapters 3–7, and in Chapter 8 a set of research questions are answered using these data with the appropriate procedures. The book takes the reader through a wide range of methods of analysis, illustrates their application with the two data sets, and concludes by putting the methods into practice in a 'real' research project.

Third, the nature of data, particularly quantitative data, is discussed rather than being taken for granted. What is accepted as being appropriate and reliable data is dependent on the ontological and epistemological assumptions that are adopted. These issues are clearly ignored in most if not all textbooks on research methods, data analysis and statistics. This will be addressed in Chapter 1.

Fourth, in addition to being concerned with the nature of data and the appropriate procedures for analyzing them, the use of the two data sets provides an excellent opportunity to combine data analysis with the interpretation of the products. In fact, in the process of answering the set of research questions in Chapter 8, it is also necessary to interpret the results. Therefore, not only will the illustrations be set in the context of real research, but also the results will have to be interpreted within this context. This extremely important aspect of data analysis is generally missing in most textbooks because the illustrations do not have a consistent context from which they are drawn.

Fifth, this is a software-free textbook. There is a growing trend in textbooks on statistics and data analysis to include instruction on how to do the various methods of analysis using one of the popular statistical software packages, such as SPSS or Minitab. If you require such a book you could consult examples such as Bryman and Cramer (1997), Fielding and Gilbert (2000), Field (2000) and Foster (2001). I have decided not to follow this trend for a number of reasons. First, while a software package such as SPSS is very popular, it is possible that you may be required to or choose to use some other software. Second, software packages are updated regularly, and this can include changes to the screen layouts. A textbook based on a particular version will soon become out of date, or would need to be revised frequently. Third, there is a common temptation to go straight to the software package without first understanding the various procedures and why they are used. Hence, this book focuses on the principles behind the procedures, on the procedures themselves, and on the purposes for which they should be used. It is not difficult to learn how to use a software package; I have found a three-hour workshop sufficient to introduce students to the setting up of a database, to entering data and to doing basic analysis. It should not be difficult to relate what is learnt in such a course, or from a suitable book, to what is covered in this book. Frankly, if you know what it is that you need to be doing, most statistical software packages are now sufficiently user-friendly for any moderately competent user to find their way about without much difficulty. In SPSS, for example, it is just a matter of finding the appropriate pull-down menu and then the method of analysis that you need. Selecting the appropriate statistics is an easy matter – that is, if you know what you should be doing. However, I have made one gesture in the direction of software. Appendix C sets out the basic steps that are used in recent versions of SPSS to carry out most of the procedures covered in the book.

The sixth difference is not as critical as the previous ones. It refers to the fact that the book is about methods of data analysis, not statistics as such. It is intended for practitioners, not just to satisfy course requirements. It is designed to complement courses and textbooks that concentrate on methods of data collection by providing a wide review of how quantitative data can be handled in the pursuit of answers to research questions. However, it does not shy away from a consideration of the equations that are used in the more basic procedures.

What are the Controversial Issues?

The following icons of social research are challenged and are either modified or destroyed in the following chapters:[3]

1. That social research must begin with one or more hypotheses.
2. That tests of significance are an essential feature of data analysis.
3. That measures of association provide explanations.

The following case will be made about the first issue:

- All social research must start out with one or more research questions.
- There are three types of research questions: 'what' questions seek descriptions; 'why' questions seek explanations; and, 'how' questions seek intervention for change.
- Only 'why' questions that are being answered with the aid of theory require the use of hypotheses.
- In any case, there are two types of hypotheses: theoretical hypotheses are derived from theory to provide tentative answers to 'why' questions; statistical hypotheses are used in the process of generalizing data from a random sample to the population from which the sample was drawn.
- A great deal of confusion is created by a general lack of recognition of the differences between these two types of hypotheses.
- Theoretical hypotheses are only relevant when certain types of 'why' questions need to be answered, and statistical hypotheses are only relevant when data come from a random sample. While some research may require both types of hypotheses, other research may require only one type, and a great deal of research requires neither type. However, all research requires research questions.

- Some research, of the theory-generating variety, ends up with hypotheses or theory rather than staring out with them.

Tests of significance are probably the most misunderstood and misused aspect of data analysis. The following argument is made about their use:

- Tests of significance can provide no help to a researcher in making decisions about the importance or meaning of research results.
- They are not measures of association.
- They are only appropriate when statistical hypotheses are being tested, that is, when population parameters are being inferred from sample statistics.
- They can only be used with sample data that are derived from a population using probability procedures.
- They are inappropriate when samples are drawn using non-probability procedures or when data come from a population; performing this statistical ritual in these circumstances has absolutely no meaning.
- They cannot be used to test theoretical hypotheses, although, in some circumstances, they may be used as a stepping-stone on the way to such testing, that is, when probability samples are being used.
- They are no help in generalizing beyond the population selected for study; further generalization is a matter of judgement based on other kinds of evidence.

The third issue is now well recognized but still causes confusion. It is concerned with the purpose of establishing correlations between variables:

- Descriptive research consists of establishing characteristics of particular phenomena, trends in these characteristics over time and patterns in the connections between phenomena.
- Measures of association establish the strength of patterns or connections between variables; they are an elaborate form of description.
- While such description may provide some understanding of phenomena and, some would argue, provide a basis for making predictions, they cannot answer 'why' questions.
- However, such patterns have to be established before explanation can be undertaken.
- Explanation tells us why patterns or trends exist.

These arguments indicate the position I have taken on some of the common misunderstandings in data analysis.

What is the Best Way to Read this Book?

The answer is simple: start at the beginning and work through to the end. The topics covered chapter by chapter build on each other. There is a developmental progression from the most elementary forms of analysis to the more complex. In addition, themes and arguments also run through the chapters. Without an overview of these, it will be very easy to take any method of analysis out of context.

I am aware that many students approach books just to find a specific concept or topic. Once the knowledge and skills dealt with in this book have been mastered, this 'dipping in' approach will no doubt be appropriate when it is necessary to be refreshed about specific types of analysis. If this is the only way the book is used, it will still be useful. However, an understanding of the 'bigger picture' is necessary to avoid making incorrect selections or interpretations of methods of data analysis.

What is Needed to Cope with it?

To understand data analysis successfully, it is very useful to have or to be able to develop a fascination with numbers, to:

- enjoy manipulating them to find answers;
- be able to understand what they are telling you; and
- have a sense of when they appear to be correct or not.

Of course, you need to have some basic numerical skills, to be able to add, subtract, multiply and divide, and you need to be able to understand the conventions used in mathematical equations, to know how to enter data into them and how to manipulate them. A short refresher course on these skills is included in the first part of Chapter 3.

To undertake data analysis in a mechanical and cookbook fashion can be not only unsatisfying but also dangerous. It is important to be able to understand when certain procedures should be used and what they are designed to achieve. It is also helpful to be able to understand what principles are involved and why certain requirements must be satisfied. I cannot guarantee that after reading through and working with this book you will feel completely confident about these things. This will only come with practical experience.

Lastly, I am not a statistician, although I have great admiration for such experts. I am a sociologist who, among other things, does social research and teaches courses on epistemology and a wide range of social research methods. As a teacher, I am constantly challenged with the task of helping students, particularly postgraduate students, to think like researchers, to develop a research imagination. This requires being able to conceptualize a problem and to design a research project that will address it. This challenge has led to two earlier books, one on the philosophy of social research, in particular on the strategies or logics of enquiry that can be used in the social sciences (Blaikie, 1993a), and the other on the many decisions that need to be considered in designing such a project (Blaikie, 2000). *Analyzing Quantitative Data* is a logical extension of these two. My task is to try to take the mystery and anxiety out of the analysis stage of social research without trivializing it in the process; to be simple but not simplistic. I shall have to leave the reader to be the judge of whether I have been successful.

Notes

[1]Cramer (1994) goes some way in this direction by identifying levels of measurement clearly but types of analysis less clearly.

[2]Some attempts have been made to use data from a particular source to illustrate the procedures. For example, Babbie et al. (2000) use data from the United States General Social Survey to explore issues. Bryman and Cramer (1997) use two projects to illustrate some procedures, and de Vaus (1995) goes partly in this direction with a chapter in which data from one of the author's own studies are used to provide an overview of the methods that have been discussed. While these are all helpful approaches to data analysis, the first example uses a data set that most individual researchers are unlikely to produce themselves, and the other two examples do not explore a data set consistently throughout the book.

[3]In order to discuss these, it is necessary to use some technical concepts that will not be elaborated until later chapters. Therefore, the discussion in this section is intended for readers who have at least some basic familiarity with the concepts of statistics.

Social Research and Data Analysis:
Demystifying Basic Concepts

Introduction

This book is about the *analysis* of certain kinds of *data*, that is, only *quantitative* data. We need to begin by discussing the three concepts that make up the main title of this book. The core concept is 'data'. On the surface, it appears to be a simple and unproblematic idea. However, lurking behind it are complex and controversial philosophical and methodological issues that need to be considered. This concept is qualified by the adjective 'quantitative', thus indicating that only one of the two main types of data in the social sciences will be discussed. Just what constitutes 'quantitative' data will be clarified. The purpose of the book is to discuss methods of 'analysis' used in the social sciences, methods by which research questions can be answered. The variety of methods that are available for basic analysis will be reviewed.

This chapter deals with three fundamental questions:

- What is the purpose of social research?
- What are data?
- What is data analysis?

The chapter begins with a discussion of the role of research objectives, research questions and hypotheses in achieving the purpose of research. This is followed by a consideration of the relationship between social reality and the data we collect, and of the types and forms of these data. Included is a discussion of 'concepts' and 'variables', the ways in which concepts can be measured, and the four levels of measurement. The chapter concludes with a review of the four main types of data analysis that are covered in subsequent chapters.[1] Let us start with the first question.

What is the Purpose of Social Research?

The aim of all scientific disciplines is to advance knowledge in their field, to provide new or better understanding of certain phenomena, to solve intellectual puzzles and/or to solve practical problems. Therefore, the critical issues for any discipline are the following:

- What constitutes scientific knowledge?
- How does scientific knowledge differ from other forms of knowledge?
- How do we judge the status of this knowledge? With what criteria?
- How do we produce new knowledge or improve existing knowledge?

In order to solve both intellectual and practical puzzles, researchers have to answer questions about *what* is going on, *why* it is happening and, perhaps, *how* it could be different. Therefore, to solve puzzles it is necessary to pose and answer questions.

The Research Problem

A social research project needs to address a *research problem*. In order to do this, research questions have to be stated and research objectives defined; together they turn a research problem into something that can be investigated. Throughout this book the following research problem will be addressed: *the apparent lack of concern about environmental issues among many people and the unwillingness of many to act responsibly with regard to these issues*. This is a very broad problem. In order to make it researchable, it is necessary to formulate a few research questions that can be investigated. These questions will be elaborated in Chapter 2. In the meantime, to illustrate the present discussion, let us examine two of them here:

- To what extent is environmentally responsible behaviour practised?
- Why are there variations in the levels of environmentally responsible behaviour?

Each research question entails the pursuit of a particular research objective.

Research Objectives

One way to approach a research problem is through a set of *research objectives*. Social research can pursue many objectives. It can explore, describe, understand, explain, predict, change, evaluate or assess aspects of social phenomena.

- To *explore* is to attempt to develop an initial rough description or, possibly, an understanding of some social phenomenon.
- To *describe* is to provide a detailed account or the precise measurement and reporting of the characteristics of some population, group or phenomenon, including establishing regularities.

- To *explain* is to establish the elements, factors or mechanisms that are responsible for producing the state of or regularities in a social phenomenon.
- To *understand* is to establish reasons for particular social action, the occurrence of an event or the course of a social episode, these reasons being derived from the ones given by social actors.
- To *predict* is to use some established understanding or explanation of a phenomenon to postulate certain outcomes under particular conditions.
- To *change* is to intervene in a social situation by manipulating some aspects of it, or by assisting the participants to do so, preferably on the basis of established understanding or explanation.
- To *evaluate* is to monitor social intervention programmes to assess whether they have achieved their desired outcomes, and to assist with problem solving and policy-making.
- To *assess social impacts* is to identify the likely social and cultural consequences of planned projects, technological change or policy actions on social structures, social processes and/or people.

The first five objectives are characteristic of *basic research*, while the last three are likely to be associated with *applied research*. Both types of social research deal with problems: basic research with theoretical problems, and applied research with social or practical problems. Basic research is concerned with advancing fundamental knowledge about the social world, in particular with description and the development and testing of theories. Applied research is concerned with practical outcomes, with trying to solve some practical problem, with helping practitioners accomplish tasks, and with the development and implementation of policy. Frequently, the results of applied research are required immediately, while basic research usually has a longer time frame.

A research project may pursue just one of these objectives or perhaps a combination of them. In the latter case, the objectives are likely to follow a sequence. For example, the four research objectives of *exploration, description, explanation* and *prediction* can occur as a sequence in terms of both the stages and the increasing complexity of research. *Exploration* may be necessary to provide clues about the patterns that need to be described in a particular phenomenon. *Exploration* usually precedes *description*, and *description* is necessary before *explanation* or *prediction* can be attempted. Whether all four objectives are pursued in a particular research project will depend on the nature of the research problem, the circumstances and the state of knowledge in the field.

The core of all social research is the sequence that begins with the *description* of characteristics and patterns in social phenomena and is followed by an *explanation* of why they occur. Descriptions of what is happening lead to questions or puzzles about why it is happening, and this calls for an explanation or some kind of understanding. The two research questions stated in the previous subsection illustrate these two research objectives. To be able to explain why people differ in their level of environmentally responsible behaviour, we need to first describe the range in levels of this behaviour. The first question is concerned with description and the second with explanation.

Research Questions

To pursue such objectives, social researchers need to pose *research questions*. Research questions define the nature and scope of a research project. They:

- focus the researcher's attention on certain puzzles or issues;
- influence the scope and depth of the research;
- point towards certain research strategies and methods of data collection and analysis;
- set expectations for outcomes.

Research questions are of three main types: 'what' questions, 'why' questions and 'how' questions:

- 'What' questions seek descriptive answers.
- 'Why' questions seek understanding or explanation.
- 'How' questions seek appropriate interventions to bring about change.

All research questions can and perhaps should be stated as one of these three types. To do so helps to make the intentions of the research clear. It is possible to formulate questions using different words, such as, 'who', 'when', 'where', 'which', 'how many' or 'how much'. While questions that begin with such words may appear to have different intentions, they are all versions of a 'what' question: 'What individuals …', 'At what time …', 'At what place …', 'In what situations …', 'In what proportion …' and 'To what extent …'. Similarly, some questions that begin with 'what' are actually 'why' questions. For example, 'What makes people behave this way?' seeks an explanation rather than description. It needs to be reworded as: 'Why do people behave this way?'.

Each research objective requires the use of a particular type of research question or, in a few cases, two types of questions. Most research objectives require 'what' questions: *exploration*, *description*, *prediction*, *evaluation* and *impact assessment*. It is only the objectives of *understanding* and *explanation*, and possibly *evaluation* and *impact assessment*, that require 'why' questions. 'How' questions are only used with the objective of *change* (see Table 1.1). Returning to our two research questions, the first is a 'what' question that seeks a descriptive answer, and the second is a 'why' question that asks for an explanation.

The Role of Hypotheses

It is a commonly held view that research should be directed towards testing *hypotheses*. While some types of social research involve the use of hypotheses, in a great deal of it hypotheses are either unnecessary or inappropriate. Clearly stated, hypotheses can be extremely useful in helping to find answers to 'why' questions. In fact, it is difficult to answer a 'why' question without having some ideas about where to look for the answer. Hence, hypotheses provide possible answers to 'why' questions.

Table 1.1   *Research questions and objectives*

Research objectives	Research questions		
	What	Why	How
Exploration	✓		
Description	✓		
Explanation		✓	
Understanding		✓	
Prediction	✓		
Intervention			✓
Evaluation	✓	✓	
Assess impacts	✓	✓	

In some types of research, hypotheses are developed at the outset to give this direction; in other types of research, the hypotheses may evolve as the research proceeds. When research starts out with one or more hypotheses, they should ideally be derived from a theory of some kind, preferably expressed in the form of a set of propositions. Hypotheses that are plucked out of thin air, or are just based on hunches, usually make limited contributions to the development of knowledge because they are unlikely to connect with the existing state of knowledge.

Hypotheses are normally not required to answer 'what' questions. Because 'what' questions seek descriptions, they can be answered in a relatively straightforward way by collecting relevant data. For example, a question such as 'What is the extent of recycling behaviour among university students?' requires specification of what behaviour will be included under 'recycling' and how it will be measured. While previous research and even theory may help us decide what behaviour is relevant to this concept, there is no need to hypothesize about the extent of this behaviour in advance of the research being undertaken. The data that are collected will answer the question. On the other hand, to answer the question 'Why are some students regular recyclers?' it would be helpful to have a possible answer to test, that is, a hypothesis.

This *theoretical* use of hypotheses should not be confused with their *statistical* use. The latter tends to dominate books on research methods and statistics. As we shall see later, a great deal of research is conducted using samples that are drawn from much larger populations. There are many practical benefits in doing this. If such samples are drawn using statistically random procedures, and if the response rate is very high, a researcher may want to generalize the results found in a sample to the population from which the sample was drawn. Statistical hypotheses perform a role in this generalization process, in making decisions about whether the characteristics, differences or relationships found in a sample can be expected to also exist in the population. Such hypotheses are *not* derived from theory and are *not* tentative answers to research questions. Their function is purely statistical. When research is conducted on a population or a non-random sample, there is no role for statistical hypotheses. However, theoretical hypotheses are relevant in *any* research that requires 'why' questions to be answered.

What are Data?

In the context of social research, the concept of *data* is generally treated as being unproblematic. It is rare to find the concept defined and even rarer to encounter any philosophical consideration of its meaning and role in research. Data are simply regarded as something we collect and analyze in order to arrive at research conclusions.

The concept is frequently equated with the notion of 'empirical evidence', that is, the products of systematic 'observations' made through the use of the human senses. Of course, in social research, observations are made mainly through the use of sight and hearing.

The concept of *observation* is used here in its philosophical sense, that is, as referring to the use of the human senses to produce 'evidence' about the 'empirical' world. This meaning needs to be distinguished from the more specific usage in social research where it refers to methods of data collection that use the sense of sight. In this latter method, 'looking' is distinguished from other major research activities such as 'listening', 'conversing', 'participating', 'experiencing', 'reading' and 'counting'. All of these activities are involved in the philosophical meaning of 'observing'.

Observations in all sciences are also made with the use of instruments, devices that extend the human senses and increase their precision. For example, a thermometer can measure temperature far more precisely and consistently than can the human sense of touch. Its construction is based on notions of hot and cold, more and less, and of an equal interval scale. In short, it has built into it many assumptions and technical ideas that are used to extend differences that can be experienced by touch. Similarly, an attitude scale, consisting of an integrated set of statements to which responses are made, provides a more precise and consistent measure than, say, listening to individuals discussing some issue.

The notion of *empirical evidence* is not as simple as it might seem. It entails complex philosophical ideas that have been vigorously contested. These disagreements centre on different claims that are made about:

- what can be observed;
- what is involved in the act of observing;
- how observations are recorded;
- what kinds of analysis can be done on them; and
- what the products of these observations mean.

There are a number of important and related issues involved in the act of observing. One concerns assumptions that are made about what it is that we observe. A second issue has to do with the act of observing, with the connection between what impinges on the human senses and what it is that produces those impressions. A third issue is concerned with the role of the observer in the process of observing. Can reality be observed directly or can we only observe its 'surface' features? Is it reality that we observe, or do we simply process some mental construction of it? Does what we observe represent what actually exists, or, in the process of observing, do we have to interpret the physical sensations in order to make them meaningful? Can we observe objectively, that is, without contaminating the impressions received by our senses, or does every act of observing also involve a process of interpretation? These are the kinds of complex issues that lie behind the generation of data. Consciously or unconsciously, every social researcher takes a stand on these issues. The position adopted is likely to be that of the particular research tradition or paradigm within which the researcher has been socialized and/or has chosen to work.

The issue of 'objectivity' is viewed differently in these research traditions. In some traditions it is regarded as an ideal towards which research should strive. It is assumed that a conscientious and well-trained researcher can achieve a satisfactory level of objectivity. The 'problem' of objectivity is dealt with by establishing rules for observing, for collecting data. In other traditions, 'objectivity' is regarded as not only being unattainable but also as being meaningless. In these traditions, the emphasis is on producing 'authentic' accounts of the social reality described by social actors rather than accurate representations of some external reality.

Collecting any kind of data involves processes of interpretation. We have to 'recognize' what we see, we have to 'know' what it is an example of, and we may have to 'relate' it to or 'compare' it with other examples. These activities require the use of concepts, both lay and technical, and whenever we use concepts we need to use meanings and definitions. For example, if we identify a particular interaction episode as involving conflict, the observer needs to have a definition of conflict and to be able to recognize when a sequence of behaviour fits with the definition. Incidents of conflict do not come with labels attached; the observer (with technical concepts) or, perhaps, the participants (with lay concepts) must do the labelling. Defining concepts and labelling social activities are interpretative processes that occur against the background of the observer's assumptions and prior knowledge and experiences. Data collected about, say, the frequency of conflict between parents and children will have been 'manufactured' by a particular researcher. While a researcher may follow rules, criteria and procedures that are regarded by her research community as being appropriate, such rules etc. are simply agreements about how research should be done and cannot guarantee 'pure' uncontaminated data. What they can achieve is comparable data between times, places and researchers.

Data and Social Reality

All major research traditions regard data as providing information about some kind of social phenomenon, and an individual datum as relating to some aspect of that phenomenon. Just what the relationship is between the data and the phenomenon depends to a large extent on the assumptions that are made about the nature of social reality, that is, the *ontological assumptions*. In turn, the procedures that are considered to be appropriate for generating data about that phenomenon depend on the assumptions that are made about how that social reality can be known, that is, the *epistemological assumptions*.

One major research tradition assumes that social reality is external to the people involved: that it is the context in which their activities occur; and that it has the capacity to constrain their actions. Knowledge of this reality can be obtained by establishing a bridge to it by the use of concepts and their measurement. Concepts identify aspects of the reality and instruments are designed to collect data relevant to the concepts. In this way, data are supposed to represent aspects of, or what is going on in, some part of reality. Only those aspects that can be measured are regarded as relevant to research. This tradition is associated with *positivism* and *critical rationalism*, and its data-gathering procedures are mainly quantitative.

A second research tradition adopts different ontological assumptions. In this case, reality is assumed to consist of layers or domains. The 'surface' or empirical layer can be observed in much the same way as the tradition just described. However, reality also has an 'underlying' layer that cannot usually be observed directly. This is the 'real' layer consisting of the structures and mechanisms that produce the regularities that can be observed on the surface. Knowledge of this 'real' layer can only be gained by constructing imaginary models of how these structures and mechanisms might operate. Then, knowing what kinds of things are worth looking for, painstaking research will hopefully produce evidence for their existence, and perhaps will eventually expose them to the surface layer. This position is known as *scientific realism*, and it uses a variety of quantitative and qualitative data-gathering procedures.

A third major research tradition adopts yet another set of ontological assumptions. Social reality is regarded as a social construction that is produced and reproduced by social actors in the course of their everyday lives. It consists of intersubjectively shared, socially constructed meaning and knowledge. This social reality does not exist as an independent, objective world that stands apart from social actors' experience of it. Rather, it is the product of the processes by which social actors together negotiate the meanings of actions and situations. It consists of mutual knowledge – meanings, cultural symbols and social institutions. Social reality is the symbolic world of meanings and interpretations. It is not some 'thing' that may be interpreted in different ways; it *is* those interpretations. However, because these meanings are intersubjective, that is, they are shared, they both facilitate and constrain social activity. With these ontological assumptions, knowledge of social reality can only be achieved by collecting social actors' accounts of *their* reality, and then redescribing these accounts in social scientific language. This position is known as *interpretivism* or *social constructionism*, and its data-gathering procedures are mainly qualitative.

This book is concerned with the first of these traditions.

Types of Data

An important issue in social research is the extent to which a researcher is removed from the phenomenon under investigation. Any 'observer' is, by definition, already one step removed from any social phenomenon by dint of the fact of viewing it from the 'outside'. This means that the processes involved in 'observing' require degrees of interpretation and manipulation. Even data generated first-hand by a researcher have already been subjected to some processing. As we have seen, there is no such thing as 'pure' data. However, not all data are first-hand. A researcher may use data that have been collected by someone else, either in a raw form or analyzed in some way. Hence, social research can be conducted that is more than one step removed from the phenomenon.

This notion of distance from the phenomenon can be categorized into three main types: primary, secondary and tertiary. *Primary data* are generated by a researcher who is responsible for the design of the study and the collection, analysis and reporting of the data. These 'new' data are used to answer specific research questions. The researcher can describe why and how they were collected. *Secondary data* are the raw data that have already been collected by someone else, either for some general information purpose, such as a government census or another official purpose, or for a specific research project. In both cases, the purpose in collecting such data may be different from that of the secondary user, particularly in the case of a previous research project. *Tertiary data* have been analyzed by either the researcher who generated them or an analyst of secondary data. In this case the raw data may not be available, only the results of this analysis.

While primary data can come from many sources, they are characterized by the fact that they are the result of direct contact between the researcher and the source, and that they have been generated by the application of particular methods by the researcher. The researcher, therefore, has control of the production and analysis, and is in a position to judge their quality. This judgement is much more difficult with secondary and tertiary data.

Secondary data can come from the same kind of sources as primary data; the researcher is just another step removed from it. The use of secondary data is often referred to as secondary analysis. It is now common for data sets to be archived and made available for analysis by other researchers. Such data sets constitute the purest form of secondary data. Most substantial surveys have potential for further analysis because they can be interrogated with different research questions.

> Secondary information consists of sources of data and other information collected by others and archived in some form. These sources include government reports, industry studies, archived data sets, and syndicated information services as well as traditional books and journals found in libraries. Secondary information offers relatively quick and inexpensive answers to many questions and is almost always the point of departure for primary research. (Stewart and Kamis, 1984: 1)

While there are obvious advantages in using secondary data, such as savings in time and cost, there are also disadvantages. The most fundamental drawback stems from the fact that this previous research was inevitably done with different aims and research questions. It may also have been based on assumptions, and even prejudices, which are not readily discernible, or which are inconsistent with those a researcher wishes to pursue. Secondly, there is the possibility that not all the areas of interest to the current researcher may have been included. Thirdly, the data may be coded in an inconvenient form. Fourthly, it may be difficult to judge the quality of secondary data; a great deal has to be taken on faith. A fifth disadvantage for some research stems from the fact that the data may be old. There is always a time lag between collection and reporting of results, and even longer before researchers are prepared to archive their data sets. Even some census data may not be published until at least two years after they were collected. However, this time lag may not be a problem in historical, comparative or theoretical studies.

With tertiary data, the researcher is even further removed from the social world and the original primary data. Published reports of research and officially collected 'statistics' invariably include tables of data that have summarized, categorized or have involved the manipulation of raw data. Strictly speaking, most government censuses report data of these kinds, and access to the original data set may not be possible. When government agencies or other bodies do their own analysis on a census, they produce genuine tertiary data. Because control of the steps involved in moving from the original primary data to tertiary data is out of the hands of the researcher, such data must be treated with caution.

Some sources of tertiary data will be more reliable than others. Analysts can adopt an orientation towards the original data, and they can be selective in what is reported. In addition, there is always the possibility of academic fraud. The further a researcher is removed from the original primary data, the greater the risk of unintentional or deliberate distortion.

The purpose of this classification is to sensitize the researcher to the nature of the data being used and its limitations. This discussion brings us back to the key issue: what are data? In particular, it highlights the problem of the gap between the researcher and the social phenomenon that is being investigated.

There is an interesting relationship between types of data and ontological assumptions. Such assumptions about the nature of the reality being investigated will not only have a bearing on what constitutes data but also determine how far a researcher is seen to be removed from that reality. This can be illustrated with reference to the operation of stock markets. All major stock markets in the world produce a numerical indicator that is used to follow movements in that particular market. For example, the New York stock exchange uses the Dow Jones index, the London exchange uses the FTSE 100, and the Tokyo exchange the Nikkei. The share prices of a selection of stocks are integrated into a summary number. This number or indicator is used to measure the behaviour of 'the market'. Trends can be calculated and, perhaps, models and theories developed about cycles or stages in these trends.

But what kind of data are these indices? The answer to this question depends on what view of reality is adopted. The notion of 'the market' is an abstract idea that can refer to an entity that exists independently of the people who buy and sell shares. Analysts frequently attribute the market with human or animal qualities: it has 'sentiments', it 'looks for directions', it acts like a bull or a bear. Hence, 'the market' can be regarded as constituting an independent reality. From these assumptions, the market indicator might be regarded as primary data; it measures the behaviour of 'the market'. The share prices are the raw data.

Another (albeit much less common) set of assumptions would be to regard the worldviews and behaviour of the people who buy and sell shares as constituting the basic social phenomenon. The decisions and actions of these people generate the fluctuating prices of shares. The stockbrokers through whom these people conduct their share transactions are equivalent to researchers who then feed the outcomes of the decisions of these people into a particular market's database from which the price of any shares, at any time, can be determined and trends plotted. Other researchers then take these average prices and do some further analysis to produce a share price index. Further researchers can then use the changes in the index to trace movements in 'the market'. Therefore, the price that individual investors pay for their parcel of shares is equivalent to primary data, the closing or average price of the shares in any particular company represents secondary data, and the share price index represents tertiary data.

This example illustrates two things. First, it shows that how data are viewed depends on the ontological assumptions about the social phenomenon being investigated. Second, it shows that what is regarded as reality determines what types of data are used. Reality can be either a reified abstraction, such as 'the market', or it can be the interpretations and activities of particular social actors, such as investors. Movements in a share price index can mean different things depending on the assumptions that are adopted. It can be a direct, primary measure of a particular reality, or it can be an indirect, tertiary measure of a different kind of reality. Hence, knowing what data refer to, and how they should be interpreted, depends on what is assumed as being the reality under investigation, and the type of data that are being used.

Forms of Data

Social science data are produced in two main forms, in *numbers* or in *words*. This distinction is usually referred to as either *quantitative* or *qualitative* data. There seems to be a common belief among many researchers, and consumers of their products, that numerical data are needed in scientific research to ensure objective and accurate results. Somehow, data in words tend to be regarded as being not only less precise but also less reliable. These views still persist in many circles, even although non-numerical data are now more widely accepted. As we shall see shortly, the distinction between words and numbers, between qualitative and quantitative data, is not a simple one.

It can be argued that all primary data start out as words. Some data are recorded in words, they remain in words throughout the analysis, and the findings are reported in words. The original words will be transformed and manipulated into other words, and these processes may be repeated more than once. The level of the language will change, moving from lay language to technical language. Nevertheless, throughout the research, the medium is always words.

In other research, the initial communication will be transformed into numbers immediately, or prior to the analysis. The former involves the use of pre-coded response categories, and the latter the post-coding of answers or information provided in words, as in the case of open-ended questions in a questionnaire. Numbers are attached to both sets of categories and the subsequent analysis will be numerical. The findings of the research will be presented in numerical summaries and tables. However, words will have to be introduced to interpret and elaborate the numerical findings. Hence, in quantitative studies, data normally begin in words, are transformed into numbers, are subjected to different levels of statistical manipulation, and are reported in both numbers and words; from words to numbers and back to words. The interesting point here is whose words were used in the first place and what process was used to generate them. In the case where responses are made into a predetermined set of categories, the questions and the categories will be in the researcher's words; the respondent only has to interpret both. However, this is a big 'only'. As Foddy (1993) and Pawson (1995, 1996) have pointed out, this is a complex process that requires much more attention and understanding than it has normally been given.

Sophisticated numerical transformations can occur as part of the analysis stage. For example, responses to a set of attitude statements, in categories ranging from 'strongly agree' to 'strongly disagree', can be numbered, say, from 1 to 5. The direction of the numbering will depend on whether a statement expresses positive or negative attitudes on the topic being investigated, and on whether positive attitudes are to be given high or low scores. Subject to an appropriate test, these scores can be combined to produce a total score. Such scores are well removed from the respondent's original reading of the words in the statements and the recording of a response in a category with a label in words.

So far, this discussion of the use of words and numbers has been confined to the collection of primary data. However, these kinds of manipulations may have already occurred in secondary data, and will certainly have occurred in tertiary data.

The controversial issue in all of this is the effect that any form of manipulation has on the relationship of the data to the reality it is supposed to measure. If all observation involves interpretation, then some kind of manipulation is involved from the very beginning. Even if a conversation is recorded unobtrusively, any attempt to understand what went on requires the researcher to make interpretations and to use concepts. How much manipulation occurs is a matter of choice.

A more important issue is the effect of transforming words into numbers. Researchers who prefer to remain qualitative through all stages of a research project may argue that it is bad enough to take lay language and manipulate it into technical language without translating either of them into the language of mathematics. A common fear about such translations is that they end up distorting the social world out of all recognition, with the result that research reports based on them become either meaningless or, possibly, dangerous if acted on.

The reason for this extended discussion of issues involved in transforming words into numbers is to highlight the inherent problems associated with interpreting quantitative data and, hence, its analysis. Because of the steps involved in transforming some kind of social reality into the language of mathematics, and the potential for losing the plot along the way, the interpretation of the results produced by quantitative analysis must be done with full awareness of the limitations involved.

Concepts and Variables

It is conventional practice to regard quantitative data as consisting of *variables*. These variables normally start out as concepts, coming from either research questions or hypotheses. First, it is necessary to define the concept in terms of the meaning it is to have in a particular research project. For example, age might be defined as 'years since birth', and education as 'the highest level of formal qualification obtained'. Unless there is some good reason to do otherwise, it is good practice to employ a definition already in use in that particular field of research. In this way, results from different studies can be easily compared.

The second step is to *operationalize* the concept to show how data related to it will be generated. This requires the specification of the procedures that will be used to classify or measure the phenomenon being investigated. For example, in order to measure a person's age, it is necessary either to ask them or to obtain the information from some kind of record, such as a birth certificate. Similarly, with education, you can either ask the person what their highest qualification is, or you can refer to appropriate documents or records. The way a concept is defined and measured has important consequences for the kinds of data analysis that can be undertaken.

The idea behind a variable is that it can have different values, that characteristics of objects, events or people can be measured along some continuum that forms a uniform numerical scale. This is the nature of metric measurement. For example, age (in years) and attitudes towards some object (in scores) are variables. However, other kinds of characteristics, such as religion, do not share this property. They are measured in terms of a set of different categories. Something can be identified as being in a particular category (e.g. female), but there is no variation within the category, only differences between categories (e.g. males and females). As there is no variability within such categories, the results of such measurement are not strictly variables. They could be called variates, but this concept also has another meaning in statistics. Therefore, I shall follow the established convention of referring to all kinds of quantitative measurement as variables. It is to the different kinds or levels of measurement that we now turn.

Levels of Measurement

In quantitative research, aspects of social reality are transformed into numbers in different ways. *Measurement* is achieved either by the assignment of objects, events or people to discrete categories, or by the identification of their characteristics on a numerical scale, according to arbitrary rules. The former is referred to here as *categorical* measurement and the latter as *metric* measurement. Within these *levels of measurement* are two further levels: nominal and ordinal, and interval and ratio, respectively.

Categorical Measurement

Everyday life would be impossible without the use of numbers. However, using numbers does not mean that we need to use complex arithmetic or mathematics. Frequently, numbers are simply used to identify objects, events or people. Equipment and other objects are given serial numbers or licence numbers so that they can be uniquely identified. Days of the month and the years of a millennium are numbered in sequence. The steps involved in assembling an object are numbered. People who make purchases in a shop can be given numbers to ensure they are served in order. In none of these examples are the numbers manipulated; they are simple used as a form of identification, and, in some cases, to establish an order or sequence. The alphabet could just as easily be used, and sometimes is, except that it is much more restricted than our usual number system as the latter has no absolute limit. This elementary way of using numbers in real life and in the social sciences is known as *categorical measurement*.

As has already been implied, categorical measurement can be of two types. One involves assigning numbers to categories that identify different types of objects, event or people; in the other, numbers are used to establish a sequence of objects, events or people. Categories can either identify differences or they can be ordered along some dimension or continuum. The former is referred to as nominal-level measurement, and the latter as ordinal-level measurement.

Nominal-level measurement

In *nominal-level measurement*, the categories must be homogeneous, mutually exclusive and exhaustive. This means that all objects, events or people allocated to a particular category must share the same characteristics, they can only be allocated to one category, and all of them can be allocated to some category in the set. The categories have no intrinsic order to them, as is the case for the categories of gender or religion. People can also be assigned numbers arbitrarily according to some criterion, such as different categories of eye colour – blue (1), brown (2), green (3), etc. However, these categories have no intrinsic order (except, of course, on the colour spectrum).

Ordinal-level measurement

The same conditions apply in *ordinal-level measurement*, with the addition that the categories *are* ordered along some continuum. For example, people can be assigned numbers in terms of the order in which they cross the finishing line in a race, they can be assigned social class categories ('upper', 'middle' and 'lower') according to their income or occupational status, or they can be assigned to age categories ('old', 'middle-aged' and 'young') according to some criterion. A progression or a hierarchy is present in each of these examples.

However, the intervals between such ordinal categories need not be equal. For example, the response categories of 'often' (1), 'occasionally' (2) and 'never' (3) cannot be assumed to be equally spaced by researchers, because it cannot be assumed that respondents regard them this way. When the numbers in brackets are assigned to these categories, they only indicate the order in the sequence, not how much of a difference there is between these categories. They could just as easily have been identified with 'A', 'B' and 'C', and these symbols certainly do not imply any difference in magnitude.

Similarly, the commonly used Likert categories for responses to attitude statements, 'strongly agree', 'agree', 'neither agree nor disagree', disagree', and 'strongly disagree', are not necessarily evenly spaced along this level of agreement continuum, although researchers frequently assume that they are. When this assumption is introduced, an ordinal-level measure becomes an interval-level measure with discrete categories.

Metric Measurement

There are more sophisticated ways in which numbers can be used than those just discussed. The introduction of the simple idea of equal or measurable intervals between positions on a continuum transforms categorical measurement into *metric measurement*. Instead of assigning objects, events or people to a set of categories, they are assigned a number from a particular kind of scale of numbers, with equal intervals between the positions on the scale. For example, we measure a person's height by assigning a number from a measuring scale. We measure intelligence by assigning a person a number from a scale that represents different levels of intelligence (IQ). Of course, with categorical measurement, it is necessary to have or to create a set of categories into which whatever is being measured can be assigned. However, these categories do not have any numerical relationships and, therefore, cannot have the rules of a number system applied to them.

Hence, the critical step in this transition from categorical to metric measurement is the mapping of the things being measured onto a scale. The scale has to exist, or be created, before the measurements are made, and these scales embody the properties and rules of a number system. Measuring a person's height clearly illustrates this. You have to have a measuring instrument, such as a long ruler or tape measure, before a person's height can be established. We can describe people as being 'tall', 'average' or 'short'. Such ordinal-level categories allow us to compare people's height only in very crude terms. Adding numbers to the categories, say '1', '2' and '3', neither adds precision to the measurement nor does it allow us to assume that the intervals between the categories are equal. Alternatively, we could line up a group of people, from the tallest to the shortest, and give them numbers in sequence. Each number simply indicates where a person is in the order and has nothing to do with the actual magnitude of their height. In addition, the differences in height between neighbouring people will vary and the number assigned to them will not indicate this. However, once we stand them beside a scale in, say, centimetres, we can get a measure of magnitude, and because they are all measured against the same scale we can make precise comparisons between any members of the group. Precision of measurement is only one of the considerations here. The important change is that much more sophisticated forms of analysis can now be used which, in turn, means that more sophisticated answers can be given to research questions.

All metric scales of measurement are human inventions. The way in which points on the scale are assigned numbers, the size of the intervals between those points, whether or not there are gradations between these points, and where the numbering starts, are all arbitrary. Scales differ in how the zero point is established. Some scales have an absolute or true zero, while for others there is no meaningful zero, that is, the position of zero is arbitrary.

Interval-level measurement

Interval-level measurement is achieved when the categories or scores on a scale are the same distance apart. Whereas in ordinal-level measurement the numbers '1', '2' and '3' only indicate relative position, say in finishing a race, in interval-level measurement, the numbers are assumed to be the same distance apart – the interval between '1' and '2' is the same as the interval between '2' and '3'. As the numbers are equally spaced on the scale, each interval has the same value.

The distinguishing feature of interval-level measurement is that the zero is arbitrary. Whatever is being measured cannot have a meaningful zero value. For example, an attitude scale may have possible scores that range from 10 to 50. Such scores could have been derived from an attitude scale of ten items, using five response categories (from 'strongly agree' to 'strongly disagree') with the categories being assigned numbers from 1 to 5 in the direction appropriate to the wording (positive or negative) of the item.[2] However, these scores could just as easily have ranged from 0 to 40 (with categories assigned numbers from 0 to 4) without altering the relative interval between any two scores. In this case, a zero score is achieved by an arbitrary decision about what numbers to assign to the response categories. It makes no sense to speak of a zero attitude, only relatively more positive or negative attitudes.

Ratio-level measurement

Ratio-level measurement is the same as interval-level measurement except that it has an absolute or true zero. For example, goals scored in football, or age in years, both have absolute or true zeros; it is possible for a team to score no goals, and a person's age is normally calculated from the time of birth – point zero.

Ratio-level measurement is not common in the social sciences and is limited to examples such as age (in years), education (in years) and income (in dollars or other currencies). This level of measurement has only a few advantages over the interval level of measurement, mainly that statements such as 'double' or 'half' can be made. For example, we can say that a person aged 60 years is twice as old as a person aged 30 years, or that an income of $20,000 is only half that of $40,000. These kinds of statements cannot be made with interval-level variables. For example, with attitude scales, such as those discussed above, it is not legitimate to say that one score (say 40) is twice as positive as another (say 20). What we can say is that one score is higher, or lower, than another by so many scale points (a score of 40 is 10 points higher than a score of 30, and the latter is 10 points higher than a score of 20) and that an interval of, say 10 points, is the same anywhere on the scale. The same applies to scales used to measure temperature. Because the commonly used temperature scales, Celsius and Fahrenheit, both have arbitrary zeros, we cannot say that a temperature of 30°C is twice as hot as 15°C, but the interval between 15°C and 30°C is the same as that between 30°C and 45°C. Similarly, not only is 30°C a different temperature than 30° Fahrenheit, but an interval of 15° is different on each scale. However, as the kelvin scale does have a true zero, the absolute minimum temperature that is possible, a temperature of 400 K is twice as hot as 200 K.

Compared to ratio-level measurement, it is the arbitrary zero that creates the limitations in interval-level measurement. In most social science research, this limitation is not critical; interval-level measurement is usually adequate for most sophisticated forms of analysis. However, we need to be aware of the limitations and avoid drawing illegitimate conclusions from interval-level data.

Discrete and Continuous Measurement

Metric scales also differ in terms of whether the points on the scale are discrete or continuous. A *discrete* or discontinuous scale usually has units in whole numbers and the intervals between the numbers are usually equal. Arithmetical procedures, such as adding, subtracting, multiplying and dividing, are permissible. On the other hand, a *continuous* scale will have an unlimited number of possible values (e.g. fractions or decimal points) between the whole numbers. An example of the former is the number of children in a family and, of the latter, a person's height in metres, centimetres, millimetres, etc. We cannot speak of a family having 1.8 children (although the average size of families in a country might be expressed in this way), but we can speak of a person being 1.8 metres in height. When continuous scales are used, the values may also be expressed in whole numbers due to rounding to the nearest number.

Review

The characteristics of the four levels of measurement are summarized in Table 1.2. They differ in their degree of precision, ranging from the least precise (nominal) to the most precise (ratio). The different characteristics, and the range of precision, mean that different mathematical procedures are appropriate at each level. It is too soon to discuss these differences here; they will emerge throughout Chapters 3–6.

However, a word of caution is appropriate. It is very easy to be seduced by the precision and sophistication of interval-level and ratio-level measurement, regardless of whether they are necessary or theoretically and philosophically appropriate. The crucial question is what is necessary in order to answer the research question under consideration. This relates to other aspects of social research, such as the choice of data sources, the method of selection from these sources and the method of data collection. The latter, of course, will have a considerable bearing on the type of analysis that can and should be used. In quantitative research, the choice of level of measurement at the data-collection

Table 1.2   *Levels of measurement*

Level	Description	Types of categories	Examples
Nominal	A set of categories for classifying objects, events or people, with no assumptions about order.	Categories are homogeneous, mutually exclusive and exhaustive.	Marital status Religion Ethnicity
Ordinal	As for nominal-level measurement, except the categories are ordered from highest to lowest.	Categories lie along a continuum but the distances between them cannot be assumed to be equal.	Frequency (often, sometimes, never) Likert scale
Interval	A set of ordered and equal-interval categories on a contrived measurement scale.	Categories may be discrete or continuous with arbitrary intervals and zero point.	Attitude score IQ score Celsius scale
Ratio	As for interval-level measurement	Categories may be discrete or continuous but with an absolute zero.	Age Income No. of children

stage, and the transformations that may be made, including data reduction, will determine the types of analysis that can be used.

Finally, it is important to note that some writers refer to categorical data as qualitative and metric data as quantitative. This is based on the idea that qualitative data lack the capacity for manipulation other than adding up the number in the categories and calculating percentages or proportions. This usage is not adopted here. Rather, 'qualitative' and 'quantitative' are used to refer to data in words and numbers, respectively. Categorical data involve the use of numbers and not words, allowing for simple numerical calculations. According to the definitions being used here, categorical data are clearly quantitative.

Transformations between Levels of Measurement

It is possible to transform metric data into categorical data but, in general, not the reverse. For example, in an attitude scale, scores can be divided into a number of ranges (e.g. 10–19, 20–29, 30–39, 40–50) and labels applied to these categories (e.g. 'low', 'moderate', 'high' and 'very high'). Thus, interval-level data can be transformed into ordinal-level data. Something similar could be done with age (in years) by creating age categories that may not cover the same range, say, 20–24, 25–34, 35–54, 55+. In this case, the transformation is from ratio level to ordinal. While such transformations may be useful for understanding particular variables, and relationships between variables, measurement precision is lost in the process, and the types of analysis that can be applied are reduced in sophistication. It is important to note, however, that if a range of ages or scores is grouped into categories of equal size, for example, 20–29, 30–39, 40–49, 50–59, 60–69, etc., the categories *can* be regarded as being at the interval level; they cover equal age intervals, thus making their midpoints equal distances apart. All that has changed is the unit of measurement, in 10-year age intervals rather than 1-year intervals.

There are a few cases in which it is possible to transform lower-level measurement to a higher level. For example, it is possible to take a set of nominal categories, such as religious denomination, and introduce an order using a particular criterion. For example, religious categories could be ordered in terms of the proportion of a population that adheres to each one, or, more complexly, in terms of some theological dimension. Similarly for categories of political party preference, although in this case dominant political ideology would replace theology. In a way, such procedures are more about analysis than measurement; they add something to the level of measurement used in order to facilitate the analysis.

The reason why careful attention must be given to level of measurement in quantitative research is that the choice of level determines the methods of analysis that can be undertaken. Therefore, in designing a research project, decisions about the level of measurement to be used for each variable need to anticipate the type of analysis that will be required to answer the relevant research question(s). Of course, for certain kinds of variables, such as gender, ethnicity and religious affiliation, there are limited options. However, for other variables, such as age and income, there are definite choices. For example, if age is pre-coded in categories of unequal age ranges, then the analysis cannot go beyond the ordinal level. However, if age was recorded in actual years, then analysis can operate at the ratio level, and transformations also made to a lower level of measurement. Such a simple decision at the data-collection stage can have significant repercussions at the data-analysis stage. The significance of the level of measurement for choice of method of analysis will structure the discussion in Chapters 3–6.

What is Data Analysis?

All social research should be directed towards answering research questions about characteristics, relationships, patterns or influences in some social phenomenon. Once appropriate data have been collected or generated, it is possible to see whether, and to what extent, the research questions can be answered. *Data analysis* is one step, and an important one, in this process. In some cases, the testing of theoretical hypotheses, that is, possible answers to 'why' research questions, is an intermediary step. In other cases, the research questions will be answered directly by an appropriate method of analysis.

The processes by which selection is made from the sources of data can also have a major impact on the choice of methods of data analysis. The major consideration in selecting data is the choice between using a population and a sample of some kind. If sampling is used, the type of data analysis that is appropriate will depend on whether probability or non-probability sampling is used. Hence, it is necessary to review briefly how and why the processes of selecting data affect the choice of methods of data analysis.

Types of Analysis

Various methods of data analysis are used to describe the characteristics of social phenomena, and to understand, explain and predict patterns in social life or in the relationships between aspects of social phenomena. In addition, one type of analysis is concerned with estimating whether characteristics and relationships found in a sample randomly drawn from a population could also be expected to exist in the population. Hence, analysis can be divided into four types: univariate descriptive, bivariate descriptive, explanatory and inferential.

Univariate Descriptive Analysis

Univariate descriptive analysis is used to represent the characteristics of some social phenomenon (e.g. student academic performance on a particular course). This can be done in a number of ways:

- by counting the frequency with which some characteristic occurs (e.g. the total marks[3] students receive on a particular course);
- by grouping scores of a certain range into categories and presenting these frequencies in pictorial or graphical form (e.g. student's total marks);
- by calculating measures of central tendency (e.g. the mean marks obtained by students on the course); and
- by graphing and/or calculating the spread of frequencies around this centre point (e.g. plotting a line graph of the frequency with which particular marks were obtained, or calculating a statistic that measures the dispersion around the mean).

There are clearly many ways in which the phenomenon of student academic performance can be described and compared. The principles of each of these methods will be elaborated later in this chapter, and they will be illustrated in later chapters.

Bivariate Descriptive Analysis

Bivariate descriptive analysis is a step along the path from univariate analysis to explanatory analysis. It involves either establishing similarities or differences between the characteristics of categories of objects, events or people, or describing patterns or connections between such characteristics.

Typically, patterns are investigated by determining the extent to which the position of objects, events or persons on one variable coincides with their position on another variable. For example, does the position of people on a measure of height coincide with their position on a measure of weight? If the tallest people are also the heaviest, and vice versa, then these two measures can be said to be associated. Sometimes this is expressed in terms of whether position on one measure is a good predictor of position on another measure, that is, whether the height of people is a good predictor of their weight.

Continuing the example about student academic performance, we can:

- compare categories in terms of averages (e.g. differences between the mean marks of female and male students, or students of different ethnic backgrounds); and
- establish the strength of the relationship between two characteristics (e.g. measuring the association between gender and honours grades, or ethnicity and grade point average).

Explanatory Analysis

To go beyond describing characteristics and establishing relationships, that is, to go beyond answering 'what' questions to addressing 'why' questions, takes us into the complex and difficult territory of *explanatory analysis* and the much disputed notion of *causation*. It is a common belief that establishing an explanation involves finding the cause or causes for the patterns and sequences in social life. Explanations are supposed to tell us why certain things occur together or follow one another in time. However, there are not only many views on how this can be achieved, but also dissenting voices that claim such a task is impossible.

There are two main views on the nature of causation: the successionist and the generative (Harré, 1972; Pawson, 1989; Pawson and Tilley, 1997). The *successionist view of causation* is based on the idea that events in the world can be explained if they follow a regular sequence. In fact, according to this view, there are no such things as causes, only connections or sequences between events in the world. For example, if we apply heat to water it will turn into steam when the temperature reaches 100°C. The event of heating is followed by another event, the change from liquid to gas. The change of status is therefore explained by the event that preceded it. Hence, the sequence of these events forms a 'natural necessity'; they could not happen otherwise. The task of science is to discover these regularities and then use them for both explanation and prediction. Explanation is achieved by pointing to prior events in the sequence, and prediction is achieved by knowing what follows in the sequence. This view is associated with the view of social science known as positivism.

While the idea of events occurring in well-established sequences implies that single events have single causes, many approaches to causal explanation recognize the possibility of multiple causes, that is, that more than one event might have to precede the event to be explained in order for it to occur. These preceding events may occur in parallel (concurrently) or in a chain reaction (sequentially), or in some combination of concurrence and sequence.

The philosophical notions of causation are frequently translated into the language of two types of conditions that are responsible for the occurrence of an event, necessary and sufficient conditions. A *necessary condition* is one that needs to be present in order for an event to occur. There may be a number of necessary conditions, but even together they may not produce an event. A *sufficient condition* is one that will lead to the occurrence of an event on its own or, perhaps, in combination with one or two other conditions. However, sufficient conditions will usually need to operate in the context of some necessary conditions. Hence, necessary conditions can be regarded as the contextual factors that need to be present and sufficient conditions as those that actually produce the event in that context. Normally, the two sets of conditions will work together. The challenge for the researcher is to find the complete set of necessary and sufficient conditions in order to explain an event. Clearly, this is an impossible task. Even trying to identify as many conditions as possible has its limitations. We need reasons for selecting possible conditions, and these are supplied by a good theory.

An elaboration of the successionist view has argued that explanation is achieved by finding a well-tested theory from which the event or pattern to be explained can be deduced once the conditions under which it is known to operate have been specified. Specifying different conditions makes it possible to predict new events or patterns and, therefore, to test the theory. However, such predictions only apply to the conditions that have been specified in the theory, not to some future time in which the conditions may not be known. Such theories are made up of statements of relationships or connections between concepts or events. It is by combining such statements into a logical argument that explanation can be achieved. This tradition is associated with the view of social science known as critical rationalism.

When research does not satisfy experimental requirements, as in survey research, it is a common practice to translate causal language into relationships between two types of variables. One variable, the values of which are to be explained, is referred to as the *dependent* or *outcome variable*, while those that are involved in producing these values are referred to as *independent* or *predictor variables*. Stated differently, the values of the dependent variable are influenced or predicted by the values of the independent variable or variables. For example, academic performance (the dependent variable) might be influenced or predicted by students' ethnicity (the independent variable).[4] In this example, there is no attempt to completely explain academic performance, only to indicate a factor that might contribute to it. Hence, it is a rather low level of causal analysis.

While it might be strengthened by the inclusion of other independent variables, this kind of research cannot produce conclusive explanations. For one thing, assumptions need to be made about the direction of influence among variables and, for another, the nature of the causal relationship is frequently left rather vague. In the case of the relationship between ethnicity and academic performance, even if there is an association, and it is possible to analyze this in terms of the influence of one variable on the other, we are still left with the problem of what it is about ethnicity that is responsible for this. The connection only makes sense when it is theorized and the theory is thoroughly tested. Something else is required to link these two variables. Such a theory might include ideas about the influence of family attitudes and experiences and the quality of early formal education. This is the core argument of those who advocate the generative view of causation.

The successionist approach has been severely criticized by the advocates of the *generative view of causation* (see, for example, Bhaskar, 1979; Pawson, 1989;

Pawson and Tilley, 1997). While successionists have restricted themselves to sequences of observable events, or the connections between concepts, the supporters of the generative position argue that events cannot be seen as being discrete and isolatable; they are part of a network or system of events. To isolate them artificially is to produce connections that may bear little relationship to how things actually behave. In addition, they argue that establishing connections or relationships is only the starting point. It is necessary to discover the underlying structures and mechanisms that are responsible for producing such connections. Observed patterns or regularities are explained by discovering the structures and mechanisms that generate the observed phenomenon. As these mechanisms may not always be obvious or readily observable, their existence may have to be postulated and then established. Explanations are produced by the 'causal powers' or 'tendencies' of things to behave in a particular way. 'A mechanism is not thus a single *variable* but an *account* of the constitution and behaviour of those things that are responsible for the manifest reality' (Pawson, 1989: 130).

The supporters of the generative view also argue that prediction is not possible because to be able to do so requires knowledge of all the conditions that are relevant to the operation of such structures and mechanisms. As social phenomena occur in open systems, it is not possible to know in advance what conditions will be operating and, therefore, to be able to predict what will occur. Hence, researchers must be content with trying to establish mechanisms and the conditions under which they operate, after the event. The philosophical tradition on which the generative view is based is scientific or critical realism.

One particular social science tradition totally rejects the idea of causation. This is based on the argument that the successionist view is only relevant to the natural sciences. Because the subject matter studied by the social sciences is fundamentally different from that of the natural sciences, the only appropriate approach is to try to understand social phenomena in terms of the reasons people can give for their actions rather than in terms of some notion of independent causes. It is the socially constructed nature of social reality that distinguishes it from natural or physical phenomena, and this difference requires the use of very different ways of understanding social life. This tradition is known as interpretivism or social constructionism. For a review of these traditions, see Blaikie (1993a, 2000).

Inferential Analysis

Inferential analysis is used with data obtained from a sample to estimate the characteristics of or patterns in the population from which the sample was drawn. This kind of analysis is only appropriate when the sample is drawn using probability or random selection procedures. There are two main types of inferential analysis: that used to estimate characteristics of a population from sample data (e.g. the mean age of its members); and that used to establish whether a pattern or a relationship found to exist in a sample could be expected to also occur in the population from which it was drawn (e.g. a relationship between ethnicity and academic performance).

Inferential analysis on sample characteristics receives limited attention in social research. Apart from some opinion polls (and even in these its use is rather rare), few social researchers actually calculate the likely population characteristics from their sample data. The sample data are usually just presented and assumed to be the same in the population. In contrast, a great deal of attention is given to testing whether relationships found in a sample can be expected to exist in a population. This is done by using *tests of significance*. Unfortunately, these tests are frequently applied beyond the situations is which they are appropriate. Their purpose is poorly understood, and they are also widely misused. The common forms of confusion are that:

- using such tests will tell you what is important in your data;
- chance factors that might adversely affect the collection of data can somehow be detected and allowed for by using these test;
- the tests tell you how closely two characteristics (variables) are associated; and
- the tests should be applied to all results, regardless of whether data were collected from a population, a random sample or a non-random sample.

These issues will be addressed in Chapter 6.

Logics of Enquiry and Data Analysis

In addition to the competing views on what constitutes causation, there is another related area of dispute in the social sciences. This centres on whether the ways of answering 'why' questions that are appropriate in the natural sciences are also appropriate in the social sciences (for a review of this issue, see Blaikie, 1993a). There are two dominant schools of thought. One argues that the logic of explanation used in the natural sciences is also appropriate in the social sciences. The other argues that the peculiar nature of the subject matter studied in the social sciences limits the kind of answers the social scientist can offer to 'why' questions. All that is possible is to understand social phenomena by establishing the reasons people give for their actions. In short, there are debates about whether it is possible to establish causal *explanations* in the social sciences or whether *understanding*, based on social actors accounts, is all that is possible and necessary.

Among those who advocate the use of the logic of explanation adopted in the natural sciences, there have been disputes about what this logic should be. The earliest view – first advocated in seventeenth century by Francis Bacon (see Bacon, 1889), with important contributions during the 1840s by William Whewell and John Stuart Mill (see Whewell, 1847; Mill, 1947) was that *inductive logic* was the appropriate scientific 'method'. Accumulated data are used to produce generalizations about the patterns or connections between events or variables. In the 1930s, this view was severely criticized and an alternative proposed by Popper (1959) in the form of a *deductive logic* of explanation. In this case, a researcher starts with a theory that provides a possible explanation, and then proceeds to test the theory by deducing from it one or more hypotheses, and then matching the hypotheses against appropriate data. More recently, both of these positions have been rejected by Harré (1961, 1970, 1972; Harré and Secord, 1972) and Bhaskar (1979) who have proposed the use of *retroductive logic*. They have argued that the inductive approach simply produces descriptions that still have to be explained by locating 'real' structures and mechanisms that produce the effects that can be observed. This is done by building models or developing pictures of these structures and mechanisms such that, if they exist and act in the way postulated, they would account for the phenomenon being examined. Structures and mechanisms are not discovered by accumulating data but by looking for evidence that would confirm their existence. These authors have argued that the discovery of atoms and viruses followed this type of logic. While the idea of atoms existed long before they were observed directly (in the 1960s), scientists, acting on the assumption that they did exist and behaved as imagined, were able to create the atomic bomb.

A fourth logic of enquiry, *abductive logic*, rejects the idea of explanation and causation in favour of understanding. Such understanding comes from 'thick' descriptions and the grasping of social actors' meanings and interpretations. These different logics of enquiry have, with some modifications, been presented as alternative research strategies, that is, as alternative ways of answering research questions, particularly 'why' questions (see Blaikie, 1993a, 2000).

The different views of causation have important consequences for the way we conduct social research and undertake data analysis. Add to that the use of different research strategies, and serious implications for data analysis become evident. The methods of analysis to be discussed in this book are really only appropriate for the successionist view of causation and the inductive and deductive research strategies. Hence, there are other ways of answering 'why' research questions that require different kinds of data analysis, and these entail different views on what constitutes data. Quantitative data analysis is only one kind of data analysis.

Summary

- Social research must start with a research problem, an intellectual puzzle or a practical problem.
- Social research is about answering three types of research questions: 'what', 'why' and 'how' questions.
- Social research pursues a range of objectives: exploration, description, explanation, understanding, prediction, intervention, evaluation and impact assessment. The objectives of explanation and understanding are expressed as 'why' questions and the objective of intervention as 'how' questions. The remaining objectives are mostly related to 'what' questions.

- Research objectives are frequently pursued in a logical sequence, the most common of which is description, explanation/understanding and intervention.
- Theoretical hypotheses provide possible answers to 'why' research questions.
- Statistical hypotheses are used to establish whether patterns found in a random sample are present in its population. This is their only role in social research.
- Data are produced by the use of the human senses, mainly sight and hearing, and through the use of instruments that extend and systematize their use. This requires agreement about rules and criteria. Such procedures do not guarantee objectivity, only comparability between times, places and researchers.
- All forms of measurement in the social sciences are socially constructed by experts, the data they produce, and the results that follow, have to be understood in terms of the assumptions and procedures adopted.
- These assumptions are both ontological and epistemological and, while they are usually taken for granted, they can be understood with reference to one of the major philosophies of social science: positivism, critical rationalism, scientific realism and interpretivism.
- There are three types of social science data: primary, secondary and tertiary. Each type has its advantages and disadvantages and varies in terms of the distance it creates between the researcher and the social reality being studied.
- Social science data can be either qualitative or quantitative, in either words or numbers. Transformations between words and numbers, or in the reverse direction, can occur at various stages in a research project.
- Quantitative data are expressed in the form of variables that are produced by operationalizing the key concepts in research questions and theoretical hypotheses.
- Concepts can be measured at four different levels. From lowest to highest, these are nominal, ordinal, interval and ratio. The first two produce categorical variables, because objects, events or people are placed into one of a set of mutually exclusive categories. The second two produce metric variables, as objects, events or people are mapped onto an established measuring scale.
- Metric variables can be either discrete or continuous. The former consist only of whole numbers, while the latter have an unlimited number of possible values between the whole numbers.
- Data can be transformed from metric to categorical. While this means some loss of information, and entails the use of less sophisticated forms of analysis, it may allow for a better understanding of the characteristics or relationships being examined.
- There are four main types of data analysis: univariate descriptive, bivariate descriptive, explanatory and inferential. The first two are concerned with characteristics and patterns in data, the third with influence between variables and the fourth with generalizing from samples to populations. Explanatory analysis is the ultimate objective in social research and is also the most complex.
- Explanation is usually associated with the idea of causation. However, this is a highly contested notion and has to be reduced to simpler ideas to be

useful in social research. One way of doing this is in terms of the influence between independent (predictor) and dependent (outcome) variables.
- Different views of causation are associated with the major logics of enquiry: inductive, deductive, retroductive and abductive. These logics also constitute different research strategies.

Notes

[1]For a more detailed discussion of many of these issues, see Blaikie (2000).

[2]For the moment we will leave aside the debates about whether such a scoring procedure is legitimate.

[3]For simplicity, marks, say out of 100, are used in these examples rather than grades (e.g. A, B, C) or grade point averages.

[4]This example is not intended to be racist. It happened to be a very 'hot' political issue in Malaysia at the time of writing.

Data Analysis in Context: Working with Two Data Sets

Introduction

In order to illustrate the methods of data analysis to be discussed in the following chapters, two data sets will be used. The research projects from which these data sets come were conducted by me in Melbourne, Australia, in the mid-1990s, one on university students and the other on urban residents. They constitute part of a six-year research programme in environmental socio-logy, under the title of 'Environmental worldviews and environmentally respon-sible behaviour'. The same variables have been used in both projects; it is just the samples that are different.

There are a number of reasons for using these data sets. First, I want to illus-trate how data analysis is conducted in the context of actual research that addresses a set of research questions. I also want data analysis to have to deal with the vagaries and limitations of actual data selection and gathering. Most books on data analysis and statistics in the social sciences discuss methods of analysis completely detached from the contexts in which they need to be applied.

Second, these are the kind of data sets that many social researchers are likely to encounter or to produce themselves. Rather than use a range of disconnected and sometimes contrived data to illustrate methods of data analysis and statis-tical procedures, I have chosen to use the same two data sets throughout the book. They were conducted on relatively low budgets and could have been pro-duced by groups of undergraduate students or by individual postgraduate students. These data sets provide some consistency and reality to the examples that are used to illustrate the procedures.

Two Samples

One of the studies was conducted in 1994 with a sample of undergraduates from a university in Melbourne. In parallel with this, another study was con-ducted with a sample of residents in the Melbourne metropolitan area (MMA). Rather than covering the whole of the MMA, the study concentrated on a representative municipality within it. Both studies used quantitative methods of data collection and analysis (more details shortly).

As part of the research programme, two similar studies were conducted in 1989 (a sample of students from the same university) and in 1990 (samples of residents from five different regions within the MMA). Some of the results of the two earlier studies have been presented in Blaikie (1992, 1993b), Blaikie and Ward (1992) and Blaikie and Drysdale (1994). These four studies were used as the basis of sample research designs in Blaikie (2000), but with a number of modifications to simplify them for that purpose. Hence, some of the details in the sample research designs based on the two 1994 studies, particularly about the timing of data collection, are different from those reported here. The details presented here represent the way the studies were actually conducted. A later study in the programme used very different methods, in-depth interviews, with a smaller non-random sample of environmental activists and people who practice environmentally responsible behaviour.

For ease of reference, the 1994 study of undergraduates is referred to as the Students or the Student sample, and the parallel study of MMA residents is referred to as the Residents or the Resident sample.

The Student and Resident samples addressed a common set of six research questions, a combination of 'what' and 'why' questions. The first two questions deal with the extent to which different environmental worldviews are held and different levels of environmentally responsible behaviour are practised. The next three questions are designed to explore well-established correlates of environmental worldviews and behaviour, namely, age and gender. The last question seeks an explanation for differences in environmentally responsible behaviour. These research questions are:

1. To what extent do students and urban residents hold different environmental worldviews?
2. To what extent do they practise environmentally responsible behaviour?
3. In what ways and to what extent is environmentally responsible behaviour related to environmental worldviews?
4. In what ways and to what extent is age related to environmental worldviews and environmentally responsible behaviour?
5. In what ways and to what extent is gender related to environmental worldviews and environmentally responsible behaviour?
6. Why are there variations in the levels of environmentally responsible behaviour?

These questions require different kinds of analysis to produce answers.[1] Questions 1 and 2 require *univariate descriptive* analysis, questions 3–5 require *bivariate descriptive* (associational) analysis, and question 6 requires *explanatory* analysis.

Chapters 3–7 draw on these two samples for examples of the various types of data analysis, and some of these examples will anticipate the analysis required to answer these research questions in Chapter 8.

The data were collected by questionnaire in the Student sample and by structured interview in the Resident sample. The questions and response categories were identical in both instruments; there were only minor variations in the formatting that was required for each method.

Descriptions of the Samples

In order to be able to make decisions about some of the methods of data analysis to be used, it is necessary to have information on the populations from which these samples were drawn and how the selection processes were undertaken.

Student Sample

The Student sample consists of a probability sample drawn from the population of all students who took classes in the Core Curriculum[2] in the second semester of 1994.[3] From the 224 classes offered in this programme at that time, a 1:4 systematic sample of 56 classes was selected. Each had an enrolment of between 20 and 25 students, thus making a population of approximately 5000 and a potential sample of about 1250. In 11 of the classes, the lecturer granted permission to have the students complete the questionnaires during class time. In the remaining classes, they were delivered one week and collected in the next or subsequent weeks. A total of 564 questionnaires were completed, giving an overall response rate of approximately 45 per cent. This ranged from nearly 100 per cent in those classes in which the questionnaire was completed during class time, down to about 15 per cent in some other classes. The data were collected over a four-week period in September and October 1994.

A significant proportion of those who completed the questionnaires (just over 8 per cent) were foreign students, mainly from South East Asia. As the study assumed an Australian context and experience, all students who had arrived in the country during the previous five years, and had not been granted permanent resident status, were excluded from the sample. This allowed for the fact that some of the foreign students had studied in Australia for a number of years, having undertaken all or part of their high school education there. Some of the latter would have remained in the sample. The final sample size was 465.

Resident Sample

The Resident sample was confined to one municipality within the Melbourne metropolitan area. Demographically, this city closely mirrored both the MMA as a whole and the state of Victoria in which it was located.[4] A two-stage sample was used. Using random numbers, 17 census collectors' districts were selected from a total of 83. Within these districts, the interviewers selected one in four households systematically, using a random start and following, snake-like, throughout the district. One adult, 18 years and over, alternating between males and females where possible, was selected from each household for inter-view. In households with more than one adult, where possible, females were selected in residences with even numbers and males in the case of odd numbers. The interviews were conducted between December 1993 and March 1994. The overall response rate was 58 per cent, giving a sample of 402.

Concepts and Variables

These two samples have a common set of concepts and variables associated with them. A selection of these variables constitutes the two data sets. Their formal and operational definitions are as follows.

Formal Definitions

Environmental Worldview: attitudes towards issues such as the preservation of wilderness environments and natural flora and fauna, the conservation of natural resources, environmental degradation, environmental impacts of economic growth, and the use of science and technology to solve environmental problems.

Willingness to Act Responsibly: expressed willingness to take actions that help to preserve nature, conserve resources and address environmental problems.[5]

Environmentally Responsible Behaviour: individual actions that help to preserve nature and conserve resources, and involvement in communal actions that confront environmental problems and seek solutions.

Age: number of years since birth.

Gender: socially constructed categories of male and female based on human biological differences.

Marital Status: the legal or de facto relationship between couples, normally of mixed gender.

Number of Children: the number of children of all ages for which a person is regarded by society as being responsible, as parent or legal guardian. This definition excludes unrecognized illegitimate children and any that have been given up for adoption.[6]

Ages of Children: the range of ages of children in the family.

Education: the highest level of qualification obtained in formal education.

Occupation: type of participation in the paid and unpaid workforce.

Religion: identification with a particular religion or religious denomination.

Religiosity: the degree to which an individual adopts religious beliefs, engages in religious practices, or regards himself or herself as a religious or spiritual person.

Political Party Preference: support of a particular political party through intended voting preference.

Operational Definitions

Environmental Worldview: by means of responses to a set of 24 attitude statements concerned with a range of environmental issues.

    a Humans have the right to modify the natural environment to suit their needs.

b Priority should be given to developing alternatives to fossil and nuclear fuel as primary energy sources.
c Rapid economic growth often creates more problems than benefits.
d Human beings were created or evolved to dominate the rest of nature.
e The balance of nature is very delicate and is easily upset.
f Through science and technology we can continue to raise our standard of living.
g Humans must live in harmony with nature in order for it to survive.
h A community's standards for the control of pollution should not be so strict that they discourage industrial development.
i Science and technology do as much harm as good.
j Because of problems with pollution, we need to decrease the use of the motor car as a major means of transportation.
k Humans need not adapt to the natural environment because they can remake it to suit their needs.
l Governments should control the rate at which raw materials are used, to ensure that they last as long as possible.
m The positive benefits of economic growth far outweigh any negative consequences.
n We cannot keep counting on science and technology to solve our problems.
o People in developed societies are going to have to adopt a more conserving life-style in the future.
p Controls should be placed on industry to protect the environment from pollution, even if it means things will cost more.
q Most of the concern about environmental problems has been over-exaggerated.
r The remaining forests in the world should be conserved at all costs.
s Most problems can be solved by applying more and better technology.
t Industry should be required to use recycled materials even when it costs less to make the same products from new raw materials.
u When humans interfere with nature it often produces disastrous consequences.
v Plants and animals exist primarily to be used by humans.
w The government should give generous financial support to research related to the development of solar energy.
x To ensure a future for succeeding generations we have to develop a no-growth economy.

These items are drawn from existing scales: six from the 'new environment paradigm' scale (Dunlap and van Liere, 1978), six from the 'dominant social paradigm' scale (Dunlap and van Liere, 1984), and eight from the Richmond and Baumgart (1981) scale, two with modifications to their wording to fit the research context. Another four have been added. Five Likert-type response categories were used: 'Strongly agree', 'Agree', 'Neither agree nor disagree', 'Disagree' and 'Strongly disagree'. These categories were assigned values from 1 to 5 in the direction that gave the highest value to responses that are pro-environment.

Willingness to Act Responsibly: by means of responses to a set of six attitude statements concerned with willingness to act in some way to protect the environment. The statements are:

1   I would be willing to give part of my income if I were certain that the money would be used to solve environmental problems.
2   I am willing to participate in demonstrations against companies that harm the environment.
3   I am willing to sign a petition in support of tougher environmental laws.
4   I would agree to an increase in taxes if the extra money was used to protect the environment.
5   I would be unwilling to take a job in a company I knew was harming the environment.
6   I am willing to contribute money to environmental organizations.

These statements have been adapted from those used in two previous studies, one in the Netherlands (Ester and Seuren, 1992) and the other in the United States (Stern et al., 1993). Again, five Likert-type response categories were used: 'Strongly agree', 'Agree', 'Neither agree nor disagree', 'Disagree' and 'Strongly disagree'. These categories were assigned values from 5 to 1 as all statements express a willingness to act in favour of the environment.

Environmentally Responsible Behaviour: by three measures. First, the degree to which the use of environmentally dangerous products is avoided. Respondents[7] were asked how frequently they avoid such products ('Regularly', 'Occasionally' and 'Never'), and they were then asked to list the products. Second, the regularity with which products made of paper, glass containers (e.g. bottles), metal containers (e.g. food and drink cans) and plastic containers were recycled. For each type of product, responses were made in the categories of 'Do not use', 'Regularly', 'Occasionally' and 'Never'. These categories were scored from 3 to 0, respectively. The responses to each type of product, as well as the total scores for all four types, were analyzed. Third, support given to environmental groups was measured by two questions: the degree of support ('Regularly', 'Occasionally' and 'Never') and the types of support. For those who provided some support, seven response categories were offered ('Donations', 'Voluntary work', 'Attend meetings', 'Financial member', 'On committees', 'Participate in demonstrations', 'Moral support' only and 'Other').

Age: by asking respondents how old they are in years.

Gender: by observation (interview) or asking whether respondents are male or female (questionnaire).

Marital Status: by asking respondents to identify with one of the following categories: 'Now married', 'De facto stable relationship', 'Never married and not in a stable relationship', 'Widowed and not remarried', 'Separated and not in a stable relationship', 'Divorced and neither remarried nor in a stable relationship'.[8]

Number of Children: by respondent's listing the ages of their biological children, and others for whom they are responsible and/or regard as theirs.

Ages of Children: by coding the age ranges into five categories: 'All under 5 years', 'All under 18', 'Five to under 18', 'Under and over 18' and 'All 18 and over'.

Education: by asking respondents to indicate which of the following categories apply to them: 'Primary only', 'Some secondary', 'Completed secondary', 'Technical qualification', 'Degree or diploma', 'Postgraduate qualification'.

Occupation: by asking respondents to write in their type of participation in the workforce. Initially, the responses were coded into the following categories: 'Manager/senior administrator', 'Professional', 'Para-professional', 'Middle manager', Self-employed – many employees', Self-employed – a few employees', 'Self-employed – on own', White-collar – senior', White-collar – junior', 'Skilled manual', 'Unskilled manual', 'Home duties', 'Pensioner', 'Unemployed' and 'Student'.

Religion: by asking respondents with which religion or religious denomination, if any, they identify. The following categories have been used: 'Catholic', 'Anglican', 'Uniting church',[9] 'Greek Orthodox', 'Baptist', 'Other' religion and 'No religion'.[10]

Religiosity: by asking respondents to what extent they regard themselves as being a religious or spiritual person. Four response categories were used: 'Very religious', 'Moderately religious', 'Somewhat religious' and 'Not religious'.[11]

Political Party Preference: by asking respondents what political party they would vote for if an election were held that day. The following categories were provided: 'Labor', 'Liberal', 'National', 'Democrats', 'Other' and 'Undecided'. These were later recoded into 'Liberal',[12] 'Undecided' and 'Conservative'.[13]

Levels of Measurement

The levels of measurement for each of the variables are as follows:

Environmental Worldview:

- a scale of total scores (interval level);
- subscale scores (interval level);[14] and
- four approximately equal (ordinal-level) categories ('Low', 'Moderate', 'High' and 'Very high') based on divisions in the distribution of the total scores.

Willingness to Act Responsibly:

- a scale of total scores (interval level); and
- four approximately equal (ordinal-level) categories ('Low', 'Moderate', 'High' and 'Very high') based on divisions in the distribution of the total scores.

Environmentally Responsible Behaviour:

(a)   Avoiding Environmentally Damaging Products (Avoid Products):

- whether avoided or not (dichotomous nominal level);
- a post-coded (nominal-level) list of 'types of products'; and
- an index (ratio level) of the 'number of products avoided'.

(b)   Recycling:

- 'frequency of recycling' categories (ordinal level) for each of the four products;
- scores (ratio level) for each product; and
- a 'recycling index' (ratio level) derived from ordinal-level measures of the frequency of recycling of the four products.

(c)   Support for Environmental Groups (Support Groups):

- level of support (ordinal level and dichotomized); and
- types of support (nominal level in an assumed order of intensity).

Age:

- in years (ratio level); and
- six (ordinal-level, approximately interval-level) age categories ('18–24', '25–34', '35–44', '45–54', '55–64' and '65+').

Gender: dichotomous categories (nominal level).
Marital Status: six categories (nominal level).
Number of Children: absolute number (ratio level).
Ages of Children: five categories (nominal level).
Education: six categories (ordinal level).
Occupation: 15 categories (nominal level).
Religion: seven categories (nominal level).
Religiosity: four categories (ordinal level).
Political Party Preference:

- six categories (nominal-level); and
- three categories ('Liberal' to 'Conservative') (ordinal level).

Some variables are measured at more than one level to facilitate different forms of analysis.

Data Reduction

It is a normal practice in social research that during the process of data entry, immediately following data entry and during the process of data analysis itself, a number of procedures will be used to reorganize or reduce the form in which the data were pre-coded in the data-gathering instruments. This can involve:

- reordering response categories used for a variable;
- reducing the number of categories by combining appropriate ones;
- reducing responses to a number of questions or attitude statements to a single score.

The elaboration of the ways in which the variables were operationalized has already hinted at a number of such procedures. In particular, the two sets of attitude statements, for Environmental Worldview and Willingness to Act Responsibly, were subjected to a form of analysis before the responses to the items were summed into a single score.

As most these procedures require knowledge of what will be covered in the next few chapters, the various forms of *data reduction* that are required will not be discussed here. Instead, they will be elaborated in detail in Chapter 7. However, in the meantime, it will be necessary to undertake some simple data reduction procedures before we get there. For example, we will be using the total scores from the Environmental Worldview statements, and we will also be using a recoding of these into four ordinal-level categories. I will explain as much as is necessary about these procedures as we go along.

Notes

[1] These research questions are modifications of those that appear in the sample research designs in Blaikie (2000), where they constitute three separate research projects, each adopting a different research strategy. The modifications allow for simpler forms of analysis.

[2] The Core Curriculum consisted of a set of 19 subjects/courses that addressed issues of relevance to a student's role as a responsible citizen. Students in all undergraduate degree programmes were required to take 4 two-hour one-semester subjects from this programme. As these subjects were taken at different points throughout a degree programme, not all students participated in the programme each semester.

[3] In Australian universities, the academic year follows the calendar, usually beginning around the end of February and running through until some time in November.

[4] As a result of amalgamations between cities in the MMA, this municipality has been combined with an adjoining one to form a new city.

[5] I accept that the wording of this concept is biased in favour of an environmental position, but I make no excuses for this. As it is purely a researcher's concept, and was not used in the questionnaire or interview schedule, it could not influence responses.

[6] The 'number of children' is an example of a superficially simple but actually complex concept to define, particularly in this era of step-families.

[7] Three concepts are now used to refer to people who agree to be involved in social and behavioural research: 'subjects', 'respondents' and 'participants'. Psychologists have traditionally used 'subjects', particularly in the context of experimental research in which people are subjected to some procedure or treatment. Sociologists have traditionally referred to people who agree to answer questions as 'respondents'. There is now a trend to use 'participants' rather than 'respondents' in order to convey a more equal relationship between the researcher and the researched. This usage is certainly appropriate in much qualitative research where the role of the researcher

is more as learner than expert, or in participatory action research were the researcher assists a community to achieve its goals. In spite of 'participant' now being regarded as more politically correct, I prefer to use 'respondent' as that is what people have been in both research projects. They did not participate in any of the design decisions; they only provided information to the researcher in response to questions asked of them.

[8]Due to the changing forms of different-sex and same-sex relationships, and the relatively limited duration of many such relationships in most contemporary societies, this variable is no longer easy to operationalize.

[9]A denomination formed as a result of a union between Methodists, Congregationalists and most Presbyterians in the early 1970s. A small 'continuing' Presbyterian church persisted after this. This denomination is similar to the United Church of Canada.

[10]In the questionnaire and interview schedule, three other categories were included: 'Jewish', 'Moslem' and 'Buddhist'. As there were generally low responses in these categories, in the initial stages of the analysis they were recoded into the 'Other' category, and during the analysis the categories were reduced even further.

[11]A more elaborate and perhaps more meaningful way to measure this variable would be to ask questions about attendance at public services of worship, type and frequency of private devotional practices, and participation in religious organizations.

[12]Meaning left of centre and including 'Labor', 'Democrats' and most of the 'Other' category. This category is also referred to as 'liberal' to distinguish it from the 'Liberal' party, which, together with the 'National' (country) party, is right of centre.

[13]This included the 'Liberal' and 'National' parties.

[14]The method by which these subscales were produced is explained in detail in Chapter 7.

Descriptive Analysis – Univariate: Looking for Characteristics

Introduction

A wide array of methods of data analysis are available in the social sciences, both quantitative and qualitative. Quantitative methods are used when the data have been collected in or are soon converted into numbers for analysis, while qualitative methods are used when data are in words and remain in words throughout the analysis. While some data begin as visual images, the classification of their analysis will depend on how they are treated in the early stages of the research: coded into numbers or remaining in words. Within both quantitative and qualitative methods, there is a wide variety of data-analysis techniques from which to choose. The choice, however, is dependent on many factors, including the nature of the data and the type of research questions that are being addressed.

In this chapter, we will encounter the most basic and commonly used methods of quantitative data analysis. While it is impossible to avoid using equations and getting involved in some mathematical procedures, the emphasis here, as in the rest of the book, is on what the methods are used for and the principles on which they are based. While computers can now do most of the calculations for us, what we need to know is what the methods do, when and how to use them and how to interpret the results.

Quantitative methods of data analysis can be divided into four main types.

- *Univariate descriptive analysis* is concerned with *summarizing* the characteristics of some phenomenon in terms of distributions on variables.
- *Bivariate descriptive analysis* is concerned with *describing* the form and strength of associations between variables, as well as *comparing* the characteristics of the same variable in different populations, or different variables in the same population.
- *Explanatory analysis* is concerned with trying to establish the direction and strength of *influence* between variables.
- *Inferential analysis* is concerned with *estimating* whether the characteristics or relationships found in a sample, or differences between samples, could be expected to exist in the population or populations from which the sample

or samples were randomly drawn; the procedures allows us to generalize sample statistics to population parameters.

While the first two are concerned with *descriptive analysis*, they are separated here as they use quite different techniques. Bivariate or associational analysis is just a sophisticated form of description. Establishing patterns or associations in data is a necessary but not a sufficient part of establishing explanations.

To put this differently, univariate descriptive analysis examines one variable at a time, while bivariate descriptive analysis deal with associations between two variables. Explanatory analysis can be either a special kind of bivariate analysis, in which the concern is with influence of one variable on another, or *multivariate analysis*, that examines the connections or influences between three or more variables.

We will be concerned with univariate descriptive analysis in this chapter, with bivariate descriptive analysis in Chapter 4, and with bivariate and multivariate explanatory analysis in Chapter 5.

Basic Mathematical Language

Before setting out on the elementary types of analysis that are discussed in this chapter, some basic mathematical concepts and symbols are defined and explained for readers who lack this knowledge or need a refresher course. Other concepts will be defined as they are introduced in the discussion of the various methods of analysis. I assume that basic arithmetical procedures, such as addition, subtraction, multiplication and division, are understood. What follows is a list of the basic symbols used in the language of data analysis. These symbols are the mathematical equivalent of nouns, adjectives, verbs and adverbs.[1]

The most commonly used *mathematical noun* in data analysis is X, and some-times Y and Z, as well as N. The letters X, Y and Z are used as shorthand to refer to values for variables. For example, X could represent a value for age (in years), Y a value for level of education achieved (in years) and Z a value for cate-gories of gender (male or female). The letter N stands for the number of items – objects, events or persons – included in the analysis.

It is possible to distinguish whether the data being analyzed come from a population or a sample. Upper-case X, Y, Z and N are commonly used for data from populations, and lower-case x, y, z and n for sample data. However, there is no consistency in the use of this convention in spite of the advantage of clarity that it brings. Where appropriate, I will use it. However, as all the data to be used for illustrations come from samples, lower-case letters will be generally used.

Mathematical nouns, such as x, can be modified by adding a *mathematical adjective*. This is done by attaching a subscript to the noun to identify to which values of a variable they refer. Thus, x_1, x_2, x_3, etc. could refer to the values of variable x for the first, second and third, etc. respondents or events. If it is required that all the values in a set of n are to be included, then the list could read $x_1, x_2, x_3, ..., x_n$. The shorthand for this list is simply x with no qualifiers.

It is also possible to include action symbols, or the equivalent of *mathematical verbs*, in data analysis. Three operators are discussed here. First, the Greek symbol sigma 'Σ' indicates that all values that follow it should be summed. Hence, Σx means that all values for variable x ($x_1, x_2, x_3,$ to x_n) are to be added together. Second, the square root symbol $\sqrt{}$ indicates that a number is required which, when multiplied by itself, will equal the number that follows the symbol. Hence, $\sqrt{9}$ is 3. When a superscript number is placed before the root symbol, it indicates that a number is required which, when multiplied by itself the number of times the superscript indicates, produces the number that follows the symbol. In other words, the cube root of 27, $\sqrt[3]{27}$, is 3.[2] Third, a superscript placed after the symbol x, such as x^2, indicates that each value for x should be multiplied by itself the number times the superscript indicates. Hence, x^2 means $x \times x$, for all values of x, x^3 means that x is to be cubed, and so on. The superscript is known as the exponent and the process is known as raising to the power indicated.

It is possible to modify the operator or mathematical verb Σ with a *mathematical adverb*. For example, modifiers in the form of small notations above and below Σ (e.g. $\sum_{i=1}^{n}$) are used to specify very precisely which values in a list are to be added together. However, as these modifiers will not be used in this book, mainly because they add unnecessarily to symbol phobia, I will spare you the agony of trying to work out what they mean.

Mathematical equations make extensive use of brackets to isolate operations, such as $(4 + 3) \times (8 - 6)$. Without the brackets it would be unclear what is required. The calculations within the brackets need to be completed first, and then the two resulting numbers multiplied, that is, $7 \times 2 = 14$. Normally, the multiplication sign is omitted and the expression becomes $(4 + 3)(8 - 6)$. Hence, adjoining brackets signify multiplication. Similarly, when a single number precedes a bracket, such as $7(8 - 6)$, multiplication is also required. This expression can also be shown correctly as $(7)(8 - 6)$. Sometimes, different-shaped brackets are used together if the order of a number of steps needs to be made clear. For example, $8[(4 + 3)(8 - 6) + 5^3]$ indicates that the parts in the curved brackets should be dealt with first (14), that 5 should be cubed (125), that these two number should then be summed (139) and the result multiplied by 8, giving a result of 1,112.

While division can by indicated by the usual sign ($\div$), equations normally use two other conventions. One is the slash sign ($/$), such that the number before the slash is to be divided by the number following it (e.g. $139/71 = 1.958$). Alternatively, a horizontal line can be used, with the number above it (the numerator) being divided by the number below it (the denominator). The latter is the more usual convention in complex equations.

Finally, in doing the calculations required to solve a mathematical equation, there is an order of priority in which the actions need to be undertaken. While it is difficult to specify these as a regular series of steps, it is possible to state them as a number of rules. The following are the two most general rules.

1. Start at the left of the equation and work to the right.
2. Complete the operations inside brackets (such as additions and subtractions) before those outside. In other words, reduce what is inside brackets to a single number before performing any operation between a bracketed section and other parts of the equation, or between what lies above and below a horizontal line.

In addition to these, other rules should also be followed for expressions within and outside brackets, as well as above and below a division line. However, these do not form a neat sequence.

3. Where possible, calculate exponents (such as squares and square roots) first. The major exception to this is where it is necessary to raise to a power (e.g. cube) or take some root (e.g. square root) of everything on one side of the equation. In this case, this will usually be the last operation.
4. Multiplications and divisions generally follow additions and subtractions and the calculation of individual exponents.
5. The last steps are likely to be a major division and/or taking a root or raising to a power.

To clarify these rules, here is an example done in stages.

$$a = \sqrt{\frac{(4+3)(8-6)+5^3}{6(8-3)-(2-7)}} = \sqrt{\frac{(7)(2)+125}{6(5)-(-5)}} = \sqrt{\frac{14+125}{30+5}}$$

$$= \sqrt{\frac{139}{35}} = \sqrt{3.971} = 1.993$$

Doing the calculations in this order reduces what looks like a complicated equation to a series of simple arithmetic steps. None of the equations to be encountered from here on will require anything more complex than this.

It important to watch out for negative signs. Normally a number with no sign in front of it is assumed to be a positive number. For example, $(4+3)$ is the same as $(+4+3)$ or, if you like, $(+4++3) = 7$. In this case, the plus sign is used in two ways, to indicate a positive number and the operation that is to be performed between two numbers. Similarly, $(8-6) = (+8-+6) = 2$, which means subtracting a positive number from another positive number. Note that the sign of a number adjoins it, while an operator is usually separated by spaces on either side. If the expression was $(-8-+6)$, the answer would be -14. Subtracting a positive number from a negative number makes an even bigger negative number. This is the same as adding two negative numbers together $(-8+-6)$.

Here are some further rules for dealing with positive and negative numbers.

- Two negatives make a positive, that is, when a negative number follows a negative operator, the operation becomes addition (e.g. $+5--6 = 11$, which is equivalent to $5 + 6$).

- A negative and a positive sign together makes a negative operation, that is, when a negative number follows a positive operator, or the reverse, the operation is subtraction (e.g. $+5 + -6 = -1$ or $+5 - +6 = -1$, or just $5 - 6$).
- Subtracting a positive number from a negative number produces an even bigger negative number ($-5 - +6 = -11$).
- Multiplying two negative numbers produces a positive number (e.g. $-5 \times -6 = +30$).
- The same is the case when a negative number is squared ($-5^2 = +25$), whereas cubing a negative number produces a negative number ($-5^3 = -125$). When raising a negative number to higher powers the rule is that when the power is an even number the result is positive, and when it is an odd number the result is negative.
- Multiplying one positive and one negative number makes a negative number (e.g. $-5 \times +2 = -10$).

With these few simple rules, you should now be ready to confront the basic methods of data analysis.

Univariate Descriptive Analysis

Before proceeding to discuss the basic methods of descriptive, explanatory and inferential analysis, we need to spend a little time examining ways in which raw data can be summarized and presented. The reasons for doing this are mainly to help the researcher to discover patterns or trends and then be able to communicate these clearly.

'What' questions can usually be answered with simple descriptions, that is, simple summaries of the characteristics of some aspect of a social phenomenon. It is by means of variables that we isolate these aspects, and it is by counting, and simple manipulation of the resulting number, that we are able to offer descriptions. More complex techniques may not be required.

While 'what' questions are important and legitimate in their own right, answers to such questions are required before we know which 'why' questions need to be asked. For example, a research question might ask: 'To what extent are aluminium cans recycled?' This could be answered by asking a random sample of people whether the cans they use are normally recycled. Alternatively, it would be possible, over a set period of time, to compare the weight of aluminium cans produced with the weight of those that are recycled. In the first case we could calculate a percentage of people who behave this way, and in the second case we could arrive at a percentage of cans that are actually recycled. In both cases, simple counting is involved to produce the answer. Then it is possible to ask a 'why' question: 'Why do people differ in their recycling behaviour?' In short, we need to describe in order to have something to explain.

Describing Distributions

The following methods for summarizing and presenting descriptive data are discussed here.

- Frequency counts across categorical data and discrete and grouped metric data.
- Summary values for frequencies and/or comparisons between categories: proportions and percentages, ratios and rates.
- Pictorial representations of distributions: bar charts and pie charts for categorical data; and histograms and line graphs for metric data.

Frequency Counts and Distributions

Frequency counts and *distributions* are used to summarize large sets of data. To establish frequencies of occurrence, data must be in categories. Frequency counts summarize data that have been collected in *nominal* categories, *ordinal* categories, in whole numbers (*discrete* data), and in *continuous* values or scores that have been grouped into categories.

Nominal categories

Raw data are usually compiled in unordered lists. For example, in the Student sample, Religion[3] was coded into seven categories and numbered from 1 to 7 as follows: 1, 'Catholic'; 2, 'Anglican'; 3, 'Uniting'; 4, 'Greek Orthodox'; 5, 'Baptist'; 6, 'Other'; and 7, 'No religion'.[4] The list of raw data is shown in Table 3.1.

It is obviously very difficult to make any sense of data that are displayed in this way. Even if the numbers were replaced by the names of the categories, it would still be extremely difficult. However, if the frequencies (f) with which each religion is represented in the sample are tallied, then it is possible to see how many respondents there are in each religious category (see Table 3.2).

It is now possible to interpret these data at a glance. Understanding a distribution can be further enhanced by calculating percentages (see the following discussion of 'Proportions and percentages' for the procedure). Now we know both the absolute number as well as the proportion out of 100 each category contributed to the sample.

There are a few points to note about this table. First, the total n for the Student sample is less than the sample size. There were 20 non-responses to the question on Religion and these have been excluded. As many of the other variables in both samples have a few non-responses there will be some variation in the totals of the tables presented. Second, while one decimal place has been used for the percentages, whole numbers would have been perfectly adequate. Not only are they easier to read and compare, but decimal places can also imply a false sense of precision in the data. Third, due to the rounding up and down of each percentage to one decimal place, the rounded percentages may not add up to exactly 100.0. Sometimes it may be 0.1 over or under. However, if a second decimal place was used, the total, rounded up, will be 100.0.

There are various *rules for rounding*. When the second decimal place is less than 5, round down; when it is more than 5, round up. However, when it is

Table 3.1   *Raw data on Religion (Students)*

2	5	1	1	6	7	7	4	7	7	1	1
1	7	1	7	1	7	1	1	6	1	6	1
7	1	1	7	6	7	2	2	7	1	7	4
3	4	1	7	6	1	1	1	7	7	4	6
4	6	1	1	2	4	1	2	2	2	1	1
4	1	7	2	7	2	1	2	2	7	1	7
4	4	7	7	7	7	7	7	1	1	7	1
6	7	1	2	6	1	7	6	1	4	6	7
7	1	7	7	1	6	7	5	7	3	7	7
3	6	1	7	7	7	1	1	3	7	7	6
1	1	2	1	7	2	1	2	1	1	7	7
2	1	7	3	3	1	7	1	7	7	3	7
7	7	7	2	1	2	4	1	6	7	7	7
1	7	1	2	7	7	7	6	1	1	6	6
2	1	7	1	7	6	7	1	1	1	7	6
1	1	1	7	7	7	7	1	7	3	1	7
1	1	1	7	6	1	7	3	1	1	2	2
1	1	1	7	7	3	1	7	5	7	1	7
6	1	3	1	7	7	1	7	2	2	1	7
7	2	5	7	5	1	1	2	1	7	7	6
5	6	6	7	7	1	5	2	1	6	3	7
2	3	1	7	1	7	1	1	1	3	1	6
7	2	5	7	7	6	1	1	1	1	1	7
7	6	7	1	7	3	3	6	1	1	7	6
3	1	2	2	7	6	1	2	3	2	2	1
4	6	1	7	7	6	4	7	1	7	3	2
7	7	2	1	1	7	3	5	3	7	2	7
4	7	6	7	6	1	2	2	7	2	2	7
7	7	2	6	2	1	3	7	2	7	1	7
2	2	7	7	7	7	6	3	7	2	7	2
1	7	6	6	7	6	7	1	1	1	7	2
6	1	2	7	5	1	3	3	1	2	1	7
1	3	4	1	1	7	1	1	1	1	7	1
7	7	6	7	2	1	6	1	7	6	1	7
3	2	4	2	3	7	7	1	1	1	1	1
2	7	6	4	3	2	1	1	2	7	1	5
7	7	1	1	1	1	1	7	1	7	7	7
											7

Table 3.2   *Distribution by Religion (both samples)*

	Students		Residents	
Religion	*f*	%	*f*	%
Catholic	139	31.2	85	21.1
Anglican	57	12.8	91	22.6
Uniting	29	6.5	55	13.7
Greek Orthodox	17	3.8	9	2.2
Baptist	11	2.5	5	1.2
Other	46	10.3	57	14.2
No religion	146	32.8	100	24.9
n	445	100.0	402	100.0

exactly 5, there are different options. The simplest one is to always round up. However, another procedure is to round to an even number. For example, 31.25 would become 31.2, as would 31.15; the first is rounded down and the second is rounded up. While usually following these rules, my method has been to examine the total after rounding up all percentages with 5 in the second place and, if the total exceeds 100.0, then round one or more of these border-line cases down to achieve the exact total. If there is a choice, I would usually adopt a conservative strategy of picking the largest number in which to make the change. Whatever rules are used, they can be applied to any number of decimal places, including rounding up or down to whole numbers.

Ordinal categories

Doing a frequency count of data in ordinal categories is essentially the same as for norminal categories. For example, respondents in both samples were asked: 'To what extent do you regard yourself as a religious or spiritual person?' Four response categories were provided: 1, 'Very religious'; 2, 'Moderately religious'; 3, 'Not very religious'; and 4, 'Not at all religious'. The frequency count is shown in Table 3.3. These categories are clearly only ordinal as the intervals between them cannot be regarded as equal. Even if some respondents regarded the intervals as equal when they responded to the categories, others may not have and researchers therefore cannot do so.

The main difference between nominal-level and ordinal-level categories is that the numbering of the former is arbitrary while, for the latter, it reflects the ordering. However, it is still not possible to manipulate the numbers used for the categories by any arithmetical procedures. Initially, all that can be done is to count the number of responses in each category and, usually, calculate percentages based on these frequencies.

However, further analysis of frequency counts of both nominal and ordinal data can include comparisons between the categories. In the case of Religion in the Student sample, we can say that 'Catholic' is the largest denomination represented (31.2 per cent), and that the largest category is 'No religion' (32.8 per cent).

By definition, ordinal categories have an underlying order at the outset. It would be unusual to reorder them in terms of another criterion, such as frequency of response. However, it is possible to make comparisons in terms of 'more or higher than' and 'less or lower than'. For example, in Table 3.3, in the Student sample, the 'Very religious' category has the lowest response (15.3 per cent), and 'Moderately religious' the highest response (33.8 per cent). It is also

Table 3.3 *Distribution by Religiosity (both samples)*

Religiosity	Students		Residents	
	f	%	*f*	%
Not at all religious	112	24.5	51	12.7
Not very religious	121	26.4	99	24.7
Moderately religious	155	33.8	155	38.7
Very religious	70	15.3	96	23.9
n	458	100.0	401	100.0

clear that nearly half of the sample say they are at least moderately religious (49.1 per cent). Hence, if numbers are used with such categories, their value indicates the position in the order; for example, that 1 is higher than 2, and that 4 is lower then 3. The numbers can mean nothing more than this.

An interesting aspect of nominal categories is that it may be possible to do a *post hoc* ordering of them on some criterion, such as their relative frequency. In the case of Religion in the Student sample, the order from highest to lowest is: 'No religion', 'Catholic', 'Other', 'Anglican', 'Uniting', 'Greek Orthodox' and 'Baptist'. The categories could have been listed in the table in this order, and they could be renumbered to correspond to it.

There is nothing very mathematical about any of this; counting and calculating percentages and, perhaps, introducing some order into the categories is about as far as you can go. Later we will see how responses on such variables (sets of nominal-level and ordinal-level categories) can be compared with other variables (interval-level and ratio-level numbers or scores).

Discrete and grouped data

It is also possible to do frequency counts of continuous data in whole numbers. For example, in the Student sample, it is possible to count the number of respondents by Age (in years) even although this is a ratio level of measurement (see Table 3.4). Because this is a sample of university students, there is a concentration in the range 18 to 21. A few older students create a long tail in the distribution. While some points (i.e. ages) are missing in the display, the level

Table 3.4   *Age distribution in years (Students)*

Age	f	%
18	84	18.3
19	113	24.6
20	88	19.1
21	45	9.8
22	42	9.1
23	13	2.8
24	17	3.7
25	13	2.8
26	5	1.1
27	3	0.7
28	5	1.1
29	6	1.3
30	3	0.7
31	3	0.7
32	5	1.1
33	4	0.9
34	3	0.7
36	1	0.2
37	3	0.7
38	2	0.4
42	1	0.2
46	1	0.2
n	460	100.0

Table 3.5   *Age distribution in five categories (Students)*

Age	f	%
18	84	18.3
19	113	24.6
20	88	19.1
21–22	87	18.9
23+	88	19.1
n	460	100.0

Table 3.6   *Age distribution in six categories (Residents)*

Age	f	%	cum f
18–24	47	11.7	47
25–34	81	20.2	128
35–44	79	19.7	207
45–54	59	14.7	266
55–64	56	14.0	322
65+	79	19.7	401
n	401	100.0	

of measurement is still ratio; all categories are separated by an interval of one unit and there is an absolute zero.

Such distributions can be collapsed into a more limited number of mutually exclusive and exhaustive categories. The reason for doing this is that:

- it may be unwieldy to present the whole range of numbers or scores;
- some numbers or scores may have a low frequency that does not warrant them being treated separately; and
- a more limited set of categories can provide a meaningful summary of the data.

In Table 3.4, it would be convenient to collapse the older ages into, say, two categories: 25 to 29 ($n = 32$); and 30 and over ($n = 26$). This could be taken further: say, 22 to 23 ($n = 55$) and 24 and over ($n = 75$); or 21 to 22 ($n = 87$) and 23 and over ($n = 88$).[5] The latter gives a fairly even distribution across six categories (see Table 3.5).

Apart from display purposes, such collapsing of categories may be useful for certain kinds of analysis, examples of which will be discussed in later chapters. However, once categories are collapsed like this, and they are used in analysis, the measurement of variables such as Age has been transformed from ratio to only ordinal level. While this severely limits the kinds of analysis that can be done, it does open up some useful methods at a lower level of sophistication. It is now possible to get a sense of the Age distribution and to make comparisons with other Age distributions in a way that is not possible if the data remain in their 'raw' form.

If the data came from a general sample or population that covers the full age range of human beings, doing a frequency count of age (in years) becomes very cumbersome and difficult to interpret; there may be more than a hundred categories to deal with. Hence, for certain purposes, it may be useful to transform such a range into a limited number of categories. For example, in the Resident sample, Age might be collapsed into six categories (see Table 3.6).

A genuine example of ratio-level measurement that can be dealt with in discrete categories is the number of children respondents have (see Table 3.7). In the Resident sample, the large percentage of respondents without children (34.8 per cent) is due to the fact that some respondents have never been married ($n = 92$). Twenty-two (5.5 per cent) described themselves as living in a stable relationship, and only three of those who have never been married indicated that they had children. Therefore, this distribution would be more meaningful if those who have never been married and do not have children ($n = 89$) are excluded. The distribution now looks rather different (see Table 3.8). The differences between Tables 3.7 and 3.8 indicate how important it is to be clear about how the percentages have been calculated. Table 3.7 shows that 28.1 per cent have two children, while Table 3.8 shows 36.1 per cent. Both are correct, but the former is based on the whole sample while the latter is based on only a subsample. Care must be taken in interpreting the meaning of such tables.

Table 3.7   *Number of children (Residents)*

No. of children	f	%
0	140	34.8
1	42	10.4
2	113	28.1
3	72	17.9
4	21	5.2
5	4	1.0
6	7	1.7
7	0	0.0
8	1	0.2
9	0	0.0
10	2	0.5
n	402	100.0

Table 3.8   *Number of children (subsample of Residents)*

No. of children	f	%
0	51	16.3
1	42	13.4
2	113	36.1
3	72	23.0
4	21	6.7
5	4	1.3
6	7	2.2
7	0	0.0
8	1	0.3
9	0	0.0
10	2	0.6
n	313	100.0

In cases where interval-level or ratio-level data have been transformed into categories, there are advantages in using categories of equal width. This makes it possible to treat the categories as at least interval-level measurement and, therefore, to be able to perform more sophisticated analysis than is possible on ordinal-level data. The categories used in Table 3.6 do not quite achieve this, as the extreme Age categories are different from the other four. However, if they had been in intervals of 10 years, starting with 0–9, 10–19, and so on, to include the whole age range, the level of measurement would be ratio. The only thing that has changed is the unit of measurement. Units of one year are not sacred for measuring Age; we could use something like months, and might if we were researching very young children. Hence, intervals of 10 years, or 15 years, do not destroy ratio-level measurement.

The interval contained within each category, and the boundaries between such categories, can vary depending on the age distribution in the population or sample, and the purpose of the research. It is up to the researcher to decide what would be most useful. Such a decision becomes clear if we wanted to compare two very different age distributions using the same categories, such as those in the two samples. As different categories have been used in Tables 3.5 and 3.6, one or both sets of categories would need to be changed to allow a meaningful comparison. Table 3.9 presents a possible solution. With the exception of the '18–19' Age category, and with '20–24' and '25–29' combined, these categories constitute ratio-level measurement. The '20–29' Age category was divided to reveal the large number of students in the '20–24' interval, and to make comparisons between the samples possible.

Table 3.9 *Comparison of Student and Resident samples by Age*

Age categories	Students		Residents	
	f	%	f	%
18–19	197	42.8	10	2.5
20–24	205	44.6	37	9.2
(20–29)	(237)	(51.5)	(75)	(18.7)
25–29	32	7.0	38	9.5
30–39	24	5.2	88	21.9
40–49	2	0.4	71	17.7
50–59	–	–	50	12.5
60–69	–	–	55	13.7
70–79	–	–	36	9.0
80–89	–	–	13	3.2
90–99	–	–	3	0.7
Totals	460	100.0	401	100.0

The procedure used to establish a set of categories of equal width is as follows:

- Establish the range of units (e.g. ages or scores) and add one to the total. In the case of Age (in years), the range could be between 0 and 99. The resulting number would be 100.
- Decide how wide each category should be, say 10, and divide the above number by this. In this case, there would be 10 categories, each including 10 years.
- Start with the lowest unit, 0 in this case, and establish the first category, i.e. 0–9. The next category would be 10–19, and so on to 90–99.

- Assign each unit to its appropriate category. A *frequency distribution* of grouped data can then be produced.[6]

If categories of varying width are required, as in Table 3.5, the number of categories, and their widths, can be established from the original frequency distribution, as in Table 3.4.

Proportions and Percentages, Ratios and Rates

In order to undertake certain types of data analysis, such as discussing the characteristics of a frequency distribution, or comparing data across categories, we need to reduce frequencies, the raw data, to some common base. This is done in two related ways: by calculating either proportions or percentages.

Proportions

The base that is used to calculate *proportions* is the unit of '1' or, perhaps '1.00'.[7] In a frequency distribution, each category will be seen to contribute a part of or a proportion of the total, that is, if we assume the total has a value of 1.00, then each category will make up a part of this. Whatever the total number is in a distribution, we assume it to be equal to 1.00. We then have to adjust the frequencies for each category so that their contributions add up to 1.00. To do this, the frequency for each category is divided by the total frequency. For example, in Table 3.5, the frequency for the first category (84) would be divided by the total (460) to produce a proportion of 0.18 (to two decimal places) or 0.183 (to three decimal places). Similarly for the other categories. The equation for this is:

$$\text{Proportion } (p) = \frac{f}{n} \tag{3.1}$$

where *f* is the frequency for any category, and *n* is the total number of responses or units for all categories.

Proportions can range from 0.00 (if none of the cases lies in a category) to 1.00 (if a category contains all the cases). Table 3.10 shows the proportions of males and females in both samples.

Percentages

A *percentage* is simply another way of expressing a proportion. In this case, the base is 100 rather than 1.00. Hence, proportions can be converted to percentages by multiplying each one by 100. In Table 3.10, 45 per cent of Students are males and 55 per cent are females. Similarly for Residents, the percentages are both 50. If the proportions had been calculated to three decimal places, the percentages could be shown to one decimal place.

Table 3.10 *Comparison of Gender proportions (both samples)*

Gender	Students		Residents	
	f	p	f	p
Males	210	0.45	200	0.50
Females	254	0.55	199	0.50
Totals	464	1.00	399	1.00

The equation for calculating percentages is the same as that for proportions, except that it is multiplied by 100.

$$\text{Percentage } (\%) = \frac{f}{n} \times 100 \qquad (3.2)$$

Percentages are more commonly used than proportions, perhaps because whole numbers are easier to read and are less prone than numbers starting with a decimal point to recording and reading errors. Why is 100 used as a base? It is just a convention, but it has all the advantages of the 'metric' system of measurement and is a big enough number to be shared meaningfully between categories.

As well as using percentages to compare the relative sizes of data in categories, it is also possible to use them as a measure of change over time. We may want to know whether, over a 50-year period, the population in one country has increased at a faster or slower rate than that in another country. At the beginning of 1950 there were 12 million in country A and 153 million in country B. At the beginning of 2000 there were 21 million and 204 million, respectively. Clearly, country A has grown by only 9 million compared to 51 million for country B. Because the two countries had different-sized populations in 1950, what we need to know is the percentage increase in both cases. To do this, we divide the increase in the population by the number at the first point of time, and then multiply by 100. The equation is:

$$\text{Percentage change} = \frac{(\text{quantity at time 2}) - (\text{quantity at time 1})}{(\text{quantity at time 1})} \times 100 \qquad (3.3)$$

The calculations for the above example are as follows.

$$\text{Country A: Percentage change} = \frac{21-12}{21} \times 100 = \frac{9}{21} \times 100 = 0.429 \times 100 = 42.9\%$$

$$\text{Country B: Percentage change} = \frac{204-153}{153} \times 100 = \frac{51}{153} \times 100 = 0.333 \times 100 = 33.3\%$$

Hence, the relative size of the population growth for country A is greater than that for country B. This may not be obvious from the raw data.

Ratios

A *ratio* is used to compare the relative size of two categories. It is calculated by dividing the frequency in the larger category by the frequency in the smaller one. For example, Table 3.2 on the distribution by Religion in the Student sample shows that there are 139 Catholics and 57 Anglicans. The ratio of Anglicans to Catholics is 1 : 2.4. We arrive at this by dividing the number of Catholics by the number of Anglicans. Hence, for every Anglican in the Student sample, there are 2.4 Catholics. It is also possible to multiply both sides of the ratio by, say, 100, to eliminate the decimal places. Hence, the ratio could be expressed as 100 : 240. In the Resident sample, the ratio is 1 : 1.07, but the other way around; for every 100 Catholics there are 107 Anglicans. All that a ratio does is to simplify the comparison by reducing the two numbers to an easily inter-preted base, usually either '1' or '100', and then making one of the categories the base.

Social scientists frequently use sex ratios to compare the relative numbers of males and females in a population or sample. In Table 3.10, the sex ratio of the Student sample would be calculated as follows.

$$\text{Ratio} = \frac{\text{number in the largest category}}{\text{number in the smallest category}} \qquad (3.4)$$

$$= \frac{254}{210} = 1.21$$

Hence, the ratio is 1 : 1.21; for every male there are 1.21 females. For large populations or samples, this might be better expressed as: for every 100 males there are 121 females.

It is possible to compare more than two categories using ratios. To do this, one category is reduced to either '1' or '100' and the rest are calculated separately in relationship to it. For example, in Table 3.2 we could compare the relative sizes of the four largest religions by making 'Greek Orthodox' the base of '1'. In the Student sample, the ratios of 'Greek Orthodox' to 'Uniting', 'Anglican' and 'Catholic' are 1 : 1.71 : 3.35 : 8.18. In the Resident sample the ratios are 1 : 6.11 : 10.11 : 9.44. However, such comparisons may have limited utility as they can just as easily be expressed in terms of percentages.

This raises the question of the differences between ratios, proportions and percentages. As we have seen, the difference between the latter two is just a matter of choice between working with a base of '1' (proportions) or a base of '100' (percentages). The latter two differ from ratios in that, for proportions and percentages, it is the total of all categories that is made the base of '1' or '100' and each category is regarded as making up a share of this base. In the case of a ratio, one of the categories is made the base of '1' or '100', or some larger round number, and the other categories are compared with it.

When data are grouped into categories, frequency counts and percentages are appropriate forms of data analysis. These are certainly the main ways of representing distributions of nominal-level and ordinal-level data, and can also be used for higher levels of measurement in discrete or grouped categories. Other more sophisticated ways of representing the character of distributions are available for use with interval-level and ratio-level data. Alternatively, in the earlier discussion of levels of measurement, we noted that many of the data-analysis procedures that are used with interval-level and ratio-level data cannot be used with nominal-level and ordinal-level data. For example, while we can say that one person is twice the age of another (ratio-level data), we cannot use this expression, or others like 'greater than' or 'higher than', with the categories of Religion (nominal-level data). However, the process of counting the frequencies in nominal categories such as Religion has introduced ratio-level assumptions. It is assumed that all members of a category are of equal value or magnitude, and that it is appropriate to map them onto our number system. In this way, two members of one category can be regarded as being twice as many as only one member of another category. This means that we can compare the size of categories using ratios even although the original level of measurement was, say, only nominal. Hence, while the calculation of ratios is only appropriate for ratio-level measurement, for certain purposes, frequencies in categories can be regarded as ratio-level.

Rates

Rates provide another variation on the idea of reducing numbers to a common base. They are used to summarize and compare events occurring in a population or category over time, or between different populations or categories. These events include such things as births, deaths, crimes or suicides. Because it can be difficult to make sense of the raw data on such events, it is necessary to reduce them to a common base such as 100, 1,000 or 100,000.

A rate is like a ratio in which the larger number is the total for a population rather than being just one category. However, in this case, each population is reduced to a common base. In effect, a rate is like a proportion or percentage but it usually has a much larger base. In other words, the number of events under consideration is divided by the total population in which they occur. Then this is multiplied by a convenient number that has been determined as the base. It is then possible to compare the relative frequency of these events across time and space. The equation for a base of 1,000 is as follows.

$$\text{Rate} = \frac{\text{number of events}}{\text{total population of events}} \times 1{,}000 \qquad (3.5)$$

Pictorial Representations

In addition to being presented in tabular form, frequency counts and distributions can be presented pictorially or graphically. The commonly used methods are bar charts and pie charts for categorical variables, and histograms and line graphs for metric variables consisting of discrete or grouped data. Some of the frequency counts and distributions presented in the previous section will be used as illustrations.

Categorical variables

In presenting frequency counts pictorially, it is important not to give a distorted impression of a distribution. It is very easy to exaggerate or minimize differences between categories by stretching or compressing the vertical scale on a chart or graph. Therefore, care must be taken to select the vertical scale carefully.

Bar charts are used to represent the frequency counts of nominal-level and ordinal-level data, or grouped data from interval-level or ratio-level variables. The bars are kept separate for the former two levels of measurement to indicate either that the categories do not lie on an underlying continuum (nominal-level data) or that the intervals between them cannot be assumed to be equal (ordinal-level data). Figure 3.1 presents a bar chart of the frequency count of the nominal data in Table 3.2, that is, Religion for the Student sample.

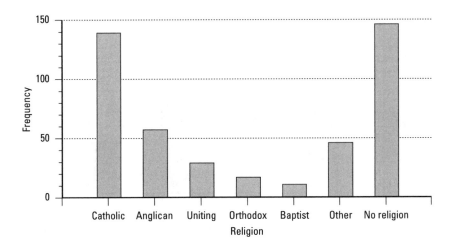

Figure 3.1   *Religion (Students): bar chart*

When only one data set is involved, it makes no difference to the relative size of the bars whether frequencies or percentages are used. The advantage of using frequencies is that it is possible to read off the size of any category, thus preserving the original character of the data. However, when comparisons are being made of the same variable between two data sets, percentages must be used if the sample sizes are different. Figure 3.2 provides a comparison of Student and Resident religious affiliation. Figure 3.3 shows a bar chart of the frequency counts of ordinal-level data in Table 3.3, that is, Religiosity for both samples.

Pie charts provide an alternative way of presenting frequency counts pictorially. The bars of a chart are replaced by segments of a circle such that the area of a segment corresponds to the frequency in that category. Figures 3.4 and 3.5

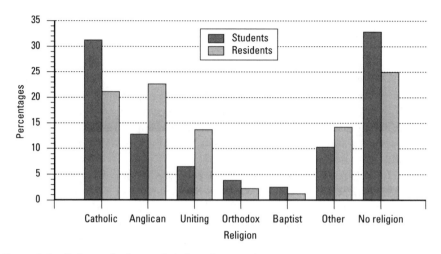

Figure 3.2   *Religion (both samples): bar chart*

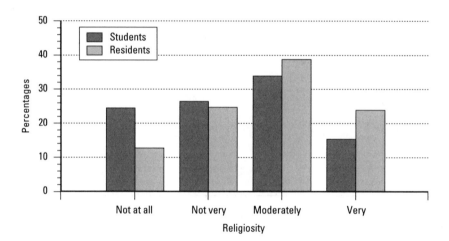

Figure 3.3   *Religiosity (both samples): bar chart*

show pie charts based on the Student distributions in Tables 3.2 and 3.3, respectively. They are alternative presentations to the bar charts in Figures 3.1 and the Student component in Figure 3.3.

Metric variables

Because of the continuous nature of their form of measurement, metric variables using discrete or grouped data can be represented pictorially either as histograms or as continuous lines.

The *histogram* is a variation on the bar chart such that the bars touch each other to create a stair pattern. Instead of having gaps between the bars, they are

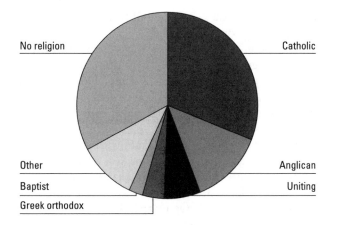

Figure 3.4   *Religion (Students): pie chart*

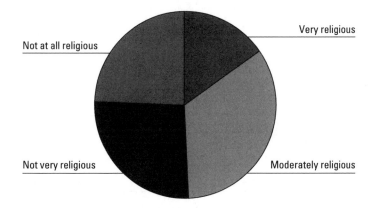

Figure 3.5   *Religiosity (Students): pie chart*

put together to convey the idea that the level of measurement is continuous, even though categories are used. When categories of differing intervals are used with such data, it is possible to present a histogram that indicates this by varying the widths of the bars. For example, in Table 3.9, the first category ('18–19') is a different width from all the others. Also, if the '20–29' category was split to give a clearer picture of the Age distribution in the Student sample, these categories would also be of a different width from those that follow. If the width of the bars does not correspond to the age interval of each category, it would be easy to misinterpret the representation of the age distribution in a histogram. The reason is that it is not just the height (or length) of the bar that is relevant in such cases. While height indicates the frequency of responses, the width of the bar represents the width of the category. It is the area included in a bar that is the true indicator of the relative frequency in each category. Hence, by adjusting the width of the bar to correspond to the interval of the category, a more accurate representation is produced.

Unfortunately, none of the software packages I am familiar with seems able to create genuine histograms or to allow for variations in the width of the categories. Of course, they could be drawn by hand! However, a perfectly good alternative is available, and that is to use line or area graphs.

Any histogram with categories of equal width or interval can be converted into a *line graph*, also known as an area graph or a frequency polygon, by joining up the midpoints of the bars in a histogram with straight lines. When many categories are involved, the line may approach a curve, or a curve could be drawn through them. Figure 3.6 provides an example of line graphs, based on the Age distributions in Table 3.9. Note that as no adjustment has been made to the width of the youngest age category to indicate that it is narrower than all the others (because the software does not allow it), there is a distortion in the representation of the size of this category.

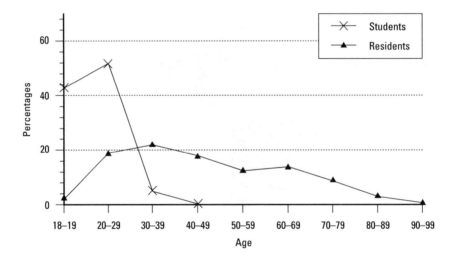

Figure 3.6 *Age (both samples): line graphs*

These four major ways of representing frequency distributions pictorially provide a range of possibilities. However, care must be taken to:

- use one that is appropriate to the level of measurement;
- faithfully represent the data and not produce a distorted impression; and
- interpret the data correctly.

Shapes of Frequency Distributions: Symmetrical, Skewed and Normal

Frequency distributions of metric variables can take on many different shapes, both symmetrical or skewed. In *symmetrical distributions*, the two halves will coincide when folded vertically along the middle (a trick used in origami to

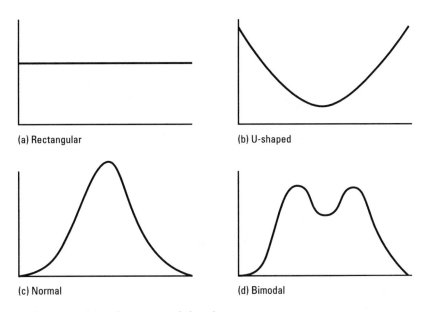

(a) Rectangular

(b) U-shaped

(c) Normal

(d) Bimodal

Figure 3.7   *Examples of symmetrical distributions*

create symmetrical shapes). *Skewed distributions* 'lean' to the lower end (*positively skewed*) or the higher end (*negatively skewed*). Figure 3.6 shows two different types of positively skewed distributions.

Symmetrical distributions can take many forms, the most common of which are shown in Figure 3.7. Figure 3.7(a) contains a rectangular distribution in which all categories have the same frequency. Figure 3.7(b) shows a U-shaped distribution in which the categories at the extremes have much higher frequencies than the middle categories. Figure 3.7(c) contains a bell-shaped distribution in which the highest frequencies are in the middle categories and the lowest frequencies at the extremes. Finally, Figure 3.7(d) contains a bimodal distribution in which there are two points with high frequencies and the lowest frequencies are at the extremes.

This is an appropriate point to introduce the notion of the *normal distribution* which, when graphed, takes the shape of a symmetrical bell-shaped distribution known as a *bell curve* or *normal curve*. The normal distribution is a theoretical notion of great importance to statisticians. It is the basis of the theory that is used to estimate population parameters from sample statistics. It is also the shape of the distribution that is required for the use of certain statistical procedures. The shape of the normal curve is determined by a complex mathematical equation and it has special mathematical properties. In theory, an infinite number of measurements are required to produce a normal distribution. However, it can be approached with particular types of data, based on measurements with very large populations or samples. While some data distributions may resemble a normal curve, they can never match it perfectly. We will come back to the characteristics of the normal curve shortly.

Measures of Central Tendency

In addition to tabular and pictorial representations of distributions, it is also possible to describe their characteristics with summary statistics known as measures of central tendency and measures of dispersion. The following measures of central tendency or central location are covered in this section:

- Categorical data, and discrete and grouped metric data: mode (nominal-level data) and median (ordinal-level data).
- Metric data: mean.

The Three Ms

Measures of central tendency are designed to indicate the 'middle' or 'most typical' point (e.g. category or score) in a distribution. The everyday term for this is the 'average'. However, there are three commonly used measures of an average: the mode, median and mean. Hence, to avoid confusion, the concept of average will not be used here. The discussion will be confined to the technical meaning of these three terms.

Mode

The *mode* is the crudest of the three measures of central tendency and has limited value. It is defined as *the value that occurs with the highest frequency* and is obtained by inspecting a distribution. For example, in Table 3.2 (Figure 3.2) the mode is 'No religion' for both Students and Residents, in Table 3.3 (Figure 3.3) it is 'Moderately religious' for both samples, in Tables 3.4 and 3.5 it is '19' years, in Table 3.6 it is the '25–34' Age category, and in Table 3.8 it is '2' children.

These examples are a mixture of levels of measurement and include nominal-level categories (Religion), categories of grouped data from a ratio-level variable (Age) and ratio-level measurement in whole numbers (Number of children). The mode can be used for all such distributions and, hence, for all four levels of measurement when the data are in categories. However, the meaning of the mode is rather different for nominal-level data than for the other three. In the former, the position of the modal category in a distribution has no significance, as the order of the categories is arbitrary. However, in the other three levels of measurement, the position of the category may have some relevance, particularly in the context of the frequencies in the other categories. For example, in Table 3.8, the modal category of '2' children does indicate an important feature of the distribution; it is the 'peak' category. The same is the case in Table 3.3, although the 'peak' is less prominent. However, in Table 3.2, while the modal category has the highest frequency, there are a number of other categories with high frequencies; these smaller categories may be just as interesting.

Distributions with two adjoining categories of the same and highest frequency are called bimodal. However, a bimodal distribution may also have two peaks or humps that are separated by at least one category and that have frequencies that are not necessarily equal. Table 3.6 is an example of bimodal ordinal-level (nearly interval-level) categories ('25–34' and '65+'), and Table 3.8 (Figure 3.5) is an example of a bimodal set of ratio-level categories ('0' and '2'). It should be clear that care must to be taken in interpreting the modal category or categories in the case of grouped data with categories of unequal width. Changing the widths of the categories can change the shape of the distribution and, perhaps, the modal category or categories.

Median

The *median is the position in a distribution above and below which half of the frequencies fall.* It splits a distribution into two equal parts; there are as many responses or scores to the left of the median as there are to the right. In short, the median is half-way 'along' a distribution. The median is not appropriate for nominal-level data, but it can be used for all the other three levels of measurement.

The simplest version of a median occurs with a set of unique scores, that is, when every score in the set is different. For example, a group of 15 children were given a standardized test for a particular ability. Their scores, arranged in order from lowest to highest, were:

68 76 79 83 87 92 97 105 108 113 118 121 134 135 139

To calculate the median score, we first calculate the median position.

$$\text{Median position} = \frac{n+1}{2} = \frac{15+1}{2} = 8 \qquad (3.6)$$

By counting 8 from either end of the array of scores, we arrive at the median score of 105. This is the middle score of this distribution of scores.

This example has an odd number of scores, which means that one score lies right in the middle. If the number was even, the median would lie half-way between two scores. In the example above, if the highest score is removed, then the median would lie half way between the scores of 97 and 105, that is, the median position would calculate as 7.5, that is, $(14 + 1)/2$. The median score is then half-way between these two score, namely, 101.

The calculation is rather different when the distribution is in categories, be they whole numbers, as with age, or grouped data, as with age categories. The distribution of Age in years in the Resident sample is displayed in Table 3.11. It shows the frequency (*f*) for each age, and the cumulative frequency (cum *f*). As there is an odd number of respondents, the median age is the age of the person who is at the half-way point in the distribution. Using equation (3.6),

$$\text{Median position} = \frac{401+1}{2} = 201$$

Therefore, the median age is that of the respondent numbered 201 in the distribution. There are 200 respondents younger than this person and 200 older.

Table 3.11 *Age in years (Residents)*

Age	f	cum f	Age	f	cum f	Age	f	cum f
18	1	1	43	7	201	68	4	346
19	9	10	44	6	207	69	3	349
20	6	16	45	12	219	70	10	359
21	8	24	46	9	228	71	1	360
22	12	36	47	8	236	72	3	363
23	8	44	48	5	241	73	5	368
24	3	47	49	3	244	74	2	370
25	4	51	50	11	255	75	5	375
26	9	60	51	3	258	76	0	375
27	6	66	52	3	261	77	5	380
28	8	74	53	3	264	78	3	383
29	11	85	54	2	266	79	2	385
30	7	92	55	4	270	80	6	391
31	6	98	56	5	275	81	2	393
32	13	111	57	5	280	82	0	393
33	9	120	58	7	287	83	2	395
34	8	128	59	7	294	84	0	395
35	12	140	60	5	299	85	1	396
36	6	146	61	6	305	86	0	396
37	10	156	62	8	313	87	1	397
38	10	166	63	3	316	88	0	397
39	7	173	64	6	322	89	1	398
40	9	182	65	8	330	90	3	401
41	7	189	66	3	333			
42	5	194	67	9	342			

To arrive at the median, we read down the cumulative frequencies until we find the category in which this respondent is located. This person is aged 43, and this the median age.

It is possible to express this median more precisely by imagining the seven respondents in this category are spread evenly across it. Or, put differently, imagine this one year is divided into seven parts, with each respondent occupying one-seventh (0.143) of the year. In the distribution, the category itself extends from 42.5 to 43.5 with the 201st respondent being at the top end of the category. That is, this person occupies the one-seventh of the year adjoining the upper boundary. Now we need to imagine the midpoint of this space as being the precise median. This is 0.072 below the upper boundary, which is 43.43 years, say 43.4 years. Another way of thinking about the median is to imagine counting the spaces in the distribution occupied by the other six respondents in the category. Together, they occupy six-sevenths (0.857) of the one-year interval, below the median position. Therefore, the median is arrived at by adding the space occupied by these respondents (0.857) to the lower boundary of the category (42.5) and then adding half of the interval of the median position (0.072). Again, this equals 43.43. Hence, we have a check on our calculations (see Figure 3.8).[8]

It may appear to be unnecessary to use this more precise method of calculating a median in this example. However, when grouped data are being used,

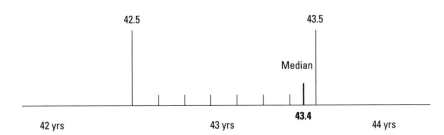

Figure 3.8 *Median to one decimal place*

in a limited number of categories, its value is more obvious. The same procedure can be used whether or not the categories are of equal width. Table 3.6 contains the same data as Table 3.11, but grouped into six categories. In this case, the 201st respondent is located in the '35–44' Age category. There are 128 respondents below this category, which means that we have to go 73 respondents into this category of 79 to find the boundary. Given that the lower boundary of the category is 34.5, that each respondent occupies 1/79 of the 10-year interval, and that the median is in the midpoint of the interval:

$$\text{Median} = 34.5 + 10(73/79) + 1/79 = 34.5 + 9.24 + 0.01 = 43.75$$

This is 0.32 years higher than the previous calculation. The reason for the difference is that the first calculation recognizes the actual distribution in the interval '35–44'. The second calculation has to assume an even distribution, when this is not strictly the case. An inspection of Table 3.11 shows that there are 45 respondents aged '35–39' and only 34 aged '40–44'. The figure would be more accurate if the width of the Age categories was smaller, say 5 years. Nevertheless, there may be some value in this more precise figure rather than simply saying the median is in the '35–44' Age category, or is the midpoint of this category, that is, 40 (or 39.5 if the width is assumed to be 9 years).

Mean

The *mean*, or *arithmetic mean*, is the most commonly used and the most useful measure of central tendency. However, it can only be calculated with interval-level and ratio-level data. As the meaning of the mean is rather more complex than that for the mode and the median, its procedural definition will be given here and a more formal definition will follow. The mean is *the sum of a set of values divided by the number of the values in the set*. Values are usually scores or frequencies.

This definition can be expressed as an equation, although it differs slightly depending on whether the data are from a sample or a population. For sample data, the equation is:

$$\text{Mean } (\bar{x}) = \frac{\text{sum of the values}}{\text{number of values}} = \frac{x_1 + x_2 + x_3 + \cdots + x_n}{n} = \frac{\Sigma x}{n} \qquad (3.7)$$

The equation for population data simply substitutes X for x, and N for n, although the symbol for the mean is different:

$$\text{Mean } (\mu) = \frac{\text{sum of the values}}{\text{number of values}} = \frac{X_1 + X_2 + X_3 + \cdots + X_n}{N} = \frac{\Sigma X}{N} \qquad (3.8)$$

Data from which means are calculated come in three main forms:

- a set of values (e.g. scores);
- an ungrouped frequency distribution (e.g. frequencies of Age in years); and
- a grouped frequency distribution (e.g. Age in categories).

For an example of the first and simplest form (scores), we can use the earlier data on the scores of children on a standardized test.

68 76 79 83 87 92 97 105 108 113 118 121 134 135 139

Assuming that this is a population,

$$\mu = \frac{\Sigma X}{N} = \frac{1555}{15} = 103.7$$

For an example of ungrouped frequencies, we can use the data in Table 3.11. First, each age is multiplied by its frequency (fx). Then these values for each age are summed (Σfx). Finally, the total is divided by the total number of respondents (see Table 3.12):

$$\bar{x} = \frac{\Sigma fx}{n} = \frac{18{,}471}{401} = 46.1 \qquad (3.9)$$

The calculation of the mean for a grouped frequency distribution is similar to that for ungrouped frequencies. We can do this from the Resident sample data in Table 3.9. In this case, the frequency in a category is multiplied by its mid-point (x_m) (see Table 3.13).

$$\bar{x} = \frac{\Sigma fx_m}{n} = \frac{18{,}557.0}{401} = 46.3 \qquad (3.10)$$

Again, it is not necessary for the width of the categories to be equal, although categories of narrow intervals will produce more accurate results. This mean is 0.2 higher than that calculated from the ungrouped frequencies. The main reason for the difference is that all ages within a category are assumed to be in

Table 3.12 *Calculation of mean Age in years (Residents)*

Age	f	fx̄	Age	f	fx̄	Age	f	fx̄
18	1	18	43	7	301	68	4	272
19	9	171	44	6	264	69	3	207
20	6	120	45	12	540	70	10	700
21	8	168	46	9	414	71	1	71
22	12	264	47	8	376	72	3	216
23	8	184	48	5	240	73	5	365
24	3	72	49	3	147	74	2	148
25	4	100	50	11	550	75	5	375
26	9	234	51	3	153	76	0	0
27	6	162	52	3	156	77	5	385
28	8	224	53	3	159	78	3	234
29	11	319	54	2	108	79	2	158
30	7	210	55	4	220	80	6	480
31	6	186	56	5	280	81	2	162
32	13	416	57	5	285	82	0	0
33	9	297	58	7	406	83	2	166
34	8	272	59	7	413	84	0	0
35	12	420	60	5	300	85	1	85
36	6	216	61	6	366	86	0	0
37	10	370	62	8	496	87	1	87
38	10	380	63	3	189	88	0	0
39	7	273	64	6	384	89	1	89
40	9	360	65	8	520	90	3	270
41	7	287	66	3	198			
42	5	210	67	9	603			

Table 3.13 *Mean of Age distributed in ten categories (Residents)*

Age	f	x_m	fx_m
18–19	10	18.5	185.0
20–24	37	22.0	814.0
25–29	38	27.0	1026.0
30–39	88	34.5	3036.0
40–49	71	44.5	3159.5
50–59	50	54.5	2725.0
60–69	55	64.5	3547.5
70–79	36	74.5	2682.0
80–89	13	84.5	1098.5
90–99	3	94.5	283.5
n	401		$\sum fx_m = 18{,}557.0$

the centre of the category; differences in the distribution within the category have to be ignored. The effect of this is clear in the highest age category, where the three persons are assumed to be aged 94.5 when they are all 90. However, it would be unusual for means calculated by these methods to differ by very much.

The mathematical character of the mean is such that if we calculate all the differences between the mean and each of the values in the distribution,

Table 3.14 *Mean of two means (both samples)*

Sample	$\bar{x}$	f	$f\bar{x}$
Students	21.16	460	9,733.60
Residents	46.06	401	18,470.06
Totals		861	28,203.66

negative differences below the mean and positive ones above it, the sum will be zero. To put this more technically, the *mean is the point in a distribution of values, the sum of the deviations from which is equal to zero*. As a result of this, it is very easy for one or a few very extreme values, either high or low, to affect the mean in a way that does not happen with the mode or median. Hence, it is sometimes recommended to use the *trimmed mean* by deleting both the upper and lower 5 per cent of values. This is based on the assumption that there is likely to be something wrong with these values as a result of errors in data recording or manipulation, or equipment malfunction. In the Resident sample, the trimmed mean would eliminate the 20 youngest and the 20 oldest respondents. However, if it can be established that the extreme values are genuine, trimming should *not* be done. In our example, if people over 80 years of age are willing to participate in social research when selected in a sample we should certainly not eliminate them or their responses.

Mean of means

Sometimes we need to produce a mean from data that are already expressed as means. If these means are based on different-sized samples or populations, we cannot simply calculate a mean of these means. This is because the means of larger samples should have a bigger influence on the overall mean than do the means of smaller samples. Simply taking the mean of the means ignores this. For example, our two samples have mean ages of 21.2 (Students; $n = 460$) and 46.1 (Residents; $n = 401$).[9] If we simply calculate the mean of these two means we get 33.6. As the samples are similar in size, calculating the mean of the means would not do much harm. However, to be strictly accurate, the sample means should be weighted according to their respective sample sizes. This is done by following the same procedure as is used to calculate the mean of an ungrouped frequency distribution (see Table 3.14).

The equation for the *weighted mean* $(\bar{x}_w)$ is:

$$\bar{x}_w = \frac{\Sigma f\bar{x}}{\Sigma f} = \frac{28,203.66}{861} = 32.8 \qquad (3.11)$$

There is a difference of 0.8 years. However, if the Student sample was half its size, and the Resident sample twice its size, the mean of the weighted means would be rather different, 40.5 in fact. You might try this as an exercise.

A similar problem arises if it is necessary to combine data in the form of percentages from different categories or samples, and a total percentage is required. Only in the case where the sizes of the categories or samples are equal is it appropriate to take the mean of the individual percentages. If the sizes are different, then each percentage needs to be weighted in terms of the total n on which it was based. The procedure for doing this is similar to that for weighting means. For example, in Table 3.9, if we wished to calculate percentages for the two samples combined, it would not be appropriate to just take the mean of the two sample percentages for each category. In the case of the '20–24' aged category, 44.6 per cent of Students and 9.2 per cent of Residents are in this age range. The mean of these two percentages is 26.9. However, the *mean weighted percentage* ($\bar{\%}_w$) for this aged category is 28.1 (see Table 3.15). The equation is:

$$\bar{\%}_w = \frac{\Sigma\%n}{\Sigma n} = \frac{24,205.2}{861} = 28.1 \tag{3.12}$$

Table 3.15 *Mean of two Age category percentages (both samples)*

Sample	%	n	%n
Students	44.6	460	20,516.0
Residents	9.2	401	3,689.2
Totals		861	24,205.2

In this case, the difference between the weighted and unweighted mean percentages is small because the two sample sizes are almost equal. However, if the Student sample was half its size, and the Resident sample twice its size, the mean weighted percentage would be 17.1.

Of course, it is possible to calculate total percentages without going through this weighting procedure, simply by adding the frequencies for the two categories, dividing this by the sum of the sample totals, and multiplying by 100. In this example, the total percentage for both samples combined is:

$$\% = \frac{\text{sum of the values in the categories}}{\text{sum of sample totals}} \times 100 \tag{3.13}$$

$$= \frac{242}{861} \times 100 = 28.1$$

The values obtained by the two methods are the same.

Comparing the Mode, Median and Mean

We are now in a position to compare these three measures of central tendency. Using Age in years in the Resident sample, and using the ungrouped distribution, the median was calculated as 43.4 years and the mean as 46.1 years. The mode depends on which version of the distribution is used: in Table 3.11 it is 32 years; and in Table 3.9 (Figure 3.6) it is in the '30–39' interval. However, neither of these modal figures is very useful.

The difference between the median and the mean tells us something about the characteristics of a distribution. In the case of Figure 3.6, the Age distribution of Students is skewed to the left; there are more respondents in the younger than in the older Age categories. The mean is affected by the tail to the right, thus making its value higher than the median, 21.2 compared with 19.9 (the mode is 19 years).

The relationship between the three Ms can be understood with reference to the normal curve. If the distribution is normal, the three Ms coincide; the modal category or score will be the same as the median and the mean. Hence, a difference between the median and mean is an indication of a skewed distribution. When the mean is higher than the median, the distribution is positively skewed (bunched to the left); when the mean is lower than the median, it is negatively skewed (bunched to the right). Software packages normally report a measure of *skewness* in which a figure of zero indicates no skew and, therefore, a coincidence between the median and the mean, and a high figure is a large skew. The values normally fall between –3 and +3, with the sign indicating a negative or positive skewness. The equation used to calculate this is:

$$SK = \frac{3(\text{mean} - \text{median})}{\text{standard deviation}} \qquad (3.14)$$

The standard deviation will be discussed shortly.

Figure 3.9 shows two distributions that approximate a normal curve. It shows the Environmental Worldview scale for Students and Residents with categories based on scores in intervals of 5. For the Students, the mean is 90.9, the median 91.3 and skewness is –0.27, while for the Residents these figures are 88.0, 87.0 and +0.07, respectively. The differences between the means and the medians (–0.4 and 1.0) reflect the direction but not the magnitude of the skewness.

When the two samples are combined, the distribution is closer to the normal curve (see Figure 3.10). Without the three lowest categories, the shape would be even better. The mean is 89.6 and the median 89.3; the difference of 0.3 is reflected in the skewness (–0.10).

Comparative Analysis Using Percentages and Means

A common form of analysis is to compare two samples or categories in terms of their distributions on the same variable. This can be done by using an appropriate measure of central tendency, preferably the mean but sometimes the median. Comparisons can also be made in terms of the proportions, percentages or rates in certain categories of a variable. Such comparisons can be useful and are very straightforward. It is just a case of comparing two numbers. For

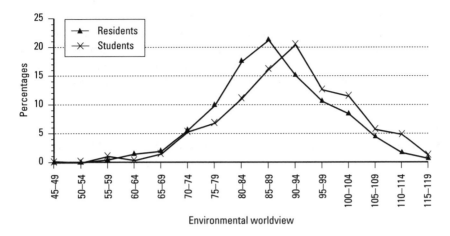

Figure 3.9 *Environmental Worldview (both samples): line graphs*

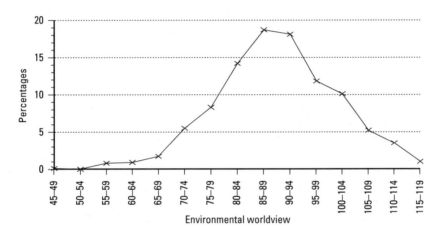

Figure 3.10 *Environmental Worldview (combined samples): line graph*

example, we can compare the percentages of males and females, or the percentage of respondents educated at university in the two samples.

If the data come from populations, the differences between the percentages and means are what the figures show. However, when the data come from probability samples, and we want to know whether the sample differences can be expected to be present in the populations from which the samples were drawn, we are faced with some further analysis and some difficult decisions. This will be discussed in Chapter 6.

Measures of Dispersion

In addition to measures of central tendency, it is also possible to describe the characteristics of a distribution in terms of how widely it is spread. This is done with *measures of dispersion* or variability. Such measures are not normally applied to nominal-level data, as the idea of spread makes very limited sense.[10] Some measures are available for ordinal-level data, and these can also be applied to interval-level and ratio-level data, while others are only suitable with the two latter types of data. The following measures of dispersion are covered in this section:

- Categorical ordinal-level data: interquartile range and percentiles.
- Metric data: range, mean deviation, standard deviation and variance.

Categorical Data

Interquartile range

While it is possible to establish the dispersion of a distribution by calculating the interval between the extreme scores or frequencies (i.e. the range), a more useful method is to take the interval within which the middle 50 per cent of all scores or respondents are included. In other words, the lowest 25 per cent of scores or frequencies, and the highest 25 per cent, are excluded from consideration. This means that the possible distorting effects of extreme scores at either end of the distribution are eliminated.

This measure is known as the *interquartile range* and is used in association with the median. It is the most commonly used method for measuring the dispersion of ordinal-level data and, while it can also be used for discrete and grouped interval-level and ratio-level data, it only allows for rather simple mathematical procedures. The two points along a distribution, 25 per cent and 75 per cent, are calculated in a similar way to the median. Instead of locating the point that divides a distribution into two equal parts, we find the points that divide the lowest 25 per cent, and the highest 25 per cent, from the rest.

If we want to calculate the interquartile range for the Age distribution in Table 3.11 (Resident sample), we have to first find the point that separates the lower 25 per cent, the first *quartile*. A similar equation to that for the median position is used.

$$\text{First quartile position } (Q_1) = \frac{401 + 1}{4} = 100.5$$

This indicates that there are, theoretically, 100.5 respondents in each quartile. Hence, the second quartile position (Q_2), which is the same as the median, is double this (201) and the third quartile (Q_3) is three times it (301.5). By inspecting the cumulative frequencies in Table 3.11, we can see that Q_1 falls in the '32' Age category (which means somewhere between 31.5 and 32.5), and Q_3 in the '61' Age category (between 60.5 and 61.5). We could simply subtract the midpoints of these two Age categories to get an approximate interquartile range (29).

However, it is possible to get a more precise figure by using the same procedure as that for calculating the median with grouped data. As there are 98 respondents below age 32, an additional 2.5 respondents are needed to takes us to Q_1. With 13 respondents in this Age category, we have to take in 0.2 of the category (2.5/13) to reach Q_1. Hence $Q_1 = 31.5 + 0.2 = 31.7$. Repeating this procedure in the 61 Age category, $Q_3 = 60.5 + 0.4 = 60.9$. Therefore, the interquartile range is 29.2 (60.9 – 31.7).

Percentiles

Calculating quartiles is a variation of calculating *percentiles*. The latter are used to divide a distribution into 100 parts but, more commonly, into deciles or 10 per cent intervals (the lowest 10 per cent, the next 10 per cent, and so on to the highest 10 per cent). If the score or frequency is calculated for all these points, this method produces a reasonably precise description of the shape of a distribution. Again, each point, at whatever interval is chosen, is calculated by the method described for the interquartile range. While percentiles or deciles have their uses, the interquartile range is the most frequently used accompaniment to the median.

Metric Data

Range

Of all the measures of dispersion, the *range* is the easiest to calculate and to understand. It is simply *the highest score or frequency minus the lowest*. In Figure 3.10 (combined samples), the highest score is 119 and the lowest is 48. Hence, the range is 71. In this case, the range is quite useful because the distribution is close to a symmetrical normal curve. However, the longish tail at the lower end leads to the midpoint of the range (83.5) being some way off both the mean (89.6) and the median (89.3).

The disadvantage of the range is that very extreme scores can affect it. This is illustrated in Table 3.4 (Student sample), which is a very skewed distribution. The oldest age is 46 and the youngest 18, giving a range of 28 and a midpoint of 32 years. However, the mean is 21.2 and the median 19.9 (skewness = +2.5). Therefore, while it may be useful to know the range, for example, when determining the number of categories required to group scores, it is very difficult to compare distributions using only this measure of dispersion. As comparing the characteristics of distributions is a major form of data analysis, some other measures are required.

Mean absolute deviation

As we have seen, a technical definition of the mean is the point in a distribution of values, the sum of the deviations from which is equal to zero. The zero is achieved because some of the deviations will be negative (those below the mean) and some will be positive (those higher than the mean). If we disregard the sign of each deviation, so that we are dealing with what are called 'absolute deviations', the sum of the absolute deviations gives an indication of the spread of a distribution: the larger the sum, the greater the spread, and vice versa. If we calculate the mean of all the absolute deviations, we have an indicator of the dispersion of the distribution. Hence, the *mean absolute deviation* is the *mean of the deviations of all values from the mean, disregarding their sign*. The equation for use with grouped data from a sample is:

$$\text{Mean absolute deviation} = \frac{\Sigma f |x - \bar{x}|}{n} \qquad (3.15)$$

where f is the frequency in a category, x is the value of a category and $\bar{x}$ is the mean. The only aspect of the equation which is new is the two vertical bars. These indicate that when the mean is subtracted from each value of x, any negative signs are ignored. Hence, $|-5| = 5$ and $|+5| = 5$.

Note that the midpoint of the category is used for x (for an example, see Table 3.13). As social research tends to use grouped data, only this equation is presented here. For data in an array of ungrouped unique scored, f is dropped from the equation.

We can illustrate the calculation of the mean absolute deviation using the data in Table 3.12 (see Table 3.16). The first column is Age (x), the second is the frequency (f), or the number of respondents in each age category, the third is the deviation of each age from the mean age ($x - \bar{x}$), and the fourth column is the third (disregarding the sign) multiplied by the second. The other columns will be dealt with shortly. The mean absolute deviation is the sum of all the individual deviations, without regard to sign (i.e the sum of the fourth column), divided by the size of the sample:

$$\text{Mean absolute deviation} = \frac{\Sigma f |x - \bar{x}|}{n} = \frac{6100.4}{401} = 15.2$$

This value provides an indication of how dispersed this Age distribution is around the mean.

Standard deviation

While the mean absolute deviation is based on a relatively simple idea, it is rarely used. Instead, the preferred method for measuring the dispersion of distributions based on interval-level and ratio-level data is the *standard deviation*. However, the standard deviation, and its sister method, the *variance*, are both derived from the mean absolute deviation.

The basic difference between the mean absolute deviation and the standard deviation is that in the latter each deviation from the mean is squared. As multiplying two negative numbers produce a positive number, squaring a negative number eliminates the negative sign. In the case of the standard deviation, the square root is taken of the result to compensate for the earlier squaring. This procedure gives the standard deviation a number of advantages over the mean absolute deviation, the most important of which is that standard deviations can

Table 3.16 Deviations from the mean of Age in years (Residents)

x	f	$x-\bar{x}$	$f|x-\bar{x}|$	$(x-\bar{x})^2$	$f(x-\bar{x})^2$	x	f	$x-\bar{x}$	$f|x-\bar{x}|$	$(x-\bar{x})^2$	$f(x-\bar{x})^2$
18	1	-28.06	28.06	787.36	787.36	55	4	8.94	35.76	79.92	319.69
19	9	-27.06	243.54	732.24	6590.19	56	5	9.94	49.70	98.80	494.02
20	6	-26.06	156.36	679.12	4074.74	57	5	10.94	54.70	119.68	598.42
21	8	-25.06	200.48	628.00	5024.03	58	7	11.94	83.58	142.56	997.95
22	12	-24.06	288.72	578.88	6946.60	59	7	12.94	90.58	167.44	1172.11
23	8	-23.06	184.48	531.76	4254.11	60	5	13.94	69.70	194.32	971.62
24	3	-22.06	66.18	486.64	1459.93	61	6	14.94	89.64	223.20	1339.22
25	4	-21.06	84.24	443.52	1774.09	62	8	15.94	127.52	254.08	2032.67
26	9	-20.06	180.54	402.40	3621.63	63	3	16.94	50.82	286.96	860.89
27	6	-19.06	114.36	363.28	2179.70	64	6	17.94	107.64	321.84	1931.06
28	8	-18.06	144.48	326.16	2609.31	65	8	18.94	151.52	358.72	2869.79
29	11	-17.06	187.66	291.04	3201.48	66	3	19.94	59.82	397.60	1192.81
30	7	-16.06	112.42	257.92	1805.47	67	9	20.94	188.46	438.48	3946.35
31	6	-15.06	90.36	226.80	1360.82	68	4	21.94	87.76	481.36	1925.45
32	13	-14.06	182.79	197.68	2569.89	69	3	22.94	68.82	526.24	1578.73
33	9	-13.06	117.54	170.56	1535.07	70	10	23.94	239.40	573.12	5731.24
34	8	-12.06	96.48	145.44	1163.55	71	1	24.94	24.94	622.00	622.00
35	12	-11.06	132.72	122.32	1467.88	72	3	25.94	77.82	672.88	2018.65
36	6	-10.06	60.36	101.20	607.22	73	5	26.94	134.70	725.76	3628.82
37	10	-9.06	90.60	82.08	820.84	74	2	27.94	55.88	780.64	1561.29
38	10	-8.06	80.60	64.96	649.64	75	5	28.94	144.70	837.52	4187.62
39	7	-7.06	49.42	49.84	348.91	76	0	29.94	0.00	896.40	0.00
40	9	-6.06	54.54	36.72	330.51	77	5	30.94	154.70	957.28	4786.42
41	7	-5.06	35.42	25.60	179.23	78	3	31.94	95.82	1020.16	3060.49
42	5	-4.06	20.30	16.48	82.42	79	2	32.94	65.88	1085.04	2170.09
43	7	-3.06	21.42	9.36	65.55	80	6	33.94	203.64	1151.92	6911.54
44	6	-2.06	12.36	4.24	25.46	81	2	34.94	69.88	1220.80	2441.61
45	12	-1.06	12.72	1.12	13.48	82	0	35.94	0.00	1291.68	0.00
46	9	-0.06	0.54	0.00	0.03	83	2	36.94	73.88	1364.56	2729.13
47	8	0.94	7.52	0.88	7.07	84	0	37.94	0.00	1439.44	0.00

(Continued)

Table 3.16 (Continued)

x	f	$x-\bar{x}$	$f\lvert x-\bar{x}\rvert$	$(x-\bar{x})^2$	$f(x-\bar{x})^2$
48	5	1.94	9.70	3.76	18.82
49	3	2.94	8.82	8.64	25.93
50	11	3.94	43.34	15.52	170.76
51	3	4.94	14.82	24.40	73.21
52	3	5.94	17.82	35.28	105.85
53	3	6.94	20.82	48.16	144.49
54	2	7.94	15.88	63.04	126.09

x	f	$x-\bar{x}$	$f\lvert x-\bar{x}\rvert$	$(x-\bar{x})^2$	$f(x-\bar{x})^2$
85	1	38.94	38.94	1516.32	1516.32
86	0	39.94	0.00	1595.20	0.00
87	1	40.94	40.94	1676.08	1676.08
88	0	41.94	0.00	1758.96	0.00
89	1	42.94	42.94	1843.84	1843.84
90	3	43.94	131.82	1930.72	5792.17

$n = 401$ $\sum f\lvert x-\bar{x}\rvert = 6{,}100.4$ $\sum f(x-\bar{x})^2 = 129{,}129.4$

be compared across different types of distributions (hence the qualification 'standard'); mean absolute deviations are not comparable.

The standard deviation can be described as *the square root of the sum of the squared deviances of all values from the mean, divided by the number of values*. The equation for grouped data from a sample is a variation of that for the mean deviation:

$$\text{Standard deviation}(s) = \sqrt{\frac{\Sigma f(x - \bar{x})^2}{n}} \qquad (3.16)$$

Again, f is eliminated in the case of data in ungrouped unique scores.

If we go back to the data presented in Table 3.16, all that is necessary is to square each of the deviations from the mean, that is, $(x - \bar{x})^2$, before it is multiplied by its frequency. The calculation is:

$$s = \sqrt{\frac{\Sigma f(x - \bar{x})^2}{n}} = \sqrt{\frac{129{,}129.4}{401}} = \sqrt{322.0} = 17.9$$

Variance

The *variance* is arrived at by squaring both sides of equation (3.16). The left side becomes s^2 and the square root sign on the right disappears. Hence the equation for the variance is:

$$\text{Variance}(s^2) = \frac{\Sigma f(x - \bar{x})^2}{n} \qquad (3.17)$$

The symbol for population standard deviations is σ and for population variances is σ^2. To change these equations for use with populations, it is just a matter of substituting X, $\bar{X}$ (or μ) and N for x, $\bar{x}$ and n, respectively. When the sample or population size is less than 40, the divisor for both the standard deviation and variance needs to be $N - 1$ or $n - 1$. The reason for this need not concern us here.

There are simpler methods than the ones just described for calculating both variance and standard deviation. Instead of calculating all the individual deviations from the mean and then squaring them, we proceed as follows.

- The value for each category is multiplied by its frequency.
- This is squared.
- These squares are added together and divided by the number of categories.
- The square of the mean is subtracted.
- Then the square root is applied to the result.

The equation for the standard deviation with grouped sample data becomes:

$$s = \sqrt{\frac{\sum fx^2}{n} - \bar{x}^2}$$

(3.18)

and for the variance:

$$s^2 = \frac{\sum fx^2}{n} - \bar{x}^2$$

(3.19)

It is necessary to be careful with the $\sum fx^2$ expression in the equation. It can be stated more clearly as $\sum f(x^2)$, and should be read backwards: square all the x values, multiply each one by its f, and then sum them. The expressions $\sum (fx)^2$ and $(\sum fx)^2$ are quite different. Subtle differences, due to the presence or absence of brackets and their positioning, are very important.

While the interquartile range is readily interpreted, the standard deviation is rather more complex. The basic idea is that if the standard deviation is small, then the spread of the distribution must be narrow; that is, the values cluster around the mean. Conversely, if the standard deviation is large, then the distribution is widely spread. However, the standard deviation really only makes sense with normal distributions.

Characteristics of the Normal Curve

Earlier we noted that the normal curve is a symmetrical distribution in which the mode, median and mean are the same. It also has some other important characteristics. As with all frequency curves, the line is determined by the frequencies at each point along the distribution; the frequencies are greatest at the mean and then decline as the values deviate from the mean. The area under the curve represents the sum of all responses or scores. In the theoretical distribution, the declining curve on either side of the mean never reaches zero frequencies; the curve goes off into infinity in both directions but never touches the base of the graph. However, empirical distributions have to stop somewhere; the extreme scores or categories must eventually have zero frequencies.

In order to discuss the normal curve, it is necessary to introduce the idea of *standard scores* or *z-scores*. The *z*-score provides a precise means of interpreting any value of a variable in which the distribution approximates the normal curve. If we want to know how a particular category or score relates to the distribution in which it is located, or if we want to compare a person's position on the distribution of two or more variables, the position or scores must be standardized. This is done by dividing the deviation from the mean of a particular category or score by the standard deviation of the distribution. The equation is:

$$\text{Standard score } (z) = \frac{\text{score} - \text{mean}}{\text{standard deviation}} = \frac{x - \bar{x}}{s} \qquad (3.20)$$

This procedure turns raw categories or scores into standard scores. The idea of z-scores also provides a useful basis for discussing the characteristics of the theoretical normal curve, also known as the *standard normal distribution*.

Converting the characteristics of an actual distribution to the standard normal distribution by means of z-scores is like converting frequencies to percentages. In the latter, frequencies are transposed to a base of 100. In converting our data to z-scores, we are simply making the mean 0 and the standard deviation 1. Hence, values to the left of the mean are negative, and to the right are positive. We simply transpose the data into a set of standard units without changing the shape of the curve.

Two points should be noted. First, this conversion can only be applied to distributions that approximate the normal curve, that is, it cannot be applied to skewed distributions. Second, it does not turn a non-normal distribution into one that resembles a normal curve. It just allows data in distributions that approximate a normal curve to be compared on the basis of standard units.

Perhaps the most important characteristic of the standard normal curve is that 68.26 per cent of the distribution lies within 1 standard deviation on either side of the mean or midpoint, 95.44 per cent lies within 2 standard deviations and 99.74 per cent lies within 3 standard deviations (see Figure 3.11). Hence, nearly 100% of the distribution lies within a total of 6 standard deviation units. These facts reveal nothing more than the particular characteristics of the normal curve. However, whenever we have a distribution that approximates the normal (as in Figure 3.10), we can estimate the percentage of the distribution that lies on either side of any category or score.

Tables have been prepared that reflect the relationship between any z-score and the shape of the standard normal curve (see Table 2 in Appendix D). The figures in Table 2 indicate the proportion of the area under the normal curve that lies between a particular positive z-score and the right-hand tail. For example, a z-score of 1.00 shows a value of 0.1587. This means that 15.87 per cent of the area lies between here and the tail. By subtracting this value from 0.5, we get the area under the curve that lies between this value of z and the mean. The reason for using 0.5 is that half the area lies on each side of the mean ($0.5000 - 0.1587 = 0.3413$ or 34.13 per cent). Note that doubling this percentage gives us the percentage that lies within ± 1 standard deviation of the mean (68.26 per cent, which is the figure given above). Therefore, the values in Table 2 can be used to indicate what proportion of a distribution lies above and below any point in the distribution, as well as between that point and the mean.

Take the example of results from a national examination. We may want to know where a particular student lies in relations to the top students and the mean mark. If the student's score has been converted to a z-score, and it happens to be +1.24,

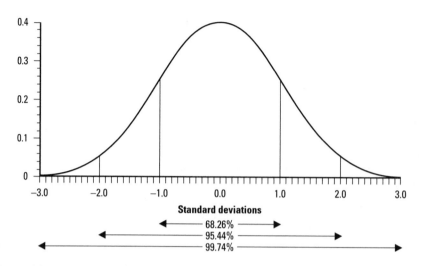

Figure 3.11 *Area covered under the normal curve by one to three standard deviations*

Table 2 indicates that 0.3925 of the distribution lies between this point and the mean (0.5000 – 0.1075). If 10,000 students sat the examination, we know that our student has 3,925 students between her and students with the mean mark. Given that the mean divides the distribution in half, which makes 5,000 students above and below the mean mark, our student has 8,925 students below her and 1,075 students above her. We do not have to have a distribution of student scores to do this, just the mean and standard deviation of the distribution and an assurance that the distribution approximates the normal curve.

While these characteristics of a normal curve remain constant, the shape of empirical curves can vary depending on the combination of their means and their standard deviations. Some curves will be 'flat' and spread, while others will be 'high' and narrow, and anything in between. The first extreme has a relatively small value for the mean and a large standard deviation, while the other extreme has a relatively high value for the mean and a much smaller standard deviation. However, there is only one normal curve for any given mean and standard deviation.

The standard normal distribution, and hence z-scores, can usually only be used with data from large populations or samples in which the variables being measured form bell-shaped distributions. Simple examples relate to human physiological features, such as height and weight, and to performance on standardized tests, such as intelligence and aptitude. With small numbers, distributions on such variables may be skewed, but with large numbers the distributions are likely to approach the normal curve. In contrast to the variables used by behavioural scientists, many of the variables used by social scientists are not normally distributed. Hence, the translation of distributions into z-scores is restricted to limited areas of research.

In order to be able to use z-scores, and other statistical procedures that require normal distributions, it is possible to transform a skewed distribution into an approximately normal one. This involves changing the intervals of the measurement scale, such as gradually increasing their width from the low to the high end of a negatively skewed distribution. What this does is stretch out the categories in which the responses are bunched at the high end of the scale, thus changing the shape of the distribution. A popular method for doing this is to use the natural logarithm of the variable.

Summary

- Univariate analysis involves describing the characteristics of distributions on variables.
- Categorical data, and discrete and grouped metric data, are described at the most basic level in terms of frequency counts.
- Frequency counts can be summarized and compared in terms of proportions, percentages, ratios and rates.
- Distributions and such summary values can also be expressed pictorially in bar charts and pie charts (categorical data), and in histograms and line graphs (discrete and grouped metric data).
- Distributions can take many shapes, ranging from symmetrical to skewed. Positively skewed distributions are clustered towards the lower end values and negatively skewed distributions are clustered towards the higher end values.
- The characteristics of a distribution can be summarized in terms of measures of central tendency and dispersion. For categorical data, and discrete and grouped metric data, the mode and the median measure central tendency. For metric data, both discrete and continuous, the mean is appropriate.
- The main measure of dispersion for categorical data, and a companion to the median, is the interquartile range. For metric data it is the standard deviation and variance.
- The normal curve is a special case of a symmetrical distribution. It is a theoretical distribution around a mean, which constitutes the peak of the curve. The curve declines on either side of the mean and approaches but never reaches zero. This distribution is extremely important in a number of the procedures used in data analysis.
- The shape of the normal curve is described in the distribution of z-scores, or standard scores, which assume a mean of 0 and a standard deviation of 1.
- Real distributions can only approach, but never replicate, the normal curve.

Notes

[1]This section of the chapter is inspired by a similar discussion in Elifson et al. (1998: 20–3).
[2]Convention does not require the number 2 to be placed before the square root symbol, that is, $\sqrt[2]{}$.

[3]I am adopting the convention of capitalizing the first letter of the variables that were measured or constructed in these samples.

[4]This set of categories for religious affiliation is typical of contemporary Australia. It reflects the Anglo-Celtic character of the early European settlers up until World War II and the subsequent waves of migration since then, initially from Europe, particularly Italy and Greece, and more recently from West and South East Asia, particularly Turkey and Vietnam.

[5]As we shall see, there are many ways in which age (in years) can be coded into categories. These procedures will be discussed in Chapter 7.

[6]This procedure is easily carried out in software packages such as SPSS.

[7]Two or three decimal places are commonly used.

[8]It has been necessary to use three decimal places here to avoid cumulative errors produced, say, by multiplying the one-seventh interval by 6. Even when two decimal places are used, the two calculations of the median do not agree. The second calculation comes to 43.41. However, using anything more than one decimal place in the final result is not justified. There is another issue here. Strictly speaking, adjoining categories cannot have the same value for their boundaries. One convention would be to start each category in this example on 0.5, that is 42.5, and end it on 0.4, that is 43.4. Thus, the width of the category would be only 0.9 years (or 0.99 if two decimal places were used). It is possible to do the calculations with these values, and the result would be marginally different. Nevertheless, given how crude a measure the median is, and the uses to which it is likely to be put, such a refinement is not justified.

[9]The missing cases have been eliminated from each sample, hence the slight differences from sample sizes used elsewhere in this discussion.

[10]Freeman (1965) has proposed the variation ratio, the proportion not in the modal category. A high proportion indicates that the mode inadequately reflects the overall distribution.

Descriptive Analysis – Bivariate: Looking for Patterns

Introduction

One of the primary tasks in social research is to establish patterns or *relationships* in the phenomenon under investigation. Many of the research questions listed in Chapter 2 are concerned with the relationships between variables, for example, between aspects of environmentalism (attitudes and behaviour), and between environmentalism and both age and gender. What does it mean to establish a relationship between two variables? How do we establish whether such a relationship exists, and how strong it is? This chapter explores the major ways in which relationships between various types of variables can be demonstrated and their strength measured.

Establishing patterns in data is just an elaborate form of description. Distributions tell us about the characteristics of single variables, while measures of association tell us about the connections between variables. *Measures of association* establish what is commonly referred to as *correlations*. However, they do not tell us anything about how one variable might influence another variable. To take this step beyond association to explanation requires either that research designs be constructed in a special way, usually as a controlled experiment, or the ability, among other things, to make assumptions about the time ordering of variables. For the moment, we will concern ourselves with the forms of relationships between variables and we will impute nothing about whether and how they might influence each other. We are simply looking for patterns. The issue of the direction of influence between variables is discussed in Chapter 5.

The *association* between two variables is described in different ways. Two variables are said to be associated if the values of one variable vary or change together with the values of the other variable. Another way of expressing this in social research is to say that respondents' positions on one variable are consistent with their positions on another variable. For example, persons with a high level of education may also have a high income, and those with a low education a low income. As level of education increases, so does level of income.

Some writers express such a relationship as the position on one variable predicting the position on the other variable. That is, if education and income are closely associated, knowing a person's level of education allows us to predict their level of income. The reverse would also be true. However, this way of expressing association between two variables tends to imply a direction of influence.

Suggesting such a direction, or wishing to make predictions, goes beyond what is necessary to understand an association.

The relationship between two variables can take different forms. Sometimes there may be *no relationship*. This means that a position or score on one variable is not associated with a position or score on the other variable. For example, persons with a high level of education are no more likely than those with a low or moderate education to have a high income. Similarly, persons with a low education are no more likely than others to have a low income. When a high position or score on one variable *is* associated with a high position or score on the other variable, and vice versa, a *positive relationship* is said to exist. Alternatively, if a high position or score on one variable is associated with a low position or score on the other variable, and vice versa, then there is a *negative relationship*. We will examine these differences shortly in the discussion of association between nominal-level and ordinal-level variables.

It is important to note that any variable to be used in the exploration of an association must have a good distribution across its categories, positions or scores. In other words, the variable must not have a restricted or *truncated range*. Take the distributions for Age in the two samples, for example. In the Student sample, the Age distribution is very truncated, that is, it is severely skewed in the positive direction: 87 per cent of the sample is in the 18–24 age category (see Figure 3.6). The result is that in the Student sample it is difficult for another variable to have much of an association with such a distribution. The limited variation in Students' Age means that the distribution on another variable has little scope to reveal any association with it. The situation is different in the Resident sample, where there is a more even distribution across the Age categories.

To illustrate how a truncated distribution can affect the association between two variables, let us examine the relationship between Environmental Worldview (EWV) and Age in the Student sample, using the appropriate measure of association. Just what this is does not need to concern us here; everything will be revealed later in the chapter. All that we need to know for now is that its value can range from −1 to +1, with 0 indicating no association, −1 a perfect negative association and +1 a perfect positive association. It turns out that the value is only 0.04, indicating a negligible association. It could be that there *is* very little association between these two variables, but the skewed age distribution prevents us from finding out. The data in the Resident sample suggest that there is at least some association as the value of the coefficient is 0.31.

About the only way there could be a relationship in the type of Age distribution found in the Student sample would be if there was a big difference in EWV between, say, those who are 20 and under and those who are 25 and over. Something dramatic would need to happen in the early 20s to bring about a dramatic change in worldview, or a very different age cohort would need to be passing through.

Some measures of association, particularly those for interval-level and ratio-level data, require that the distributions on both variables also approximate the normal curve. When this is not the case, some researchers apply transformations to distributions to make them resemble a normal curve, thus allowing procedures to be used that have this requirement. However, methods for doing this will not be discussed here.

The methods used to establish an association between two variables depend on the level of measurement of the variables. In general, a number of measures can be used with nominal-level data, ordinal-level data requires its own particular measure and interval-level and ratio-level data use very different measures. We will examine the following:

- contingency coefficient, phi and Cramér's V (nominal-level);
- gamma (ordinal-level data and categorized interval-level and ratio-level data); and
- covariance and Pearson's correlation coefficient (interval-level and ratio-level data).

Association with Nominal-Level and Ordinal-Level Variables

The measures of association discussed here are appropriate for the two lowest levels of measurement and for variables at a higher level of measurement that have been converted to categories (such as Age), that is, for any categorical data. In fact, if an association is to be established between variables at different levels of measurement (e.g. one nominal-level and the other interval-level), it may be necessary to convert the variable at the higher level of measurement into categories. In other words, the appropriate measure of association is likely to be determined by the lower level of measurement. There are exceptions to this that will be discussed in due course.

Contingency Tables

Relationships between combinations of nominal-level and ordinal-level variables are best understood with the use of *contingency tables*. Such tables set out, category by category, the extent to which two variables are or are not related. This is done by *cross-tabulating* the distributions of the two variables. Before proceeding to a discussion of how to construct a contingency table, we need to describe and label its parts (see Figure 4.1).

Tables are made up of columns and rows that produce cells at the intersection of each one. Each variable has a name (called a 'variable label' in SPSS speak) and a set of categories with labels (called 'value labels'). The size of the table is determined by the number of categories in each variable. Figure 4.1 is an example of a 2 by 2 table: there are two categories for each variable, thus making four cells. Each cell will contain certain data, perhaps a frequency count or a percentage, or both. Each value label produces either a row or a column of the table, and each row and column has a total. These are known as row *marginals* or column marginals. In the bottom right-hand corner of a table is the

Table number and title			
	Column variable label		
Row variable label	Value label	Value label	Row totals
Value label	Cell values	Cell values	Row marginal
Value label	Cell values	Cell values	Row marginal
Column totals	Column marginal	Column marginal	Table total

Figure 4.1   *Parts of a table*

Table 4.1   *Religion by Gender (Residents; observed and expected frequencies, and percentages)*

Gender	Religion					
	Catholic	Anglican	Protestant	Other	No religion	Total
Male	34 (40%)	44 (49%)	27 (45%)	28 (43%)	67 (67%)	200 (50%)
	[42.6]	[44.6]	[30.1]	[32.6]	[50.1]	
Female	51 (60%)	45 (51%)	33 (55%)	37 (57%)	33 (33%)	199 (50%)
	[42.4]	[44.4]	[29.9]	[32.4]	[49.9]	
Totals	85 (100%)	89 (100%)	60 (100%)	65 (100%)	100 (100%)	399 (100%)

'table total', which is the sum of the row or column marginals and, therefore, is the sum of all the cells.

As an example of a simple table, let us take two variables from the Resident sample, Religion and Gender. If we want to see if there is any relationship between these two variables, we can construct a table of cells in which, for each of the categories of Religion, we can see the number of respondents who are male and female. The distributions on these two variables were shown previously in Tables 3.2 and 3.10. For simplicity, Religion has been recoded into five categories, 'Catholic', 'Anglican', 'Protestant', 'Other' and 'No religion', thus producing a 2 by 5 table[1] (see Table 4.1).

Table 4.1 reports the 'observed' frequencies (the plain numbers), 'expected' frequencies (in square brackets) and percentages (in parentheses) for males and females in the five categories of religion. 'Observed' simply means what the research results show. We can see that of the 100 respondents who have 'No religion', 67 are males and 33 are females. It would appear as if more males than females have 'no religion'. However, this is deceptive; we cannot simply compare the raw data to draw such conclusions. There are two main ways to proceed.

The first is to see how many males and females there would be in each of these cells of the table if they were evenly distributed, that is, if there was no relationship. These are called the 'expected' frequencies and are calculated by multiplying the row and column marginals and dividing by the table total. For example, the expected frequency for males who stated they have 'No religion' is 200 multiplied by 100 and then divided by 399, which equals 50.1. The expected frequencies for the other cells are calculated in the same way. The differences between observed and expected frequencies form the basis of a number of statistical procedures that we shall encounter shortly. In the meantime, we shall use them to interpret the data in this table.

Reading down the 'Anglican' column of the table, we can see that the observed and expected frequencies in each cell are almost the same. This means that the number of males and females who are 'Anglican' is almost the same as we would expect if males and females were distributed in this category in the same way as they are in the sample. It turns out that there are 50 per cent of males and females in the sample and, among the 'Anglicans', 49 per cent are males and 51 per cent are females. However, when we compare the observed and expected frequencies in the other columns, differences are evident. Compared with the overall male/female composition of the sample, females are overrepresented among 'Catholics', 'Protestants' and 'Other' religions, and underrepresented in the 'No religion' category when the observed frequency is higher than the expected, there is overrepresentation, and vice versa. While these differences are only small, they do indicate a trend in the data.

It is also possible to interpret the data in this table by using percentages rather than frequencies. Percentages are commonly used to present such data. In order to discover whether or not there may be some relationship between these variables, we need to compare the percentage in each cell either with its row marginal, or with percentages in the other categories in the same row. If we find that the cell value is lower than the marginal, we can say that there is underrepresentation in that cell. A higher cell value indicates that there is overrepresentation. If we compare the percentage of 'Catholic' males with males in the row marginal, that is, with the percentage of all males in the sample, we find an underrepresentation (40 per cent compared with 50 per cent). However, when comparisons are made for 'No religion' males, we find the cell value is higher than the marginal value (67 compared with 50), and vice versa for the females (33 compared with 50). Hence, males are overrepresented and females underrepresented among respondents with 'No religion'. The reverse is the case for the 'Other' religion category. Comparing these pairs of percentages establishes how much the frequency in any cell deviates from the sample distribution on that variable. This procedure simply confirms what we found by comparing observed and expected frequencies. In this latter case, we were also looking for deviations from the overall distribution. We can either use the raw data and expected frequencies, or percentages to do this.

The percentages can also be compared along the rows. For example, we can see that 43 per cent of respondents in the 'Other' religion category are males compared with 67 per cent in the 'No religion' category. This also suggests under- and overrepresentation. The direct comparison of percentages across the rows is particularly useful in 2 by 2 tables.

It is possible to calculate percentages in a table like Table 4.1 in the other direction, that is, across the rows rather than down the columns. In associational analysis, this is optional and may be determined by what a researcher wants to say about a particular association. The only change will be in the way the association is discussed, that is, by comparing the categories of Religion across the Gender categories, rather than the other way around. However, as we shall see, in analysis that explores influence between variables, the direction in which the percentages are calculated is critical. More on this later.

Contingency tables are also used for ordinal-level variables, and interval-level and ratio-level variables that have been coded into categories. In short, they are used for any categorical variables. This means that variables at different levels of measurement can be included in the same table. For example, in Table 4.2, the EWV of Residents has been recoded into four categories, each including the following range of scores: 'Low' (56–79), 'Moderate' (80–89), 'High' (90–99) and 'Very high' (100–119); and Age has been recoded into three categories: 18–34, 35–54 and 55 +. Ignore the alphabetic identification of the cells for the moment.

Following the method of interpretation used for Table 4.1, we find that younger people tend to have 'Very high' scores (although they are also reasonably well represented in the three other EWV categories), middle-aged people tend to have 'Very high' and, more particularly, 'High' scores, and older people have 'Moderate' and, more particularly, 'Low' scores. Clearly, there is some association between these two variables, with the suggestion of a curve rather than a straight line. It is possible to describe this relationship in terms of percentage differences. However, it is difficult to judge the strength of the relationship from such comparisons. It is necessary to turn to other forms of analysis to achieve this, as we shall see shortly.

Forms of Association

An association between two variables can take various forms:

- positive or negative;
- linear or curvilinear; and
- symmetrical or asymmetrical.

Positive and Negative

Positive and negative associations are illustrated using a simplified form of Table 4.2. Environmental Worldview (recoded into two categories) is cross-tabulated with

Table 4.2   *Environmental Worldview by Age (Residents; observed frequencies and percentages)*

Environmental Worldview	Age			Total
	18–34	35–54	55+	
Low	a 21 (16%)	b 16 (12%)	c 42 (31%)	79 (20%)
Moderate	d 45 (35%)	e 46 (33%)	f 65 (48%)	156 (39%)
High	g 30 (23%)	h 52 (38%)	i 22 (16%)	104 (26%)
Very high	j 32 (25%)	k 24 (17%)	l 6 (4%)	62 (15%)
Total	128 (100%)	138 (100%)	135 (100%)	401 (100%)

Table 4.3 *Environmental Worldview by Age*
            (percentages)

(a) No relationship

EWV	Age			Total
	18–34	35–54	55+	
Low	47	47	47	47
High	53	53	53	53
Totals	100	100	100	100
n	(128)	(138)	(135)	(401)

(c) Strong negative relationship

EWV	Age			Total
	18–34	35–54	55+	
Low	6	47	**86**	47
High	**94**	53	14	53
Totals	100	100	100	100
n	(128)	(138)	(135)	(401)

(b) Strong positive relationship

EWV	Age			Total
	18–34	35–54	55+	
Low	**91**	47	5	47
High	9	53	**95**	53
Totals	100	100	100	100
n	(128)	(138)	(135)	(401)

(d) Actual relationship (Residents)

EWV	Age			Total
	18–34	35–54	55+	
Low	45	30	**67**	47
High	**55**	**70**	33	53
Totals	100	100	100	100
n	(128)	(138)	(135)	(401)

Age (in three categories) giving a simple 2 by 3 table. Table 4.3 presents four examples of the different ways in which these two variables could be related, as well as their actual relationship in the Resident sample.

Table 4.3(a) indicates how the table would appear if there was *no relationship*; cell percentages in each row are the same as the row marginal percentage. Table 4.3(b) shows what a strong *positive relationship* would look like. This is indicated by the cells in which there is overrepresentation, that is, in which there are more respondents than would be expected if there was no association. This relationship is described as positive because the oldest age category ('high') is associated with a 'High' score on the EWV scale, and the youngest age category ('low') is associated with a 'Low' score. The reverse is the case in Table 4.3(c). Older age is associated with a 'Low' score' and younger age with a 'High' score. Hence, as the variable categories are defined, this is a *negative relationship*.

It is possible to imagine a diagonal drawn across Tables 4.3(b) and 4.3(c), in the former, from the top left-hand cell to the bottom right-hand cell, and in the latter, from the bottom left-hand cell to the top right-hand cell. It is in the two corner cells of the table to which the line goes that the overrepresentation occurs. This line would be in the other direction (bottom left-hand corner to top right-hand corner) if the order of the categories for one of the variables had been reversed. Hence, the direction of the line does not indicate whether a relationship is positive or negative; it is necessary to look closely at the order of the categories.

In order to help recognize the patterns in cross-tabulations, in all subsequent tables, cells in which there is overrepresentation will be shown in bold, and if the percentage exceeds the marginal by at least 20 per cent, it will be shown in italics as well as bold.

Linear and Curvilinear

Tables 4.3(b) and 4.3(c) represent positive and negative *linear relationships*. Table 4.3(d), which reports the actual form of the relationship in the Resident sample, is clearly also negative: as Age increases, EWV score decreases. However, there is a suggestion in 4.3(d) that the actual relationship is *curvilinear*. The overrepresentation starts in the bottom left-hand cell, then goes across into the '35–54' and 'High' cell, and then goes up to the top right-hand cell. A line through these cells forms a simple curve. In fact, the Age category with the greatest overrepresentation among the three 'High' EWV cells is '35–54'. The overrepresentation is much less in the '18–34' age 'High' cell. This can only be explored with a wider range of categories on both variables. See what you can make of the pattern of the relationship in Table 4.2. Note that the table is constructed differently than Table 4.3.

There are other ways of identifying whether an association is linear or curved. We shall do this later in the chapter with these two variables in their continuous rather than categorical forms.

Symmetrical and Asymmetrical

The third way in which an association can be described is in terms of symmetry – whether it is symmetrical or asymmetrical. The measures of association that are discussed in this chapter are referred to as *symmetrical*, which means that the relationship can be examined from the point of view of either of the variables. All that is being established is whether the variables *are* associated, and to what extent. No assumptions are made about whether one variable has an influence on the other. However, there is another set of measures that are used when it *is* possible or desirable to assume that there is a direction of influence between two variables, when it *can* be assumed that a person's position on one variable influences their position on the other variable. For example, it can be argued that a person's level of education has an influence on their income, or on the type and status of occupation that they occupy. These measures of association are referred to as being *asymmetrical*. The variables are examined from only one point of view.

Measures of Association for Categorical Variables

The inspection of contingency tables can indicate whether or not there is an association between two variables and, perhaps, can provide a rough idea of the strength of a relationship. It is clear that the associations in Tables 4.3(b) and 4.3(c) are stronger than in Table 4.3(d). The percentage differences between 'High' and 'Low' EWV categories for extreme age categories are smaller in the latter than in the two former parts of the table. However, while percentage differences can give some indication of the strength of association, what is needed is a summary measure that can not only indicate this, but also be used to make comparisons with associations between other variables. This problem is dealt with by the use of *measures of association*.

Nominal-level Variables

Measures of association for nominal-level variables usually produce a number between 0 and 1. A value of zero indicates little or no association, while 1 indicates a perfect association or relationship.

Different coefficients are required for different levels of measurement. Four major measures of association are used with categorical data. Three of them, the contingency coefficient, the phi coefficient and Cramér's V, can be used with both nominal-level and ordinal-level data, although they are particularly appropriate when one or both variables are nominal. All are based on the differences between the observed and expected frequencies in the cells of a contingency table. Another coefficient, gamma, can only be used when both variables are at ordinal level, or with interval-level or ratio-level variables that have been coded into categories. Some exceptions to the uses of these coefficients will be encountered in due course.

Contingency coefficient

The *contingency coefficient* is derived from *chi-square* (χ^2, pronounced 'kie' to rhyme with 'tie'). First, it is necessary to explain how χ^2 is calculated for different-sized tables. It is based on the squared difference between the observed (O) and the expected (E) frequencies, divided by E, for every cell of a contingency table. This calculation provides an indication of how much each individual cell contributes to the overall association between the variables. The total χ^2 value for all cells provides the basis for a measure of overall association. If E and O are the same in all cells of a table, there will be no association between the variables. The extent to which they are different indicates some kind of association. The larger the total χ^2, the stronger is the association. The equation is:

$$\chi^2 = \sum \frac{(O - E)^2}{E} \qquad (4.1)$$

χ^2 can be calculated for tables of any size. All the necessary information is available in Table 4.1 to be able to calculate the total χ^2 value.[2] In the top left-hand cell,

$$\chi^2 = \frac{(34 - 42.6)^2}{42.6} \ 1.7385$$

Repeating this procedure for all ten cells produces the following figures, set out in the order of their cell position in the table.

$$1.7385 + 0.0084 + 0.3144 + 0.6442 + 5.6809$$
$$+ 1.7473 + 0.0084 + 0.3160 + 0.6475 + 5.7094 = 16.8150$$

It is no coincidence that the χ^2 values for the two cells in each column are very similar. This is inevitable when there are only two categories for a variable. It is also worth noting that it is the two cells in the 'No religion' column that make the greatest contributions, 68 per cent of the total χ^2 in fact. As we have already noted, there is a considerable difference between males and females in this category.

This method can be used with a contingency table of any size. However, a 2 by 2 table is a special case in which a different procedure can be used, particularly when N (or n) is greater than 40. The equation includes what is known as a correction for continuity, which is supposed to improve its efficiency. It is also easier to calculate.

If the four cells in a 2 by 2 table are identified as a, b, c and d, as follows,

the equation for a sample is:

$$\chi^2 = \frac{n([a \times d] - [b \times c] - n/2)^2}{(a + b)(c + d)(a + c)(b + d)} \tag{4.2}$$

The expressions '$a \times d$' and '$b \times c$' simply indicate that the diagonally opposite cell values should be multiplied. The square brackets mean that this calculation should be done before any others in the numerator (top line). The denominator (bottom line) simply means that all four marginals are multiplied in pairs. Let us explore this by recoding Religion into two categories, 'Some religion' and 'No religion'.

Table 4.4 is a simplified 2 by 2 version of Table 4.1. We can calculate χ^2 using the above equation:

$$\chi^2 = \frac{399([133 \times 33] - [67 \times 166] - 399/2)^2}{200 \times 199 \times 299 \times 100} = \frac{399(-6932.5)^2}{1,190,020,000} = 16.114$$

While this value is lower than for the 2 by 5 table, it is higher than the value that would be arrived at by using the previous method (15.245 with the 2 by 2 data). This is due to the continuity correction that the 2 by 2 equation contains.

There are some restrictions on when the χ^2 can be calculated legitimately. This is because cells with small expected frequencies can produce inflated χ^2 values. Therefore, for tables of 2 by 3 and larger, the following rules must be followed:

- Not more than 20 per cent of the expected frequencies can be less than 5.
- No expected frequency can be less than 1.

Table 4.4 *Religion by Gender (Residents; observed frequencies)*

	Religion		
Gender	Some religion	No religion	Total
Male	*a* 133	*b* 67	200
Female	*c* 166	*d* 33	199
Totals	299	100	399

In the case of 2 by 2 tables, all the expected frequencies should be at least 5.

In order to satisfy these rules, it may be necessary to collapse some categories in a table, if this is meaningful, particularly those that have small marginal totals. However, not much can be done in the case of 2 by 2 tables. These rules can be a problem when the table total is small, or one or both of the variables is badly skewed. It is these requirements that make it necessary to use relatively large samples or populations when it is expected that the analysis of the data will require the use of contingency tables.

Now that we can calculate χ^2, we can return to the contingency coefficient. This is the most basic measure of association between two nominal-level variables. It is derived directly from the total χ^2 in a contingency table. However, as the magnitude of the total χ^2 can be influenced by the table total, the χ^2 has to be modified to take this into account. Hence, the equation for the contingency coefficient (C), for data from a sample, is:

$$C = \sqrt{\frac{\chi^2}{n + \chi^2}}$$ (4.3)

For data from a population, n is replaced by N.

Returning to Table 4.1 and the χ^2 value calculated for it above, we can now get an indication of the strength of this relationship using the equation for the contingency coefficient:[3]

$$C = \sqrt{\frac{16.8150}{399 + 16.8150}} = \sqrt{\frac{16.8150}{415.8150}} = \sqrt{0.0404} = 0.201$$

The values for the contingency coefficient range from 0 to 1.

The coefficient has a number of strengths. It can be used with nominal-level data, and it can detect an association regardless of whether it is linear curvilinear or more complex. However, it has some major limitations. While it produces a value of 0 if there is no association, it can never produce a value of 1 for a perfect association. This means that it is only possible to compare contingency coefficients across tables of the same size.

Standardized contingency coefficient

The upper limit, or maximum value, of the contingency coefficient is dependent on the size of the table. For example, in a 2 by 2 table the maximum possible value is 0.707 and in a 3 by 3 table, 0.816. It is only with tables larger than 5 by 5 that the upper limit exceeds 0.900. These values can be calculated using the following equation. The one for a 'square' table, that is, one with the same number of rows and columns, is

$$\text{Upper limit } (L) = \sqrt{\frac{r-1}{r}} \qquad (4.4)$$

where r is the number of rows or columns. If the table is not square, then

$$L = \sqrt[4]{\frac{r-1}{r} \times \frac{c-1}{c}} \qquad (4.5)$$

where r is the number of rows and c is the number of columns.

There is a simple solution to the problem of the variation in the upper limits of the contingency coefficient. They can be standardized by dividing them by their upper limit. This makes all maximum values, regardless of the table size or shape, equal to 1.[4] These *standardized coefficients* (C_s) can be compared between tables of any size. As we shall see, other attempts have been made to overcome this problem, namely the use of Cramér's V (see below).

If we calculate the upper limit for Table 4.1 we find that it is 0.795 (you might like to try this as an exercise). Then applying this correction to the C that we have just calculated, $C_s = 0.201/0.795 = 0.253$. This coefficient *can* be compared with others that use a χ^2-based procedure.

The second limitation derives from the requirements for the computation of χ^2. The table must be of a form that meets these requirements before the contingency coefficient can be calculated. The third limitation is that C cannot really be compared with many other measures of association, mainly because they can normally only detect linear relations (see the next section for a discussion of this issue).

Before leaving the contingency coefficient, it is necessary to outline the convention to be followed in the rest of the book for indicating the strength of an association, based on the value of the coefficient. This convention will be used for *all* measures of association.[5]

0.00	None
0.01–0.09	Negligible
0.10–0.29	Weak
0.30–0.59	Moderate
0.60–0.74	Strong
0.75–0.99	Very strong
1.00	Perfect

Phi

For 2 by 2 tables, or tables in which one variable is in two categories, a special version of the contingency coefficient should be used, known as *phi* (ϕ), pronounced to rhyme with 'pie'. It uses a simplified version of the equation for the contingency coefficient:

$$\phi = \sqrt{\frac{\chi^2}{n}} \qquad (4.6)$$

For this size of table, or any table with one dichotomized variable, phi ranges from 0 to 1, but when applied to larger tables, its maximum value can exceed 1. Hence, it should only be used with 2 by 2, or 2 by *c* or *r* by 2 tables.

This means that we could have used ϕ in Table 4.1, the 2 by 5 version. Using the χ^2 value for this table (16.8150), ϕ can be calculated as follows.

$$\phi = \sqrt{\frac{16.8150}{399}} = \sqrt{0.0421} = 0.205$$

The 2 by 2 version of the table (Table 4.4) produced a χ^2 of 16.114. Hence,

$$\phi = \sqrt{\frac{16.114}{399}} = \sqrt{0.0404} = 0.201$$

While the two values are not identical, the difference is only in the third decimal place, or in the second if rounded to two places, so that 0.205 becomes 0.21. This difference is of no consequence.

Cramér's V

The most commonly used measure of association for categorical variables, particularly at the nominal level, is *Cramér's V*. Again, it is a variation of the contingency coefficient and it is designed to yield values between 0 and 1. The denominator is replaced by the smaller of the two values $r - 1$ and $c - 1$:

$$V = \sqrt{\frac{\chi^2}{n \times (\text{smaller of } r - 1 \text{ and } c - 1)}} \qquad (4.7)$$

Applying this equation to Table 4.1, we get

$$V = \sqrt{\frac{16.8150}{399 \times (2 - 1)}} = 0.205$$

Note that this calculation ends up being the same as that for ϕ (see above). The reason is that one variable, Gender, is dichotomized, giving the value of 1 for the $r-1$ component of the equation. In a table with at least three categories for both variables, this component would be at least 2. Hence, for Table 4.1, $C = 0.201$, $C_s = 0.253$, $\phi = 0.205$ and $V = 0.205$.

When it is possible to use more than one of these coefficients, it is not always easy to know which one is the most appropriate. They all are. However, it is not advisable to use C except with large tables, and ϕ cannot be used if both variables have more than two categories. In my experience, Cramér's V appears to be a conservative measure and C_s usually produces a higher figure. Cramér's V is the most commonly used measure where ϕ cannot be used.

There are no exact answers to the calculation of the strength of association between categorical variables. Different statisticians have devised different methods, each with its own strengths and weaknesses. In the end, we are looking for a general indication upon which a judgement can be made as to the importance of the results of the analysis.

Ordinal-level Variables

Gamma

There is a more appropriate measure of association for use with contingency tables that have two ordinal-level variables, namely, Goodman and Kruskal's *gamma* (γ or G). It is based on the idea of comparing every possible pair of respondents in a sample or population to see whether their positions on the two variables are concordant or discordant. For example, the age and attitudes of two respondents, A and B, can be compared to see whether, say, older age is associated with a higher attitude score. If B is older than A, and has a higher score, this pair would be regarded as concordant. Similarly, there would be concordance if B is younger and has a lower score. If neither is the case, the pair would be discordant. In other words, we are looking for the level of consistency in the pattern of responses on two variables. If every pair is concordant, there is a perfect relationship, that is, there is absolute consistency in the way all respondents are located on the two variables. On the other hand, if every pair is discordant, there is no relationship. Hence, the balance between concordant and discordant pairs determines the relative strength of a relationship.

Gamma ranges from -0.1 to $+0.1$. The equation is:

$$G = \frac{C-D}{C+D} \tag{4.8}$$

where C is the number of *concordant pairs* and D the number of *discordant pairs*. The equation is deceptively simple. However, the work involved in manually comparing every pair in a large sample is horrendous. While computers can now do this in the blink of an eye, there is a manual computational method that can be used with contingency tables.

The method for calculating gamma will be demonstrated with the data in Table 4.2, in which both variables are ordinal, although based on higher levels

Table 4.5   *Calculation of gamma (from Table 4.2)*

Focal cell	Paired cells	Concordant pairs		
a	*e, f, h, i, k, l*	21 (46 + 65 + 52 + 22 + 24 + 6)	=	4,515
b	*f, i, l*	16 (65 + 22 + 6)	=	1,488
d	*h, i, k, l*	45 (52 + 22 + 24 + 6)	=	4,680
e	*i, l*	46 (22 + 6)	=	1,288
g	*k, l*	30 (24 + 6)	=	900
h	*l*	52 (6)	=	312
		Total	=	13,183

Focal cell	Paired cells	Discordant pairs		
j	*b, c, e, f, h, i*	32 (16 + 42 + 46 + 65 + 52 + 22)	=	7,776
k	*c, f, i*	24 (42 + 65 + 22)	=	3,096
g	*b, c, e, f*	30 (16 + 42 + 46 + 65)	=	5,070
h	*c, f*	52 (42 + 65)	=	5,564
d	*b, c*	45 (16 + 42)	=	2,610
e	*c*	46 (42)	=	1,932
		Total	=	26,048

of measurement. We have already noted that the percentages in the cells suggest a negative and slightly curvilinear relationship. As we shall see, this may cause some slight problems. The cells have been assigned letters for convenience of reference in calculating gamma.

To calculate the concordant pairs (C), we start at one end of the positive diagonal, that is, at the '18–34' years and 'Low' EWV cell (*a*) and work towards the '55 +' years and 'Very high' EWV cell (*l*). We start by focusing on the respondents in cell *a*, and compare them with those in all the cells to the right of and below *a*, that is, *e, f, h, i, k* and *l*.[6] Respondents in these latter cells are older and have higher EWV scores than respondents in *a*. The number of concordant pairs here is arrived at by multiplying the number in *a* by the sum of the numbers in the other six cells. Now we move to cell *b* and identify the cells in which respondents are older and have higher scores, that is, *f, i* and *l*. The same calculation is done. We now do the same by focusing on cells *d, e, g* and *h* in turn. The number of concordant pairs is the sum of these products (see Table 4.5).

To calculate the discordant pairs (D), we work from one end of the negative diagonal. This diagonal runs from the cell that links the '18–34' years and 'Very high' EWV cell (*j*), to the '55 +' years and 'Low' EWV cell (*c*). This time we start by focusing on the respondents in cell *j* and compare them with those in cells to the right and above *j*, that is, *b, c, e, f, h* and *i*. Respondents in these latter cells are older and have lower EWV scores than respondents in cell *j*. The number in *j* is then multiplied by the sum of the other six cells. Next we focus on cell *k* and multiply it by the sum of its discordant cells *c, f* and *i*. Then we move to cells *g, h, d* and *e* in turn, and do similar calculations. The sum of all these products is the total number of discordant pairs (see Table 4.5).

We can now calculate gamma for Table 4.2:

$$G = \frac{C - D}{C + D} = \frac{13{,}183 - 26{,}048}{26{,}048 + 13{,}183} = \frac{-12{,}865}{39{,}231} = -0.328$$

The coefficient indicates a moderate, negative association between these two variables.

While G is the most appropriate measure of association for Table 4.2, it is also possible to use C, C_s and V, particularly if the form of association is not linear. The χ^2 for this table is 49.706, and this produces the following values for these measures of association; $C = 0.332$, $C_s = 0.396$ and $V = 0.249$ (you may like to calculate these as an exercise). It would be inappropriate to use ϕ with this table. When the relationship is linear, in theory, gamma should produce a higher value than these other coefficients. However, as there is a tendency towards a curve in this relationship, with the exception of V, which tends to be rather conservative, the other coefficients are about the same as or higher than gamma.

Gamma has two main limitations. Firstly, it can only detect linear relationships while C, C_s, ϕ and V can all detect any kind of relationship. Therefore, when a curvilinear or other form of relationship is present, it is useful to also use these other coefficients with categorical data. However, this disadvantage is not peculiar to gamma (more on this shortly). The second disadvantage is that gamma ignores all tied pairs, that is, when the members of a pair have the same scores or positions on one or both variables. When there are many tied pairs, gamma will overestimate the strength of the relationship. Kendall's tau-*b* and Somer's *d* can be used in such cases. I will discuss tau-b here and return to Somer's *d* in the next chapter.[7] In spite of these limitations, gamma is widely used with ordinal-level data.

Kendall's tau-b

Kendall's tau-b (τ_b) is an alternative measure of association to gamma, particularly in square tables, where there is the same number of rows and columns. It allows for ties on both variables. The equation is a variation on the one for gamma:

$$\tau_b = \frac{C - D}{\sqrt{(C + D + T_x)(C + D + T_y)}} \tag{4.9}$$

where T_x is the number of ties on one variable and T_y the number of ties on the other.

Using the same example as for gamma (see Tables 4.2 and 4.5), we already know the values for $C - D$ (12,865) and $C + D$ (39,231). To calculate T_x, the ties on Age, we multiply cell *a* by the sum of the other three cells in the column (*d*, *g* and *j*), repeat the same procedure in the other two columns, then sum the results. T_y, the ties on EWV, is arrived at using the same procedure along each row. Hence,

$$T_x = 21(45 + 30 + 32) + 16(46 + 52 + 24) + 42(65 + 22 + 6) = 8105$$
$$T_y = 21(16 + 42) + 45(46 + 65) + 30(52 + 22) + 32(24 + 6) = 9393$$

Now entering these figures in the equation,

$$\tau_b = \frac{C - D}{\sqrt{(C + D + T_x)(C + D + T_y)}} = \frac{12{,}865}{\sqrt{(39{,}231 + 8105)(39{,}231 + 9393)}}$$

$$= \frac{12{,}865}{\sqrt{47{,}336 \times 48{,}624}} = \frac{12{,}865}{47{,}975.68} = 0.268$$

This value is more conservative than that for gamma (0.328). As a result of the ties being included, tau-b will never be larger than gamma.

Other Methods for Ranked Data

Two other coefficients are available for use when objects or individuals can be ranked in two ordered series, rather than in ordered categories. Suppose a class of students is rank-ordered according to their performance on both their mid-semester test and their end-of-semester examination. If we wanted to know how consistent the students' performances were, we could use one of two tests: *Spearman's rank correlation coefficient* (r_s), known as rho, or *Kendall's rank correlation coefficient* known as tau (τ).[8] These coefficients may be useful with small numbers where persons or items have unique ranks. See Siegel and Castellan (1988) and Elifson et al. (1998) for a discussion.

Combinations of Categorical and Metric Variables

We have noted that if a measure of association is required in a contingency table that combines nominal-level or ordinal-level with interval-level or ratio-level variables, such as EWV and Gender, then it may be necessary to transform the continuous variable (e.g. EWV) into a categorical variable.[9] Of course, when a measure of association is required between two continuous variables, it is possible to transform both into the categorical form (as in Table 4.2) and then use G or even C_s or V.

Coding interval-level and ratio-level variables into categories, and creating contingency tables, will usually allow the form of the relationship to be determined. However, these measures of association are not as powerful as those that have been developed for use with interval-level and ratio-level variables. They are likely to produce more conservative or lower values than the more powerful measures (this will be discussed in the next section). However, C_s and V have one distinct advantage: they can detect any pattern in the relationship between two variables, while the more powerful measures can only detect linear relationships. Hence, if a relationship is curvilinear, or if it is suspected to be so, it may be useful to recode metric variables into categories and use C_s or V.

Association with Interval-Level and Ratio-Level Variables

We now turn to measures of association that are appropriate when both variables are metric, that is, they are either interval-level or ratio-level. The same measures can be used with variables at both levels of measurement. As the measures of association discussed in this section of the chapter are only designed to detect linear relationships, it is important to first establish what form a relationship takes in order to know whether the measure is appropriate and to be able to interpret the results.

Scatter diagrams

We have seen how the nature or pattern of a relationship can be detected in a cross-tabulation. However, with interval-level and ratio-level variables, this would require transforming them into categorical variables. Instead, it is possible to construct a *scatter diagram* by plotting all points of intersection between the two variables. In other words, the combination of each person's position on the two variables is plotted.

Figure 4.2 shows a scatter diagram for the relationship between EWV and Age in the Resident sample. This is a real rather than a contrived scatter diagram. It indicates a clustering of responses among the over 50s at the lower end of the EWV scale. Between 40 and 50, the clustering tends to move up the scale. However, under 40 years, the clustering is not as consistent; it is spread from the middle to higher scores. In fact, there is evidence of a slight curve at this end of the diagram. In other words, rather than the younger respondents having high EWV scores, they, and those up to about 40, tend to be clustered around moderate scores. The most conservative line we could draw to represent this clustering would start as a 'flat' line through moderate scores for the younger respondents, and then 'drop off' to lower scores in older age. It would be a 'bent' rather than a straight line.[10] You might like to compare Figure 4.2 with Table 4.2. However, the coefficients to be discussed in this section cannot detect the 'bend'; they can only assume a straight line, from reasonably high scores among the younger respondents to rather low scores among the older respondents.

It is a common practice to simplify such scatter diagrams into a line that represents the shape of the association, be it straight or curved. However, this can lead to the loss of important information, as is evident in Figure 4.2. It is possible to view this relationship as either linear or curvilinear. While the

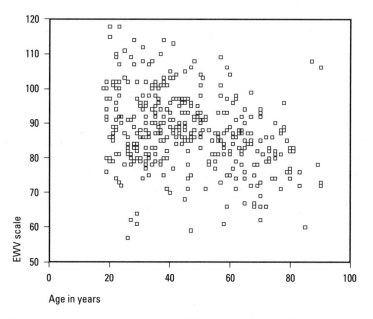

Figure 4.2   *Scatter diagram: Environmental Worldview by Age (Residents)*

latter may be a more accurate representation, it may be forcing the data into a pattern that overlooks important differences. It is clear that younger people in the sample have a range of attitudes towards the environment. They may even be divided into two main groups, and these groups may be related to some other variable, such as education. It is always important to inspect scatter diagrams and contingency tables very carefully for diversity as well as for associations, for in the dispersion may be clues to important patterns in the data.

Covariance

Another way of thinking about any association is how much commonality there is in, say, the responses of a sample or population on two variables. Or, to put this more technically, how much does the variance on one variable coincide with the variance on the other variable? This is what is meant by *covariance*.

In examining the characteristics of single continuous (metric) variables, we explored the notion of variance in terms of the sum of the deviations of individual scores from the mean score. We found that this principle is also contained in the idea of mean absolute deviation and standard deviation (see pp. 79–84). This same idea can be used to examine the relationship between two variables. However, in this case, the deviations from the means of the scores on both variables are multiplied together. For sample data, this is expressed as $(x - \bar{x})(y - \bar{y})$. To arrive at the covariance, the products of the two deviations are summed for all respondents, and this is divided by n, or preferably $n - 1$ (see the discussion on variance):

$$\text{Covariance } (Cov_{xy}) = \frac{\sum(x - \bar{x})(y - \bar{y})}{n - 1} \tag{4.10}$$

Unfortunately, this coefficient has limited value on its own as the size of the covariance is dependent on the units of measurement used. Large units (such as Age in 10-year intervals) produce larger values than when smaller units are used (such as Age in years). However, covariance provides the major ingredient in the most commonly used measure of association for continuous variables, Pearson's r. In fact, all that this latter measure does is standardize the covariance.

Pearson's r

There is one measure of association, commonly referred to as the *correlation coefficient*, which is almost universally used with interval-level and ratio-level variables. It is Pearson's r or, more technically, *Pearson's product moment correlation coefficient*. The latter term identifies its use in bivariate analysis.

Pearson's r represents the extent to which individuals, events, etc., occupy the same relative position on two variables. This coefficient builds on the idea of covariance, of how much the variance on one variable coincides with the variance of the other variable – in other words, how much they vary together, how much they are related, that is, co-related.

Peasron's r is produced by standardizing the covariance. This is done by dividing the covariance by the product of the standard deviations of the two variables. The display below begins with a simple version of this procedure and is followed by the more elaborate versions that include the calculation of the covariance component as well as the two variances.

$$\text{Pearson's } r = \frac{Cov_{xy}}{s_x \, s_y} \tag{4.11}$$

$$= \frac{\sum(x - \bar{x})(y - \bar{y})}{(n - 1) \, s_x \, s_y} \tag{4.12}$$

$$= \frac{\sum(x - \bar{x})(y - \bar{y})}{\sqrt{[\sum(x_i - \bar{x})^2 \sum(y_i - \bar{y})^2]}} \tag{4.13}$$

This correlation coefficient ranges from -1 to $+1$. Its sign is determined by whether one or other of the deviations from the mean is negative; if both are positive or negative, the sign will be positive; if both are different, the sign will be negative.

There are two commonly used ways of calculating r, the mean deviation method and the raw score method. The former allows for a clearer understanding of the principles involved, while the latter is easier for manual calculations. They will both be illustrated using a subsample of 21 respondents from the Resident sample.[11] Figure 4.3 shows a scatter diagram of the relationship between Age and EWV in this subsample.

Table 4.6 provides the data required to use the *mean deviation method*. The equation for this method is (4.13). Substituting the data in the equation we get:

$$= \frac{-4{,}781.38}{\sqrt{5{,}188.95 \times 4{,}918.95}} = \frac{-4{,}781.38}{5{,}052.15} = -0.946$$

The equation for the *raw score method* is:

$$r = \frac{n(\sum xy) - (\sum x)(\sum y)}{\sqrt{[n(\sum x^2) - (\sum x)^2][n(\sum y^2) - (\sum y)^2]}} \qquad (4.14)$$

Entering the data in Table 4.7 into this equation we get:

$$r = \frac{(21 \times 83{,}527) - (988 \times 1877)}{\sqrt{(21 \times 51{,}672 - 988^2)(21 \times 172{,}687) - 1877^2}}$$

$$= \frac{1{,}754{,}067 - 1{,}854{,}476}{\sqrt{(1{,}085{,}112 - 976{,}144)(3{,}626{,}427 - 3{,}523{,}129)}} = \frac{-100{,}409}{106{,}095.13} = -0.946$$

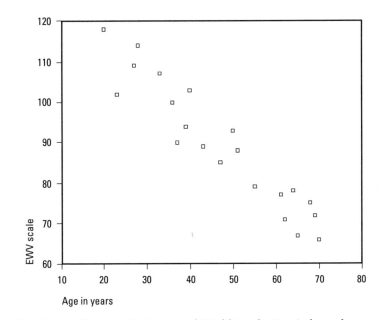

Figure 4.3   *Scatter diagram: Environmental Worldview by Age (subsample of Residents)*

Table 4.6 *Mean deviation method for computing r (sub-sample of Residents)*

Respondent	Age			EWV score			
	x	$x - \bar{x}$	$(x - \bar{x})^2$	y	$y - \bar{y}$	$(y - \bar{y})^2$	$(x - \bar{x})(y - \bar{y})$
1	20	−27.05	731.57	118	28.62	819.05	−774.08
2	23	−24.05	578.29	102	12.62	159.24	−303.46
3	27	−20.05	401.91	109	19.62	384.91	−393.32
4	28	−19.05	362.81	114	24.62	606.10	−468.93
5	33	−14.05	197.34	107	17.62	310.43	−247.51
6	36	−11.05	122.05	100	10.62	122.76	−117.32
7	37	−10.05	100.95	90	0.62	0.38	−6.22
8	39	−8.05	64.76	94	4.62	21.34	−37.17
9	40	−7.05	49.67	103	13.62	185.48	−95.98
10	43	−4.05	16.38	89	−0.38	0.15	1.54
11	47	−0.05	0.00	85	−4.38	19.19	0.21
12	50	2.95	8.72	93	3.62	13.10	10.68
13	51	3.95	15.62	88	−1.38	1.91	−5.46
14	55	7.95	63.24	79	−10.38	107.76	−82.55
15	61	13.95	194.67	77	−12.38	153.29	−172.74
16	62	14.95	223.57	71	−18.38	337.86	−274.84
17	64	16.95	287.38	78	−11.38	129.53	−192.93
18	65	17.95	322.29	67	−22.38	500.91	−401.79
19	68	20.95	439.00	75	−14.38	206.81	−301.32
20	69	21.95	481.91	72	−17.38	302.10	−381.55
21	70	22.95	526.81	66	−23.38	546.67	−536.65
Σ	988		5,188.95	1877		4,981.95	−4781.38
	$\bar{x} = 47.05$			$\bar{y} = 89.38$			

Table 4.7 *Raw score method for computing r (subsample of Residents)*

Respondent	Age		EWV score		
	x	x^2	y	y^2	xy
1	20	400	118	13,924	2,360
2	23	529	102	10,404	2,346
3	27	729	109	11,881	2,943
4	28	784	114	12,996	3,192
5	33	1,089	107	11,449	3,531
6	36	1,296	100	10,000	3,600
7	37	1,369	90	8,100	3,330
8	39	1,521	94	8,836	3,666
9	40	1,600	103	10,609	4,120
10	43	1,849	89	7,921	3,827
11	47	2,209	85	7,225	3,995
12	50	2,500	93	8,649	4,650
13	51	2,601	88	7,744	4,488
14	55	3,025	79	6,241	4,345
15	61	3,721	77	5,929	4,697
16	62	3,844	71	5,041	4,402
17	64	4,096	78	6,084	4,992
18	65	4,225	67	4,489	4,355
19	68	4,624	75	5,625	5,100
20	69	4,761	72	5,184	4,968
21	70	4,900	66	4,356	4,620
$n = 21$	$\sum x = 988$	$\sum x^2 = 51,672$	$\sum y = 1877$	$\sum y^2 = 172,687$	$\sum xy = 83,527$

The Pearson correlation coefficient for this example is extremely high. The scatter diagram indicates what a distribution would need to be like to achieve such a value. Note that if these two variables were perfectly correlated (negatively), the ages would decrease in perfect order, in the same way as the EWV scores increase. An inspection of either Tables 4.6 or 4.7 indicates that when Age is in order, from youngest to oldest, the EWV scores do not decrease uniformly. This accounts for the scatter in Figure 4.3.

It is also possible to calculate Pearson's r from the z-scores of both variables. In this case, the equation is:

$$\text{Pearson's } r = \frac{\sum(z_x \, z_y)}{n} \qquad (4.15)$$

The attention given to Pearson's r here is intended to reinforce the idea that it is a universal and extremely useful coefficient. It also forms the basis of many other types of data analysis.

A measure of the actual 'overlap' between these two variables can be obtained by squaring r. Hence, in the example of the association between EWV and Age (Figure 4.3), $r^2 = 0.896$. Translated, this means that 89.6 per cent of the variance of the two variables is common. Put differently, knowing a person's position or score on one variable gives an 89.6 per cent chance of predicting their position or score on the other variable. Of course, in real research this figure is usually much lower. For example, in the actual relationship between these two variables in the Resident sample, $r = -0.308$ and $r^2 = 0.095$. Hence, only 9.5 per cent of the variance is in common.

In the earlier discussion of the contingency coefficient, I provided a convention for describing the strength of any association. Cohen (1988) has provided a simpler scheme for Pearson's r in which a coefficient of approximately 0.1 is regarded as 'small', 0.3 as 'medium' and 0.5 or more as 'large'.

When used in bivariate relationships, r is sometimes referred to as a *zero-order correlation coefficient*. This distinguishes its bivariate use from use in multivariate analysis. We shall return to this in the next chapter.

Comparing the Measures

It is very important to select a measure of association that is appropriate for the levels of measurement of the variables being analyzed. Nevertheless, we have already noted that there is some flexibility in their application. For example, a number of measures are available when both variables are nominal: ϕ for tables where at least one variable is dichotomized, and C, C_s and V for tables with variables in three or more categories. These coefficients can also be used for ordinal-level data, although G is more appropriate if the association is linear. Pearson's r is the most commonly used measure when both variables are interval or ratio.

However, when a set of ordinal-level categories can be assumed to approximate interval-level data, it is possible to also use r, albeit with some caution.

Now let us examine an example in which it is possible to use all of these measures (except for ϕ). We can then compare the values of the various coefficients. EWV and Age have been coded into categories of approximately equal intervals, EWV into four categories and Age into six categories. In Chapter 3 we noted that converting such variables into categories of equal width does not destroy the interval-level character of the data. However, it must be noted that the categories used for both variables do not completely conform to the interval-level requirements. The extreme categories, which incorporate the tails of the distributions, are not the same width as the other categories of the variable; with one exception, the 18–24 Age category, they are all wider, although of uniform width. In spite of this, I believe it is useful to apply Pearson's r to the categorical as well as to the continuous form of these two variables.[12]

First, let us compare the values of r for this association, for both the continuous and categorical forms of the variables. In the Resident sample, r is −0.31 for both forms of measurement. This illustrates that recoding scores (e.g. EWV) or discrete continuous measures (e.g. Age) into categories may not affect the value of the correlation coefficient.

Here is another example in which all the measures of association can be compared. Table 4.8 reports a contingency table for two continuous variables that have been categorized, Education and Age (Residents). Education was originally an ordinal-level variable, but is now dichotomized, and Age was a ratio-level variable, now in six categories. As we have seen, even in its categorical form, Age closely approximates at least an interval-level variable. Any variable that is dichotomized, regardless of its original level of measurement, is amenable to the use of measures of association appropriate for interval-level and ratio-level data. Hence, the whole range of measures of association can be applied to this cross-tabulation.

An inspection of the table shows a genuine curvilinear relationship; the extreme Age categories ('18–24', '55–64', '65 +') are overrepresented in the 'No university education' category, and the middle Aged categories (25–54) are overrepresented in the 'University educated' category. It is possible to trace a curve through these overrepresented categories. Clearly, there is some association. However, when we compare C, C_s, V, G and r we find a discrepancy; G and r are very different from the other coefficients (C = 0.290, C_s = 0.361, V = 0.303, ϕ = 0.303, G = −0.182, r = −0.138).[13] The latter two are lower because they cannot detect the curve.

The curve in this relationship is even more marked when five education categories are used; postgraduate qualification is definitely more common among the '35–44' and '45–54' Age categories. In this case, ϕ cannot be used and r must be used with caution as the intervals in the ordinal-level measurement of Education are certainly not equal. The coefficients for this form of the contingency table are: C = 0.408, C_s = 0.451, V = 0.225, G = −0.151, r = −0.160.

Table 4.8   *Education by Age (percentages; Residents)*

Education	Age						Total
	18–24	25–34	35–44	45–54	55–64	65+	
No uni. edn	77	42	43	53	63	78	58
Uni. edn	23	58	57	47	37	22	42
Totals	100	100	100	100	100	100	100
n	47	81	77	58	56	78	397

Hence, in both cases, the measures that can only detect linear relationships, G and r, produce much more conservative and less useful results. Even the added power of r is of no value in such cases. The choice is between C_s and V; use the former if you want the most 'flattering' value and the latter if you wish to be more conservative.

Association Between Categorical and Metric Variables

When two variables are at the same level of measurement, the choice of measure of association is straightforward. When they are both nominal, there are two main possibilities. When they are both ordinal, the choice will depend on whether the association is linear or not. When both variables are metric (interval or ratio) there is really no choice; Pearson's r is it. However, invariably in social research we have to deal with variables at different levels of measurement when we are trying to establish associations. There are a number of strategies available, most of which we have already discussed. What follows here is mainly a summary of the methods that can be used when one variable is categorical and the other is metric.

Code Metric Variable to Ordinal Categories

A common strategy is to reduce the metric variable to a set of ordinal-level categories. This is done using recoding techniques that were discussed earlier for EWV scores (originally interval) and Age (originally ratio).

Dichotomize the Categorical Variable

If the categorical variable is already dichotomized, or can be recoded into two categories, it is possible to use the measure of association appropriate to interval-level and ratio-level variables, namely, Pearson's r. This is an acceptable practice, the technical reasons for which do not need to concern us here.

Summary

- Associational analysis is an elaborate form of description in which the patterns or connections between variables are investigated. Such connections are expressed statistically as measures of association, or correlation coefficients, which indicate the extent of common variance between two variables. Establishing the strength of such associations provides some understanding of social phenomena and is a necessary step towards explanatory analysis.
- The choice of measure of association depends of the levels of measurement of the two variables. The measures discussed in this chapter are used under the following circumstances.

    1. Nominal-level variable with nominal-level variable:

        (a) three or more categories on each variable-Cramér's V and standardized contingency coefficient (C_s);
        (b) one or both variables are dichotomies-phi (ϕ);

    2. Nominal-level variable with ordinal-level variable;
       as for 1.
    3. Ordinal-level variable with ordinal-level variable:

        (a) ordered categories-gamma (G) and Kendall's tau-b;
            Somer's d (asymmetric version; not discussed) can also be used;
        (b) ordered items with small samples-Spearman's rho and Kendall's tau (not discussed).

    4. Metric-level variable with metric-level variable;
       Pearson's r.
    5. Nominal-level variable with metric-level variable:

        (a) recode metric-level variable to ordinal categories-use 1(a) above;
        (b) if nominal-level variable is a dichotomy: Pearson's r;
        (c) if nominal-level variable can be dichotomized sensibly-Pearson's r.

    6. Ordinal-level variable with metric-level variable:

        (a) recode metric-level variable to ordinal categories-use 3(a) above;
        (b) if ordinal-level variable can be dichotomized sensibly-Pearson's r.

Notes

[1]It is conventional to give the number of rows first. Hence, 2 by 5 means that the table has 2 rows and 5 columns.

[2]Note that the expected values have been rounded in Table 4.1 to one decimal place, and that more decimal places are needed in order to produce the accrate results given here.

[3]Normally, two decimal places are sufficient for any measure of association. I have included a third decimal place here just to facilitate comparisons.

[4]I am indebted to my former mentor in statistics, Oscar Roberts, for this simple solution. I have used it extensively (see, for example, Blaikie, 1968, 1969, 1979, 1993b; Blaikie and Ward, 1992) without any negative feedback from statistical experts and continue to be surprised that it is not widely used.

[5]A number of different conventions are used in the literature, and some writers suggest that different conventions be used for different types of coefficients. You may wish to follow some other practice.

[6]Again, it is also possible to start by focusing on cell l and then working in the other direction. The result will be the same.

[7]Somer's d can be used as a symmetrical measure of association as well as an asymmetrical measure of influence. However, different values will be produced for each purpose.

[8]The difference between tau and tau-b is that the former deals with small samples where objects or individuals are ranked on two variables, while the latter has been adapted to handle ordered categories, each of which contains a number of objects or individuals.

[9]There are other alternatives when the nominal variable is in just two categories, or has been recoded into two categories. We shall discuss these later.

[10]The curvilinear nature of this relationship has been established in a combination of the 1989/90 samples, similar to those being used in this book (see Chapter 2). Calculating the mean EWV scores for six Age categories, and plotting them in a graph, revealed a definite curve in the relationship (see Blaikie, 1992). The highest EWV mean occurred in the '25–34' Age category for males and in the '35–44' Age category for females.

[11]These are 'real' respondents, but their selection from the Resident sample was not random; the purpose of the selection is purely illustrative.

[12]I need to make it clear that I am not advocating wholesale infringement of the requirements of measures of association, only a pragmatic approach when it can be justified. There is considerable disagreement between the purists and the pragmatists on whether it is appropriate to use Pearson's r on ordinal-level data, such as the Likert response categories to attitude statements. I think it can be justified as long as it is carried out with caution. In fact, it could be argued that the EWV scale is only ordinal because any score is the sum of arbitrarily numbered ordinal-level responses categories used with Likert-type items (usually ranging from 'Strongly agree' to 'Strongly disagree').

[13]Note that C, C_s and V detect any differences between observed and expected frequencies in a cross-tabulation; they cannot detect the direction of a relationship, if one exists. Hence their values are always positive, ranging between 0 and 1.

Explanatory Analysis: Looking for Influences

Introduction

The ultimate and most challenging objective in quantitative social research is to establish the elements, factors or mechanisms that are responsible for producing the state of some social phenomenon, or regularities and trends in it, that is, to explain why social phenomena are as they are or behave as they do. In other words, social researchers want to be able to answer 'why' questions. The common-sense way of expressing this is in terms of causes. However, the language of causation is rather complex and has been contested philosophically.

As we have seen in the previous chapter, the establishment of associations between variables is an important part of descriptive analysis. The existence of an association is a necessary but not a sufficient condition for explanatory analysis. Association on its own does not allow us to infer that one variable has an influence on the other. While it may be possible to make limited predictions on the basis of well-established associations, the fact that two variables may vary together consistently does not necessarily mean that one is the cause of the other. Something more is required.

Huff (1954) referred to the faulty causal inference from correlations as the *post hoc fallacy*. He offered the example of the association between having a university education and having a high income. While the association between education and income may not be perfect (for example, because some wealthy people do not have a university education), we cannot assume that it was going to university that led these people to be in the higher income brackets. They may have been economically successfully without it, either because they are smart or they come from wealthy families – the smart can be rich and money breeds money. Hence, the attributes that made it possible for these people to go to university could be the same attributes that have given them a high income, such as inherited wealth. The problem is to know what the relative contributions of ability, education and economic advantage are to being economically successful. It is to this problem that this chapter is directed.

This brings us back to the discussion on causation in Chapter 1, in particular, the distinction between the successionist and generative views. What follows in this chapter is based on the successionist view. It examines the influence of one variable on another, of a predictor variable on an outcome variable, or a number of predictor variables working in parallel or sequence. In general, this type of quantitative data analysis is unsuitable for the testing of explanations based on the generative view.[1]

The Use of Controlled Experiments

In social research, it is generally accepted that *causality* can only be inferred when the following three criteria have been met:

- The two variables must be associated.
- The causal variable must produce its influence before the outcome occurs.
- Other possible explanations must be eliminated, such as a third variable that influences both variables under consideration.

It is not easy to fulfil these criteria in cross-sectional research, particularly the second and third.

It is generally felt that the most effective way of fulfilling these criteria is to conduct a controlled experiment. An *experiment* involves testing hypotheses about possible causes. In its most basic form, such an experiment involves measuring some phenomenon, then modifying some aspect of a situation through an intervention of some kind, and then remeasuring the phenomenon to see if any change has occurred. From this basic idea, a variety of more elaborate experimental designs have been developed, the most common of which involves the use of a control group. Before and after measurements are also made on this group without any intervention.

What experiments attempt to do is to establish a connection between a variable that is regarded as the cause and another that is regarded as the effect, to control the order in which things happen (to ensure that the hypothesized cause precedes the effect), and to eliminate alternative explanations (to control their possible influences). In short, controlled experiments are a structured form of a longitudinal study that is designed to satisfy the criteria for inferring causation.

In experiments, the time order of the variables is artificially manipulated. For example, the knowledge children have about HIV/AIDS can be measured at one point in time, the children can then be exposed to an education programme on the topic, and then their level of knowledge measured again. A control group could have its knowledge measured at the same times as the experimental group, but not be exposed to the education programme. Assuming that other factors that could affect their knowledge have been controlled, or can be assumed to have been absent during this time period, then the extent to which the education programme has improved the children's knowledge can be assessed.

Take another example. A lecturer may want to know whether teaching a course with a particular textbook helps students to achieve higher grades than teaching without a textbook. The lecturer could split the class into two, say, by matching students according to their academic ability (assuming this is possible), and then conducting one class with the textbook and one without. The average grades of the two classes, and the distribution of the grades, can then be compared at the end of the course. This experiment sounds simple enough, but what the lecturer cannot do by conducting such an experiment in a non-laboratory situation is to control for other influences on the students during the course of the semester. For example, the students from the two classes may talk to each other, and those in the class not using the textbook may read it anyway. Even if the lecturer asked the students not to do this, and they conformed, other factors may influence one group and not the other between the beginning and end of the experiment, thus confounding the results.

Sometimes the influence of one variable on another can occur with the passage of time in a natural rather than an artificial experimental setting. The best that most social scientists can hope for is that a naturally occurring situation lends itself to some kind of 'before and after' study. For example, it may be possible to gauge the effects of a sudden increase in tourism on a given town if relevant features of it can be studied both before and after the increase occurs. Assuming that other factors have not had an effect on the town during this period, such as an economic recession in the country, then the effect of tourism can be gauged. However, such pseudo-experiments fall short of the ideal experimental requirements, mainly because of the researcher's lack of ability to control other possible influences on the community during this time period.

While experiments are reasonably common in the behavioural sciences, such as psychology, they are rather rare in disciplines such as sociology and political science. This is largely the result of these disciplines being concerned with different phenomena. It is easier to conduct experiments on individuals, and perhaps small groups, under different conditions, than it is to conduct experiments on larger groups, organizations, communities or societies. The latter naturally occurring social phenomena cannot be manipulated experimentally. Therefore, I shall not discuss data analysis associated with social experiments, except in so far as other general methods may be appropriate.[2]

Explanation in Cross-Sectional Research

In social research, it may be very difficult or even impossible to undertake longitudinal research even in a natural setting. Instead, a great deal of social research has used what is commonly called a *cross-sectional design*. This simply means that all the variables are measured at the same time, as in social surveys. This is in fact what was done in the two samples being used here to illustrate data-analysis techniques. If 'why' questions are to answered with these data, assumptions have to be made about the time ordering of the variables – that there is some kind of order or sequence in the way variables relate to each other.

One of the problems in the social sciences is that the phenomenon we want to explain may have a number of 'causes' that interact with each other and/or are connected in a sequence or network, and that these 'causes' may act differently under different conditions. It is impossible to reduce all this to a combination of experimental and control groups, and if such a thing was attempted, it is likely to produce artificial distortions in the phenomenon.

Whether social research is cross-sectional, or includes some longitudinal features, it is a conventional practice to divide variables into two types: *independent* or *predictor* variables and *dependent* or *outcome* variables (see Chapter 1). Some writers have argued that the concepts of 'independent' and 'dependent' are only appropriate in controlled experiments and that other concepts should be used in cross-sectional research. Certainly, when the objective of research is prediction, the use of predictor and outcome is appropriate. We shall encounter some of these later in the chapter. I will follow the predictor/outcome usage throughout the rest of the book.[3] However, it would also be appropriate to call predictor variables *explanatory* variables when explanation rather than prediction is the concern.

As has already been indicated, in order to differentiate between predictor/explanatory and outcome variables, some assumptions have to be made about the direction of influence and about the time ordering of the variables. In the Student and Resident samples, it might be argued that Environmental Worldview is a predictor variable and the various forms of Environmentally Responsible Behaviour are outcome variables. This is based on the common assumption that attitudes influence behaviour. However, this is only an assumption, as the reverse may be the case in some situations. For example, it is possible that by being encouraged to engage in Environmentally Responsible Behaviour, perhaps through some incentive scheme, people may begin to change their views on environmental issues. The influence may be in the opposite direction.

This brings us to a critical issue. Any attempt to establish influence between variables in cross-sectional research of necessity requires assumptions to be made. As we know, it is one thing to establish associations between Age or Gender and variables such as EWV, but quite another to claim that either Age or Gender 'influences' EWV. But what does it mean to say that a person's Age influences their EWV? Certainly a person's age does not cause them to hold a particular worldview. Whatever influence growing older has on such attitudes is much more complex than one variable (e.g. Age) statistically influencing another (e.g. EWV). There must be social process and cognitive mechanisms at work.

It may be that being a person of a particular age has meant that certain experiences, different from those of other age cohorts, have led a person to hold certain views and to behave in certain ways. 'Age' simply becomes shorthand for these different experiences. Hence, the classification of variables as either 'independent' or 'dependent', or as 'predictor' and 'outcome', masks the theoretical complexities that lie behind the variables themselves. Having said this, additional understanding, beyond bivariate association, can be obtained by analyzing three or more variables together. This will be illustrated by going back to the variables used to illustrate the methods of associational analysis.

With this somewhat sceptical view of the assumptions that are commonly made about the direction of influence between variables, let us review the major attempts that have been made to answer 'why' questions using cross-sectional data.

Bivariate Analysis

Explanatory analysis can be conducted on both bivariate and multivariate relationships. In the previous chapter on associational analysis, only bivariate relationships were examined. Consideration of multivariate associations was deferred to this chapter as such analysis inevitably explores directions of influence. Before we consider multivariate analysis, we will concern ourselves in this section with the simpler case of *bivariate explanatoty analysis*. The following methods are reviewed: lambda (nominal-level variables), Somer's *d* (ordinal-level variables) and bivariate regression (metric variables).

In the discussion of associational analysis in Chapter 4, we noted that measures are divided into two types, *symmetrical* and *asymmetrical*. Symmetrical measures assume that a relationship can be examined for the point of view of either of the variables; that no direction of influence is inferred. Asymmetrical measures make assumptions about the direction of influence, and the value of the coefficient will usually vary depending on which direction is being considered. It is important to note that this analysis is based on assumptions, not a demonstrated direction of influence. Asymmetrical measures are concerned with the prediction of one variable by another, rather than with genuine explanation. They take us only a limited distance beyond associational analysis. As we shall see, much more is required to produce convincing explanations with cross-sectional data.

Influence Between Categorical Variables

Procedures are available for both nominal-level and ordinal-level data, lambda for the former and Somer's *d* for the latter. While they are both based on a fairly simple idea, they are asymmetric measures of association. Note that while symmetric versions of both lambda and Somer's *d* are available, only the asymmetric versions are discussed here.

Nominal-level Variables: lambda

In Chapter 4, we discussed four measures of association that are suitable for two nominal-level variables, the contingency coefficient (C), the standardized contingency coefficient (C_s), Cramér's *V* and phi (ϕ). These measures simply indicate the degree of dependence between two variables; they are symmetrical procedures in that no direction of influence is implied. A measure that can allow us to predict the position on one nominal-level variable from another is Goodman and Kruskal's *lambda* (λ). One variable has to be designated the predictor and the other the outcome. The value of lambda can vary, depending on how the variables are identified.[4]

Lambda can be used with any size of contingency table. It tells us how helpful is it to know the distribution on the predictor variable when predicting the distribution on the outcome variable. Lambda is based on two types of predictions and the possible errors involved in making them. The first prediction or guess just uses the information provided by the distribution on the outcome variable, and the second prediction then takes into account knowledge of the distribution on the predictor variable. Lambda allows us to calculate the reduction in prediction errors when knowledge of the predictor variable is taken into account. This is based on the logic of the *proportional reduction in error* (PRE). These two predictions are expressed as two rules.

Rule I: Predict the modal category of the outcome variable.
Rule II: Predict the modal outcome category for each predictor variable category.

While these rules appear to be complex, the ideas contained in them are quite simple, as we shall see.

Lambda provides a coefficient that expresses the reduction in prediction errors. It ranges from 0 to 1, zero meaning that the distribution on the predictor variable has no value in predicting the distribution on the outcome variable, and 1 meaning that there is complete predictability. Lambda is calculated as follows.

$$\lambda = \frac{(\text{errors using Rule I}) - (\text{errors using Rule II})}{\text{errors using Rule I}} \tag{5.1}$$

Let us consider an example. How useful is it to know a person's religion in order to predict their occupation?[5] Table 5.1 is the result of simplifying the distributions on these two variables in the Resident sample.[6] Occupation, the outcome variable, has been recoded into four categories and Religion, the predictor variable, has been recoded into five categories. The 'Protestant' category, which includes 'Uniting' and 'Baptist', comes closest to what Weber (1958) had in mind when he referred to the inheritors of Calvinist theology.

In the example, Rule I requires that the modal occupational category, the category with the highest frequency, be identified; it is 'Professional/managerial'. This is shown by the marginal totals at the right of Table 5.1; there are 138 in this category. Rule II requires that the modal occupational category be identified in each of the categories of Religion. For the categories of 'Catholic', 'Anglican' and 'Other religion' it is 'White collar/self-employed', while for 'Protestant' and 'No religion' it is 'Professional/managerial'. According to Rule I, we have made 263 prediction errors in the occupational categories outside the modal category, this being the sum of the non-modal occupational categories (122 + 74 + 67). According to Rule II, we have made 256 prediction errors, this being the sum of all the non-modal occupational categories for each of the Religion categories (61 + 58 + 31 + 44 + 62). By comparing these two totals, we can establish that the prediction errors have been reduced by only 7 when knowledge of the distribution on Religion is introduced.

Table 5.1   *Occupation by Religion (Residents; observed frequencies and percentages)*

Occupation	Catholic	Anglican	Protestant	Other	No religion	Total
			Religion			
Professional/ managerial	22 (26%)	30 (33%)	29 (48%)	19 (29%)	38 (38%)	138 (34%)
White-collar/ self-employed	24 (28%)	33 (36%)	18 (30%)	21 (32%)	26 (26%)	122 (30%)
Manual	17 (20%)	14 (15%)	7 (12%)	14 (22%)	22 (22%)	74 (18%)
Not employed	22 (26%)	14 (15%)	6 (10%)	11 (17%)	14 (14%)	67 (17%)
Totals	85 (100%)	91 (100%)	60 (100%)	65 (100%)	100 (100%)	401 (100%)

Using the information from the example,

$$\lambda = \frac{263 - 256}{263} = \frac{7}{263} = 0.027$$

Thus by using Rule II we eliminate only 2.7 per cent of the prediction errors made by using Rule I. What this means is that we have not learnt very much about the occupational distribution by knowing a respondent's Religion. Using relevant symmetrical measures of association on the data in Table 5.1, we find that Cramér's V is 0.12, and C_s is 0.23. In general, asymmetrical measures produce lower values than symmetrical ones.

A close examination of Table 5.1 shows that there are differences between 'Catholics' and 'Protestants', the categories with which Weber (1958) was originally concerned. Certainly, their percentage differences on all the Occupation categories are greater than between any of the other categories of Religion. Table 5.2 presents these two Religion categories as a subsample for which lambda can be calculated as follows.

$$\lambda = \frac{94 - 92}{94} = \frac{2}{94} = 0.021$$

In this case the coefficient is even smaller; there is only a 2.1 per cent reduction in prediction errors.

It is important to note that if the direction of prediction was the reverse of the one just discussed, that is, using Occupation to predict Religion, the value of lambda is only 0.050. Such a prediction only makes theoretical sense if we can assume that people choose a religion related to their occupational status.

Lambda has some strengths and limitations. Its strengths are that it can be used with nominal-level variables, the distributions on these variables need not be normal, and it can be applied to contingency tables of any size. However, it has two major limitations. The first is that as the coefficient has no sign, the direction of the relationship is not clear. This would have to be obtained from an inspection of the table. The second limitation arises from a particular case of the application of the two rules. Lambda will always be 0 whenever all the

Table 5.2 *Occupation by Religion (subsample of Residents)*

Occupation	Religion		Total
	Catholic	Protestant	
Professional/ managerial	22 (26%)	29 (48%)	51 (35%)
White collar/ self-employed	24 (28%)	18 (30%)	42 (29%)
Manual	17 (20%)	7 (12%)	24 (17%)
Not employed	22 (26%)	6 (10%)	28 (19%)
Totals	85 (100%)	60 (100%)	145 (100%)

within-category modes of the predictor variable are in the same row as the modal category of the outcome variable. For example, if we collapse Table 5.2 to a 2 by 2 table, with Catholics and Protestants cross-tabulated against 'Professional/managerial' and all 'Other' occupations (see Table 5.3), the calculation is as follows:

$$\lambda = \frac{51 - 51}{51} = \frac{0}{51} = 0.00$$

An inspection of the percentages in the table indicates that Catholics are considerably less likely than Protestants to have 'Professional/managerial' occupations; only about a quarter of Catholics (26 per cent) compared with about half of the Protestants (48 per cent). In fact there is a weak association ($\phi = 0.23$). However, lambda cannot detect any possible influence. It is a rather crude measure, mainly because it is based on a very insensitive measure of central tendency, the mode.

A somewhat simpler method for calculating lambda is available and is useful for tables with many rows and columns. Instead of using the errors (i.e. the sum of the values in the non-modal categories), it uses the values of the modal categories. Expressed in words, the equation is:

$$\lambda = \frac{\begin{array}{c}\text{sum of the within-category modes} \quad \text{model frequency of}\\ \text{of the predictor variable} \quad \text{the outcome vaiable}\end{array}}{\text{sample size} - \text{model frequency of the outcome variable}} \qquad (5.2)$$

This procedure can be illustrated with the data from Table 5.1.

$$\lambda = \frac{(24 + 33 + 29 + 21 + 38) - 138}{401 - 138} = \frac{7}{263} = 0.027$$

This agrees with the previous procedure.

Table 5.3   *Occupation by Religion (subsample of Residents;*
2 by 2 table)

Occupation	Religion		
	Catholic	Protestant	Total
Professional/ managerial	22 (26%)	29 (48%)	51 (35%)
Other	63 (74%)	31 (52%)	94 (65%)
Totals	85 (100%)	60 (100%)	145 (100%)

Ordinal-level Variables: Somer's d

The most suitable measure for predicting the influence of one ordinal-level variable on another is *Somer's d*. It uses a procedure similar to gamma in that it is based on pair-by-pair comparisons. In fact, its equation is a variation of that for gamma. The difference is that it includes tied pairs on the outcome variable, shown by T_d in the equation below. As with gamma, it is necessary to determine the number of *concordant* (C) and *discordant* (D) pairs. The equation is:

$$d = \frac{C - D}{C + D + T_d} \tag{5.3}$$

where C is the number of concordant pairs, D is the number of discordant pairs, and T_d is the pairs with different values on the predictor variable but with the same values on the outcome variable.

The rationale for including T_d in the denominator of the equation is that a tie on the outcome variable will not contribute to the influence between the variables. In other words, the predictor variable exerts no influence on the outcome variable in these instances. It is assumed that including ties on the outcome variable in the equation gives a more accurate measure of the strength of the influence between the two variables. As a result, Somer's *d* is more conservative than gamma; *d* will always be equal to or less than G.

To illustrate the method used to calculate Somer's *d*, we can use the categorical versions of Age and EWV, and the same table that provided the illustration for the calculation of gamma (see Table 4.2). However, now we assume that Age is the predictor variable and EWV is the outcome variable, that is, Age is assumed to have an influence on EWV. The numbers of concordant and discordant pairs are calculated in the same way and, as before, are 13,183 and 26,048, respectively (see Table 4.5). To calculate T_d, we multiply each cell, in each column, by the sum of the values in the cells below it. This means that cell *a* is multiplied by the sum of cells *d*, *g* and *j*, then *d* is multiplied by *g* plus *j*, then *g* is multiplied by *j*. Similarly, *b* is multiplied by the sum of *e*, *h* and *k*, *e* is multiplied by the sum of *h* and *k*, and *h* is multiplied by *k*. The same calculation is done in the third column. All of these products are summed. Therefore,

$$T_d = 21(45 + 30 + 32) + 45(30 + 32) + (30 \times 32) + 16(46 + 52 + 24) + 46(52 + 24) + (52 \times 24) + 42(65 + 22 + 6) + 65(22 + 6) + (22 \times 6) = 18,551$$

Then entering these figures in the equation, we get:

$$d = \frac{C - D}{C + D + T_d} = \frac{13,183 - 26,048}{26,048 + 13,183 + 18,551} = \frac{-12,865}{57,782} = -0.22$$

The sign of the coefficient indicates that the influence of Age on EWV is negative; the older a person becomes, the lower their EWV becomes.

Another equation can be used that requires less calculation – see Siegel and Castellan (1988: 303–7) for details. It is:

$$d = \frac{2(C - D)}{n^2 - \text{sum of the squares of the marginals for the outcome variable}} \tag{5.4}$$

$$= \frac{2(13,183 - 26,048)}{401^2 - (79^2 + 156^2 + 104^2 + 62^2)} = \frac{-25,730}{160,801 - 45,237} = \frac{-25,730}{115,164} = -0.22$$

The marginals in the example are for the rows. Notice that this figure is lower than gamma (calculated as –0.33) for the same cross-tabulation. If we wished to reverse the predictor and outcome variables, a different set of tied pairs would be calculated (by working down the columns rather than along the rows in Table 4.2), thus producing a different coefficient. In this case it is –0.24. However, this direction of influence makes even less sense than in the example used to calculate lambda. Holding a particular Environmental World-view cannot influence a person's Age.

Influence Between Metric Variables: Bivariate Regression

We now come to the most popular measure of influence between two variables, *bivariate regression*, also referred to as simple linear or ordinary least-squares (OLS) regression.[7] The popularity of regression stems from the fact that, because it requires both variables to be metric, it has more power to measure influence than the measures we have just discussed. Hence, many researchers will make every effort to measure variables at interval-level or ratio-level just to be able to use regression analysis. Multiple regression will be dealt with later in this chapter.

Just as with Pearson's r, the commonest form of regression analysis assumes that the relationship between two variables is linear, that is, that an increase in the values on one variable is associated with *either* an increase (positive relationship) or a decrease (negative relationship) on the other variable, and that the changes in value on both variables occur at the same rate. Regression is based on the idea of fitting a straight line to a scatter plot of the pairing of values on the two variables. The *regression line* represents the best estimate of the relationship between two variables, or, more precisely, how the values on one variable predict or influence the values on the other variable. Prediction implies influence.

When the metric versions of Age and EWV are used, a scatter plot reveals a tendency for older persons to have relatively low EWV scores, for younger persons to have relatively high scores, and for middle-aged persons to have more average scores (see Figure 4.2). While Pearson's *r* provides us with a coefficient to measure how consistent this pattern is in a population or sample, that is, how much variance two variables share in common, regression describes the characteristics of a line that best represents the influence of one variable on the other. In bivariate regression, the regression coefficient (*R*) has the same value as Pearson's *r*. However, *r* is a symmetric measure, while *R* is an asymmetric measure.

Before examining the relationship between Age and EWV, let us explore a contrived example of two variables that would usually be perfectly related. Employees in a company are allowed to work very flexible hours per week. They can work for between 2 and 5 days a week, for between 7 and 9 hours a day. While a majority work 8 hours a day for 5 days a week, others work different combinations of days and hours per day. Table 5.4 provides the data for a sample of 10 employees who are all on the same hourly rate, but who work different arrangements. The scatter plot (Figure 5.1) indicates that the points form a straight line. The relationship is perfectly linear.

Table 5.4   *Working hours per week and weekly wage*

Employee	Hours worked	Weekly wages ($)
A	14	210
B	16	240
C	21	315
D	24	360
E	27	405
F	28	420
G	32	480
H	36	540
I	40	600
J	45	675

Regression analysis can be used to describe the nature of this relationship. However, to do so, it is necessary to identify one variable as the predictor and the other then becomes the outcome variable. As with the examples earlier in this chapter, the description of the relationship will be different, depending on how the variables are identified. In this example, hours worked per week is regarded as the predictor variable (usually referred to as the *x* variable) and wages per week is the outcome variable (the *y* variable). In other words, it is assumed that the hours worked determines the wages. It would be possible to

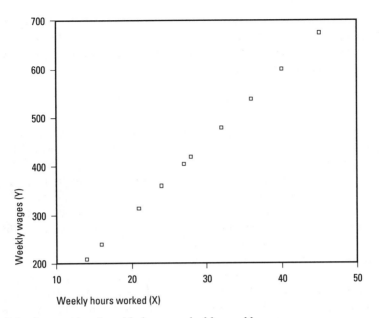

Figure 5.1 *Scatter plot of weekly hours worked by weekly wages*

view this relationship differently, in terms of the desired level of wages determining the hours that need to be worked. When the assumed direction of influence is different, the regression calculation and results will also be different.

The regression line that joins up the points in Figure 5.1 can be described in the same way as on any straight-line graph. The equation for a positive relationship is:

$$y = a + bx \qquad (5.5)$$

where x and y are the two variables (predictor and outcome, respectively), b represents the slope of the line, and a the point at which the line intersects the vertical or Y axis. Hence, in words:

$$y = \text{intercept} + (\text{slope} \times x)$$

The slope of the line indicates the extent to which a change in the predictor variable produces a change in the outcome variable. For example, a change of one unit of x may produce a change of two units of y, or one unit, or only half a unit. In the first example, $b = 2.0$, in the second, $b = 1.0$, and in the third, $b = 0.5$. The slope of the line will be steepest in the first example, flattest in the third example, and at 45° in the second.

Coming back to the example of the relationship between hours worked and wages, it is possible to establish the values of a and b without doing any calculations. First, a must be zero because if no hours are worked, no wages are received. If the line was extended in the lower left direction it would intersect the both the X and Y axes at zero.[8] Second, b must be 15.00, because all workers in this sample receive $15 per hour. Therefore, substituting the values for a and b in the equation, we get:

$$y = 0 + 15x = 15x$$

With this information, it is now possible to predict the wages (y) that any worker will receive if the number of hours worked (x) is known. If a worker works 35 hours a week, his/her weekly wages would be $15 \times 35 = \$525$.

Of course, we could have arrived at this answer without the help of regression analysis because we know what the weekly wage is. Unfortunately, social science data are not normally like this. A scatter plot is usually scattered; that is, the points do not fall along a perfect line. The challenge is to find a line that would best represent this scatter.

Why do we want to find such a line? The main reason is that it allows us to make a prediction about a person's position on the outcome variable, given that we know their position on the predictor variable. Knowing a person's Age would allow us to predict their EWV score. If the relationship between Age and EWV was a perfect one (all the points in the scatter plot falling in a straight line), then we could make an absolutely accurate prediction. However, if the relationship is not perfect, we can only make the best possible estimate of a person's position on the outcome variable. Regression analysis provides us with the best estimate of how well a particular predictor variable predicts a particular outcome variable.

Two Methods of Regression Analysis

Let us take another example where the points in a plot all cluster around a straight line. In the discussion on Pearson's correlation coefficient, an example was presented based on a subsample of Residents (see Figure 4.3). We can also do a regression analysis on these data (see Tables 4.6 and 4.7). Just as there are two methods for calculating Pearson's r by hand, so there are also two methods for doing regression analysis, the raw score method and the mean deviation method. The calculation for the raw score method is simpler, although the logic behind it is not as obvious as it is for the mean deviation method. Before illustrating both methods, we need to review the principles behind regression analysis.

It is possible to draw a line on Figure 4.3 that would run down between the points. We could then measure the vertical distance from each point to this line. The best line would be the one for which the total of these distances is the smallest. However, as we saw with calculating r, to avoid the problem caused by some of these measurements being negative (the ones above the line), the practice is to square all the measurements. Hence, this is known as the method of least squares. Rather than trying to locate the best line by trial and error, regression analysis calculates its position.

Let us look at the *mean deviation method* first. Table 4.6 provides us with all the information needed. To calculate a, we have to rearrange and adapt equation (5.5), as follows:

$$a = \bar{y} - b\bar{x} \tag{5.6}$$

where $\bar{x}$ and $\bar{y}$ are the means of all the values of x and y, respectively. The minus sign is used when the relationship, that is, the slope of the line, is negative. To calculate a, we must first calculate b using the following equation.

$$b = \frac{\Sigma(x - \bar{x})(y - \bar{y})}{\Sigma(x - \bar{x})^2} \tag{5.7}$$

Inserting the data from Table 4.7, we get:

$$b = \frac{-4781.3810}{5188.9524} = -0.9215$$

Now, entering the known information in the equation for a, we get:

$$a = 89.3810 - (-0.9215)47.0476 = 89.3810 + 43.3522 = 132.73$$

Hence, the best estimate of the regression line indicates that for every year of increase in Age, there is a corresponding decrease of 0.92 in EWV score. It also suggests that, at least in theory, all children are born with a potential EWV score of 133 (rounded). In fact, the method of measurement used to produce the EWV scores has a maximum of 120. Hence, this point of intersection of the line with the Y axis is purely theoretical and makes no sense in practice. We can only entertain the range of scores between the possible maximum and minimum, that is, from 24 to 120. This example illustrates that in most social research the intercept is of very little interest, particularly for interval-level variables in which the zero is arbitrary.

The *raw score method* uses the following equation to calculate b.

$$b = \frac{n(\Sigma xy) - (\Sigma x)(\Sigma y)}{n(\Sigma x^2) - (\Sigma x)^2} \tag{5.8}$$

Now inserting the data from Table 4.7 we get:

$$b = \frac{21 \times 83{,}527 - 988 \times 1877}{21 \times 51{,}672 - 988^2} = \frac{1{,}754{,}067 - 1{,}854{,}476}{1{,}085{,}112 - 976{,}144} = \frac{-100{,}409}{108{,}968} = -0.9215$$

It is worth noting that these equations for calculating b are very similar to those used to calculate Pearson's r. The numerator is the same, as is part of the denominator. Hence, the same table of data can be used for both.

As we shall discover later in discussing multiple regression, b becomes much more useful if it is standardized. All values of it are dependent on the measurement scale used. For example, Age and EWV are measured on different scales and, if regressed, will produce values for b that cannot be compared with variables using different scales. The solution is standardization, which means transforming the values of b to z-scores. By definition, z-scores have a mean of 0 and a standard deviation of 1. This means that not only is the slope of the regression line standardized, its intercept is also transformed to become zero. Standardization is achieved by multiplying b by the ratio of the standard deviations of the two variables, with the predictor over the outcome. The standardized value is known as *beta* (β). Thus,

$$\beta = b \times \frac{s_p}{s_o} \tag{5.9}$$

where s_p is the standard deviation of the predictor variable and s_o is the standard deviation of the outcome variable. In bivariate regression, *beta* has the same value as Pearson's r. The methods used to calculate these coefficients are just different ways of arriving at the same answer.

Coefficients

Two further calculations are required to complete regression analysis. First, it is possible for this line to be produced by different combinations of respondents' scores. For example, it is possible for the scatter plot to be much more dispersed than in Figure 4.3 and yet for the same line to be produced. Hence, we need a measure of how well the line 'fits' the data, or, put differently, how much of the variation between the two variables the line explains. To do this, the value of the regression coefficient (R) is squared. Note that in bivariate regression, R indicates the extent to which the predictor accounts for the outcome. In multiple regression, R is like a *multiple correlation coefficient* between all the independent predictor variables and the outcome variable. R-squared (R^2) is known as the *coefficient of multiple determination* and indicates the total amount of variance explained by all the predictor variables. More on this later in the chapter.

As we saw in Chapter 4, the value of Pearson's r for the relationship between these two variables was calculated as −0.946. Therefore, by squaring this value and turning it into a percentage, we know that the regression line explains 89.6 per cent of the variance. We need to note that this remarkably high figure is not normally found in social science data and is the result of this example being contrived for illustrative purposes.

The second calculation provides a measure of how well the regression line predicts values of y, given the values of x. The first step is to calculate the unexplained variation. This is based on how close the points in a scatter plot are to the regression line. If they are all on the line, all the variation between the two variables is accounted for. However, in practice, the deviations from the line may be considerable. To calculate the unexplained variation, it is necessary to calculate the sum of the vertical distances between each point in the scatter plot and the regression line using the method of least squares. To calculate the individual deviations, for each value of x, we have to find the value of y if the point had fallen on the regression line. The difference between this calculated point for y and its actual value is a measure of the error involved in predicting

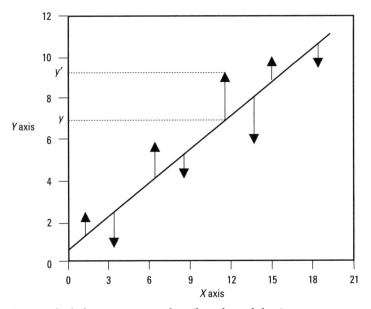

Figure 5.2 *Residuals from a regression line (hypothetical data)*

a value of y from a value of x, referred to as the *residual*. These values are represented by the length of the arrows in Figure 5:2. As some of these values will be negative (the arrows pointing up), they are all squared before they are added together. The expression for the unexplained variation is $\Sigma(y - y')^2$, where y is the value for the point on the regression line (the tail of the arrow) and y' is the actual value (the head of the arrow). In Figure 5.2, the values for the fifth point up the line are y = 7.0 and y' = 9.2, making a residual of −2.2. This value would need to be squared and then added to the sum of similar values for each of the other seven points.

In order to be able to compare this value with others, it is possible to calculate the *standard error of the estimate*. This has similar properties to the standard deviation of the mean: the smaller its value, the less dispersed the points are about the regression line. The equation used to calculate this is:

$$se_{\text{est } y} = \sqrt{\frac{\Sigma(y - y')^2}{n - 2}} \qquad (5.10)$$

Table 5.5 provides the data needed to calculate both the unexplained variation and the standard error of the estimate. The values of y' for each value of x are calculated from the standard regression line equation, y' = a + bx. Substituting the data in the equation, we get:

$$se_{\text{est } y} = \sqrt{\frac{513.130}{21 - 2}} = 5.20$$

Table 5.5   *Unexplained variation and standard error of the estimate (subsample of Residents)*

Respondent	x	y	y′	y − y′	(y − y′)²
1	20	118	114.304	3.696	13.660
2	23	102	111.540	−9.540	91.006
3	27	109	107.854	1.146	1.314
4	28	114	106.932	7.068	49.950
5	33	107	102.325	4.675	21.854
6	36	100	99.561	0.439	0.193
7	37	90	98.639	−8.639	74.639
8	39	94	96.796	−2.796	7.820
9	40	103	95.875	7.125	50.765
10	43	89	93.111	−4.111	16.897
11	47	85	89.425	−4.425	19.579
12	50	93	86.660	6.340	40.190
13	51	88	85.739	2.261	5.112
14	55	79	82.053	−3.053	9.322
15	61	77	76.524	0.476	0.226
16	62	71	75.603	−4.603	21.188
17	64	78	73.760	4.240	17.977
18	65	67	72.839	−5.839	34.090
19	68	75	70.074	4.926	24.263
20	69	72	69.153	2.847	8.106
21	70	66	68.231	−2.231	4.979
$n = 21$	$\Sigma x = 988$	$\Sigma y = 1877$			$\Sigma(y - y')^2 = 513.130$

One way of dealing with these residuals, or the unexplained variance, is to introduce an error term into the equation. Hence, the more correct equation for calculating the regression line is:

$$y = a + bx + \varepsilon \qquad (5.11)$$

where ε is an error term that represents all the other influences on y that are not accounted for by x, that is, it is the error in making the prediction. However, this equation is not commonly used and the error is dealt with in terms of the coefficient of determination and the standard error of the estimate.

An Example

Now back to the real world. If we take all the data in the Resident sample, and apply regression analysis to Age and EWV, the picture is rather different (see Figure 4.2). There is a considerable dispersion among the points and only a tendency towards a linear pattern. Applying regression analysis to these data produces the following:

$$a = 96.490; \quad b = -0.185; \quad r = -0.308; \quad R^2 = 0.095; \quad se_{est\,y} = 10.26.$$

These values are very different from those for the subsample. They tell us that the regression line cuts the Y axis on the graph at the EWV score of 96.5

(rounded); that for every year of increase in Age, the EWV score decreases by 0.185; that only 9.5 per cent of the variance is accounted for; and that the standard error of the estimate is 10.26.

Points to Watch For

First, it is worth checking to see if there are any *outliers* in the scatter plot. Outliers are points that are very deviant from the dominant pattern. For example, in Figure 4.2, there are two points in the top right-hand area, four in the bottom left-hand area, and one in the centre at the bottom that are out of character. In small samples, such outliers can have a big impact on the value of r and on the regression analysis. Consideration might be given to excluding them, particularly if there is reason to believe that they are the result of errors of some sort, such as in coding or data entry.

When these seven outliers are excluded from the analysis, the results are:

$$a = 98.396; \quad b = -0.221; \quad r = -0.380; \quad R^2 = 0.145; \quad se_{est\ y} = 9.56.$$

This produces some improvement in the proportion of explained variation (coefficient of determination) and in the ability of the regression line to predict y values (standard error of the estimate). A procedure is available in SPSS for identifying outliers by specifying the number of standard deviations from the regression line beyond which cases or respondents should be excluded from the analysis. In effect, these are the cases for which the predicted value of y (EWV score), based on the regression line, deviates widely from the actual value. When 2 standard deviations were specified, 18 cases became candidates for exclusion. They included the 7 arrived at by an inspection of the scatter plot, plus 8 respondents with high EWV scores (mostly aged between 20 and 40) and 3 older persons with low scores. In fact, removing all 18 does improve the level of explained variation and the predictive capacity, but also flattens the regression line. The results are:

$$a = 96.515; \quad b = -0.187; \quad r = -0.349; \quad R^2 = 0.122; \quad se_{est\ y} = 8.88.$$

For more details on how to deal with outliers, or cases with high residuals, see Fielding and Gilbert (2000), Hair et al. (1998) and Miles and Shevlin (2001).

A word of caution is in order. It is possible to improve the regression analysis and produce 'neater' results by excluding outliers, those that lie outside some arbitrary boundary. However, this has to be tempered with a concern for retaining the validity of the data. For example, we might suspect that the two very elderly respondents who have high EWV scores (top right-hand corner of the scatter plot) might have misunderstood how to respond to the items in the EWV scale. However, it is also possible that they are both keen environmentalists who just happen to be different from others in their age cohort. Hence, this kind of manipulation should not be undertaken lightly, or simply by using arbitrary rules.

Second, the scatter plot should be inspected to see whether there is a pattern in the spread of points around the line. For example, at one end of the line, the points may cluster closely to it, while at the other end they may be very dispersed. The ideal is a uniform spread on both sides along the length of the line. The latter is referred to as *homoscedasticity* and the former as *heteroscedasticity*. For the calculations of both r and regression, homoscedasticity is a requirement. In its absence, caution must be exercised in interpreting the results.

Third, it is important to check the distributions of both variables. If one is widely dispersed and the other is not (particularly if it is badly skewed as well), the correlation coefficient will be smaller than if they were both widely dispersed. Such a combination may also produce a curvilinear relationship or even an L-shaped pattern. The type of regression analysis being discussed here cannot handle such patterns.

There is another issue that needs to be considered. As we have seen, bivariate regression analysis endeavours to establish how well positions on one variable can predict positions on another variable. It is possible, of course, that some other variables are also involved. Hence, it may be appropriate to examine more than one predictor variable. In other words, we can also do multiple regression analysis, and this will be discussed later in the chapter.

Influence Between Categorical and Metric Variables

Just as there are procedures for dealing with associations between categorical and metric variables, so there are similar procedures for such combinations in explanatory analysis.

Coding to a Lower Level

In discussing methods of analysis to establish association between two variables at fundamentally different levels of measurement (categorical and metric), it was suggested that one strategy is to code the metric variable into categories, and then use methods appropriate for two categorical variables. The same applies to explanatory analysis. However, there are a number of alternatives to this that can also be used.

Means Analysis

Another method can be used when the predictor variable is nominal, ordinal or dichotomous and the outcome variable is metric. This involves calculating the mean on the outcome variable for each of the categories of the predictor variable. For example, if Gender is the predictor variable and EWV the outcome variable, the mean EWV score can be calculated for males and females separately. A comparison of the means can give an indication of the influence of Gender on EWV.

It is also possible to measure the level of influence by using a coefficient known as *eta* (η). Just as r^2 indicates the proportion of the variance that is common to two variables, so eta-squared (η^2) is the proportion of variance in the outcome (interval-level or ratio-level) variable that is explained by differences among the categories of the predictor (nominal-level or ordinal-level) variable. Put differently, η^2 is a regression coefficient for a non-linear regression line (a curve) that is assumed to pass through all the means of the categories of the predictor variable.

The results of undertaking this type of analysis with Gender and EWV in the Resident sample is: for males, $\bar{x} = 86.4$ $(n = 199)$; for females, $\bar{x} = 89.5$ $(n = 200)$; $\eta = 0.14$; and $\eta^2 = 0.021$. The difference between the means is only 3.1, and only 2.1 per cent of the variance has been explained. Another dichotomized example is education coded as 'University educated' and 'Non-university educated': for the 'University educated', $\bar{x} = 89.6$ $(n = 167)$; for the 'Non-university educated', $\bar{x} = 86.8$ $(n = 231)$; $\eta = 0.13$; and $\eta^2 = 0.016$. In this case, the difference between the means is 2.8, with 1.6 per cent of the variance explained. Clearly, in both examples, the influence is very weak.

Similar analysis can be done with a predictor variable that has a limited number of nominal-level or ordinal-level categories. For example, with Education coded into five categories, the difference in the means between the lowest and highest education categories is 6.3 and $\eta = 0.195$ (see Table 5.6). With one exception ('Technical certificate') the mean EWV scores increase as education increases, thus suggesting that Education has some influence on EWV. The exception can be accounted for if 'Technical certificate' is taken to be a lower category than 'Completed secondary'. These certificates are largely associated with apprenticeships in trades that can be entered before secondary education is completed. It might be argued that the academic level achieved for the certificate is not as high as that required to complete secondary education. If these assumptions are correct, the order of 'Completed secondary' and 'Technical certificate' could be reversed, thus producing a perfect linear relationship.

Table 5.6   *A means analysis of Education and Environmental Worldview (Residents)*

Education	Environmental Worldview		
	$\bar{x}$	s	n
Primary/some secondary	84.3	9.4	74
Completed secondary	89.1	11.4	96
Technical certificate	86.3	11.3	61
Degree/diploma	89.4	10.7	143
Postgraduate qualification	90.5	8.6	24
Total	88.0	10.8	398

Dummy Variables

When the outcome variable is metric and the predictor variable is dichotomized, can be sensibly dichotomized, or consists of a number of categories, it is possible to use regression analysis with *dummy variables*. Methods appropriate for metric variables can be applied to such dichotomies. This is a very convenient trick. It is achieved by assuming that one category is coded as 0 and the other as 1, and that this creates interval-level measurement. When a set of categories is involved, it is possible to dichotomize each category against all the others. For example, in Table 5.6, the 'Primary/some secondary' category can be dichotomized against all the other Education categories combined. This can be repeated with each category in turn, thus producing five separate dichotomies. In effect, this categorical variable is turned into five different dichotomized variables. As we shall see later, regression analysis can be conducted on any four of these dichotomies with the outcome. As this method of analysis takes us into procedures that are used in multivariate regression, its discussion will be postponed until later in the next section of this chapter.

Multivariate Analysis

The basis for any attempt to establish connections or patterns in quantitative data is bivariate relationships. The challenge is to see if two variables vary together and how strong either the association between them is or the influence of one on the other. For more sophisticated analysis, we usually want to establish networks of relationships between variables. This provides a better understanding of how things are connected and influence each other in the social world. However, some kinds of multivariate analysis sit on the border between associational and explanatory analysis. This is because in using data from cross-sectional research as a surrogate for data from longitudinal or experimental research, multivariate analysis has to work with an assumed ordering of variables. In this section the following methods are reviewed: three-way contingency tables (categorical variables) and partial correlation and multiple regression (metric variables).

Trivariate Analysis

To begin this exploration, let us initially extend the relationship between two variables to include a third variable, that is, *trivariate analysis*. There are a number of reasons for introducing a third variable (or even a fourth or fifth) into the analysis. For the most part, the task is to see how the three variables are interrelated and, more particularly, what influence they have on each other.

Forms of Relationships

Let us assume three variables, A, B and C, with C being the outcome variable. What we want to discover is whether A and B have an influence on C, and if so, how. There are a number of theoretical possibilities (see Figure 5.3).

(i) A has an influence on C, but B does not.[9]
(ii) A and B separately have an influence on C, but they are not themselves associated.
(iii) Both B and C are outcomes of A. This means that any association between B and C is *spurious* because they are both outcomes of A.

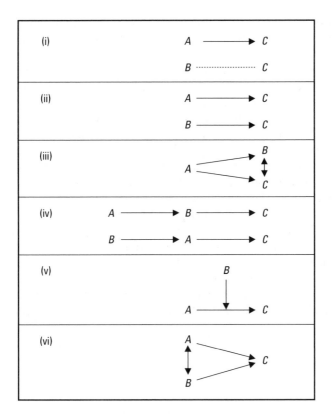

Figure 5.3   *Possible forms of relationships between three variables*

(iv)   The influence is in a sequence, *A* influences *B* which in turn influences C, or *B* influences *A* which in turn influences C. In this combination the middle variable is known as an *intervening variable*.

 (v)   *B* has an effect on the influence of *A* on C, that is, *B* changes the form of the relationship between *A* and C. In this case, *B* is regarded as a *moderating variable* and the influence of *B* on C involves an interaction effect.

(vi)   Both *A* and *B* have an influence on C while they are themselves associated. The question here is: what is their relative influence? This issue is a major concern of multivariate analysis and, of course, can include more than two predictor variables.

Interacting Variables

Concerning (V), two variables are said to *interact* when their association is not uniform across all categories of a third variable, that is, the influence of one variable on another is contingent on the presence of a third variable. For example, we may be interested in the influence of Religion on people's support of political parties (Political Party Preference) and wish to know whether there are Gender differences in this relationship. If it turns out that the influence is stronger for males than females, we would conclude that there is a statistical interaction between Religion and Political Party Preference (PPP). What this means is that the influence of Religion on PPP is not as simple as it seems. Gender is a moderating variable.

Interaction is explored by examining differences between a measure of association or influence in a bivariate relationship and similar measures for different segments of the sample or population. For example, if we wish to know whether the association between A and C is moderated by B, we could not only examine this association, but we could also see what happens to it for different categories within B. These are known as *conditional associations*. If the strength of association or influence between A and C is more or less the same for each category of B, we would conclude that B is not a moderating variable on the overall association. However, if there are differences in the strength of association or influence within each category of B, then B can be considered to be a moderating variable, and there is interaction between A and C. This kind of analysis relies entirely on comparing a number of associations or influences, both full and conditional, and inferring interaction from the changes in the coefficients.

The logic of Trivariate Analysis

To illustrate the logic of the analysis for spuriousness, for intervening and moderating variables, and for multiple influences, let us imagine possible coefficients for the types of relationships outlined in Figure 5.3. Table 5.7 sets out the forms of the relationships, the methods of statistical control, possible coefficients of influence and the conclusion to be drawn. The values of these coefficients are purely hypothetical and may not even be possible in practice. Their purpose is simply to illustrate what could happen and what it means. It is assumed that all relationships are linear.

The three pairs of bivariate relationships between A, B and C, as shown in Table 5.7(a), are moderate to strong.[10] This means that it is worth proceeding with an exploration of possible forms of trivariate relationships between them. If there had been little or no influence between one or more pairs of variables, there would be no point in exploring their interrelationships. The first test is to see whether the relationship between B and C is spurious, that is, whether this association is the result of each being influenced by a third variable, A (see Table 5.7(b)). If the influence of A on B and of A on C is high, then there is the possibility of a spurious relationship between B and C. If both of the measures of influence of A on the other two variables are low, then it is certain that A is not responsible for the association between B and C. For example, a strong association between Willingness to Act (B) and Environmentally Responsible Behaviour (ERB, C) may be the result of both variables being strongly influenced by EWV (A). This means that the strong association betweem Willingness to Act and ERB is spurious because it is mainly the result of the influence of EWV on both of them. However, is social research, the issue of spuriousness is usually

Table 5.7   *Forms of relationships between three variables*

Form	Method of control	Coefficients	Conclusion
(a) Bivariate	No control	A —— 0.45 ——▶ C	
		B —— 0.55 ——▶ C	It is worth proceeding
		A —— 0.60 ——▶ B	
(b) Spurious	B with C by A		B with C could be spurious
			B with C is not spurious
(c) Intervening	A on C by B		B is intervening
			B is not intervening
(d) Moderating	Category X of B	A —— 0.80 ——▶ C	B is moderator of A with C
	Category Y of B	A —— 0.10 ——▶ C	
	Category X of B	A —— 0.60 ——▶ C	B is not moderator
	Category Y of B	A —— 0.55 ——▶ C	
(e) Multiple	No control		Separate influence
			Combined influence

not black and white. Low to moderate coefficients tend to leave the issue open for further analysis.

Once these preliminaries are settled, there are three further issues to be examined. First, does one variable intervene between the other two, that is, is the influence of one variable on another dependent on the third variable creating a link, or stepping-stone, between them? The first of the two examples in Table 5.7(c) indicates that the influence of A on B and then of B on C is very much higher than that of A on C directly. This suggests that B intervenes between A and C. In the second example, B is not an intervening variable as the influence of A on C is strong on its own. For example, if EWV (A) has a weak influence on ERB (C), but there is a strong influence on both EWV on Willingness to Act (B) and then of Willingness to Act on ERB, Willingness to Act can be regarded as an intervening variable between EWV and ERB. However, if the strengths of these coefficients are reversed, or if they were all fairly similar, say moderate, then Willingness to Act would not intervene. In short, it is only when the coefficients through the intermediate variable are both higher than that between the first and last variables, that an intervening variable can be said to be present.

In order to establish whether one variable, say B, moderates the influence of one variable on another, say A on C, it is necessary to examine their relationship for different categories of B, say two categories (see Table 5.7(d)). If there is a substantial difference between the coefficients for the influence of A on C for the two categories of B, say one is very strong and the other is weak, we can conclude that B moderates this relationship. The strength of the influence is dependent on category X of B and not on category Y. Hence, B is a moderating variable. For example, a moderate influence of EWV (A) on ERB (C) might be due to differences in Willingness to Act (B) across categories of EWV. There may be a very strong Willingness to Act among those with above average EWV scores but a variation from high to low amongst those with below average scores; the coefficient for the former will be strong and for the latter, weak or negligible. Hence, Willingness to Act is a moderating variable. However, if both of these EWV categories (above and below average scores) have a similar level of influence on ERB, then Willingness to Act does not moderate the influence of EWV on ERB.

Another interest in trivariate relationships is whether two predictor variables (A and B) separately or together influence the outcome variable (C) (see Table 5.7(e)). The first step in this direction is to examine the coefficients for each pair of relationships. If the association between the two predictor variables is negligible, it is possible to conclude that the two predictors have an independent influence; if there is a strong association between them, then their influence is probably combined. For example, if there was a negligible association between EWV (A) and Willingness to Act (B), but both have a moderate influence on ERB (C), the conclusion would be that their influence is not related. However, a moderate association between EWV and Willingness to Act, and moderate influences of both on ERB, would suggest that their influence is combined.

A common form of multivariate analysis, multiple regression, is designed to establish the relative influence that a set of predictor variables has on an outcome variable. This procedure can indicate the contribution of each predictor variable when the influence of all the other predictors is controlled.

Each of the five forms of relationships between three variables constitutes an analytical model. It is up to the researcher to select a model to structure the analysis of a particular data set, preferably on theoretical grounds. The values of the coefficients will then determine whether or not the model is appropriate for the data. If not, other models can be tried. Sorting out the forms of bivariate relationships requires a clear understanding of the logic of the relationships and a careful inspection of the values of the bivariate coefficients.

When categorical variables are involved, a comparison of cell percentages is also a useful procedure.

The logic of the various relationships between these three variables is the same regardless of the levels of measurement. We have already encountered methods of analysis for all types of variables, including combinations of variables at different levels of measurement. However, as with bivariate analysis, multivariate analysis is more cumbersome with categorical variables than it is with metric variables. Some examples of both methods will be discussed shortly. For an alternative approach to spuriousness, and intervening and moderating variables with categorical data, see Bryman and Cramer (1997: 239–50).

Relationships in bivariate analysis are often referred to as *zero-order relationships*. When a third variable is introduced as a control, the analysis deals with *first-order relationships*, and adding a fourth variable as a control leads to *second-order relationships*. Most of what follows deals with first-order relationships.

Influence Between Categorical Variables

One way of doing trivariate analysis with categorical variables is to use *three-way contingency tables*. While this type of analysis is usually done using measures of association, it makes sense to use measures of influence as the logic of the analysis is to discover influences.

Three-way Contingency Tables

In Chapter 4, contingency tables were used to establish associations between two categorical variables. Earlier in this chapter we also used contingency tables to examine bivariate relationships between combinations of nominal-level and ordinal-level variables in order to establish the degree of influence of predictor variables on outcome variables. In three-way contingency tables, the cross-tabulation between two variables is controlled by a third variable. This involves creating two or more conditional tables, one for each of the categories of the third variable. By comparing the measures of association or influence between the conditional tables with that for the bivariate relationship in the full table, it is possible to work out what form the relationships between the three variables take. These comparisons can be confirmed by calculating the differences between cell percentages in the conditional and full tables.

An example

Let us examine the relationship between two categorical variables, Age and EWV, with two other categorical variables, Gender and Education, as separate controls (Resident sample). Environmental Worldview, the outcome variable, has been coded into four categories ('Low', 'Moderate', 'High' and 'Very high'), and Age, the main predictor variable, has been coded into three categories

('18–34', 35–54, '55+'). Education has been recoded into three categories: 'Low' (primary, some secondary and technical certificate), 'Moderate' (completed secondary) and 'High' (university educated). What we wish to discover is whether the influence (or association) between Age and EWV is spurious, or whether either Gender or Education is an intervening or moderating variable. To do this, we shall explore a number of three-way contingency tables.

First, we need to examine the bivariate influence and association between Age and EWV (see Table 5.8). The appropriate coefficients are Somer's d for influence and gamma for association. The standardized contingency coefficient is also included for comparison, even though it is more appropriate with nominal-level variables. It is clear that Age has an influence on EWV ($d = -0.24$) and that there is a moderate association ($G = -0.33$; $C_s = 0.39$). The association is almost linear, with younger people tending to have 'Very high' EWV scores, middle-aged people having 'High' scores and older people having 'Moderate' or 'Low' scores.

Table 5.8   *Environmental Worldview and Age (Residents)*

EWV	Age			Total
	18–34	35–54	55+	
Low	16	12	**31**	20
Moderate	35	33	**48**	39
High	24	**38**	16	26
Very high	**25**	17	5	15
Total	100	100	100	100
n	128	138	135	401

Somer's $d = -0.24$ ($G = -0.33$; $C_s = 0.39$)

Age can be a difficult variable to interpret in cross-sectional research as there is always the dilemma of either viewing changes in Age as a developmental process, or regarding it as an indicator of the different experiences of each age cohort as their biographies intersect with history in different ways. One of these differences in life experiences is level of education. Younger people have greater educational opportunities and higher educational expectations than were available for older people. Therefore, it is possible that Education is confounding the association between Age and EWV, that is, if Education is also associated with EWV. Gender can also enter into this possible network of associations. To save space, only the bivariate influences and associations between these variables are given, including Age with EWV for comparison:

Age with EWV	d (EWV outcome)	$= -0.24$	($G = -0.33$; $C_s = 0.39$)
Gender with EWV	d (EWV outcome)	$= 0.15$	($G = 0.21$; $C_s = 0.28$)
Education with EWV	d (EWV outcome)	$= 0.17$	($G = 0.23$; $C_s = 0.23$)
Age with Education	d (Educn outcome)	$= -0.18$	($G = -0.28$; $C_s = 0.34$)
Gender with Education	d (Educn outcome)	$= 0.06$	($G = 0.08$; $C_s = 0.19$)
Age with Gender			($G = 0.02$; $C_s = 0.03$)

There is some influence of both Gender and Education on EWV, but less than Age. Age also has an influence on Education, no doubt reflecting the point just made. While it makes no sense to examine any kind of influence between Age and Gender, we can note that the low coefficients of association indicate that there is a Gender balance across the three Age categories. It is also evident that there is very little difference between males and females in terms of their Education: males are slightly more inclined to have a 'Low' Education and females a 'Moderate' Education; and there is a Gender balance in terms of 'High' Education. These data need to be taken into account in interpreting three-way contingency tables involving these variables.

Table 5.9   *Environmental Worldview and Age controlled for Education (Residents)*

Education	EWV	Age			Total
		18–34	35–54	55+	
Low	Low	14	22	**35**	27
	Moderate	38	38	**51**	44
	High	**28**	**32**	10	20
	Very high	**21**	8	4	9
	Total	100	100	100	100
	n	29	37	69	135
Moderate	Low	**20**	7	**22**	17
	Moderate	34	37	**44**	38
	High	22	**30**	**30**	26
	Very High	**24**	**26**	4	19
	Total	100	100	100	100
	n	41	27	27	95
High	Low	15	7	**32**	15
	Moderate	35	30	**45**	35
	High	22	**44**	18	31
	Very High	**28**	**20**	5	19
	Total	100	100	100	100
	n	58	71	38	167

In view of the bivariate analyses, Education and Gender will be used as controls on the relationship between Age and EWV. Table 5.9 shows three conditional tables with Education as the control variable: 'Low' (primary/some secondary/technical certificate); 'Moderate' (completed secondary); and 'High' (university educated). By inspecting the percentages in the three conditional tables, we find the same slightly curvilinear pattern that was found in the bivariate relationship, particularly for those with 'High' Education. In this conditional table, the younger respondents tend to have 'Very high' EWV scores, the middle-aged respondents tend to have 'High' scores and the older respondents tend to have 'Moderate' and, more particularly, 'Low' scores. For the 'Low' education conditional table, the relationship is linear. However, in the 'Moderate' education conditional table, the pattern is more complex. While it tends to be curvilinear, the distribution is more dispersed and there is an exception in the

Table 5.10 *Environmental Worldview and Age controlled for Gender (Residents)*

Gender	EWV	Age 18–34	35–54	55+	Total
Males	Low	22	18	**42**	27
	Moderate	36	30	**43**	37
	High	16	**31**	12	20
	Very high	**27**	**21**	3	16
	Total	100	100	100	100
	n	64	67	69	200
Females	Low	11	6	**18**	12
	Moderate	34	37	**54**	42
	High	31	44	22	33
	Very High	**23**	13	6	14
	Total	100	100	100	101
	n	64	70	65	199

'18–34' and 'Low' EWV score cell, in which there is overrepresentation. The coefficients reflect these patterns, and are as follows.[11]

Age with EWV	d (EWV outcome) = –0.24	(G = –0.33; C_s = 0.39)
'Low' education	d (EWV outcome) = –0.30	(G = –0.42; C_s = 0.41)
'Moderate' education	d (EWV outcome) = –0.11	(G = –0.15; C_s = 0.33)
'High' education	d (EWV outcome) = –0.19	(G = –0.25; C_s = 0.42)

It is clear that respondents with 'Low' education contribute more to the relationship between Age and EWV than the other Education categories, while those with a 'Moderate' education make the least contribution. In other words, the relationship is stronger for those with 'Low' education, followed by those with 'High' education and then those with 'Moderate' education. This analysis suggests that Education is a moderating variable.

While it is not critical to this analysis, it is worth noting that about half (51 per cent) of those with 'Low' Education are aged 55 and over, that approaching half (43 per cent) of those with 'Moderate' Education are aged 18–34, and that a similar proportion (42 per cent) of those with 'High' Education are aged 35–54. This is not unexpected as some older respondents would be less likely to have had the same educational opportunities as younger respondents today, that the youngest respondents (18–20), if they are at university, will not yet have completed their studies, and that some middle-aged respondents (35–54) will either have completed a university education or may have taken up first or further university studies later in life, particularly postgraduate studies. These factors account for the different distributions across the three Age categories in each of the conditional tables.

Table 5.10 shows two conditional cross-tabulations of Age with EWV, one for males and the other for females. As with the full table, there is a consistent curvilinear pattern in both conditional tables. The coefficients are as follows.

Age with EWV	d (EWV outcome) = −0.24	(G = −0.33; C_s = 0.39)
Males only	d (EWV outcome) = −0.26	(G = −0.34; C_s = 0.43)
Females only	d (EWV outcome) = −0.22	(G = −0.31; C_s = 0.36)

Controlling for Gender reveals very little difference between males and females: the relationship is only slightly stronger for males than females. This confirms that Gender is not a moderating variable on this relationship and it could hardly be a candidate as an intervening variable.

While this use of three-way contingency tables provides only a weak form of explanatory analysis, it does provide a better understanding of how variables interact than can be gained from the more powerful multiple regression analysis. Fortunately, when the analysis uses lambda (nominal-level variables) and Somer's d (ordinal-level variables) as the measures of influence, it is not necessary to satisfy the normal requirements for chi-square analysis on contingency tables, that is, that fewer than 20 per cent of expected frequencies can be less than 5 and no expected frequency can be less than 1. However, care needs to be taken when the numbers in any cells get very small. In this situation, it may be advisable to combine categories with smaller numbers even if some information is lost. However, care must be exercised when the analysis involves ordinal-level variables as combining categories can change the form of an association.

Other Methods

Loglinear analysis can be applied to relationships between two or more categorical variables. It is particularly useful when four or five variables are involved. However, in contrast to the analysis of three-way contingency tables just elaborated, loglinear analysis requires the formulation of models in order to explore the relationships in the data. These models are derived from theory and are developed iteratively until the best fit with the data is found.

The basis of this method is the calculation of expected cell values in the same manner as occurs in chi-square analysis (see Chapter 4). A model is constructed in which the expected frequencies in the cells of the table are those that would occur if there were no associations between the variables. However, while this is a simple procedure for bivariate contingency tables it is much more complex in contingency tables with three or more variables. It is difficult to do manually but, fortunately, it can be done automatically by statistical packages.

As with the use of three-way contingency tables, loglinear analysis lies on the border between association and explanatory analysis. Its purpose is to discover whether there is any interaction between a set of variables rather than to establish influence between a set of predictor variables and an outcome variable. Nevertheless, it provides a useful extension to the multivariate analysis of categorical variables. While it is beyond the scope of this book to deal with this method, a detailed elaboration can be found in Gilbert (1993).

Influence Between Metric Variables

It is much easier to conduct multivariate analysis with metric variables than it is with categorical variables. Most of this subsection is devoted to a discussion of multiple regression as this has become the major method of choice. However, a brief consideration of partial correlation precedes this as it is an important aspect of multiple regression.

Partial Correlation

Partial correlation is the metric equivalent of three-way contingency tables. It allows a researcher to examine the effect of one variable, the control, on the relationship between two other variables. It is possible to test for spuriousness, and an intervening or moderating variable (see Table 5.7). However, the analysis is much simpler than that required in three-way contingency tables. After computing Pearson's *r* for all three bivariate associations, say *A* with *B*, *A* with *C*, and *B* with *C*, the possible effect of *B* on the association between *A* and *C* is explored by computing a partial correlation coefficient to remove the association that *B* has with both *A* and C.

The first possibility is that *B* is strongly associated with *A* (say, 0.75) but has a very weak association with C (say, 0.10). Therefore, *B* cannot affect the association between *A* and C. A second possibility occurs when *B* is strongly associated with both *A* and C. When the effect of *B* is removed, the partial correlation between *A* and C could become very weak (say, 0.05). This would suggest that the association between the latter is spurious as both are related to *B*. A third possibility is that controlling for *B* could reduce the strength of association between *A* and C. In social research, this is the most likely possibility. The difficult question is: what does it mean? It could be that the association between *A* and C is partly spurious, that *B* is an intervening variable between *A* and C, that the strength of the latter association is dependent on *B* providing the link, or that *B* has a moderating effect, that is, *B* changes the form of the association between *A* and C. The only way that this can be settled is by examining both the zero-order and the first-order coefficients, and considering the logic of the relationships themselves (see Table 5.7).

Multiple Regression

Of all the methods available in the social sciences for multivariate explanatory analysis, *multiple regression* is the most widely used.[12] Multiple regression is a method for analyzing the relationship between a single, metric outcome variable and two or more predictor variables. Just as with bivariate regression, predictions can be made about the outcome variable, based on the observed values of the predictor variables. The analysis establishes the relative magnitudes of the contributions of each predictor variable. It is assumed that using more than one predictor variable leads to better predictions.

In addition to prediction, it is also possible to use multiple regression for explanatory analysis. It is possible to assess the influence of each predictor variable by statistically controlling the influence of all the others. In other words, the analysis tells us what happens when one of the predictor variables changes while all the other predictor variables remain the same. Hence, the independent influence of all the predictor variables can be established and their total influence can also be measured. It is then possible to see what proportion of the variance in the outcome variable is explained by each predictor variable, and by a set of them together.

It is important to note that regression analysis requires that the outcome variable is metric. Normally, the predictor variables will also be metric but, as we shall see, it is possible to work with categorical variables. When the outcome variable is categorical, a different method of analysis must be used, namely, logistic regression. We shall return to this later in the chapter.

The statistical purists may argue that the only satisfactory way to hold variables constant, and to control for extraneous variables, is to conduct randomized experiments. However, given that it is not possible to design experiments for many of the problems that social scientists wish to investigate, multiple regression provides a useful alternative. There are, nevertheless, some limitations. First, it must be possible to assume that all the relationships between each of the predictor variables and the outcome variable are linear. Second, it must be possible to measure all the variables that might have an effect on the outcome variable. Third, it must be possible to measure these variables precisely. In practice, it would be rare to meet the second and third requirements fully, even though the third is an aspiration of quantitative social research.

The issue of what we assume is being measured by a variable is extremely important in regression analysis, particularly multiple regression. Frequently, variables are just shorthand for complex social processes. Being clear about what we are measuring, and having appropriate methods for doing it, involves philosophical, theoretical and methodological considerations. Measuring any concept in the social sciences is a complex process, with the result that the techniques that are involved in the analysis of quantitative variables cannot capture the meanings and assumptions that are built into them. This interpretation is a separate process.

The principles behind multiple regression are exactly the same as for bivariate regression. The expression $y = a + bx$ is extended to include a combination of bs and xs for every predictor variable. In the case of two predictor variables, the equation is written as:

$$y = a + b_1 x_1 + b_2 x_2 + \ldots \tag{5.12}$$

where y is the value on the outcome variable, a is the intercept on the Y axis, x_1 and x_2 are the corresponding values on the two predictor variables, and b_1 and b_2 are their respective slopes. Additional predictor variables and their slopes can be added to the equation. Whereas it was possible to draw a simple graph of the regression line between two variables, the graphical representation of a multiple regression is rather more complex and needs to be in one more dimension than there are predictor variables.

Table 5.11   *Regression of Environmental Worldview on Age, Gender and Education*
(Residents)

Predictor variables	$\bar{x}$	s	r	Slope (b)	Std error	*Beta*	Tolerance	VIF
Age	46.01	18.20	−0.308	−0.164	0.030	−0.274	0.93	1.08
Gender[a]	0.50	0.50	0.143	2.500	1.030	0.116	0.99	1.01
Education[b]	0.66	0.47	0.186	2.243	1.127	0.099	0.92	1.09
$n = 395$ Constant = 92.82			$R = 0.346$ $R^2 = 0.119$			Standard error of the estimate = 10.17		

[a]Female coded '1'.

[b]'Completed secondary/diploma/degree/postgraduate qualification' coded '1'.

In discussing bivariate regression earlier in the chapter, dummy variables were introduced to make it possible to include categorical predictor variables in the analysis. It is possible to use a categorical predictor variable in simple regression as long as it can be recoded into two categories (dichotomized), with one category assigned the value '1' and the other '0'. However, when it is necessary or desirable to use more than two categories of a nominal-level or ordinal-level predictor variable, multiple regression must be used. Take the variable Education, for example. In the Resident sample, Education was coded into five categories: 'Primary/some secondary', 'Technical certificate', 'Completed secondary', 'Degree/diploma' and 'Postgraduate qualification'. It is possible to dichotomize these categories into 'University educated' versus 'No university education', as was done earlier (see Table 4.8). However, Table 5.6 suggests that more homogeneous categories would be produced if the dichotomy was based on a combination of 'Primary/some secondary' and 'Technical certificate' against the other three categories. This will be used here.

An example

It is now possible to take the example of simple regression between Age and EWV a step further by introducing additional predictor variables. As with the analysis of three-way contingency tables, let us start with two more variables, Gender and Education. The question is, what are the relative strengths of their contributions in explaining a person's level of EWV? Gender, as a dichotomized variable, is coded '1' for 'Female' and '0' for 'Male'; and Education is dichotomized as 'High' (completed secondary/diploma/degree/postgraduate qualification), coded '1', and 'Low' (primary/some secondary/technical certificate), coded '0'.

The results of multiple regression analysis, using these three predictor variables, are shown in Table 5.11. While the means and standard deviations of these variables, and their Pearson's r (with EWV), are not normally shown in such a table, they are included here mainly to show what happens with dichotomized or dummy variables, to confirm the distributions on the two dichotomized variables, Gender and Education, and to compare r with the *beta* coefficient. The means indicate that there is a gender balance in the sample ($\bar{x} = 0.50$), and that the 'High' education category has about two-thirds of the sample in it ($\bar{x} = 0.66$).

The critical question in this analysis is whether knowing the Gender and Education of our respondents increases our ability to predict or explain their EWV score. To do this we need to compare R^2 and the standard error of the estimate shown in Table 5.11 with the bivariate regression done with Age alone (see pp. 132–3).[13] The bivariate regression produced an R^2 of 0.095, which indicates that 9.5 per cent of the variance was explained, whereas in the multiple regression 11.9 per cent of the variance was explained ($R^2 = 0.119$). There is a slight reduction in the standard error of the estimate, from 10.26 to 10.17. What is also evident is that the regression line for Age is now slightly flatter than it was in the bivariate analysis ($b = -0.164$ compared with -0.185). This means that for every year of Age, the EWV score now decreases by 0.164 rather than 0.185. While it is not particularly important, note that a, the point at which the combined regression effects of the predictor variables intersect with the Y axis (referred to in multiple regression as the 'constant'), has been reduced from 96.49 to 92.82. In other words, it has moved towards the EWV mean of 87.99.

We now know what the total effect of the three predictor variables is on the outcome variable. However, we can also assess the individual contributions of the three variables. If we examine the unstandardized coefficients (b) for each of the predictor variables (see Table 5.11), we find -0.164 for Age, 2.500 for Gender and 2.243 for Education. We have already interpreted the coefficient for Age. What do the other two mean? They indicate that, on average, females have EWV scores 2.500 higher than males and that, on average, those in the 'High' education category have EWV scores 2.243 higher than those in the 'Low' education category.

There is a second more complex factor to consider. Because predictor variables usually have different units of measurement, it is not possible to compare the unstandardized b coefficients in the hope of assessing the relative influence of these variables. For example, we cannot say that Gender has a bigger influence on EWV than Age just because its b is 2.500 compared with -0.164 for Age. Gender is measured as either '1' or '0' while Age ranges from 18 to 90 years. To make such comparisons, the b coefficients have to be standardized. This is done by converting them into standard deviation units. They tell us how many standard deviation units the outcome variable changes for an increase in one standard deviation unit in the predictor variable.[14] The standardised coefficients are referred to as *beta* coefficients.

In Table 5.11 we can see that the *beta* for Age is -0.274, for Gender it is 0.116 and for Education it is 0.099. Now we are in a position to compare the relative influences of the three predictor variables on the outcome variable. Clearly, Age has more influence than the other two variables, with Education having the least influence. This may be the result of the fact that there is some association between Age and Education ($r = -0.273$): older people tend to be less well educated than younger people.

There is some similarity between these *beta* coefficients and the corresponding values for Pearson's r (see Table 5.11). They are measures of two different kinds of relationships between two variables, association (r) and influence *(beta)*. However, apart from the differences in the mathematics, the magnitude of the *beta* coefficients is the result of the influence of all the other predictor variables in the analysis being controlled statistically. Pearson's *r* is a measure of the relationship regardless of the associations of other variables.

Collinearity

There is an important feature of multiple regression that needs to be mentioned here. When sets of predictor variables are themselves highly correlated, the regression procedure is unable to sort out the contributions of each one. It will usually rely on the variable with the highest *R* and then assume that the other variable (or variables) make little or no contribution. This is known as the problem of *collinearity*, or multiple collinearity. In order to determine whether this is the case, we can examine two diagnostics, *tolerance* and the *variance inflation factor* (VIF). A tolerance value of 1 indicates that the variable is not correlated with the other(s), and a value of 0 that it is perfectly correlated. Likewise, a VIF value of more than 2 indicates a close correlation, and a value approaching 1 indicates little or no association. The simplest way to interpret these values is to hope that they are both about 1 (low or no collinearity) and to look very carefully as they deviate in both directions away from 1.[15] Of course, we can check the values of Pearson's *r* to confirm this. When there are only two predictor variables, there will be consistency between *r* and the diagnostics. However, when there are more than two predictors, the *r* values may not provide a reliable indicator of the degree of collinearity.

The diagnostics are shown in the right-hand columns of Table 5.11. The values for both are all close to 1, indicating a low level of correlation between the variables. This is confirmed by the values of *r* for Age with Gender (−0.06) and Gender with Education (0.11), but not as clearly for Age with Education (−0.27). While the diagnostic values for the latter two variables are further from 1 than the others, the difference is not as great as might be expected. Nevertheless, with this possible exception, it can be assumed that the three variables make relatively independent contributions to the explanation of EWV.

Multiple-category dummy variables

Before exploring a more complex example of multiple regression, we need to review the use of dummy variables with multiple-category, categorical predictor variables. Let us use the same three predictor variables, but this time creating four dummy variables for Education. To do this, each of the education categories is dichotomized against all the others in turn. For example, 'Primary/some secondary' can be coded as '1' and all the other categories as '0'; and similarly for each of the other categories. When such a variable is entered into the regression analysis, the number of dummy variables needs to be one less than the number of categories. The category that is not included becomes the *reference category* against which the *b* coefficient for each of the other categories is compared. In this case, the reference category is 'Postgraduate qualification'.

Table 5.12 provides the additional information on these Education categories. The first thing to note is how to interpret the *b* coefficients for the four

Table 5.12 *Regression of Environmental Worldview on Age, Gender and Education in five categories (Residents)*

Predictor variables	$\bar{x}$	s	r	Slope (b)	Std error	Beta	Tolerance	VIF
Age	46.01	18.20	−0.308	−0.164	0.030	−0.274	0.91	1.10
Gender	0.50	0.50	0.143	2.677	1.047	0.124	0.96	1.04
Primary/some sec.[a]	0.19	0.39	−0.166	−4.805	2.406	−0.174	0.30	3.36
Technical cert.[a]	0.15	0.36	−0.066	−3.220	2.468	−0.108	0.33	3.03
Completed sec.[a]	0.24	0.43	0.069	−2.459	2.338	−0.097	0.27	3.78
Degree/diploma[a]	0.36	0.48	0.093	−1.778	2.252	−0.079	0.23	4.45

$n = 395$ Constant $= 96.80$ $R = 0.352$ $R^2 = 0.124$ Standard error of the estimate $= 10.18$

[a]Compared with 'Postgraduate qualification'.

Education dummy variables. The missing category, 'Postgraduate qualification', is, in effect, '0' and the values of the other four categories have to be compared with it. They are all negative, indicating that respondents in each category have lower mean EWV scores than those with 'Postgraduate qualifications'. Also, the differences decrease as the level of education increases, with those in the lowest education category having an average EWV score of 4.805 less than those in the highest category. There is clearly a linear relationship between EWV and this set of ordinal-level education categories (see Table 5.6 for a comparison of means).

What can we learn from the data on the four dummy Education variables? Without going into technical details, we would have to conclude that while the difference between the top and bottom education categories has some interest, overall the dichotomized version of the Education variable is as useful as the four dummy variables. The only relevant difference is that R^2 has increased slightly with the four dummy variables (0.124 compared with 0.119). How-ever, the situation might be different when dummy variables are based on categories from nominal-level variables.

While the coefficients for Age remains the same, the Gender coefficients have increased slightly (*beta* from 0.117 to 0.124), and the constant has also increased (from 92.816 to 96.800). Another important change has occurred in the collinearity diagnostics; they indicate that the four Education dummy vari-ables are probably correlated among themselves as well as with Age and Gender. The correlation matrix for these variables provides some support for this (see Table 5.13). The pairs of variables with the higher coefficients are as would be expected, although not uniformly across all the Education dummy variables. For example, there is a weak association between Age and 'Primary/some secondary' education ($r = 0.26$), 'Completed secondary' ($r = -0.16$) and 'Degree/diploma' ($r = -0.14$).

Perhaps it is now time to get in at the deep end and try swimming in a multiple regression with more predictor variables, and with some nominal-level data. Table 5.14 adds Marital Status, Religion and Political Party Preference to Table 5.11. Marital Status has been recoded into five categories: 'Married', 'Separated or divorced', 'Widowed', 'Stable relationship' and 'Never married'. Dummy variables cover the first four categories and are compared with 'Never married'. Religion has been recoded into four categories: 'Protestant',[16]

Table 5.13   *Correlation matrix for Age, Gender and six Education dummy variables (Residents)*

	1	2	3	4	5	6	7
1 Age	1.00						
2 Gender	−0.06	1.00					
3 Primary/some sec.	0.26	0.03	1.00				
4 Technical certificate	0.07	−0.17	−0.20	1.00			
5 Completed secondary	−0.16	0.13	−0.27	−0.24	1.00		
6 Degree/diploma	−0.14	−0.02	−0.36	−0.32	−0.42	1.00	
7 Postgraduate	0.02	0.02	−0.12	−0.11	−0.14	−0.19	1.00

Table 5.14   *Regression of Environmental Worldview on Age, Gender and Education, Marital Status, Religion and Political Party Preference (Residents)*

Predictor variables	Slope (b)	Standard error	Beta	Tolerance	VIF
Age	−0.134	0.037	−0.220	0.54	1.86
Gender	3.504	0.996	0.163	0.91	1.09
Education[a]	1.956	1.061	0.086	0.90	1.12
Married[b]	0.957	1.342	0.044	0.52	1.94
Separated or divorced[b]	3.375	2.181	0.077	0.79	1.27
Widowed[b]	0.352	2.562	0.008	0.57	1.75
Stable relationship[b]	3.332	2.248	0.072	0.84	1.20
Protestant[c]	−0.123	1.386	−0.006	0.51	1.97
Catholic[c]	−5.644	1.479	−0.215	0.61	1.63
Other religions[c]	−4.191	1.556	−0.144	0.69	1.46
Liberal parties[d]	4.274	1.184	−0.192	0.69	1.45
Conservative parties[d]	−3.850	1.248	−0.165	0.68	1.47

$n = 395$;   Constant = 95.89 $R = 0.521$ $R^2 = 0.272$ Standard error of the estimate = 9.35

[a] 'Completed secondary/diploma/degree/postgraduate qualification' coded '1'
[b] Compared to 'Never married'.
[c] Compared to 'No religion'.
[d] Compared to 'Undecided'.

'Catholic', 'Other religions'[17] and 'No religion'. Dummy variables have been created from the first three categories and are compared with 'No religion'. Political Party Preference has been recoded into three categories: 'Conservative' parties,[18] 'Liberal' parties[19] and 'Undecided'. The first two categories have been converted into dummy variables and are compared with 'Undecided'.

Now to interpret Table 5.14. The first thing to note is that R^2 has increased from 0.119 (Table 5.11) to 0.272. Hence, this set of predictor variables can explain 27.2 per cent of the variance in the outcome variable. The best that has been achieved up to this point is 12.4 per cent. Second, the constant has been reduced to 95.89, between the previous two figures. Third, the *beta* coefficients for Age and Education are now somewhat lower (from −0.274 to −0.220, and from 0.099 to 0.086, respectively), but for Gender marginally higher (from 0.116 to 0.163). Fourth, Marital Status makes very little contribution. While the dummy variables 'Separated or divorced' (*beta* = −0.077) and 'Stable relationship' (*beta* = 0.072) make minor contributions, the other Marital Status dummy variables do not. Fifth, Religion seems to make some contribution, but only from the 'Catholic' and 'Other religion' dummy variables. Sixth, Political Party Preference also makes a contribution (for 'Liberal' *beta* = −0.192, and for 'Conservative' *beta* = −0.165).

We could add further predictor variables into the analysis. However, this is really not the way to try to explain any variable. The selection of predictor variables should be informed by theory rather than a process of trial and error. It is possible to give theoretical rationales for the variables included in Table 5.14, but this is not the place to do it (see Chapter 8). It should be evident from this discussion on multiple regression that while categorical variables can be included using dichotomous or dummy variables, their interpretation is more complex than metric variables.

Other Methods

The methods that have been discussed in this chapter have concentrated on explanatory analysis that involves one or more predictor variables and one outcome variable. We have dealt with combinations of categorical and metric variables and have explored ways of handling combinations of variables at different levels of measurement. While these methods include those that are the most commonly used in the analysis of data from social surveys, other more advanced multivariate methods are available. Some of these are concerned with explanatory analysis in terms of the influence of a set of predictor variables on an outcome variable. Such methods are sometimes referred to as *dependence techniques*. Those discussed in this chapter belong to this category. Other methods of multivariate analysis deal with the interrelationships between a number of variables and involve the simultaneous analysis of all the variables in the set with no assumptions about direction of influence. These methods go beyond the bivariate correlations of all pairs of variables in the set and are known as *interdependence techniques*.

In addition to the methods that have been discussed in this chapter, a range of more advanced methods of multivariate analysis is available. However, these methods are beyond the scope of this book. Most of the more important ones are simply outlined briefly below, with suggestions for further reading. Perhaps the most detailed treatment of multivariate techniques of analysis available is to be found in Hair et al. (1998). A book that is highly recommended for any reader who wishes to use more advanced methods.

Dependence Techniques

The major distinguishing feature of these various methods is the particular combination of different levels of measurement, categorical and metric, of the predictor and outcome variables, and the number of variables of each type that can be handled. While some of the methods are alternatives, most work with a unique combination of variables.

Analysis of variance

Analysis of variance (ANOVA) is used to make comparisons between two or more groups to see if they differ on the outcome variable. The groups are the equivalent of a multi-category predictor variable for which separate means on the outcome variable can be calculated. Hence, the outcome variable must be metric. This will be discussed and illustrated in Chapter 6 in the context of testing the significance of differences between means. See, for example, Field (2000: Chapters 7–9) or Wright (1997: Chapter 6).

Multiple analysis of variance

Multiple analysis of variance (MANOVA) is an extension of ANOVA in which comparisons can be made between groups (the predictor variable) across two or more outcome variables. The predictor variable is the equivalent of a categorical variable and the outcome variables need to be metric. Both ANOVA and MANOVA are particularly useful in experimental research. See, for example, Field (2000: Chapter 10) or Hair et al. (1998: Chapter 6).

Logistic regression

Logistic regression is equivalent to multiple regression but has an outcome variable that is dichotomous. The predictor variables can be either categorical or metric. It predicts to which of two categories a person is likely to belong, given the information contained in the predictors. See, for example, Hair et al. (1998: Chapter 5), Scott (1995), Agresti and Finlay (1997: Chapter 15), Miles and Shevlin (2001: Chapter 6) or Gilbert (1993: Chapter 10).

Logit logistic regression

This method is the same as logistic regression except that there are more than two categories in the outcome variable.

Multiple discriminant analysis

This method is an alternative to the two forms of logistic regression. It can handle a single outcome variable in dichotomous or multichotomous categories, and a number of metric predictor variables. See, for example, Hair et al. (1998: Chapter 5).

Structural equation modelling

This method, sometimes referred to as LISREL after the commonly used software package, is an extension of several multivariate techniques, particularly multiple regression and factor analysis. Whereas other dependence techniques can deal with only one predictor variable at a time, structural equation modelling can handle the relationships between a series or network of interrelated predictor variables. It can estimate a series of separate, but interdependent, multiple regression equations simultaneously. The form of the relationships can be specified in a path diagram in which an outcome variable in one relationship can become a predictor variable in the next relationship in the series. The final outcome variable must be metric but the predictor variables can be either categorical or metric. See, for example, Hair et al. (1998), Hayduk (1996); Kaplan (2000) or Kelloway (1998).[20]

Interdependence Techniques

These multivatiate techniques are not concerned with influence or explanation, but rather with how a set of variables relate to each other. They search for what a set of variables has in common and reduce them to one or a few factors or dimensions.

Factor analysis

Factor analysis is an interdependence technique in which a large set of variables is considered simultaneously in terms of their bivariate relationships. It is used to discover the underlying patterns or relationships in a large number of variables and can reduce these variables to a smaller set of factors or new variates. Factor analysis is not concerned with predicting an outcome variable. The original variables all need to be metric, although the method is commonly applied to ordinal-level variables in which it is reasonable to assume equal intervals between the categories. Exploratory factor analysis will be discussed in detail in Chapter 7. See, for example, Hair et al. (1998: Chapter 3), Field (2000: Chapter 11), Gorsuch (1983), Lewis-Beck (1994) or Kim and Mueller (1978a, 1978b).

Cluster analysis

Cluster analysis is a technique for classifying a set of individuals or objects into a smaller number of mutually exclusive groups, based on the similarities among them. The aim is to maximize the homogeneity within clusters while maximizing the heterogeneity between clusters. Whereas factor analysis is concerned with grouping variables together as factors, cluster analysis is concerned with grouping individuals or objects together in terms of some criterion. The measurement of this criterion variable must be metric. See, for example, Hair et al. (1998: Chapter 9) or Aldenderfer and Blashfield (1984).

Multidimensional scaling

Multidimensional scaling, or perceptual mapping, identifies key dimensions underlying people's judgements and perceptions, such as their evaluations of objects, comparison of physical qualities or perceptions of objects, people or issues. It transforms such judgements and perceptions into distances represented in multidimensional space. It can determine the dimensions people use, their relative importance and how the objects etc. are related perceptually. Whereas in cluster analysis the researcher must specify the variable on which the clusters are to be based, multidimensional scaling is like having the outcome variable (judgements or perceptions) and then working out what the independent variables (perceptual dimensions) might be. This technique can handle both metric (ratings) and ordinal-level (rankings) input data and can produce an output in metric data. See, for example, Hair et al. (1998: Chapter 10).

Summary

- Explanatory analysis is concerned with answering 'why' research questions about the patterns or connections between variables. It builds on bivariate descriptive (associational) analysis to achieve the ultimate objective in quantitative social research.
- Because of the philosophical complexities associated with the notion of causation, social researchers limit their discussions to statistical influence among variables. To do this, variables are labelled as either predictors (independent) or outcomes (dependent). Procedures are used to demonstrate the extent of influence of one or more predictor variables on an outcome variable.
- While it may be more convincing to conduct explanatory analysis using controlled experiments, social researchers usually have to be content with techniques that have been designed for cross-sectional research. This involves making assumptions about the time order of variables and using statistical rather than experimental controls.
- In bivariate explanatory analysis, three main methods are used to demonstrate influence between variables. The choice of method depends on the levels of measurement of the variables.

  1. Nominal-level predictor and nominal-level outcome; lambda (equations (5.1) and (5.2)).
  2. Ordinal-level predictor and ordinal-level outcome; Somer's d (5.3).
  3. Interval-level predictor and interval-level outcome; bivariate regression (5.5).
  4. Nominal-level predictor and ordinal-level outcome; lambda.
  5. Nominal-level predictor and metric-level outcome:

     (a) code outcome to ordinal-level-lambda;
     (b) conduct means analysis-eta; or
     (c) use regression with dummy variables (bivariate regression for a dichotomized predictor and multiple regression with multichotomous predictors).

  6. Ordinal-level predictor and metric-level outcome; as for 5, but using Somer's d for (a).
  7. Metric-level predictor and nominal-level outcome; code predictor to ordinal-level-lambda.
  8. Metric-level predictor and ordinal-level outcome; code predictor to ordinal-level-Somer's d.

- In multivariate analysis, in which the influence of a predictor variable on an outcome variable is controlled by a third variable, and all the variables are categorical, three-way contingency tables are used. While the control variable can be either nominal or ordinal, the method of analysis depends on the level of measurement of the other two variables. Methods of association or influence can be used. Whether the relationship between the predictor and outcome variables is regarded as being spurious, or the control variable intervenes or is a moderator, will depend on the relative values of the coefficients for the controlled and uncontrolled relationships.

    9. Nominal-level predictor and nominal-level outcome;
        lambda (5.1), Cramér's V (4.7) or C_s (4.3). (Loglinear analysis.)
    10. Ordinal-level predictor and ordinal-level outcome;
        Somer's d (5.3) or gamma (4.8). (Loglinear analysis.)
    11. A combination of nominal-level and ordinal-level variables;
        as for 9. (Loglinear analysis.)
    12. A combination of metric-level and categorical-level predictor and outcome variables;
        code the metric-level variable to ordinal level categories and use 10 or 11.
    13. Metric-level predictor and outcome variables;
        partial correlation.

- When multivariate analysis is used to establish the relative influence of two or more predictor variables on an outcome variable, the following methods are used.

    14. Two or more groups compared on a metric-level outcome variable;
        ANOVA (not discussed).
    15. Two or more groups compared on two or more metric-level outcome variables;
        MANOVA (not discussed).
    16. Metric-level predictor and outcome variables;
        multiple regression (5.12).
    17. Metric-level and/or categorical-level predictors and metric-level outcome;
        multiple regression with categorical-level predictors as dummy variables.
    18. Metric-level and/or categorical-level predictors and dichotomous outcome;
        logistic regression (not discussed).
    19. Metric-level and/or categorical-level predictors and multichotomous outcome;
        logit logistic regression (not discussed).
    20. Metric predictors and categorical outcome;
        multiple discriminant analysis (not discussed).
    21. A network of interrelated categorical and metric predictors and a final metric-level outcome variable;
        structural equation modelling (not discussed).

Notes

[1] See Pawson and Tilley (1997) for ideas related to this view.

[2] Should you require information on the variety of experimental models that can be used, and how data from them can be analyzed, see Campbell and Stanley (1963) and Cook and Campbell (1979) for classic discussions of experiments in social research, and Kidder and Judd (1986: Chapters 4 and 5), Neuman (2000: Chapter 9) and Maxim (1999: Chapter 8) for useful reviews.

[3] However, computer programs such as SPSS use 'independent' and 'dependent'.

[4] While lambda can also be used as a symmetrical procedure and with any variables in categories, both nominal and ordinal, it tends to be a rather conservative measure, that is, it tends to produce rather low coefficients. It is better to use gamma when both variables are ordinal.

[5] This relationship, particularly the possible differences in occupation between Protestants and Catholics, has fascinated sociologists for more than fifty years following the publication in English of Weber's *The Protestant Ethic and the Spirit of Capitalism* (Weber, 1958); see, for example, Lenski (1961), Blaikie (1969), and Mol (1971).

[6] In constructing contingency tables in which assumptions are made about the direction of influence of one variable on another, it is conventional to place the predictor (independent) variable in the columns and the outcome (dependent) variable in the rows, and then calculate the percentages down the columns. This convention need not be followed in associational analysis.

[7] For examples of more technical discussions of bivariate and multiple regression than is possible here, see Allison (1999), Hair et al. (1998), Lewis-Beck (1993) and Miles and Shevlin (2001).

[8] This is not obvious in Figure 5.1 because SPSS has shortened both axes to save space.

[9] There is, of course, another possibility in which neither A nor B has an influence on C. In this case, there is no point in proceeding with any further analysis.

[10] The double-headed arrows indicate association, while the single-headed arrows indicate influence. It is possible to do these forms of analysis using only measures of association. However, the logic is clearer when measures of both association and influence are used.

[11] While it is not a strictly correct procedure, it is interesting to note the equivalent values for r: 0.27, 0.32, 0.13 and 0.22. They closely resemble those for Somer's d.

[12] In some sociology journals, and in the *American Sociological Review* in particular, it appears that the use of multiple regression is almost mandatory in order to get a research article published.

[13] These figures are based on the analysis without the exclusion of outliers.

[14] Standard deviation units sound a bit mysterious but were explained in (Chapter 3, p. 80, 83).

[15] It is not really necessary to use both diagnostics as one is the reciprocal of the other. However, as both are given by SPSS, they are used here.

[16] This includes 'Anglican' ($n = 91$), 'Uniting' ($n = 55$) and 'Baptist' ($n = 5$).

[17] This includes 'Greek Orthodox' ($n = 9$), 'Jewish' ($n = 5$), 'Moslem' ($n = 1$) and 'Buddhist' ($n = 51$).

[18] This includes the Liberal Party ($n = 123$) and the National Party (although no respondent in this urban sample intended to vote for the latter, a party with a mainly rural constituency).

[19] This includes the Australian Labor Party ($n = 94$), the Australian Democrats ($n = 24$) and 'Other' parties, most of which are left of centre. 'Liberal' here should not be confused with the name of one of the conservative parties.

[20] For examples of pioneering work on path analysis and structural equation modelling, see Blalock (1964), Duncan (1966, 1969), Land (1969), Hesse (1969), Goldberger and Duncan (1973) and Asher (1983).

Inferential Analysis: From Sample to Population

Introduction

Inferential analysis is used to generalize the results obtained from a random (probability) sample back to the population from which the sample was drawn. This analysis is only required when:

- a sample is drawn by a random procedure; and
- the response rate is very high.

Hence, this type of analysis is *not* appropriate when:

- non-probability methods of selection are used;
- the response rate is less than, say, 85 per cent, unless independent evidence is available to indicate that the sample is reasonably representative; and
- the data are obtained from a population.

There are some technical concepts here that will be explained in due course. However, I have made these assertions at the beginning because there is a great deal of confusion in the literature about when inferential analysis should be used in social research, with the result that it is often applied inappropriately and unnecessarily.

There are a number of other common misunderstandings when inferential analysis is applied to measures of association or influence between two variables.

1. Inferential procedures are not a substitute for measures of association. Many studies appear to use inferential analysis in making decisions about whether a relationship should be taken seriously, and ignore measures of association or influence in the process.
2. An inspection of many textbooks on statistics in the social sciences reveals that a substantial part of the book (usually at least 50 per cent and frequently much more) is devoted to inferential analysis, and the theory behind it. This gives the impression that this is the most important method of data analysis. Wrong! We might describe this as an inferential obsession. Inferential techniques are necessary under very particular circumstances, and in these situations they are only a supplement to the more basic techniques of analysis, such as those that have been dealt with in previous chapters.

3. In reading many textbooks on statistics it would be very easy to come to the conclusion that using inferential analysis is all that is required in the testing of hypotheses. If inferential analysis is not appropriate for data obtained from a population, then how do you test hypotheses in such a situation? I will show later that inferential analysis is only relevant to a very particular role for hypotheses in social research.

4. Inferential analysis is sometimes presented as determining whether results obtained have occurred 'other than by chance'. Sometimes the notion of 'chance' in this context is meant to refer to results occurring by accident or through some random error in the procedures. As we shall see, chance is involved in the theory behind inferential analysis, but it does not refer to accidents or errors.

Having stated these points boldly, we can now proceed to locate this analysis in its appropriate place and to confine it to the very specific uses for which it was developed. As inferential analysis is only relevant when probability samples are used, let us begin by discussing sampling procedures.

Sampling

All social research involves decisions about how to select data from whatever the source or sources may be. When data are obtained separately from a number of individuals, social units or social artefacts, the researcher has the choice of either taking the whole population or selecting a sample from the population. If sampling is used, then a choice must be made from a variety of methods.

It is a common practice in social research to work with samples rather than populations, particularly when the population under consideration is very large, such as a country, a region or an urban area. It is tedious and expensive to study such large populations. It is also unnecessary as samples of between 1000 and 2000 provide adequate information about most populations in most circumstances. However, there is a price to pay when samples are used: first, it is not possible to be absolutely confident that what a sample shows also exists in the population; second, it adds considerable complication to the analysis.

Populations and Samples

In order to apply a sampling technique, it is necessary to define the *population* (also called the target population, universe or sampling frame) from which the sample is to be drawn. A population is an aggregate of all units or cases that conform to some designated set of criteria. *Population elements* are single members or units of a population; they can be such things as people, social actions, events, places or times. A *census* is a count of all population elements and is used to describe the characteristics of a population.

A population is defined according to the purposes of the research being undertaken. It can be whatever the researcher needs it to be. It may be large, as in the case of a national census. It may be small, such as the students on an introductory university course. In addition, populations are not just collections of people; they can be made up of many types of elements. Here are some examples of populations.

- The citizens of a country at a particular time.
- The university students of a country at a particular time.
- First-year university students at a particular university.
- Telephone subscribers in a particular city.
- People of a particular age living in a particular geographical area.
- All the issues of a newspaper published over a 12-month period.
- Only the Saturday issues of the newspaper during this period.
- Only articles in such newspapers that report domestic violence.

A *sample* is a selection of elements (members or units) from a population and is used to make statements about the whole population. The ideal sample is one that provides a perfect representation of a population, with all the relevant features of the population included in the sample in the same proportions. However, while this ideal can be approached, it is difficult to achieve fully in practice. In some research designs, a sample may be selected deliberately that does *not* represent a scaled-down version of the population.

In a *probability sample*, every population element must have a known and non-zero chance of being selected. Most types of probability sample will also give every element an equal chance of being selected. A *non-probability sample* does *not* give every population element a chance of selection. The relationship between the size of the sample and the size of the population is the *sampling ratio* or *sampling fraction*.

Sampling is used for a variety of reasons. Studying a whole population may be slow and tedious; it can be expensive and is sometimes impossible; it may also be unnecessary. Given limited resources, sampling can not only reduce the costs of a study, but also, given a fixed budget, increase the breadth of coverage. However, as mentioned earlier, there is a price to pay when it comes to analyzing the data.

The complexity that the use of samples introduces into the analysis of the data occurs when it is necessary to estimate the characteristics of or patterns in the population from those found in the sample. This is technically known as estimating *population parameters* from *sample statistics* and involves the use of methods of *inferential statistics*. However, it is only possible to make such estimations when probability sampling is used and when it has been possible to obtain data from all or most of the elements selected.

Probability Samples

To be able to use the results obtained from a sample to draw conclusions about a population, the sample must be selected using probability techniques. To reiterate, a random or probability sample is one in which every population element has a known (usually equal) and non-zero chance of being selected. As long as this principle is satisfied in the selection of population elements, it is possible to generalize the data obtained from a sample to the population from which it was drawn.

Inferential analysis is a collection of methods for estimating what the population characteristics (parameters) might be, given what is known about the sample's characteristics (statistics), or for establishing whether patterns or relationships, both association and influence, or differences between categories or collectivities that exist in a sample could also be expected to exist in the population.

It is possible to draw many probability samples from a population. The possible combinations of population elements that can be selected from a large population are almost infinite. The ideal sample is one that has a combination of population elements that are a miniature version of the population, that is, that represent it in all respects. However, the use of probability procedures cannot guarantee this. Some samples may be very bad replicas of the population. It is a matter of chance which combination of elements is drawn. In short, using probability procedures does not guarantee that a sample accurately represents a population. As we shall see, there are ways of ensuring that certain population parameters are represented in the correct proportions, but this is usually limited to one parameter, such as gender or ethnicity, and two or three at the very most.

There are a few technical terms that need to be elaborated here.

- Samples can be selected with or without replacement. If replacement is used, after each population element is drawn, the element is 'put back' and is available for selection again. Selection without replacement means that once a population element is selected it is not 'put back' and is not available for selection again. Sampling without replacement is the most common in social research.
- A sample that is not representative is called a *biased sample*. The extent to which a sample statistic does not accurately represent the population parameter is its *error of estimation* or *sampling error*. Because population parameters are usually not known, it may be impossible to calculate the error of estimation. A biased sample produces errors in its estimates of population characteristics.

The fact that it is usually impossible to achieve a perfectly representative sample creates one of the most complex problems in social research; namely, how to generalize from a sample to a population when the sample might be biased. If all probability samples were accurate replicas of the population from which they were drawn, we would not need to use inferential analysis. In such a situation, the characteristics and patterns found in a sample can be assumed to be the same as those in the population. The only difference is that the sample is smaller.

If a population's characteristics are not known, it is impossible to know to what extent a sample is biased. Therefore, we have to find a way of estimating the likelihood of a sample not being an accurate representation of a population. In other words, we need to know what the chances are that our estimates of population characteristics are inaccurate. To do this, we have to turn to what is known as *probability theory*, which is based on the theoretical chances of not drawing a representative sample.

Probability Theory

The jump from sample statistics to population parameters is made possible by the use of probability theory. While it is not necessary to go into the details of this theory here,[1] there are some points that need to be covered in order to be able to understand what lies behind the methods of inferential analysis. In terms of a particular population parameter, say age, probability theory allows us to estimate the distribution of the mean age produced from all possible samples. It turns out that the possible sample means will tend to be clustered around the population mean age. However, some samples may have means that are very different from the population mean. A distribution of these means will take the shape of a normal curve.

Let us try a hypothetical example using a population of 20 and age as the variable (see Table 6.1). The age of each member of the population is shown

Table 6.1   *Hypothetical sampling*

No.	Age	f	Samples of four				Total	Mean
1	18	4	85	20	55	27	187	46.75
2	20	5	55	52	18	65	190	47.50
3	25	2	65	40	18	80	203	50.75
4	27	5	55	30	27	64	176	44.00
5	30	6	60	75	48	18	201	50.25
6	33	2	45	85	33	80	243	60.75
7	35	4	30	35	50	55	170	42.50
8	40	4	40	30	65	35	170	42.50
9	45	2	50	20	65	30	165	41.25
10	48	6	55	25	75	64	219	54.75
11	50	4	48	64	30	27	169	42.25
12	52	1	50	33	60	20	163	40.75
13	55	6	27	75	70	48	220	55.00
14	60	5	70	35	80	60	245	61.25
15	64	4	35	27	20	60	142	35.50
16	65	6	40	70	64	30	204	51.00
17	70	4	48	75	65	50	238	59.50
18	75	4	25	70	60	55	210	52.50
19	80	3	48	65	85	45	243	60.75
20	85	3	48	40	20	18	127	31.50
Total	977							971.00
Mean	48.85							48.55

(ranging from 18 to 85). Using a table of random numbers, twenty samples of size 4 were drawn and the frequency with which each member of the population was selected is shown (ranging from 1 to 6). The mean age of each sample is shown in the right-hand column (ranging from 31.75 to 61.25). At the foot of the table is the mean age of the population (48.85) and the mean of the sample means (48.55).[2]

With only 20 samples, we could not expect the distribution to look like a normal curve. When five-year intervals are used, it certainly does not, but it approaches a crude normal curve with ten-year intervals (see Figure 6.1). By increasing the number of samples the distribution would not only look more like a normal curve, there would also be a greater 'bunching' around the population mean.

A number of points need to be noted. First, the mean of the sample means is a very good approximation of the population mean; the difference in this case is only 0.30 years. If more samples were drawn, the gap should be even narrower; if all possible samples of size 4 were drawn we would expect the two means to

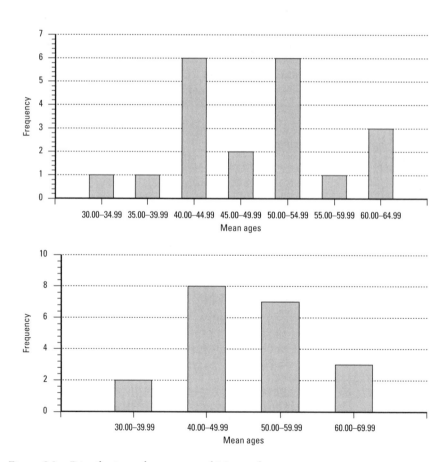

Figure 6.1   *Distributions of mean ages of 20 samples*

coincide. You could try a simple test of this by drawing 20 more samples and calculating the mean of the means. Second, using a random selection procedure does not guarantee that the sample means will be the same as the population mean. In fact, no sample replicates the population mean; the closest is 47.50, still 1.35 years away (sample number 2), and the most extreme is 17.35 years away (sample number 20). Of course, this example creates such extreme differences because the samples are very small. The larger the samples, the closer the mean of the sample means will be to the population mean and the less dispersed will be the distribution of all sample means. You could test this by drawing twenty samples of size 8 from this same data set; forty samples of size 12 would be even better.

This example begins to illustrate some of the principles behind probability theory. One important principle is known as the *central limit theorem*. This says that when many probability samples are drawn from a population, increasing the sample size will increase the possibility of the distribution of sample means approaching the normal curve and the overall mean of the sample means approaching the population mean. This is true regardless of the shape of the distribution of the population values. Just how big such samples should be cannot be determined precisely. Some writers suggest that it could be as small as 30, as long as the population distribution on critical variables is not unusual (see, for example, Freund and Perles, 1999: 276). Hence, if all possible samples of a particular size are drawn from a population, the following will be the case.

1. If the means of one of the variables from these samples are plotted, the distribution will form a normal curve. This will happen regardless of the form of the distribution of this variable in the population and in the samples. It is only the sample means that are relevant here.
2. The mean of all these means will be the same as the mean for the population from which the samples were drawn except, perhaps, for very small samples.
3. As the sample size is increased, the dispersion of the sample means decreases. There will be a greater clustering around the population mean and shorter tails in the distribution. The standard deviation of this distribution is known as the *standard error of the mean*. It decreases as the sample size is increased.
4. The relationship between sample size and the standard error of the mean is not linear. Increases in the sample size lead to decreasing reductions in the standard error of the mean. This is because the standard error is inversely proportional to the square root of the sample size. In other words, the effect of increasing the sample size gradually diminishes until further increases do not produce useful gains in reducing the dispersion of the means (see Table 6.2 and Figure 6.3).

These characteristics of the distribution of sample means allow us to conclude that when the estimate of a population parameter is based on only one sample, the larger the sample the closer the estimate will be. Therefore, the accuracy of estimates of population parameters depends on the sample size.

Sample Size

For these reasons, the general rule for samples is the bigger the better. However, increasing the sample size is subject to the 'law' of diminishing returns. Large gains are made initially, but they decrease as the sample size increases. There comes a point where the cost of further increases outweighs the gain in the accuracy with which the population parameters or patterns can be estimated. As stated previously, in studies of large populations, a sample of around 1000 may be satisfactory and one of 2000 will be very satisfactory. Problems only begin to arise when research is attempted with smaller samples. Note that we have been able to do useful analysis with our two samples of Students and Residents, one of 410 and the other of 465. My rule of thumb when advising students is to say that 300 may be adequate, 500 would be better and 1000 would be even better. However, there are many factors that need to be taken into account when determining the sample size.

Before discussing these, there is one point that needs to be made very clear. The decision on sample size has nothing to do with the ratio of the size of the sample to the population. There seems to be a common belief (at least I seem to come across it at regular intervals and in many contexts) that samples should normally be about 10 per cent of the population. This is *not* the rule of thumb that should be used. Here are three important considerations.

- First, decisions about sample sizes depend on how widely dispersed are the population characteristics. In our example, if all members of the population were the same age, we would need a sample of only one to estimate the mean age of the population. As the age distribution becomes wider, so the sample size must be increased, that is, if age is a critical variable. Given that the age distributions in the populations from which the Student and Resident samples were drawn are very different, I could have decided to work with a smaller sample of Students. However, age is not the only variable under consideration in this research.
- Second, we need to know what the risks are in making an incorrect estimation of a population parameter. In other words, how much sampling error can be tolerated? If the consequences of being wrong are serious, the sample size will need to be larger than where they are not as serious. For example, making an inaccurate estimate of the mean age of a population may not be as serious as determining whether a drug is safe to use.
- Third, the various methods of data analysis have different requirements as far as the minimum number is concerned. This is particularly critical when nominal-level data are analyzed using cross-tabulations. This consideration is independent of the accuracy of the estimate of population characteristics.

The general rule is that nominal-level data require larger numbers than ordinal-level data and certainly larger than the methods appropriate for interval-level and ratio-level data.[3] A rule of thumb for nominal-level data is that the cells of a cross-tabulation need an average of 10. Hence, the sample size can be determined by the combination of the number of categories in two variables. In practice, this means taking the table to be used in the analysis with the greatest number of cells. For example, if the two variables each have six categories, there would be 36 cells in a cross-tabulation based on them; the sample size would need to be 360 ($6 \times 6 \times 10$). If you wish to undertake multivariate analysis with nominal-level variables, this number must be multiplied by the number of categories in the third variable. In this same example, if the third variable had four categories, the sample size would need to be 1440. Textbooks on statistics usually specify the minimum numbers required for metric-level analysis and they are usually quite small, such as 30.

Response Rate

At the beginning of the chapter I raised the issue of the need to achieve a very high *response rate* before it is appropriate to use inferential analysis, 85 per cent in fact. I attribute this figure to one of my statistical mentors. The reason for insisting on such a high figure is that as the response rate declines, the possibility of a sample becoming unreliable, or being even more biased, increases. If non-respondents or non-contacts are not typical of the sample as a whole, their absence will change the characteristics of the remaining sample. For example, if non-respondents tend to be elderly people, then the age distribution of the sample will be distorted and its ability to accurately estimate the mean age of the population will be jeopardized. It is bad enough having to accept the risk of being wrong in estimating population parameters from a sample with 100 per cent coverage. To then run the risk of distortion due to non-responses or non-contacts is to compound the problem in a way that probability theory cannot rescue.

Unfortunately, achieving very high response rates is frequently very difficult in much social research. Two strategies can be adopted to compensate for this, both of which are compromises. One is to collect as much data as possible on the non-responses and non-contacts. In interview studies it may be possible to get some basic information on people who refuse to participate (e.g. age, gender, socio-economic circumstances) and on those who could not be contacted (perhaps from people who know them). If their profile is similar to that of the rest of the sample, there is some justification for using inferential analysis. The second strategy can be used where at least some of the basic characteristics of the population are known. This may be possible in surveys of residential areas that correspond to the subdivisions in which census data are collected and published. A comparison of the sample and population distributions on critical variables will give some indication of the extent to which the sample is biased.

You may already be curious about our two samples, neither of which achieved the high response rate that has been proposed. However, in the Student sample we were able to make some approximate comparisons with the undergraduate student body in terms of its gender composition, age distribution and representation across the various faculties. Only minor variations were evident. Similarly, census data on a number of key variables were available for the urban area from which the Resident sample was drawn. Again, there were only minor variations. Hence, the application of inferential analysis can be justified.

Response rate is also relevant in studies based on populations. However, lower response rates can be more readily tolerated, as inferential analysis is not required.[4] Response rates of less than 50 per cent with samples are common and it is rare to find evidence presented to establish the representativeness of the sample. It is no wonder that some writers have argued that methods of inferential analysis are given far too much weight in data analysis and that their use should either be severely restricted or abandoned (see, for example, Selvin, 1957; Labovitz, 1970). While I do not want to go that far, I observe that some of the methods are used in a ritualistic manner, often inappropriately, and apparently with little or no understanding of their purpose. In contrast to this, however, too many opinion polls and surveys of voting intentions fail to use inferential analysis when it is essential.

Sampling Methods

There are two main methods for selecting probability samples in the social sciences, with a third method that can be combined with either of them. The first, *simple random sampling*, involves a selection process that gives every possible sample of a particular size the same chance of selection. Each element of a population must be able to be identified and numbered. Once the sample size has been decided, numbers are selected using a table of random digits until the desired total is reached. The size of the sample determines the number of columns of digits that must be used in the table. Only the combinations of digits relevant to the size of the sample are used in the selection. The selected numbers then determine which population elements are to be included in the sample.

The second method, *systematic sampling*, avoids having to number the whole population. If the population elements can be listed, they can be counted and a sampling ratio determined. For example, if the population has 20,000 elements (say all students enrolled in a particular university) and a sample of 500 is required, the sampling ratio will be 1 : 40. In effect, the list is then divided into bunches or zones of 40 and one selection is made in each zone. The only really random aspect of this method is the selection of a number within the first zone. This can be done by using a table of random numbers, or even less sophisticated methods like drawing numbered objects out of a 'hat'. Counting down the list to the number selected then determines the first population element in the sample. All that is then required to select the rest of the sample is to continue counting down the list 'systematically' in intervals corresponding to the sampling ratio, for example, 40.

There are potential dangers in this method that could introduce unnecessary bias. For example, there may be patterns or cycles in the list that correspond to the sampling interval. This could happen in a residential area designed on a 'grid iron' pattern with the same number of residences in each block. If the number of residences corresponds to the sampling interval, then residences in exactly the same position would be selected from each block. This may have some bearing on the aims of the research. There are two things that can be done to avoid this problem and to introduce greater randomness into the selection process. The first is to change the selection at regular intervals. The second is to double or treble the size of the zones and then to make two or three random selections at the outset. These two methods can also be combined.

All probability sampling can be undertaken using one of these methods. However, there is a third method that can be used in combination with either of them: *stratified sampling*. If a researcher wants to ensure that particular categories in the population (e.g. gender or ethnicity) are represented in the sample in the same proportions as in the population, and if it is possible to classify all members of the population into the categories of such a variable, then the population can be stratified according to these categories. Simple random or systematic sampling can then be used in each stratum. It is possible to stratify on more than one characteristic. For example, having established categories of males and females, strata for ethnicity could be established within each one, thus ensuring that the sample proportions are the same as those in the population on these two variables. On their own, the other two methods cannot guarantee this.

There is a variation of stratified sampling that is also useful under certain conditions. If there is a big variation in the size of the strata, using the same sampling ratio in each one may produce very small numbers in some strata. For example, the variables of ethnicity and religious affiliation can have relatively small categories in some populations. It is possible to use different sampling ratios in each stratum to compensate for this, even to the point of producing approximately equal numbers from all strata. However, if this method is adopted, the strata must be kept separate throughout the analysis. The reason for this is that they constitute separate samples each giving its members different chances of being selected, higher in the small strata and lower in the large ones. Combining them infringes the key principle of probability sampling.

There are two other choices to be made in sampling. The first is whether to select only one population element at a time, or whether to select them in clusters (*cluster sampling*). The second is whether the sample will be drawn in one stage or in more than one (*multi-stage sampling*). It is beyond the scope of the present discussion to go into these variations in detail. Separately, or perhaps together, they allow for creative sampling designs. Figure 6.2 reviews the combinations of these sampling techniques for both probability and non-probability sampling. What we do need to note is that various methods of sampling, and their combinations, have implications for the kind of inferential analysis that is appropriate. This can become very complex; only basic differences will be discussed here.[5]

Not only can software packages not distinguish whether data were obtained from a population, a probability sample or a non-probability sample, in a situation where a probability sample is used, they cannot possibly know anything about the method of sampling used. They appear to assume that simple random procedures were used. This assumption is probably satisfactory if there are minimal risks in being wrong in making estimates of population parameters. However, if there are serious risks, it would be wise to do the inferential analysis by hand when other sampling techniques, or combinations of them, have been

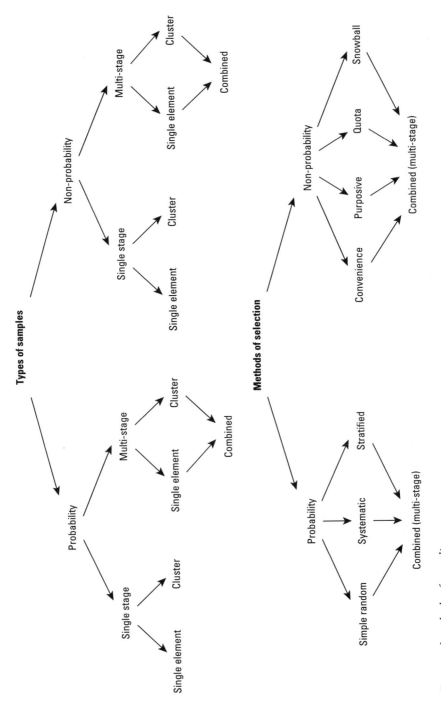

Figure 6.2   *Types and methods of sampling*

used. Just because the software presents inferential analysis, or can be requested to do so, makes it very easy to use inferential analysis when it is inappropriate. The researcher has to know when this should and should not be used; the software cannot tell you.

Parametric and Non-Parametric Tests

Before we proceed to discuss specific inferential procedures, there is a common distinction between types of procedure that need to be reviewed. As for all methods of analysis, the level of measurement used for the variables being analyzed determines which inferential procedures are appropriate. The classification that I have been using, nominal and ordinal (categorical variables) and interval and ratio (metric variables), is still relevant. However, there is another classification that has some relationship to these, namely, parametric and non-parametric. Here we are concerned with the characteristics of the data rather than the level of measurement, although the two are related.

Some tests of significance can only be used when the distribution on a variable in a population approximates a normal distribution. Other tests, such as those used to compare samples from different populations, may require that the variables under consideration have approximately the same variance (the same spread in their distributions) in both populations. Tests with these requirements are referred to as *parametric tests*. When we cannot assume that the population from which our sample was drawn meets these requirements, other types of tests have to be used, namely, *non-parametric tests* or *distribution-free tests*.

Whether or not a variable can meet these requirements will depend to some extent on its level of measurement, that is, on how the observations were transformed into numbers. Metric variables have the possibility of meeting these requirements, although whether they do will depend on the characteristics of the population. For example, we know that the population from which the Resident sample was drawn is approximately normally distributed in terms of Age, but we know that this is not the case in the Student population. The Age distribution in the latter population is badly skewed because that is the nature of this population. When Age is the variable under consideration, a parametric test could be used with the Resident sample but not with the Student sample. Of course, if the analysis involves an association with another variable, its distribution in the population also has to be considered. When variables are categorical, non-parametric tests must be used. We cannot even think about a distribution across a set of nominal-level categories, and it would be inappropriate to do so with ordinal-level categories. Siegel (1956) brought together an array of non-parametric tests that has made the analysis of distribution-free data both possible and legitimate. While there are ways of transforming the distributions of metric variables that do not meet the normality assumption, creating dummy variables from categorical data also avoids the problem of meeting the parametric assumptions and allows for the use of parametric methods, particularly regression analysis.

A major problem in deciding whether parametric assumptions have been satisfied is that it is the population characteristics, not those of the sample, which are relevant. If this information about the population is not available, our only alternative is to examine the characteristics of the sample and hope that it is reasonably representative.

Inference in Univariate Descriptive Analysis

When data from a single variable, such as age, are obtained from a probability sample, and the population value is required, inferential analysis must be used. This involves estimating the population parameter by determining a range of possible values around the sample statistic within which it is expected to fall, and then estimating the likelihood that it falls within that range. For example, to establish the mean age of a population from a sample mean of, say, 49 years, we would specify a margin of error, say plus or minus 3 years. The size of this margin has to be calculated for that particular sample. This means that we would expect the population mean to lie between 46 and 52 years. However, we cannot be absolutely certain about this. We also need to specify how likely this is to be the case. This is normally stated as a 95 per cent level of confidence, although 99 per cent and 99.9 per cent levels are also used. In other words, we say that we are 95 per cent confident that the population mean lies between these two values. This is the only way that we can estimate a population parameter from a sample statistic.

The only circumstance under which we could say that the sample and population means are the same would be if we had a perfectly representative sample. Even using the most appropriate probability procedures, we may have selected a very biased sample, in which case our sample value may lie outside the estimated range. Our value may be among the 5 per cent (or 1 per cent or 0.1 per cent) about which we cannot be confident. By saying that we are 95 per cent confident that is does not lie outside the range, we are still allowing for a 5 per cent possibility that it does.

There are two key concepts in this analysis, confidence level and confidence interval. *Confidence level*, or degree of confidence, refers to the level of probability that we wish to set, say, 95 per cent, also referred to as the 0.05 *significance level*.[6] It indicates how confident we are, or need to be, about our population estimate. *Confidence interval* refers to the range of values around the sample value within which we expect the population value to lie. The two extremes of this range are known as *confidence limits*.

Now you may be wondering why we do not set the confidence level as high as possible, thus reducing the chance of being wrong. Well, this is always the aim, but there is a price to pay. The higher you set the level of confidence, the wider will be the confidence interval, and vice versa. It is possible to be very confident about the population estimate but it may not be very precise. Similarly, it is possible to make the confidence interval very narrow but this will reduce the level of confidence. The only way that a confidence level can be high and the confidence interval narrow is to use big samples. In other words, not only are the confidence level and confidence interval inversely related, they are both affected by the size of the sample. In addition, they are affected by the method of sampling used.

We can now turn to the methods used to calculate confidence intervals for both categorical and metric data, with either percentages or proportions for the former and means for the latter.

Categorical Variables

So far, we have been using means and standard deviations of sample data to illustrate the principles behind inferential analysis. We will come to the methods for calculating the confidence intervals of means shortly. First, we need to discuss the calculations that can be used with categorical data. The most common sample statistic in this case is a percentage, although to do the calculations this needs to be expressed as a proportion. You will recall from Chapter 3 that moving between a percentage and a proportion is just a matter of moving the decimal place; for example, 65 per cent is the same as a proportion of 0.65.

To calculate the confidence interval around a proportion, we need to first estimate the *standard error of the proportion*, the equivalent of the standard error of the mean. This is given by

$$\text{estimated standard error of the proportion } (se_p) = \sqrt{\frac{p\,(1-p)}{n}} \qquad (6.1)$$

where p is the sample proportion and n the sample size. The upper and lower limits of the confidence interval (CI) can then be calculated:

$$CI = p \pm (z \times se_p) \qquad (6.2)$$

In this equation, z is determined by the confidence level that is selected: 1.96 for 95 per cent, 2.58 for 99 per cent and 3.29 for 99.9 per cent. These figures can be thought of as the standard deviation that corresponds to a particular area under the bell-curve (see Figure 3.11). This means that we have to go 1.96 standard deviations on either side of the proportion in order to include 95 per cent of the proportions of all possible samples. This leaves 2.5 per cent under each tail of the curve. Similarly, we have to go 2.58 standard deviations to include 99 per cent and leave 0.5 per cent under each tail, and 3.29 standard deviations to include 99.9 per cent and leave 0.05 per cent under each tail. These figures can be checked by consulting the table of z values (see Table 2 in Appendix D).

Take the example of the percentage of respondents who are aged 65 and over in the Resident sample (19.7 per cent; see Table 3.11). If we want to estimate their percentage in the population, we need to calculate the confidence interval around the sample percentage/proportion. Let us set the confidence level at 95 per cent. Then

$$se_p = \sqrt{\frac{p(1-p)}{n}} = \sqrt{\frac{0.197(1-0.197)}{401}} = \sqrt{\frac{0.1582}{401}} = 0.020$$

and our confidence interval is

$$p \pm (z \times se_p) = 0.197 \pm (1.96 \times 0.020) = 0.197 \pm 0.039$$

Hence, we can be 95 per cent confident that the population proportion lies between 0.158 and 0.236, or between 15.8 per cent and 23.6 per cent. The confidence limits are 3.9 per cent on either side of the sample percentage (19.7), making a confidence interval of 7.8 per cent.

But what about other parameters? Let us try two others, the proportion of females (0.501; Table 3.10) and the proportion who have children (0.652; Table 3.7). For the proportion of females, we get

$$se_p = \sqrt{\frac{p(1-p)}{n}} = \sqrt{\frac{0.501(1-0.501)}{399}} = \sqrt{\frac{0.2500}{399}} = 0.025$$

with confidence interval

$$p \pm (z \times se_p) = 0.501 \pm (1.96 \times 0.025) = 0.501 \pm 0.049$$

Therefore, the confidence interval is between 0.452 and 0.550, or between 45.2 per cent and 55.0 per cent. Here, the confidence limits are 4.9 per cent on either side of the sample percentage (50.1), giving a confidence interval of 9.8 per cent.

For the proportion who have children, we get

$$se_p = \sqrt{\frac{p(1-p)}{n}} = \sqrt{\frac{0.652(1-0652)}{402}} = \sqrt{\frac{0.2270}{402}} = 0.0238$$

and confidence interval

$$p \pm (z \times se_p) = 0.652 \pm (1.96 \times 0.0238) = 0.652 \pm 0.0466$$

This means that the confidence interval is 9.3 per cent and the confidence limits are 60.5 per cent and 69.8 per cent.

If we set the confidence level at 99.9 per cent, the confidence interval will increase. For example, for the proportion who are 65 and over, the value of se_p remains the same but the confidence interval is wider because the z value is higher: we get

$$CI = p \pm (z \times se_p) = 0.197 \pm (3.29 \times 0.020) = 0.197 \pm 0.065$$

which produces confidence limits of 13.2 per cent and 26.2 per cent. This confidence interval (13.0 per cent) is nearly twice as wide as for the 95 per cent confidence level, thus illustrating that setting the confidence level higher leads to a wider confidence interval. You may like to calculate the confidence intervals for females and those with children with the confidence level set at 99.9 per cent, and all three examples at 99 per cent.

If the sample was smaller, say only half the size, the confidence intervals would all be wider, and vice versa. The reason for this is that the sample size changes the divisor in the equation for the standard error. You could try calculating them. It is obvious that a table could be constructed for this sample covering the confidence intervals for a full range of percentages, for each confidence level. How about trying this for intervals of 10 per cent.

Metric Variables

The procedure for estimating population means from sample means is very similar to the one for proportions and percentages. However, estimating the *standard error of the mean* (the standard deviation of the mean of all sample means) is a simpler calculation:

$$\text{estimated standard error of the mean } se_m = \frac{s}{\sqrt{n}} \qquad (6.3)$$

where s is the sample standard deviation. Then the confidence interval is

$$CI = \bar{x} \pm (z \times se_m). \qquad (6.4)$$

When the population is small and the sample is a major fraction of the population, an adjustment needs to be made to the estimated standard error of the mean. It is multiplied by the square root of the population size minus the sample size, divided by the population size: $\sqrt{(N - n)/N}$. This is called the finite population correction factor.

To estimate the mean Age of the population from which the Resident sample was drawn ($\bar{x} = 46.06$; $s = 17.97$), at a 95 per cent confidence level, we would first have to calculate the estimated standard error of the mean:

$$se_m = \frac{s}{\sqrt{n}} = \frac{17.97}{\sqrt{401}} = \frac{17.97}{20.025} = 0.897$$

Then

$$CI = \bar{x} \pm (z \times se_m) = 46.06 \pm (1.96 \times 0.897) = 46.06 \pm 1.76$$

Hence, we estimate that the population mean lies between 44.30 and 47.82. If we set the confidence level at 99.9 per cent, the confidence interval would be between 43.12 and 49.00. You can check this by substituting 3.29 for 1.96 in the above equation, and 2.58 if you want the confidence interval at the 99 per cent level.

To illustrate how the confidence level and sample size affect the size of the confidence interval, Table 6.2 reports the intervals for the three major levels of confidence with samples ranging from 100 to 2000. The mean Age (46.06) and standard deviation (17.97) are assumed to remain the same in all samples. These figures clearly illustrate that the more confident you want to be in your estimate of a population mean, the less precise will be the estimate, and the larger the sample size the more precise the estimate. The major gains from increasing the sample size occur up to about 400, and beyond 1000 increases produce very limited gains. Figure 6.3 plots the size of the confidence interval for each sample size, using all three confidence levels. It must be noted that this analysis is illustrative only. Different sample characteristics with different distributions (standard deviations) will produce different patterns.

Table 6.2 *Variations in confidence intervals of mean Age by confidence level and sample size (Residents)*

Sample size	95% (0.05)	99% (0.01)	99.9% (0.001)
100	7.04	9.26	11.82
200	4.98	6.55	8.36
300	4.07	5.34	6.83
400	3.52	4.63	5.91
500	3.15	4.14	5.29
600	2.88	3.78	4.83
700	2.66	3.50	4.47
800	2.49	3.27	4.18
900	2.35	3.09	3.94
1000	2.23	2.93	3.74
1100	2.12	2.79	3.57
1200	2.03	2.67	3.41
1300	1.95	2.57	3.28
1400	1.88	2.47	3.16
1500	1.82	2.39	3.05
1600	1.76	2.31	2.96
1700	1.71	2.24	2.87
1800	1.66	2.18	2.79
1900	1.62	2.12	2.71
2000	1.57	2.07	2.64

If the sample size is 40 or less, it is more appropriate to use values of the *t* statistic (see Table 3 in Appendix D) rather than *z* values for the confidence level. Because we normally have to use the sample standard deviation as an estimate of the standard error of the mean, and because this estimate becomes less reliable with small samples, *t* values produce more reliable but more conservative confidence intervals. For example, whereas the *z* value for a 95 per cent confidence level is 1.96, the *t* value gradually increases as the sample size

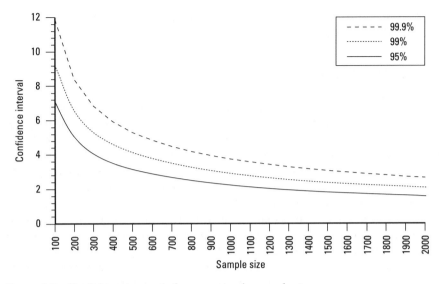

Figure 6.3   *Confidence intervals for mean Age by sample size*
(Resident sample)

falls below 40. It happens to be 2.04 for samples of size 30, 2.09 for 20, 2.23 for 10 and 2.57 for 5. These larger values lead to wider confidence intervals and, hence, less precise estimates. Compared with behavioural scientists, social researchers are unlikely to use samples as small as this. Hence, z values will normally be used to calculate confidence intervals around sample means.

Establishing confidence intervals is the only inferential procedure that we need to be concerned with in univariate descriptive analysis. It is interesting to note that few researchers use this procedure and seem to assume that population data are the same as sample data. To recapitulate, if you are working with a population, if the method of sampling is not a probability procedure, or if the response rate is low, you should not concern yourself with such estimates. In the first situation, it is not necessary. In the other two, all you can talk about legitimately is your sample data – it is not possible to generalize statistically beyond it.

Inference in Bivariate Descriptive Analysis

When analysis is concerned with relationships between two variables, different inferential procedures are required. These are commonly referred to as tests of significance, a much misunderstood and misused procedure.

A *test of significance* tells us whether the relationship that we have found in a sample could also be expected to exist in the population from which the sample was drawn. Just as in the case of estimating population characteristics from probability samples, it is necessary to set a confidence level. However, as we shall see, setting the level in this case is more complex than for univariate descriptive analysis.

Testing Statistical Hypotheses

Two types of hypotheses are used in social research, theoretical hypotheses and statistical hypotheses. *Statistical hypotheses* deal only with the specific problem of estimating whether a relationship found in a probability sample also exists in the population. They are an essential part of testing for significance. However, as not all social research uses probability samples, and hypotheses are frequently used in all kinds of research, another type of hypothesis is also used.

The more important form of hypothesis testing is concerned with the implications of a theory that offers an explanation, that purports to answer a 'why' research question (see Blaikie, 2000, Chapter 3). A *theoretical hypothesis* is a tentative answer to a 'why' question. This type of hypothesis, which should preferably be derived from some theory, does not have strict statistical rules for its testing. It is necessary to make a judgement, on the basis of the evidence, as to how well the data match the form of the proposition in the hypothesis. Therefore, while such hypotheses may state a relationship between two concepts, which become variables in research, the method for testing theoretical hypotheses should not be confused with that used for statistical hypotheses. All that the testing of a statistical hypothesis contributes is to establish whether or not what was found in a probability sample can also be expected to exist in the population and, if so, how confident we can be about this.

If we do use a probability sample in our research, and we manage to establish that an association can be expected to exist in the population, we still have to decide whether this allows us to reject or corroborate our theoretical hypothesis. This will be based on a judgement about the patterns and strengths of associations or influences and not on what the level of significance might be. Therefore, when we work with probability samples, and we are trying to answer a 'why' research question, we will need to work with both types of hypotheses.

For example, if a reasonably strong association has been established between Gender and Environmental Worldview, and if we want to explain why such a relationship exists, we could develop a theory that will propose an answer. The theory might suggest that in so far as women see themselves as the primary care-givers in their families and communities, they will be concerned about the effects of environmental problems on the health of people. Their level of environmental responsibility will be high and will be localized. On the other hand, men, as well as women who do not see their primary role as care-giver, are likely to have a lower level of concern and, if their concern is high, it will be directed towards global or regional rather than local problems. Of course, such a theory requires much greater elaboration than is possible here. The testing of the implications of this theory requires a range of data but fairly simple data analysis. If the study is based on a population, the decision as to whether the theory should be rejected will depend on the strength of the associations between Gender and the nature and type of environmental concern. Only if the data come from a probability sample (with a very high response rate) will inferential analysis be required, in which case its only role will be to estimate whether these associations are likely to be present in the population. As we shall see, subject to the consideration of sample size, strong associations are usually significant, that is, they are likely to be present in the population, while weak associations may not be significant. The bigger the sample, the more likely weak associations will be significant.

Null and Alternative Hypotheses

In order to establish whether a relationship found in a sample can also be expected to exist in the population, two forms of statistical hypotheses are used, a null hypothesis and alternative hypotheses. A *null hypothesis* states that the relationship does not exist in the population. It is usually denoted as H_0. As we are likely to be more interested in establishing whether some form of relationship exists, we normally try to reject the null hypothesis. An *alternative hypothesis* states that a relationship does exist, usually the one that we expect is most likely to be the case.[7] It can be stated in three different ways. First, it may simply state that a relationship *does* exist, but without specifying its form, that is, whether it is positive or negative. This is a non-directional alternative hypothesis. Second, it may state a positive relationship, that is, as values on one variable increase the values on the other variable also increase. Third, it may state a negative or inverse relationship, that is, as the values on one variable increase the values on the other decrease. Alternative hypotheses are usually designated as H_A if only one alternative is proposed, or as H_1, H_2, etc. if there is more than one. For example, one alternative hypothesis might propose a positive relationship and another a negative relationship.

While a non-directional alternative hypothesis can be used if we are unsure what form a relationship might take in the population, if we are dealing with linear relationships it is just as easy to propose two alternative hypotheses, one for each direction. In practice, however, we would examine the form of the relationship in the sample and propose that form as our alternative. To repeat once again, what we want to know in this type of analysis is whether what we have found in the sample also exists in the population.

Let us examine an example of a null and an alternative hypothesis. If our sample data shows that there is a positive association between EWV and Willingness to Act to protect the environment, and if we are working with a probability sample, we need to establish whether the nature of the association found in the sample could be expected in the population. To do this, we first establish the null form of the statistical hypothesis.

H_0: There is no association between EWV and Willingness to Act.

If we are uncertain about the form of the relationship in the population, we could state the alternative hypothesis in a non-directional form. It would read:

H_A: There is an association between EWV and Willingness to Act.

We could also state two alternative hypotheses to cover the two possible directions of the relationship, positive and negative.

H_1: There is a positive association between EWV and Willingness to Act. (EWV varies directly with Willingness to Act.)

H_2: There is a negative association between EWV and Willingness to Act. (EWV varies inversely with Willingness to Act.)

However, on the basis of what we have found in our sample, we can be confident in proposing only one alternative hypothesis in a directional form.

H_A: There is a positive linear association between EWV and Willingness to Act.

To state the alternative hypothesis as both positive and linear is being very precise. If this is the form of the association in the sample, we have good grounds for doing this. In fact, it makes no sense to do anything else, and there is nothing else we *could* test.

Having determined what the hypotheses are to be, the task is now to decide which one is correct. Is there or is there not an association in the population? And if there is, is it in the form that we have hypothesized? As both hypotheses cannot be true, we have to decide which one will not be rejected; one of them has to be rejected in favour of the other. The aim is to reject the null hypothesis in favour of the alternative, to establish whether there is likely to be an association rather than no association. This is what a test of significance is designed to help us to do.

Type I and Type II Errors

As with the establishment of confidence intervals, we also have to set a confidence level to make a decision about whether the null hypothesis can be rejected. We have to decide how confident we want to be in rejecting the null hypothesis. However, there is a dilemma in setting this level, usually referred to as making either a type I error or a type II error (see Table 6.3). A *type I error* involves rejecting the null hypothesis when it is actually true, which means claiming that an association exists in the population when it does not; a *type II error* involves not rejecting the null hypothesis when it is actually false, which means claiming that an association does not exist when it does. The latter is more common than the former. If we set the level of confidence at 95 per cent, we may mistakenly reject the null hypothesis 5 per cent of the time. If we do not want to make this mistake, we should set the level as high as possible, say 99.9 per cent, thus running only a 0.1 per cent risk. The problem is that the higher we set the level, the greater is the risk of a type II error. Conversely, the lower we set the level, the greater is the possibility of committing a type I error and the lower the possibility of committing a type II error. It seems like a no-win situation.

For example, a study conducted with a rather small random sample may have shown that a new but expensive method of teaching is effective in raising the

Table 6.3 *Type I and Type II Errors*

	Decision	
The null hypothesis	Reject	Accept
Is really true	Incorrect rejection **Type I error**	Correct failure to reject
Is really false	Correct rejection	Incorrect failure to reject **Type II error**

performance of all students, and particularly the weaker ones. It is possible that this sample does not represent the population and may have produced very 'deviant' results. This could mean that if the teaching method were introduced universally in schools it might produce little or no improvement. Clearly, there is a need for caution in claiming that it will make big improvements. Rejecting the null hypothesis when it is true could lead to a great deal of unnecessary expense in implementing such a teaching method.

The convention in the social sciences is to set the level at 95 per cent, unless there is an important reason for wanting to avoid rejecting the null hypothesis when it is true. Again, just a gentle reminder about what we are trying to do here. We know from probability theory that it is possible that our sample is highly unrepresentative of the population from which it was drawn. It may be one of those 'deviant' samples that produces results that are out at the tails of the normal curve produced by the distribution of results from all possible samples. Therefore, we have to protect ourselves from claiming something on the basis of our sample that is not the case in the population. We have to strike a balance between committing a type I error and a type II error. We can only *estimate* what exists in the population, and we can only do this by setting a level of confidence with which we make our statements about the population. There is no other way.

One-tailed and Two-tailed Tests

The form in which an alternative hypothesis is stated, that is, as either directional or non-directional, has a bearing on how we deal with confidence levels. When the alternative hypothesis is non-directional, it has to be rejected in favour of the alternative on the possibility that its values lie in either extreme of the sampling distribution. This means that if the confidence level was set at 95 per cent, there would be a 2.5 per cent possibility that the sample's values lie under the tail at the lower end of the distribution of all possible sample values and another 2.5 per cent possibility that they lie at the higher end of the distribution. In other words, we are trying to reject the possibility that our sample's values lie at either extreme. However, if a direction is specified in the alternative hypothesis, then we are trying to reject the possibility that our sample's values lie at only one extreme of the distribution of all possible sample values. In this case, all 5 per cent of our lack of confidence is at one extreme of the distribution.

Putting all the eggs of our uncertainty at only one extreme of the sampling distribution basket makes it easier to reject the null hypothesis. As our area of uncertainty lies on only one side of the sampling distribution, the 5 per cent region of uncertainty at one extreme of a one-tailed test is larger than the 2.5 per cent region at the same extreme, as is the case with a non-directional hypothesis. This is why it is easier to reject the null hypothesis in favour of a directional rather than a non-directional alternative hypothesis.

The convention is to describe the testing of a non-directional alternative hypothesis as being *two-tailed* or two-sided, and a directional alternative as being *one-tailed* or one-sided. This simply refers to the fact that the region of uncertainty is in both tails of the distribution for non-directional alternative hypotheses and in only one tail for directional hypotheses. As the testing of statistical hypotheses usually requires us to consult a table of critical values, we need to be clear in reading such tables as to whether we need a one-tailed or two-tailed test.

The Process of Testing Statistical Hypotheses

With the discussion of the technical features of hypothesis testing behind us, it is now possible to examine the five basic steps that are commonly followed in testing a statistical hypothesis.

1. *State the null and alternative hypotheses.* The form of the alternative hypothesis (or hypotheses) will determine whether the test needs to be one-tailed or two-tailed.
2. *Select the level of significance* with type I and type II errors in mind: normally 0.05, but 0.01 or 0.001 are also possible.
3. *Identify the appropriate test statistic,* according to the level of measurement and the type of analysis. The choice is usually between the chi-square, z-score, t statistic or F statistic (more on this soon).
4. *Compute the value of the test statistic* using the appropriate procedure.
5. *Make a decision* as to whether to reject or not reject the null hypothesis.

These steps will be elaborated shortly.

Some statisticians have argued that these or similar steps should be followed rigidly (see, for example, Agresti and Finlay, 1997: 159; Berenson and Levine, 1999: 422, 425, 465; Fielding and Gilbert, 2000: 249–56; Freund and Perles, 1999: 324–39; Lind et al., 2000: 267–71; Salkind, 2000: 185–6). Some even argue that decisions about the first three steps should be made before the research is commenced and should determine the size and nature of the sample.

The reason for such advice is to counter a rather common practice of collecting data on many variables and then dredging the data for significant relationships. These are then used to determine what is worth discussing. This mindless and mechanical approach to research is certainly to be rejected. In my view, both extremes are undesirable. Setting probability levels and deciding on the appropriate test before the data are collected, and certainly before the analysis is conducted, can be regarded as adding a degree of objectivity to the research and as avoiding *post hoc* interpretations. However, if our ultimate aim is to test theoretical hypotheses, and if we need to use statistical hypotheses as stepping-stones to this destination, then we should be more interested in how confident we can be in using our sample data to talk about our population. The ultimate testing of theoretical hypotheses will follow this. While we need to make allowances for the possible impact of committing either type I or type II errors, our judgement about theoretical hypotheses can only be assisted by being as confident as possible about the population parameters of interest. Setting a rigid level of confidence in advance may not serve this purpose. It is better to examine the sample characteristics and patterns relevant to our research questions, and to answer the questions in the light of all available information, including how confident we can be in making inferences from our sample to the population.

Testing Hypotheses Under Different Conditions

Textbooks on statistics generally use a conventional array of concepts to refer to the variety of conditions under which tests of significance can be applied (see, for example, Siegel, 1956; Siegel and Castellan, 1988). They include distinguishing between 'one-sample cases', 'two-sample cases' and '*k*-sample cases' (the latter meaning many samples). When two or more samples are involved, they are also referred to as 'dependent', 'matched' or 'related' samples' and 'independent or 'unrelated' samples. I do not intend to follow these conventions. First, most of them apply to experimental designs that are rare in social research. Second, I have always found them to be extremely confusing, coming as they do from the discipline of statistics. For example, the concepts of 'sample' and 'population' are used in highly technical ways, that are different from the definitions on pages 160–1, and do not relate well to the practice of social research. However, as they are commonly used, including in software packages such as SPSS, I shall try to explain them and show how they are related to the concepts I will be using.

There are two dimensions to the traditional classification. The first refers to the nature of the samples and the second to the number of samples involved. *Independent samples* are drawn from different populations, although this can also mean from different groups or categories in the same population. An example of samples from different populations would be our Student and Resident samples, and of different groups or categories would be males and females in the Resident sample. Even although these two latter categories come from one sample drawn from one population, inferential analysis tests to see whether males and females come from different populations. I translate this to mean different categories in the same population. *Dependent samples* can be of two kinds. They can be separate samples in which the members of one are matched against the members of the other, perhaps to form an experimental and a control group. This is usually done in pairs in terms of the characteristics that need to be controlled in an experiment. The second kind of dependent sample refers to experimental designs in which data from one sample are collected at two points in time, usually before and after some treatment or intervention. Therefore, independence and dependence can relate to either one or more samples, or to one or more populations. Don't be surprised if confusion is beginning to set in!

The situation is further complicated when the number of samples is introduced. *One-sample tests* are used to establish whether the value for a particular variable in a sample is different from some known or assumed population value. This is sometimes stated in terms of whether or not the sample comes from a population with a particular mean. *Two-sample tests* are used to establish either whether the values for the same variable measured in two samples are different in the populations from which they were drawn, or whether, in terms of the same variable, two categories of the same sample could have been drawn from different 'populations'. The former can be illustrated in terms of the mean Age in the Student and Resident samples, and the latter in terms of the mean Age of males and females, say, in the Resident sample. The latter seems to assume that in drawing our sample of Residents we were also drawing a sample of males from males in the population and a sample of females from females in the population. This usage requires us to think about two 'populations' (males and females) existing within a population (Residents).

To avoid the confusion that this schema can create, my emphasis will be on 'variables' and 'categories' within a variable. Translated, our concerns will be with differences between the values of a variable:

- for two categories within the same sample (e.g. the EWV of male and female Residents);
- in different samples (e.g. EWV of Students and Residents); or
- in the same categories in different samples (e.g. EWV of male Students and male Residents).

In the first case, the task is to establish whether differences between categories within a sample can be expected to exist within a population. In the second and third cases, it is to establish whether differences between two samples also exist between the two populations. I shall refer to the first as *within-sample comparisons* and the second as *between-sample comparisons*.[8]

So far I have been referring to comparisons between categories and samples. This is because much of the testing is for differences between means. It is also possible to test for associations between two variables, but these are confined to within-sample situations. When dealing with categorical data, when at least one variable is dichotomized, such as gender, testing for an association is analogous to comparing the means of two categories (conventionally referred to as 'two independent samples'). If both variables have more than two categories, testing for an association is analogous to comparing means across more than two categories (conventionally referred to as '*k* independent samples'). When the data are in the form of metric measurement, the analogy with means analysis disappears. In this case, the focus is on testing the significance of correlation coefficients in bivariate analysis and, in multivariate analysis, on coefficients such as *beta* in methods such as multiple regression.

I have chosen not to discuss two procedures that appear in many textbooks on statistics. The first is the 'one-sample' or 'single-sample' convention used to establish whether a particular sample characteristic differs significantly from a known population parameter or reference value. Some writers give the impression that if the sample is not based on probability procedures, we can still establish whether the sample value for some variable is different from 'the general population' (see, for example, Cramer, 1994: 10–11; Balnaves and Caputi, 2001: 180–1). Others express this as finding out whether a particular random sample could have come from some specified population with a particular distribution (Siegel, 1956: 35; Siegel and Castellan, 1988: Chapter 4). This is sometimes expressed as a test for 'goodness of fit'. For example, the mean age of a population may be 37 years and you want to know whether the mean age of your sample, which is 34 years, is significantly different from the population mean. However, there seems to be little point in trying to establish whether the null or an alternative hypothesis is correct with a single variable, or to predict what a population value will be on some variable. If the sample was drawn by probability procedures, then calculating a confidence interval will answer the question. If you know the population mean, and it falls outside the sample confidence limits, then it is likely to be different from the sample mean (at whatever confidence level you have set). All this means is that you do not have a representative sample. Of course, if you do not know the population mean, you can only estimate what it might be, given a certain confidence level.

What seems to be common about the examples used to illustrate 'one-sample' testing is that the sample was *not* drawn by probability procedures. Sometimes the researcher wants to know whether a non-probability sample is representative, although the problem is not usually stated this way. Alternatively, it may be the accuracy of the population value that is being challenged; perhaps a claim by some manufacturer about how long a product can last. In either case, if a non-probability sample is used, neither of these procedures is legitimate.

The second procedure that I will not be discussing concerns the basic element in experimental designs, or before and after studies, in which one variable is measured with one sample at different times or under two different conditions. In this situation, it is possible to compare the two scores for each individual and the mean scores of all members of the sample. The testing procedure is usually referred to as a 'one-sample' test of means, as a 'dependent-sample' test or as a 'paired-sample' test. A variation on this is where different samples are used at different times or under different conditions. The latter testing procedure is referred to as a 'two-sample' test, 'independent-samples' test or 'unpaired-samples' test. These tests are also used when two groups within a sample are compared on some variable, such as men and women, and when two different samples are compared. It is on these latter uses that I shall concentrate.[9]

Some Critical Issues

Before we proceed to discuss the methods that are used to make a decision between a null and an alternative hypothesis, there are a number of points that need to be noted. First, it is sometimes argued that significant relationships based on large samples should be treated with suspicion or at least some caution. The impression is given that there is something wrong with being able to achieve a desired level of significance simply by increasing the size of the sample. To me this seems to be muddle-headed. Of course there is a connection between sample size and the ability to estimate population parameters, or to be confident about a particular relationship in a probability sample. We can be more confident about our results from large samples and we have to be less confident, and therefore more cautious, when small samples are used. Working with large samples does not mean that you may unfairly 'prove' your hypothesis. They just give you more confidence in estimating the population parameters. What we need to focus on in the analysis of association and influence is the strength of the associations, provided they are significant, because these will be relevant to the testing of our theoretical hypotheses. Significant but weak relationships produced by large samples may not be very useful and may mean that the theoretical hypotheses must be rejected.

Second, the language used in many textbooks on statistics to refer to the testing for significance is couched around the notion of 'chance'. No doubt this is derived from the way statisticians talk about probability theory, particularly when they use examples about the likelihood (or chance) of tossed coins coming down heads. A perfectly balanced coin, tossed many times, is likely to come down heads 50 per cent of the time. This is sometimes described as a law of probability or chance. Hence, what we want to know is whether a characteristic of our sample (e.g. mean age), or a relationship between two variables, could just have occurred by chance. Now, the correct interpretation of such a statement is whether these results could have come from a probability sample which is very unrepresentative, that is, the values the sample produces lie at the extremes of the distribution of values for all possible samples. Chance is related to the way random selection procedures operate.

Somehow this principle gets lost in rather confusing language. I will cite just two examples from textbooks that I happen to have at hand. The first comes from Andrew Siegel (1994: 337).[10] He states:

> Hypothesis testing uses data to decide between two possibilities (called *hypotheses*). It can tell you whether the results you're witnessing are just coincidence (and could reasonably be due to chance) or are likely to be real.

The first sentence confuses statistical and theoretical hypotheses; we use data to test theoretical hypotheses, not to choose between the null and alternative hypotheses. The latter is decided by tests of significance. Then the statement goes on to contrast what is 'real' with what might be just a 'coincidence', a chance happening. This conveys the impression that some things happen because they are supposed to happen that way and other things happen for no good reason, that is, by chance. This is not what we are concerned with when we are testing statistical hypotheses. We are concerned with whether we might have drawn a 'dud' sample and what the consequences might be if we place too much reliance on it.

A more satisfactory statement comes from Siegel and Castellan (1998: 2), although even here what is meant by 'chance' is very vague.

A common problem for statistical inference is to determine, in terms of a probability, whether observed differences between two samples signify that the populations sampled are themselves really different. Now, even if we collect two groups of scores by taking random samples from the same population, we are likely to find that the scores differ to some extent. Differences may occur simply because of the operation of chance. How can we determine in any given case whether the observed differences between two samples are due merely to chance or are caused by other factors? The procedures of statistical inference enable us to determine whether the observed differences are within the range which easily could have occurred by chance or not.

Unfortunately, it is not clear how 'chance' is operating here. It is the fickleness of random sampling procedures that is the bogey. At the same time, the impression is given that 'other factors' are the problem when it is these factors that should be the focus of our attention. In other words, the fixation on 'chance' deflects attention from the factors that *do* produce the difference. Perhaps this is why tests of significance generally receive more attention than, say, measures of association.

Another example goes in a different direction, and comes from Salkind (2000). While Salkind's book purports to help people who are afraid of statistics, it warns the reader that no concept creates 'more confusion for the beginning statistics student than the concept of statistical significance' (2000: 171). The discussion of significance uses the argument that as 'our world is not a perfect one, we must allow for some leeway in how confident we are that only those factors we identify could cause any difference between groups'. While we may be pretty sure we know what the factors are, we 'cannot be absolutely, 100%, positively, unequivocally, indisputably (get the picture?) sure. There's always a chance, no matter how small, that you are wrong' (2000: 172). Other factors may be at work.

> So what do you do? In most scientific endeavours that involve testing hypotheses … there is bound to be a certain amount of error that cannot be controlled – this is the chance factor. … The level of chance or risk that you are willing to take is expressed as a significance level, a term that unnecessarily strikes fear in the hearts of even strong men and women. (Salkind, 2000: 173)

Unfortunately, the presence of other factors that may have an influence, or errors that cannot be controlled, have nothing to do with tests of significance. Only sampling error does. However, 'other factors' and 'errors' are relevant when we are trying to establish strength of association or level of influence, that is, when we are trying to explain or predict an outcome variable, and when we are testing a theoretical hypothesis. But tests of significance cannot tell you if you have overlooked 'other factors' or if there are errors in your measurements. They can only help you to generalize from your (probability) sample to the population, and they cannot help you to test a theoretical hypothesis.

The third issue is an extension of the previous two, particularly the confusion over the use of 'sample' and 'population'. One of the procedures we shall discuss shortly concerns establishing whether difference in the means on the same variable in two different samples could be expected to exist in the populations.

Sometimes this idea is completely distorted and is used to establish whether the difference in the means for two categories in a population could have occurred by chance. Let me illustrate from Siegel (1994: 372–5). An example is used in which the mean salaries of 15 women and 22 men in a department within a company are compared to see if the difference in the means 'is within the usual random variation or not' (1994: 373). Apparently the company is being sued for gender discrimination. It turns out that the mean annual salary for women in the department is \$24,467 and for men is \$33,095, a difference of \$8,628. The author then asks 'whether such a large difference as found here could reasonably be the result of a *random* allocation of salaries to men and women, or if there is a need for some other explanation for the apparent inequity' (1994: 373). The analysis conducted suggests that this difference is significant at the 0.001 level. Therefore, as the allocation of salaries between men and women is not random, the author concludes that there must be some other explanation.

> So what might cause the salary difference? One explanation is that management, in out-dated, selfish, and illegal ways, has deliberately decided to pay people less if they are women than if they are men, looking only at the person's gender. However, it is not the only plausible explanation. The salary difference might be due to some other factor that (1) determines salary and (2) is linked to gender. In its defence, the firm might argue that it pays solely on the basis of *education and experience*, and it is not to be blamed for the fact that its pool of applicants consisted of better-educated and more experienced men as compared to the women. This argument basically shifts the blame from the firm to society in general. (Siegel, 1994: 374–5)

There are a number of points to be made here.

- First, the data come from a population, the staff in a particular department of a firm. However, the discussion (not reported above) suggests that both the men and women in this department come from two 'idealized' populations of people in similar circumstances. If there *are* such populations, then the two samples were not drawn randomly. How could we draw such samples randomly? Therefore, it is not possible to generalize the data back to those populations; they *come* from a population, defined as the employees in this department in this firm.
- Second, what is 'usual random variation' or 'random allocation'? These notions make no sense except, perhaps, in the context of some abstract statistical theory. Salaries are not usually allocated randomly (although we may sometimes be surprised at the salaries some people receive). How could we possibly know what random variation is usual? Inferential analysis cannot tell us.
- Third, to say that this difference is statistically significant is meaningless. The samples were not randomly selected from any population. The difference between the two means *is* the difference. Deciding whether the difference is too big, or whether there should be a difference at all, cannot be settled or even assisted by this kind of analysis. Applying inferential analysis to population data not only is wrong, but also cannot provide an explanation for the difference in mean salaries. As the author clearly illustrates, you have to look somewhere else.

Many other such examples could be cited from textbooks on statistics, particularly in discussions relevant to behavioural research with small samples. Remember, anything over 30, or sometimes 40, is regarded as a large sample in this kind of research. Frequently, these are just 'convenience' samples or small populations. At best, they consist of matched pairs or random selection into experimental groups. Convenience samples must be ruled out of court because the selection is not based on probability procedures. Also, matched pairs are usually not randomly selected from a population. Any results from such studies cannot be generalized statistically to any wider population. Selection to experimental groups could be made randomly from a designated population, but I suspect this rarely happens. Behavioural researchers are no doubt desperate to have their research regarded as important, even though their samples might be very small and without probability selection methods. By applying tests of significance, usually illegitimately, they try to create the impression that their results can be generalized. Perhaps they can, but by judgement rather than statistically.

To recapitulate, tests of significance are only relevant when we are trying to estimate whether the results we have obtained in a probability sample (or samples) are also present in the population (or populations) from which the sample (or samples) was (were) drawn. Such tests have nothing to do with the importance of the findings, with the degree of completeness of an explanation or with handling errors that may have inadvertently crept into our research. Following this idea should help to avoid much of the confusion and angst associated with the concept of significance and its role in testing statistical hypotheses and, perhaps, help to avoid the misuse of these procedures.

Categorical Variables

Because different measures of association are appropriate for nominal-level variables (e.g. C_s and Cramér's V) and ordinal-level variables (e.g. gamma), different tests of significance have been devised to go with them. While it is usually best to use the appropriate test, it is also possible to use the chi-square test, which is appropriate for nominal-level data, with ordinal-level data as well, but this involves regarding the ordinal-level variable as nominal.[11]

Nominal-level Data

In Chapter 4, we discussed chi-square in some detail when we were concerned with establishing the level of association between two nominal-level variables. It was derived by comparing the observed (O) and expected (E) frequencies in every cell of a contingency table and was calculated using equation (4.1), repeated here for convenience:

$$\chi^2 = \Sigma \frac{(O - E)^2}{E}$$

We then used the total chi-square value to calculate the contingency coefficient, in both its raw (C) and standardized (C_s) versions, and Cramér's V.

What we want to know is whether the level of association indicated by such coefficients in a probability sample could be expected to be present in the population from which the sample was drawn. We already know that the level of association is dependent on the differences between the observed and expected frequencies, as expressed in the total chi-square value for any contingency table. This total chi-square value can also be used to test the significance of the association – that is, whether, at a particular level of confidence, the association is also present in the population.

There are two steps involved in this; first, to determine the number of degrees of freedom; and, second, to compare the chi-square value with those in a table of critical values. The notion of *degrees of freedom* (*df*) refers to the number of values that are free to vary when certain restrictions are placed on the data. In a contingency table, the number of degrees of freedom is related to the number of cells in the table. Take the example of a 2 by 2 table, such as Table 4.4. Given that we know the sample total, the marginal totals, that is, the numbers with 'Some religion' and 'No religion', and the number of 'Males' and 'Females', once we know how many 'Males' have 'Some religion' the numbers in all the other cells of the table can be calculated. Hence, only one cell in the table is free to vary and, once its value is fixed, the other three values have been determined. Therefore, a 2 by 2 table has only one degree of freedom.

As larger tables have more cells that can vary, they have more degrees of freedom. This is calculated by subtracting 1 from the number of categories on each side of the table and multiplying the two numbers. If c represents the number of columns and r the number of rows, then the number of degrees of freedom is $(c - 1) \times (r - 1)$. In a 3 by 4 table the number of degrees of freedom is $2 \times 3 = 6$.

We need to know the number of degrees of freedom in order to be able to establish whether the total chi-square for a table exceeds the critical value for the confidence level we have set (see Table 1 in Appendix D). We already know that the total chi-square value for Table 4.4 is 16.114 (see p. 98) and we know that this table has only 1 degree of freedom. If we set the confidence level at 95 per cent (the 0.05 level of significance), we find that the critical chi-square value is 5.02 for a two-tailed test. To be significant, our value would need to be equal to or higher than this critical value for a non-directional alternative hypothesis (two-tailed). As our value exceeds this critical value, we can say that the association between Religion and Gender is significant. In fact, our chi-square value would make it significant at the 0.001 level as it exceeds the critical value of 12.12. The phi coefficient tells us that the strength of the association is 0.20. Hence, there is a 99.9 per cent probability that an association of this strength exists in the population. What it does not tell us is whether an association of this strength is important.

We can do a similar analysis on this association using the data in Table 4.1. In this case, the total chi-square value is 16.8150 (see p. 97) and there are 4 degrees of freedom. From the table of critical values we find that the level of significance certainly exceeds the 0.05 level (critical value is 11.14) and also exceeds the 0.01 level (14.86). Hence, we can be 99 per cent confident that an association of this strength ($C = 0.20$; $C_s = 0.25$; see pp. 99 and 100) can be found in the population. Note that as the number of degrees of freedom increases, a higher chi-square value is required to achieve a given level of significance. That is why the larger table for this association has only achieved a 0.01 level of significance.

If our alternative hypothesis was directional, such as 'women are more likely than men to profess a religious affiliation', a one-tailed test would be appropriate. In the 2 by 2 table, the total chi-square would have to equal or exceed a critical value of 3.84 for the association to be significant at the 0.05 level and 10.83 at the 0.001 level. In the 2 by 5 version of the table, the critical values for a one-tailed test would be 9.49 at the 0.05 level and 13.28 at the 0.01 level. Therefore, this directional alternative hypothesis is significant at the 0.01 level. It should be clear that having a directional or a non-directional alternative hypothesis can make a difference as to whether an association turns out to be significant or not.[12]

Ordinal-level Data

While it is possible to use the chi-square to test the level of significance of all tables with categorical data, given that gamma is now a popular and appropriate coefficient for measuring the association between two ordinal-level variables, it is worth reviewing an approximate test of significance that has been developed specifically for it (see Siegel and Castellan, 1988: 296–8). As this procedure produces a conservative estimate of the 'true' level of significance, we may end up claiming a lower level of significance than is the case, thus not rejecting the null hypothesis when it is false (type II error). We have already calculated the value for gamma for the data reported in Table 4.2 for the association between Age and EWV. It was -0.328, a moderate, negative association (see p. 104). The following equation is used to test the null hypothesis by producing a value for z.[13]

$$z = G \sqrt{\frac{C + D}{n(1 - G^2)}} \qquad (6.5)$$

where C is the number of concordant pairs and D is the number of discordant pairs. We can arrive at the value for z by substituting the known values in this equation (see Table 4.5):

$$z = -0.328 \times \sqrt{\frac{13,183 + 26,048}{401(1 - [-0.328^2])}} = -0.328 \times \sqrt{\frac{39,231}{401 \times 0.8924}}$$

$$= -0.328 \times \sqrt{109.629} = -3.433$$

As the same level of significance will apply to both positive and negative associations, we can ignore the negative sign here. This z-score produces a level of significance beyond the 0.001 level (both one-tailed and two-tailed) (see Table 2 in Appendix D).

In the same table, if we calculate the level of significance using chi-square, with a total value of 49.706 and 6 degrees of freedom ($df = (c - 1)(r - 1) = 3 \times 2$), the level of significance is also well beyond the 0.001 level for both a one-tailed and a two-tailed test (see Table 1 in Appendix D). Therefore, for linear relationships, the two methods produce the same results. If a relationship is non-linear, gamma might be non-significant while a test based on chi-square may be significant. This is because gamma can only detect linear relationships while measures based on chi-square can detect any form of relationship. Taking this into consideration, the only time a choice of test might be critical is when the results are close to the 0.05 level.

Apart from the chi-square test, a range of other tests is available for use with nominal-level and ordinal-level data. Still the most complete discussion of these tests is to be found in Siegel and Castellan (1988). However, many are designed for small samples (usually less than 40) under experimental conditions.[14] A number of these tests require individuals to be rank-ordered according to their score or position on a particular variable. As ordinal-level data in most social research involve grouping respondents into a set of ordered categories, such as level of education by qualifications, these tests may not be very useful. Such data are in ordered categories rather than being ordered individuals. The latter is only feasible with small samples. While I strongly recommend the use of Siegel and Castellan (1998) if what is discussed here does not meet your requirements, it is important to recognize that much of it is written for psychologists rather than for social researchers.[15] It is worth noting that only a few of these tests are available in software packages such as SPSS.

Metric Variables

Different tests of significance are required when data are either at the interval or ratio level of measurement. These tests receive much greater attention than those just discussed, no doubt because of the assumption that metric variables are superior to categorical variables. Given that Pearson's r is the most commonly used measure of association for metric variables, what we need is a test of significance for this coefficient. However, as different tests are required when means are compared, we shall discuss these first.

Comparing Means

The type of means analysis to be discussed here constitutes a form of associational analysis. Like associational analysis, means analysis is an elaborate form of description involving comparison. Comparisons can be made in various ways:

- between the means of two variables within a sample;
- between the means of one variable for two categories of another variable within a sample; and
- between the means of one variable across two samples.

The first two are within-sample comparisons, while the third involves a between-sample comparison. For the second, where the difference between means for one variable is produced for categories of another variable, we are really looking to see whether there is an association between the two categories and this variable, for example, between Gender and EWV.

In testing the significance of a difference between two means within the same sample, we are trying to establish whether the difference found between the categories is the result of our sample not being representative, or whether it is due to a real difference between the categories in the population. This analysis requires the setting up of a null and an alternative hypothesis. The task of the analysis is to try to reject the null hypothesis in favour of the alternative form that is supported by the data.

Whether the analysis concerns within-sample or between-sample comparisons, the same procedure can be used when only two means are involved. The appropriate test is the group t test.[16] If the parametric requirements of this test are not met, an alternative is the Mann–Whitney U test or its equivalent, the Wilcoxon test. When more than two means are compared, analysis of variance can be used. Reviews of these three tests follow.

Group t test

The *group t test* is sometimes known as 'Student's t test' due to the pseudonym used by its creator, William Gossett, when he first published it. The t test is based on a similar set of critical values to the z-scores. What we are trying to establish is whether the value (for t or z) that we arrive at by the relevant procedure indicates that our sample characteristic or pattern lies in the extreme tails of the normal curve of all possible samples – that is, that this value indicates that the particular sample characteristic or pattern is not significant. The distribution of values of z corresponds to the shape of a theoretical normal curve with a mean of 0 and a standard deviation of 1. Similarly, the distribution of values of t represents a theoretical symmetrical distribution with a mean of 0 but, in this case, a standard deviation that decreases towards 1 as the degrees of freedom increase. When the degrees of freedom exceed 100, the t distribution approximates the z distribution. When there are fewer degrees of freedom (i.e. the samples are smaller), the tails of the distribution spread out further. Hence, for smaller degrees of freedom, the proportion of the area beyond a specific value of t is greater than that beyond the corresponding value of z. The t test is more commonly used than the z test because the former uses the sample standard deviation while the latter requires either knowledge of the population standard deviation or some way of estimating it. The table of t values (see Table 3 in Appendix D) is used in the same way as that for chi-square values.

In order to use the group t test, two requirements have to be met:

- The variable must have a normal distribution in both categories.
- The standard deviations of both categories should be approximately the same.

When the size of both categories is large, and there is approximately the same number in each one, the requirement for normal distributions is less important. If these requirements cannot be met, there are three alternatives. The first is to just use the group *t* test regardless. This is likely to produce a conservative result, which means that the null hypothesis may not be rejected when it is false (type II error). The second alternative is to do some normalizing transformation of the variable or variables. The third is to use a non-parametric test, such as the Mann–Whitney *U* test. The latter will be discussed shortly.

Earlier in the chapter we encountered two notions, the standard error of the proportion and the standard error of the mean. The latter refers to the standard deviation of the mean of all possible sample means. We need to use a similar idea here, the *standard error of the difference*. Using the central limit theorem (see p. 165), we know that if we draw enough samples of the same size from a population, the distribution of the differences between the means of a variable, for two subsamples, will approach the normal curve, and that the mean of all these differences will be the same as the difference between the means of the two categories of a variable in the population. As we may not know the variances of the two means in the population, we again have to use the sample variances as our best guess. Because there are two variances in this case, the equation for the standard error of the difference is different from those used for the standard error of the mean or the proportion.

In contrast to its use in contingency tables, the notion of degrees of freedom works differently with metric variables. Now the sample size determines the number of degrees of freedom, which is equal to $n - 1$. The logic in both cases is similar. To recapitulate, in the case of a contingency table with a certain sample size, the values in all but one of the categories of each variable can vary in order that both rows and columns will add up to the marginals, and the sum of both sets of marginals will add up to the sample size. Once all category values apart from this last one are decided, the value of the last category is automatically determined. It has no freedom to vary, while all the other categories do. In the case of metric variables, if the mean of a set of values in a sample is known, then all but one of the values is free to vary. The value of the last one will be determined because it, together with all the other values, must produce the mean. Hence, the number of degrees of freedom is one less than the sample size. When categories of a variable are being compared within a sample, each category's degrees of freedom will need to be calculated, being one less than the total *n* in the category.

The equation for the group *t* test is:

$$t = \frac{\text{difference between the means}}{\text{estimated standard error of the difference}} = \frac{\bar{x}_1 - \bar{x}_2}{se_d} \qquad (6.6)$$

To calculate the estimated standard error of the difference when the standard deviations of the two groups are approximately equal, the two standard deviations are pooled together. This produces a *pooled estimate* of the standard deviation of the difference between the means.

$$s_p = \sqrt{\frac{n_1 s_1^2 + n_2 s_2^2}{n_1 + n_2}} \qquad (6.7)$$

where s_1 and s_2 are the standard deviation of the first and second categories respectively, and n_1 and n_2 are numbers of values in the first and second categories respectively. When the sizes of the two categories are roughly equal, s_p is simply the square-root of the mean of the two standard deviations:

$$s_p = \sqrt{\frac{s_1^2 + s_2^2}{2}} \qquad (6.8)$$

The pooled estimate can now be entered in the equation

$$se_d = s_p \sqrt{\frac{1}{n_1} + \frac{1}{n_2}} \qquad (6.9)$$

and t can be calculated by inserting this value in equation (6.6).

When the standard deviations of the two groups are not approximately the same, the following equation can be used to arrive at the estimated standard error of the difference:

$$s_p = \sqrt{\frac{s_1^2}{n_1} + \frac{s_2^2}{n_2}} \qquad (6.10)$$

Once the estimated standard error of the difference is known, its value can be inserted in equation (6.6).

Note that when the size of the two categories is large, moderate departures from normal distributions on the variable can be tolerated by the pooled procedure for arriving at the t value.[17] In other words, this procedure is robust in that it is less sensitive than some to deviations from the normality requirement.

To arrive at the critical value for t, we must calculate the number of degrees of freedom. Two different procedures are used depending on whether or not the sizes of the categories are equal. If they are equal, there are $n_1 + n_2 - 2$ degrees of freedom. Because the standard deviations have been pooled, the normal $n - 1$ degrees of freedom have also been pooled for the two categories, that is, added together. When the two ns are different, the number of degrees of freedom is the smaller of $n_1 - 1$ and $n_2 - 1$. The reason for this is that the smaller the degrees of freedom, the more difficult it is to reject the null hypothesis, thus producing a more conservative outcome. Using the larger n, or even averaging the two, will make it more likely that the test will be significant.[18]

Now to try some examples from the data sets. A within-sample difference will be calculated using the mean EWV scores for male and female Students. A between-sample difference will compare the mean EWV scores of Students and Residents.

The mean EWV scores are 87.27 for males and 93.94 for females (Students). Clearly, the difference is not large (6.67) but the question is whether it could also be expected to be present in the population of students from this particular university. The standard deviations for male and female students will be considered to be approximately equal, 11.50 for males and 10.94 for females.[19] Given that the two categories have different ns, we need to use the following equation to calculate the pooled estimates of the standard deviation.

$$s_{\mathrm{p}} = \sqrt{\frac{n_1 s_1^2 + n_2 s_2^2}{n_1 + n_2}} = \sqrt{\frac{(210 \times 11.50^2) + (254 \times 10.94^2)}{210 + 254}}$$

$$= \sqrt{\frac{27{,}775.50 + 30{,}399.63}{464}} = \sqrt{125.377} = 11.197$$

We can check this figure by observing that it lies between the standard deviations for males and females, and even though the sizes of these two groups are not the same, it should be somewhere near the mean of the two values (which is 11.22). Now we can calculate the estimated standard error of the difference:

$$se_{\mathrm{d}} = s_{\mathrm{p}} \times \sqrt{\frac{1}{n_1} + \frac{1}{n_2}} = 11.197 \times \sqrt{\frac{1}{210} + \frac{1}{254}} = 11.197 \times \sqrt{0.0087} = 1.044$$

With this value, it is possible to calculate t:

$$t = \frac{\bar{x}_1 - \bar{x}_2}{se_{\mathrm{d}}} = \frac{-6.67}{1.044} = -6.39$$

The negative sign can be ignored as the order of the means is arbitrary. With 462 degrees of freedom $(n_1 + n_2 - 2)$ and a one-tailed significance level of 0.05 (because we expect the difference to be in the same direction in the population), the critical value of t is 1.97 (see Table 3 in Appendix D). As our value exceeds this value we can be 95 per cent confident that this difference exists in the population. In fact, we could be 99.9 per cent confident with either a one-tailed or a two-tailed test. Therefore, we can conclude that the difference between the mean EWV scores for male and female Students, with females having a higher mean score than males, can be expected in the population at an extremely high level of confidence.

It is also possible to calculate a confidence interval around this difference in the means. It is ± 2.05 at the 95 per cent level of confidence and ± 3.46 at the 99.9 per cent level. Note that the latter interval takes in slightly over half of the difference between the means, and it indicates that the difference is expected to be between 3.21 and 10.13. The difference is between 4.61 and 8.72 at the 95 per cent level.

We can also test the difference in the EWV means for males and females in the Resident sample. The means are 86.44 for males ($s = 11.52$; $n = 200$) and 89.52 for females ($s = 9.75$; $n = 199$), a difference of 3.08. In this case the ns

can be regarded as being equal but the standard deviations are not. This requires the use of different equations to calculate the pooled estimate of the standard deviation and the estimate of the standard error of the difference. You may wish to try this as an exercise. The value of t is 2.89 and, with 397 degrees of freedom, the difference is significant at the 99 per cent level of confidence for either a one-tailed or a two-tailed test.

In the second example, we wish to know whether the difference in mean EWV scores between the Student and Resident samples can be expected to exist in the populations from which they were randomly drawn. The mean for the Students is 90.91 ($s = 11.65$; $n = 465$) and for the Residents is 87.97 ($s = 10.76$; $n = 402$), a difference of 2.94. We could regard the standard deviations as being approximately equal (the difference is only 0.89) but the sample sizes are different. The procedure is as follows:

$$s_p = \sqrt{\frac{n_1 s_1{}^2 + n_2 s_2{}^2}{n_1 + n_2}} = \sqrt{\frac{(465 \times 11.65^2) + (402 \times 10.76^2)}{465 + 402}}$$

$$= \sqrt{\frac{63,110.96 + 46,542.60}{867}} = \sqrt{126.475} = 11.246$$

$$se_d = s_p \times \sqrt{\frac{1}{n_1} + \frac{1}{n_2}} = 11.246 \sqrt{\frac{1}{465} + \frac{1}{402}} = 11.246 \times \sqrt{0.00464} = 0.766$$

$$t = \frac{\bar{x}_1 - \bar{x}_2}{se_d} = \frac{2.94}{0.766} = 3.84$$

$$df = n_1 + n_2 - 2 = 465 + 402 - 2 = 865$$

Using a one-tailed test, the value for t exceeds the critical value at the 0.001 level of significance (3.30) and therefore allows us to reject the null hypothesis, that there is no difference in the population means, and to say that we are 99.9 per cent confident that there is such a difference. However, in this particular case, this does not say very much as the sample difference is only 2.94. We could calculate a confidence interval for this difference to help clarify the situation. In the end, we need to focus on the difference rather than the level of significance or confidence level. The latter is only a step along the way to interpreting such a result, not an end in itself. The same applies when it is measures of association with which we are concerned.

Mann–Whitney U test

The *Mann–Whitney U test* is a distribution-free test that is appropriate either when the parametric requirements of the t test cannot be met (in particular, when the distribution of the population on the variable being considered is not normal) or with ordinal-level variables. This test is used when members of two categories can be ranked in terms of their scores on the same variable. Hence, the data may be metric but the procedure is non-parametric. It is regarded as the most powerful of the non-parametric tests because it makes use of most of the information in the data. The Mann–Whitney U test is associated with the *Wilcoxon test*. They are identified by the name of their originator and involve slightly different procedures for their calculation.

Let us begin with a simple example to illustrate the procedure for the Mann–Whitney version of the test, with a small sample (defined as 20 or less). This sample has 12 members in two categories, 'A' ($n = 5$) and 'B' ($n = 7$), with scores on a hypothetical variable. The members of both categories can be ranged together in terms of their scores as follows.

Score	7	8	10	12	14	16	17	19	20	21	22	25
Rank	1	2	3	4	5	6	7	8	9	10	11	12
Category	B	B	B	A	B	B	A	B	A	A	B	A

The value of U is determined by the number of times a score from one category precedes a score from the other category, using the following equation.

$$U = n_1 n_2 + \frac{n_1(n_1 + 1)}{2} - R_1 \qquad (6.11)$$

where R_1 is the sum of the ranks assigned to category A. Here

$$R_1 = 4 + 7 + 9 + 10 + 12 = 42$$

Therefore,

$$U = 5 \times 7 + \frac{5(5 + 1)}{2} - 42 = 35 + 15 - 42 = 8$$

Tables provided in Siegel (1956) indicate that a two-tailed test for this value of U, with categories of this size, is not significant ($p = 0.15$, a confidence level of only 85 per cent).[20]

I have not appended a table for such small samples as they are unlikely to occur in social research. As the sample size increases, the distribution of U approaches the normal curve. Hence, as long as *ns* for both categories are approximately equal and one exceeds 20, the z statistic can be used to establish the significance of the difference between two categories of ranked data.

With larger samples, it is likely that ties will occur, that is, that some respondents will have the same score. This is not a problem if the ties occur within a category, but they can be when the ties occur across the categories. Although the effect of ties may be negligible, it is possible to include a correction for this in the calculations. Consideration should be given to including the correction when there are many ties, or when the uncorrected value for U is on the borderline of the desired level of significance. If the correction is not done, the test will be conservative, that is, it will decrease the probability of committing a type I error and increase the probability of committing a type II error. As SPSS provides both the uncorrected and the corrected values for U, it is easy to see what effect ties have in any situation.

To calculate the value of z for large samples, the equation is

$$z = \frac{R_1 - R_E}{se_U} \qquad (6.12)$$

where R_1 is the sum of the ranks for the first category (say, males), R_E is the expected sum of ranks if there is no difference (the null hypothesis),

$$R_E = \frac{n_1(n_1 + n_2 + 1)}{2} \qquad (6.13)$$

and se_U is the standard error of the ranks,

$$se_U = \sqrt{\frac{n_1 n_2(n_1 + n_2 + 1)}{12}} \qquad (6.14)$$

To correct for ties, a different equation is used to calculate se_U:

$$se_U = \sqrt{\frac{n_1 n_2}{n(n-1)}\left(\frac{n^3 - n}{12} - \Sigma T\right)} \qquad (6.15)$$

where $n = n_1 + n_2$ and $T = (t^3 - t)/12$ (where t is the number of scores tied for any rank).

Let us now illustrate the Mann–Whitney U test with data from the Student sample on the assumption that the EWV scores are not normally distributed. We immediately encounter a problem. Establishing the rank order of scores can be very tedious to do manually with large samples such as ours. Therefore, I will select a 1 : 10 probability sample of the sample. This still preserves its randomness but may make it more difficult to reject the null hypothesis. Table 6.4 shows the ranked EWV scores for males and females. We know that $n_1 = 21$, $n_2 = 25$, $n = 46$ and $R_1 = 457$. Therefore,

$$R_E = \frac{n_1(n_1 + n_2 + 1)}{2} = \frac{21(21 + 25 + 1)}{2} = 493.50$$

The equation for standard error of the difference without the correction for ties is:

$$se_U = \sqrt{\frac{n_1 n_2 (n_1 + n_2 + 1)}{12}} = \sqrt{\frac{21 \times 25(21 + 25 + 1)}{12}} = \sqrt{2056.25} = 45.35$$

Table 6.4 *Ranked Environmental Worldview scores by Gender (subsample of Students)*

Males (A)		Females (B)	
Scores	Rank	Scores	Rank
72	1	74	2
76	4	76	4
76	4	83	9
79	6	83	9
80	7	85	11.5
83	9	86	14
85	11.5	89	18
86	14	90	20
86	14	90	20
87	16	90	20
88	17	92	23.5
91	22	92	23.5
94	29	93	26
95	32.5	93	26
95	32.5	93	26
96	35.5	94	29
97	37	94	29
100	38	95	32.5
106	40.5	95	32.5
106	40.5	96	35.5
115	46	103	39
		107	42
		111	43.5
		111	43.5
		113	45
$n_1 = 21$	$R_1 = 457$	$n_1 = 25$	$R_2 = 624$

In order to include the correction, we have to first calculate ΣT. The following scores are tied: 76 (3), 83 (3), 85 (2), 86 (3), 90 (3), 92 (2), 93 (3), 94 (3), 95 (4), 96 (2), 106 (2) and 111 (2). This makes 12 values for T, the first of which is $(t^3 - t)/12 = (3^3 - 3)/12 = 2.0$. When two scores are tied, $T = 0.5$, and when there are four tied scores, $T = 5.0$. Therefore,

$$\Sigma T = 2.0 + 2.0 + 0.5 + 2.0 + 2.0 + 0.5 + 2.0 + 2.0 + 5.0 + 0.5 + 0.5 + 0.5 = 19.5.$$

Hence,

$$se_U = \sqrt{\frac{n_1 n_2}{n(n-1)}\left(\frac{n^3 - n}{12} - \Sigma T\right)} = \sqrt{\frac{21 \times 25}{46 \times 45}\left(\frac{46^3 \times 46}{12} - 19.5\right)}$$

$$= \sqrt{0.253623 \times 8088.00} = \sqrt{2051.30} = 45.29$$

Now we can calculate z, firstly without the correction for ties.

$$z = \frac{R_1 - R_E}{se_U} = \frac{457.00 - 493.50}{45.35} = -0.805$$

And then including the correction.

$$z = \frac{457.00 - 493.50}{45.29} = -0.806$$

Clearly, the correction for ties makes a negligible difference in this example. Both values for z are not significant for both two-tailed and one-tailed tests. Therefore, we cannot reject the null hypothesis that there is no difference in EWV scores for this subsample of males and females. This is not surprising, as the difference between the means is only 2.98 (males = 90.14; females = 93.12). In the whole sample, the difference is 6.67 (males = 87.27; females = 93.94). An inspection of the data shows that the subsample did not include males with low scores. Hence, our subsample is not representative of the original sample. In addition, the fact that the subsample is much smaller makes it more difficult to establish a significant difference. For an exercise, you could do a group t test on the sub-sample, on the assumption that EWV is normally distributed in the population, and compare the results with that obtained by using the Mann–Whitney U test. You will need to calculate the two standard deviations by hand.

When the Mann–Whitney U test is done on the whole of the Student sample (using SPSS of course) the z value is −6.05, and this is significant at the 0.001 level for both one-tailed and two-tailed tests. This result is consistent with that for the group t test discussed above.

Analysis of variance

Analysis of variance (ANOVA) tests the significance of the differences between more than two means. This can be between the means of an outcome variable for different categories of a predictor variable, such as mean EWV scores for three or more Age categories or Religion categories (within-sample comparisons). It can also be used to compare the means of one outcome variable between two or more different samples (between-sample comparisons). The former test is known as *one-way analysis of variance* because the categories across which the means are compared come from only one predictor variable, such as Age.

It would be possible to do a series of group t tests with each pair of categories or samples when more than two are involved. However, this is not recommended for a number of reasons. While it might work for only three categories or samples, as the number increases the pairs multiply very rapidly. For example, 10 categories or samples produce 45 pairs.

The one-way ANOVA requires certain assumptions to be met in order to be able to use the F *statistic* to establish whether or not differences between the means are significant.

- The populations, or the categories within a population, must have normal distributions on the variable in question.
- The standard deviations for this variable in the population, or the categories within a population, must be equal.
- The selection into the samples or categories must have been independent, that is, no pairing or similar procedures must have been used.

Unfortunately, we rarely know these parameters in the populations we have sampled. We can only rely on the characteristics in our samples and, as we know, samples may not be representative. Hence, it is necessary to be pragmatic and use this procedure when the samples have *reasonably* normal distributions and *reasonable* equivalence between standard deviations.

It is also possible to do *two-way analysis of variance*, or even more than two-way. This usually involves a combination of categories for which the means on a variable are compared. For example, it would be possible to do an analysis of variance with Gender (two categories) and Age (three categories). We would end up comparing the means, say of EWV scores, across six categories: 'young females', 'middle-aged females', 'older females', 'young males', 'middle-aged males' and 'older males'. This analysis would allow us to sort out the interaction between Gender and Age in terms of their association with EWV.

When two categories in one sample or two samples are compared on a number of variables, a different procedure is required, known as *multivariate analysis of variance* (MANOVA). For example, males and females could be compared in terms of their mean EWV scores, their mean Willingness to Act scores and their mean Recycling scores. To put this differently, Gender could be regarded as the predictor variable and the others as a set of outcome variables. These two more advanced forms of ANOVA procedures are beyond the scope and purpose of this book. See the discussion of 'Other methods' of multivariate analysis near the end of Chapter 5 for further reading.

Now back to one-way analysis of variance. One-way ANOVA is used to establish whether differences between three or more sample means could be expected in the population. The test is based on a comparison between two kinds of variance. One is within-category or *within-sample variance*. This is the dispersion around the mean for each category or sample, for example, the variance of the mean for each of three Age categories. The second is the variation between the categories or samples, that is, how different the means are from each other, known as *between-sample variance*. Comparison is achieved by establishing the ratio between these two types of variance. This produces an F value that can be compared with a table of Fisher's F statistics (Table 4, Appendix D):

$$F = \frac{\text{between-sample variability}}{\text{within-sample variability}} \qquad (6.16)$$

A table of F statistics lists the critical values, for a range of significance levels and degrees of freedom, when the null hypothesis is true. As with other test statistics, if the value calculated for F exceeds the critical value, the null hypothesis (that there is no difference between the population means) can be rejected.

Three points need to be noted. First, the variances are estimates of the variances in the population or populations. Second, while 'sample' is used to identify the type of variability, this is intended to include 'category' in the case where the means are calculated for the categories of a variable. Third, 'variability', as in between-sample variability, has a different meaning than 'comparison', as in between-sample comparisons. The latter identifies the categories or samples that are to be compared, while the former refers to the characteristics of the variable being compared.

A few steps are involved in obtaining an F value. First, we have to calculate the size of the 'total sample', which is the sum of the sizes of the individual categories or samples. For within-sample comparisons, if the categories include all the sample, this will be the same as the actual sample size; for between-sample comparisons, it will be the sum of the sizes of all the samples. Second, we also need a grand mean, or a weighted mean. Each mean is multiplied by its category or sample size, these products are summed and then divided by the total sample size (n_t). The weighted mean can be found from the following equation:

$$\text{Weighted mean } (\bar{x}_w) = \frac{n_1\bar{x}_1 + n_2\bar{x}_2 + n_3\bar{x}_3 + \dots}{n_t} \tag{6.17}$$

Now we can calculate the between-sample variability. For each sample, the difference between the sample mean and the weighted mean is squared and multiplied by the sample/category size. These products are summed and then divided by the degrees of freedom, which is one less than the number of categories or samples.

$$\text{Between-sample variability} = \frac{n_1(\bar{x}_1 - \bar{x}_w)^2 + n_2(\bar{x}_2 - \bar{x}_w)^2 + n_3(\bar{x}_3 - \bar{x}_w)^2 + \dots}{c - 1} \tag{6.18}$$

where n_1, n_2, n_3, etc. are the sizes of the respective categories or samples, $\bar{x}_1$, $\bar{x}_2$, $\bar{x}_3$, etc. are their means, and c is the number of categories or samples.

The within-sample variability is based on the variance or standard deviation of the mean for each category or sample. Using standard deviation rather than variance, each standard deviation is squared and then multiplied by one less than its sample/category size. These products are then summed and this is divided by the number of degrees of freedom. The equation is:

$$\text{Within-sample variability} = \frac{(n_1 - 1)\, s_1^2 + (n_2 - 1)\, s_2^2 + (n_3 - 1)\, s_3^3 + \dots}{n_t - c} \tag{6.19}$$

where s_1, s_2, s_3 are the standard deviations of the respective categories or samples and their squares are the respective variances.

Now it is possible to calculate a value for F using equation (6.16). We can illustrate this procedure by using the mean EWV scores for the three Age categories, '18–34', '35–54' and '55 +' (Resident sample). The required information for the three Age categories is: $\bar{x}_1 = 90.11$, $\bar{x}_2 = 90.54$, $\bar{x}_3 = 83.34$, $s_1 = 11.91$, $s_2 = 9.28$, $s_3 = 9.55$, $n_1 = 128$, $n_2 = 138$ and $n_3 = 135$. We know that the distribution of EWV scores approaches the normal curve, and their distributions in the three Age categories, as indicated by the standard deviations, are reasonably similar. Substituting the values from our example in the above equations, we can calculate the value for F:

$$\text{Weighted mean } (\bar{x}_w) = \frac{(128 \times 90.11) + (138 \times 90.54) + (135 \times 83.34)}{401}$$

$$= \frac{11{,}534.08 + 12{,}494.52 + 11{,}250.90}{401} = \frac{35{,}279.50}{401} = 87.98$$

$$\text{Between-sample variability} = \frac{128(90.11 - 87.98)^2 + 138(90.54 - 87.98)^2 + 135(83.34 - 87.98)^2}{2}$$

$$= \frac{581.38 + 905.24 + 2905.00}{2} = \frac{4391.62}{2} = 2195.81$$

$$\text{Within-sample variability} = \frac{(128 - 1)\, 11.91^2 + (138 - 1)\, 9.28^2 + (135 - 1)\, 9.55^2}{401 - 3}$$

$$= \frac{18{,}014.71 + 11{,}798.22 + 12{,}221.14}{398} = \frac{42{,}034.06}{398} = 105.61$$

$$F = \frac{\text{between-sample variability}}{\text{within-sample variability}} = \frac{2{,}195.81}{105.61} = 20.791$$

Let us set the significance level at 0.05. In order to read the table of critical values for F, we must make use of the two degrees of freedom calculated above, one for the between-sample variability ($c - 1 = 2$) and the other for the within-sample variability ($n_t - c = 398$). Reading from Table 4 in Appendix D, we find that the critical F value is approximately 3.00. As our value clearly exceeds this, we can reject the null hypothesis that there is no difference between the means. In fact, we can also reject the null hypothesis at the 0.01 level, where the critical value is approximately 4.60.

Test of Significance for Pearson's r

Whenever we use a measure of association between metric variables, such as Pearson's r, with data from a probability sample, we need to apply inferential analysis in the form of a test of significance. Again, the t test is appropriate, using the equation

$$t = r\sqrt{\frac{n - 2}{1 - r^2}} \tag{6.20}$$

where r is a particular correlation coefficient. This is obviously a simpler procedure than the one we have just been through to test the difference between means.

We can illustrate this test by returning to the association between Age and EWV, but this time with the metric versions of these variables and with the

Resident sample. With Pearson's $r = -0.308$ and $n = 401$, we have

$$t = r\sqrt{\frac{n-2}{1-r^2}} = -0.308\sqrt{\frac{401-2}{1-0.308^2}} = -0.308\sqrt{\frac{399}{0.9051}} = -6.467$$

With 399 degrees of freedom $(n - 2)$, a two-tailed test is significant well beyond the 0.001 level (Table 3, Appendix D). Ignore the negative sign. Therefore, the null hypothesis, that there is no association, can be rejected and the conclusion drawn that there is an association in the population, usually represented by ρ (rho). In other words, there is a 99.9 per cent probability that the correlation coefficient is greater than zero in the population ($p < 0.001$). While we do not know precisely what ρ is, it is possible to calculate confidence limits around r at some level of probability, perhaps 0.001 in this case. The procedure for this is the same as for calculating a confidence interval around a sample mean (see Edwards, 1954: 307).

Inference in Explanatory Analysis

It is also necessary to test the significance of asymmetrical coefficients that are designed to indicate an influence between predictor and outcome variables, that is, when they are based on probability samples.

Nominal-level Data

In Chapter 5, we reviewed the use of Goodman and Kruskal's lambda (λ) for establishing influence between two nominal-level variables. Because of some complexities in the procedure, it is necessary to test the hypothesis that the reduction of error is a particular value rather than zero. In other words, the null hypothesis is not strictly null; it has to specify a value. With relatively large samples, λ approaches a normal distribution for all samples of a particular size. The estimated standard error of λ can be calculated as follows:[21]

$$se_\lambda = \sqrt{\frac{\left(n - \frac{\text{sum of within-category}}{\text{modes of the predictor}}\right)\left(\frac{\text{sum of within-category}}{\text{modes of the predictor}} + \frac{\text{modal } f \text{ of}}{\text{the outcome}} - 2 \times \frac{\text{modal } f \text{ in the row with the}}{\text{modal } f \text{ of the outcome}}\right)}{(n - \text{modal } f \text{ of the outcome})^3}} \quad (6.21)$$

With this value, we can then calculate a value for z:

$$z = \frac{\lambda - \text{predicted value of } \lambda}{se_\lambda} \quad (6.22)$$

We can go back to Table 5.1 and its discussion in Chapter 5 to illustrate this procedure. The value of λ was calculated as 0.027, which represents very little influence. It would not be surprising if it were not significant. The 'sum of within-category modes of the predictor' is the sum of the modes in each column of Table 5.1 (24 + 33 + 29 + 21 + 38 = 145). The 'modal f of the outcome' is the highest frequency in the Total column at the right of the Table (138, for 'Professional/managerial'). The 'modal f in the row with the modal f of the outcome' is the highest frequency of the first row because that is the row of the 'modal f of the outcome' (38, for 'No religion'). Now we have all the ingredients for the equation for the standard error of λ:

$$se_\lambda = \sqrt{\frac{(401 - 145)(145 + 138 - 38)}{(401 - 138)^3}} = \sqrt{\frac{62,720}{18,191,447}} = \sqrt{0.0034} = 0.059$$

If we were to predict the value of λ to be 0.10,

$$z = \frac{\lambda - \text{predicted value of } \lambda}{se\lambda} = \frac{0.027 - 0.10}{0.059} = \frac{-0.073}{0.059} = -1.24$$

Using Table 2 in Appendix D, with the 0.05 level of significance and a one-tailed test (because we predicted a value for λ), we find a p-value of 0.1075. This means that we must reject the hypothesis that Religion has an influence of 0.10 on Occupation, in the population.

Ordinal-level Data

In Chapter 5 we discussed the use of Somer's d for establishing influence between two ordinal-level variables. As with the test for lambda, this test is also not straightforward. However, it is possible to arrive at an approximation.[22]

To calculate z, we require the value for Somer's d that is being tested, and its variance. The equation is:

$$z = \frac{d}{\sqrt{var_d}} \tag{6.23}$$

To calculate Somer's d, we had to establish the number of concordant pairs (C), the number of discordant pairs (D) and the number of tied pairs (T_d) (see pp. 102–4). The calculation of var_d follows a similar but more detailed procedure. Taking each cell in the table in turn, the values in all the cells outside its own column and row are taken together and multiplied by that cell's value. However, some cells are given a positive value and some a negative value. Positive values are given to the values in the cells that are below and to the right and that are above and to the left, while negative values are given to the cells that are below and to the left and that are above and to the right. To simplify, this, I shall refer to each cell's relationship to its 'diagonal' cells, those off its own row and column. Of course, not all cells have all four combinations. For example, the top, left-hand cell can only be related to cells below and to its right. Similarly, each of the cells in the other three corners of the table can only relate to cells in one direction from it. Other cells on the margins of the table will only relate to cells in two directions, while all others will relate in four directions. Put in words, the equation for the estimate of the variance of d is:

$$var_d = \frac{4 \times \sum(\text{each cell multiplied by the sum of its diagonal cells squared})}{[\text{total squared} - \sum(\text{each column marginal squared})]^2} \qquad (6.24)$$

Using the data presented in Table 4.2, Table 6.5 shows each cell multiplied by the sum of its 'diagonal' cells. Hence,

$$var_d = \frac{4 \times 7,181,228}{[401^2 - (128^2 + 138^2 + 135^2)]^2} = \frac{28,724,912}{[160,801 - 53,653]^2} = 0.0025$$

and

$$z = \frac{d}{\sqrt{var_d}} = \frac{0.223}{\sqrt{0.0025}} = 4.460$$

where d is based on equations (5.3) or (5.4) (pp. 124–5), calculated to three decimal places. With a one-tailed test, this value for z is significant at the 0.001 level (see Table 2 in Appendix D).[23]

This is a very tedious procedure to do by hand, particularly with large tables, and there is plenty of scope for making errors. However, if it can be assumed that the distribution of the population across the categories of both variables is uniform, a much simpler equation can be used (see Siegel and Castellan, 1988: 308). Even when the distribution is not exactly uniform, the following equation provides a reasonable estimate of the variance of d:

$$var_d = \frac{4(r^2 - 1)(c + 1)}{9nr^2(c - 1)} \qquad (6.25)$$

where r is the number of rows, c is the number of columns and n is the table total.

In our example, the distribution across the Age categories is close to uniform, but the EWV categories are much less so. Unless we need to be extremely precise, it would be appropriate to use this simpler equation in this situation. We can compare the two procedures by substituting the relevant information from the same example in equation (6.25).

$$var_d = \frac{4(4^2 - 1)(3 + 1)}{9 \times 401 \times 4^2(3 - 1)} = \frac{240}{115,488} = 0.00208$$

Table 6.5 *Cells and their 'diagonals' in Table 4.2*

Cell	Cell value	Sum of 'diagonals'	Total
a	21	$(^e 46 + {}^f 65 + {}^h 52 + {}^i 22 + {}^k 24 + {}^l 6)^2 =$	970,725
b	16	$(^f 65 + {}^i 22 + {}^l 6 - {}^d 45 - {}^g 30 - {}^j 32)^2 =$	3,136
c	42	$(- {}^d 45 - {}^e 46 - {}^g 30 - {}^h 52 - {}^j 32 - {}^k 24)^2 =$	2,202,522
d	45	$(^h 52 + {}^i 22 + {}^k 24 + {}^l 6 - {}^b 16 - {}^c 42)^2 =$	95,220
e	46	$(^i 22 + {}^l 6 + {}^a 21 - {}^g 30 - {}^j 32 - {}^c 42)^2 =$	139,150
f	65	$(^a 21 + {}^b 16 - {}^g 30 - {}^h 52 - {}^j 32 - {}^k 24)^2 =$	663,065
g	30	$(^k 24 + {}^l 6 - {}^b 16 - {}^c 42 - {}^e 46 - {}^f 65)^2 =$	579,630
h	52	$(^l 6 + {}^a 21 + {}^d 45 - {}^j 32 - {}^c 42 - {}^f 65)^2 =$	233,428
i	22	$(^a 21 + {}^b 16 + {}^d 45 + {}^e 46 - {}^j 32 - {}^k 24)^2 =$	114,048
j	32	$(- {}^b 16 - {}^c 42 - {}^e 46 - {}^f 65 - {}^h 52 - {}^i 22)^2 =$	1,889,568
k	24	$(^a 21 + {}^d 45 + {}^g 30 - {}^c 42 - {}^f 65 - {}^i 22)^2 =$	26,136
l	6	$(^a 21 + {}^b 16 + {}^d 45 + {}^e 46 + {}^g 30 + {}^h 52)^2 =$	264,600
Total			7,181,228

and

$$z = \frac{d}{\sqrt{var_d}} = \frac{0.223}{\sqrt{0.00208}} = 4.884$$

This value for z is close to the previous value, and the difference has no bearing on the test. Again, when the value of z is close to the critical value for the boundary between two levels of significance, particularly the 0.05 level, small differences may be important and the more tedious calculation would be more appropriate (assuming it cannot be done by computer software).

Metric Variables

The only tests to be discussed for influence between metric variables are those required for bivariate and multiple regression. I will not attempt to illustrate any of these procedures, as multiple regression in particular, like factor analysis, is not something that you are likely to do by hand, including the various tests of significance.

Bivariate Regression

A test of the significance of a regression coefficient is a test for the slope of the regression line *b*. In bivariate regression, testing the significance of *b* is similar to testing the significance of Pearson's *r*. As we have seen, when *b* is standardized in bivariate regression, it has the same value as Pearson's *r*.

In testing the significance of a correlation coefficient we are usually trying to reject the null hypothesis that it is equal to zero. When we are testing the significance of the slope of a regression line, we are trying to reject the null hypothesis that the slope is flat. A flat slope has a value of zero, whether it is standardized or not. The *t* test is appropriate.

It is also possible to calculate a confidence interval around the value of *b*. As with previous calculations of confidence limits, we must first have an estimate of the *standard error of the slope*. Then

$$CI = b \pm (z \times se_s) \qquad\qquad (6.26)$$

where se_s is the standard error of the slope. The value of z will be determined by the confidence level set, being 1.96 for the 0.05 level.

Multiple Regression

Testing for significance in multiple regression is rather more complex. First, in the same way as we would test the significance of r in a bivariate relationship, we can test the significance of R, the total or multiple correlation coefficient between a set of predictor variables and the outcome variable. In this case, the F test is appropriate. A special table can be used to determine whether the F value produced exceeds the relevant critical value for the size of sample and the number of predictor variables (see, for example, Siegel, 1994: 490–5). This will establish whether an R of this size can be expected to exist in the population. Second, perhaps a more valuable figure is the *adjusted* R^2 (see Miles and Shevlin, 2001: 32–3). As we already know, by squaring R we can determine the proportion or percentage of the variance that is explained by a set of predictor variables. The adjusted R^2 estimates what this percentage is likely to be in the population. Third, if R turns out to be significant, it is then possible to examine the significance of each *beta* coefficient. This allows us to estimate for each predictor variable, after the influence of all the other variables is taken into account, whether it makes a contribution to the explained variance in the population, that is, whether it is sufficiently different from zero to be able to reject the null hypothesis. The t test is appropriate here. Note, however, that if R turns out not to be significant, an examination of the significance of the predictor variables would not be legitimate. Therefore, for multiple regression, we have three different but related ways of estimating whether what we found in a sample can be expected to be present in the population from which it was drawn. To summarize:

- Test the significance of R, the multiple correlation coefficient, using the F statistic.
- Use the adjusted R^2 as an estimate of proportion of the variance explained in the population.
- If R is significant, examine the significance of each predictor variable, using a t test.

Summary

- Inferential analysis is a collection of methods for generalizing the characteristics, relationships and differences discovered in data from a probability sample to the population from which the sample was drawn.
- This analysis is not appropriate with non-probability samples, with probability samples with poor response rates, or with populations.

- In a probability sample, every population element must have a known and non-zero chance of being selected.
- In selecting a probability sample, the aim is to produce a smaller version of the population in all respects. However, random selection procedures cannot guarantee this. Probability samples can be biased and this can produce errors in the estimation of population parameters.
- However, there is a solution to this problem, which is based on the central limit theorem. This theorem states that the distribution of *all* possible sample means approaches the normal curve and the overall mean of these sample means approaches the population mean. The larger the samples used, the more likely this will happen and the narrower will be the dispersion (standard error) of the sample means. This occurs regardless of the shape of the distribution of the population values.
- Therefore, the accuracy of estimates of population parameters depends largely on the sample size and *not* on the ratio of the sample size to the population size.
- The level of measurement of the variables, and the characteristics of their distributions, together determine what methods of inferential analysis are appropriate. Parametric tests can only be used when population distributions are approximately normal, but non-parametric or distribution-free tests can be used when they are not normally distributed.
- In all inferential analysis it is necessary to set a level of confidence (a percentage) or a level of probability (a proportion) as part of the estimation process. These state how confident we wish to be about our estimate of a population's parameter. The usual level of confidence is 95 per cent (0.05 level of probability or significance), although 99 per cent (0.01 level) and 99.9 per cent (0.001) are also used. These levels allow for a small probability that the sample has produced values that lie at the extremes of the distribution of all possible sample values.
- In univariate descriptive analysis, inferential statistics determine the confidence interval around a sample value (proportion or percentage with categorical variables and mean with metric variables) within which the population value is expected to lie, at the level of confidence set.
- In bivariate descriptive (associational) and explanatory analyses, tests of significance are used to estimate whether the relationships found in a sample can also be expected to exist in the population from which the sample was randomly drawn.
- Statistical hypotheses, in both the null and alternative forms, specify the possible forms of a relationship in a population. Tests of significance are used to establish whether it is possible to reject the null form of the hypothesis in favour of either a directional or a non-directional alternative.
- This decision requires the setting of a level of confidence, and this entails the possibility of committing either of two types of errors. A type I error occurs when the null hypothesis is rejected when it is true, and a type II error occurs when the null hypothesis is not rejected when it is false. The latter error is more common than the former.

- When a non-directional alternative hypothesis is entertained, a two-tailed test of significance should be used. When the alternative hypothesis is directional, the test must be one-tailed.
- The testing for differences (say, between means) can occur for the values of one variable; for the categories of another variable, within the same sample; between samples; and between the same category in different samples.
- The following tests are appropriate for associational analysis.

  1. Nominal-level variable with nominal-level variable; chi-square test (4.1) for C_s or V.
  2. Nominal-level variable with ordinal-level variable; as for 1.
  3. Ordinal-level variable with ordinal-level variable; z test for G (6.5).
  4. Metric-level variable with metric-level variable; t test for r (6.20).
  5. Nominal-level variable with metric-level variable:

     (a) recode metric-level variable into ordinal-level categories-use 1 above;
     (b) If nominal-level variable is a dichotomy, or can be dichotomized sensibly-t test for r (6.20);
     (c) conduct means analysis:
         comparison of two means-group t test if parametric requirements are met, or Mann-Whiney U test or Wilcoxon test (equation (6.11) or (6.12)) if not;
         comparison of more than two means-F test with one-way ANOVA (6.16).

  6. Ordinal-level variable with metric-level variable;

     (a) recode metric-level variable into ordinal categories-z test for G (6.5).
     (b) conduct means analysis as for 5(c).

- The following tests are appropriate for explanatory analysis.

  7. Nominal-level predictor and nominal-level outcome; z test for lambda (6.22).
  8. Nominal-level predictor and ordinal-level outcome; as for 7.
  9. Ordinal-level predictor and ordinal-level outcome; z test for Somer's d (6.23).
  10. Interval-level predictor and interval-level outcome;

     (a) bivariate regression-t test for R (6.20);
     (b) multiple regression-F test for R.

11. Nominal-level or ordinal-level predictors and interval-level outcome; use dummy variables with 10(b), and use F test for R.
12. Nominal-level, ordinal-level and metric-level predictors and interval-level outcome;
    combine 10(b) and 11.

- Tests of significance must be treated with caution as the ability to reach a desired level of significance depends on the sample size; with large samples, small differences can be highly significant. Therefore, instead of just relying on tests of significance, it is preferable to construct confidence intervals around sample values. This makes it possible to see the range of possible population values in both descriptive and associational analysis. In bivariate descriptive analysis, this procedure makes it easier to understand the extent to which differences within or between populations are likely and also if they are meaningful.

Notes

[1] For a detailed and readable discussion of probability and statistics, see Siegel (1994: Chapter 6).

[2] This is a case where it is legitimate to calculate the mean of means as the sample sizes are all the same.

[3] It is the restrictions on the calculation of chi-square that determine the need for larger sample sizes. Ordinal-level data that involve the use of other methods of analysis can use somewhat smaller samples, although still much larger than is required for the higher levels of measurement.

[4] I once managed an 86 per cent response rate from a population, using a mailed questionnaire, a method prone to low response rates. However, this was only possible because of the nature of the population (members of a professional occupation), the timeliness of the study for the participants and a great deal of follow-up work. I have never managed such a high response in studies involving the use of samples. As a general rule, neither do most social researchers.

[5] See Kish (1965) for a detailed treatment of this.

[6] Percentages are used to state the confidence level while probabilities are used to state the level of significance. The present discussion will use percentages, as I believe they convey a clearer meaning. However, in later analysis I will use the 0.05 level of significance, and 0.01 for the 99 per cent confidence level and 0.001 for the 99.9 level.

[7] The alternative hypothesis is sometimes called the research hypothesis because it is what we expect to be the outcome. However, this is to inflate a statistical hypothesis to the status of a theoretical hypothesis.

[8] This follows closely Wright's (1997) practice. He also avoids the use of these confusing conventions and refers to 'variables' and 'groups', such as two variables within one group, or one variable with two groups. As a sociologist, I prefer to use 'category' rather than 'group' as the former avoids inappropriate connotations associated with *social* groups, that is, groups in which social processes occur. Categories are simply collectivities – collections of people, cases, objects, etc., that have been created for the purpose of the research and which do not necessarily occur naturally. For example, males and females are categories rather than *social* groups. In any survey, few if any will have interacted with each other, either casually or over time. However, this is a minor difference from Wright's usage compared to the complexities of the usual conventions.

[9] You should now be thoroughly confused by these different types of tests and the conditions to which they apply. While it is partly for this reason that I am going to limit the discussion of

the testing of means, I also believe that much of the confusion must be attributed to way these issues are dealt with, not to your deficiency in understanding.

[10]Not to be confused with the author of the classic text on non-parametric statistics, Sidney Siegel (1956).

[11]Most textbooks on statistics give very little attention to tests of significance for categorical variables. They concentrate mainly on tests that should be used with metric variables. The major exception is Siegel and Castellan (1988) and Siegel (1956) before that.

[12]It is frustrating to find that the tables at the back of many textbooks on statistics do not specify whether the values are for one-tailed or two-tailed tests. This serious oversight can lead to errors of interpretation.

[13]The component of the equation in front of the square root sign, shown here as only G, is normally shown as $(G - \gamma)$, where γ is the population parameter of the variable in question (see Siegel and Castellan, 1988: 296–7; Elifson et al., 1998: 351–2). In testing the null hypothesis here, the population parameter is assumed to be 0, making this component of the equation $(G - 0)$. There seems to be no point in showing that zero is to be subtracted from G, except to make it clear that the focus is on the null hypothesis. I have chosen to leave it out.

[14]Note that they use the concept 'categorical' to refer to only nominal-level data while I use it to refer to both nominal-level and ordinal-level data. The reason for the different usage is that I define ordinal-level data as ordered categories, whereas they use 'ordinal' to refer to the rank ordering of individuals.

[15]Elifson et al. (1998) has a chapter on statistical inference for ordinal-level variables, and it also focuses on tests for experiments.

[16]Other versions of the *t* test are also used. For example, the paired *t* test is used in experimental designs.

[17]Statisticians usually define large as being beyond 30 or 40. This would mean that each category would need to exceed this.

[18]Statistical software packages have more complex procedures and better ways of arriving at the degrees of freedom in this situation. This method is suitable for hand calculation.

[19]SPSS provides a test for the equality of variances (the square of the standard deviation) and it shows the difference not to be significant (it is well below the 0.05 level). Therefore the assumption of approximate equality is justified.

[20]Different tables can be found in Siegel and Castellan (1988) and in Elifson et al. (1998) for small samples.

[21]This may seem complex but I can assure you that in statistical notation it would be unintelligible to most people. If you doubt me, try reading the equation at the foot of p. 300 in Siegel and Castellan (1988).

[22]Because of the obsession with the analysis of metric variables, few statistical textbooks deal with either lambda or Somer's *d*. The outstanding exception is Siegel and Castellan (1988). However, their discussion of them is not very accessible to the statistical novice.

[23]Note that the Table does not include *z* values of this size. In fact, z values beyond 3.11 simply indicate that a one-tailed test exceeds the 0.001 level.

Data Reduction: Preparing to Answer
Research Questions

Introduction

Before proceeding to apply the methods of data analysis discussed in Chapters 3–6 to answering the six research questions set out in Chapter 2, some preliminary analysis is required. This includes:

- creating scales and indexes;
- recoding variables; and
- describing the characteristics of the samples.

Data reduction reduces responses to a number of questions to a single score or number. This is done by using scaling techniques and by constructing indexes. The result is that instead of having to analyze the responses to each question separately, answers to related questions can be dealt with as a single variable.

Variables are recoded for a number of reasons, but mainly to tidy up or reorder distributions, or to transform variables from one level of measurement to another. In the latter case, it is mainly a matter of grouping a range of numbers (such as Age in years) or scores (such as Environmental Worldview) into a set of categories, that is, transposing metric measurement into categorical.

As a preliminary step in most empirical research, a description is prepared of the basic socio-demographic characteristics of the population or sample from which the data were obtained. This will provide a background to the subsequent analysis. Some or all of the following might be included when the data are obtained from individuals: gender, age, marital status, education, income, religion and ethnicity. In preparation for what follows in Chapter 8, this preliminary analysis will be presented at the end of this chapter.

Scales and Indexes

Two scales and three indexes have been constructed to reduce the data in the two samples. They are:

- Environmental Worldview scales and subscales;
- Willingness to Act Responsibly towards the environment scale;
- Avoiding Environmentally Damaging Products index;
- Recycling waste products index; and
- Support for Environmental Groups index.

Scales and indexes are used to combine a number of separate measures into a combined measure, normally resulting in at least interval-level measurement. While the two terms are frequently used interchangeably, I am using them to identify combined measures that have been tested for unidimensionality (scales) and those that have not (indexes). A scale is unidimensional when all its components contribute to the measurement of the particular variable, and only to that variable. The fact that statements appear to be concerned with the same topic does not mean that people will have interpreted and responded to them in a manner consistent with the meaning behind the variable that is being measured. It is this consistency in the responses that has to be demonstrated. I will discuss some of the methods used for this shortly.

Indexes, on the other hand, have not had this analysis applied to them. The numbers that have been assigned to the response categories of each component of the index are simply summed. The researcher must have some reason for believing that the components are all measuring the same thing, usually based on their manifest content. The three indexes to be used in this analysis will be elaborated in the next section.

While scales should be constructed from metric-level variables, it is a common practice to use ordinal-level measures and regard them as being interval. For example, many scales are created from responses to a number of statements or items in which the response categories form only ordinal-level measurement. Commonly used categories are 'Strongly agree', 'Agree', 'Neither agree nor disagree', 'Disagree' and 'Strongly disagree'. If these categories are assigned numbers, say from 1 to 5, it is only possible to sum the responses to a set of statements if the intervals between these categories are assumed to be equal, that is, as constituting interval-level measurement. While this assumption is not strictly correct, its adoption is quite general and few attitude scales have been constructed without it.

Creating Scales

In both the Student and Resident samples, *scales* were used to measure EWV and Willingness to Act. We will begin by creating a scale and three subscales for the former and then a scale for the latter.

Environmental Worldview Scales and Subscales

These scales have been developed from responses to 24 statements that express views on environmental issues. The same set of statements was used in two earlier studies (see Blaikie, 1992, 1993b; Blaikie and Ward, 1992) and is listed in Chapter 2. Such attitude statements are usually referred to as *items*, and this convention will be followed here.

Responses to these items were made in the five Likert categories that have already been discussed ('Strongly agree', 'Agree', 'Neither agree nor disagree', 'Disagree' and 'Strongly disagree'). Weights or scores were assigned to the categories giving a pro-environment response 5 and an anti-environment response 1. The wording of the items varied between pro- and anti-environment positions, an important requirement for avoiding unthinking responses.

Based on the assumption that the response categories constitute interval-level measurement, it is possible to produce a total score for the responses to the 24 statements. These scores were used in the earlier analysis. However, before a set of such scores is summed, it is necessary to demonstrate that the items are all measuring the same thing. A total score will have no meaning if it is made up of responses that relate to different dimensions or factors. There are a number of ways in which this can be done. In spite of the fact that these 24 statements were drawn from a number of existing scales, and have been used in earlier studies, it is necessary to demonstrate unidimensionality with these particular samples.

Pre-testing the Items

Some work was done on this task before the items were administered to the previous student sample in 1989. They were pre-tested on a diverse sample of 30 and then subjected to item analysis to establish the degree to which responses to each item are consistent with the total score based on them. This was done by dividing the sample into four quartiles or equal-sized categories, based on each respondent's total score. The response pattern of the top 25 per cent of respondents was compared with the responses of the bottom 25 per cent. The assumption behind the analysis is that if the responses to these items are consistent, that is, if respondents with pro-environmental total scores responded in a pro-environmental way to all the items, and vice versa, then a case could be made for including all the items in the scale. To do this, the mean score[1] for each item was calculated separately for respondents in each of the two extreme quartiles. If an item's mean was inconsistent with the position of these respondents with extreme mean scores, for example, if the respondents in the quartile with the highest overall mean scores had a low mean score on an item, and vice versa, then that item would need to be examined. It could be that the item had been weighted in the wrong direction, or that it is measuring some other variable. Fortunately, no such items were identified among the 24. In practice, a decision on marginal cases would be better deferred until the scale has been used with larger samples, particularly if removing them would create a shortage of items.[2]

Once the items had been administered to the two samples (along with the rest of the questionnaire in which they were located), and before any analysis was done, four further procedures were applied: item-to-item correlations; item-to-total correlations; the alpha test for reliability; and factor analysis. To do this, the data from the two samples were combined ($n = 867$).

Item-to-item Correlations

The first clues that we can get about possible patterns of relationships between the items come from a correlation matrix for all the items (see Table 7.1). It is worth looking for both the lowest and highest coefficients. The following items have coefficients of 0.10 or less:

'b' with 'f' (0.00), 'i' (0.08), 'n' (0.09), 's' (0.07) and 'x' (0.07);
'f' with 'b' (0.00), 'e' (0.10), 'g' (0.10), 'p' (0.09) and 'w' (0.07);
's' with 'b' (0.07), 'r' (0.08) and 'w' (0.04);
'x' with 'b' (0.07), 'k' (0.09), 'l' (0.10) and 'v' (0.10).

Some combinations have been repeated to show how four items, 'b', 'f', 's' and 'x', stand out from the rest. The strongest associations are for:

'c' with 'm' (0.43);
'd' with 'a' (0.45) and 'v' (0.52);
'q' with 'j' (0.41), 'm' (0.41), 'p' (0.42) and 'r' (0.41);
's' with 'f' (0.43) and 'n' (0.41);
't' with 'p' (0.47) and 'r' (0.41).

We shall find that the first two and the last two of these combinations appear again later.

It should be obvious that it is very difficult to interpret all these figures. In fact, factor analysis was developed to do this mathematically for us, and we shall wait to see what it can produce. In the meantime, some other types of exploratory analysis can be done.

Item-to-total Correlations

In the second procedure, the distribution of responses to each item is correlated with the distribution of the total scores of the responses to all 24 items. This is known as item-to-total correlation and is a simple way to test for unidimensionality. As with item analysis, summing each respondent's scores on all the items is done on the assumption that the items all measure the same thing. The method then explores whether this is the case.

A low correlation coefficient between responses to any item and the total score can suggest two things: that the item is measuring some other variable; or that the item itself is unreliable, that is, there is something peculiar about its wording that could have led to different interpretations and, hence, inconsistent responses.

In the analysis of the items designed to measure EWV, I have adopted the criterion that a correlation coefficient of less than 0.50 between any item and the total score needs to be examined[3] (see Table 7.2). If this was the only method available for establishing the scale, we could consider excluding any items with lower coefficients. However, other procedures can also be used.

Table 7.1   Correlation matrix of 24 items (both samples)

Item	a	b	c	d	e	f	g	h	i	j	k	l	m	n	o	p	q	r	s	t	u	v	w	x
a	1.00																							
b	0.13	1.00																						
c	0.20	0.17	1.00																					
d	0.45	0.18	0.20	1.00																				
e	0.25	0.21	0.20	0.18	1.00																			
f	0.27	0.00	0.26	0.18	0.10	1.00																		
g	0.22	0.24	0.20	0.27	0.27	0.10	1.00																	
h	0.28	0.20	0.27	0.25	0.19	0.23	0.19	1.00																
i	0.20	0.08	0.33	0.20	0.18	0.31	0.17	0.19	1.00															
j	0.24	0.23	0.32	0.22	0.26	0.20	0.26	0.28	0.26	1.00														
k	0.35	0.21	0.22	0.34	0.20	0.19	0.30	0.27	0.16	0.28	1.00													
l	0.17	0.12	0.16	0.14	0.28	0.11	0.24	0.14	0.17	0.30	0.15	1.00												
m	0.28	0.29	0.43	0.31	0.25	0.25	0.26	0.36	0.28	0.32	0.31	0.20	1.00											
n	0.19	0.09	0.24	0.19	0.11	0.32	0.21	0.18	0.32	0.28	0.20	0.17	0.26	1.00										
o	0.16	0.27	0.29	0.16	0.23	0.21	0.26	0.20	0.26	0.34	0.21	0.21	0.38	0.30	1.00									
p	0.22	0.32	0.27	0.24	0.28	0.09	0.32	0.29	0.17	0.35	0.25	0.27	0.33	0.21	0.31	1.00								
q	0.30	0.26	0.29	0.28	0.30	0.19	0.32	0.34	0.22	0.41	0.32	0.26	0.41	0.25	0.36	0.42	1.00							
r	0.24	0.18	0.22	0.24	0.30	0.13	0.26	0.28	0.22	0.29	0.20	0.26	0.29	0.16	0.24	0.34	0.41	1.00						
s	0.26	0.07	0.27	0.26	0.11	0.43	0.14	0.23	0.27	0.29	0.24	0.11	0.28	0.41	0.20	0.14	0.23	0.08	1.00					
t	0.21	0.23	0.24	0.17	0.27	0.13	0.29	0.23	0.22	0.31	0.16	0.30	0.26	0.22	0.31	0.47	0.38	0.41	0.11	1.00				
u	0.30	0.11	0.28	0.13	0.34	0.16	0.25	0.20	0.33	0.22	0.20	0.21	0.26	0.24	0.21	0.23	0.23	0.25	0.17	0.27	1.00			
v	0.35	0.24	0.21	0.52	0.21	0.11	0.31	0.23	0.14	0.22	0.39	0.14	0.29	0.20	0.24	0.29	0.31	0.25	0.21	0.24	0.16	1.00		
w	0.18	0.30	0.18	0.17	0.22	0.07	0.30	0.22	0.13	0.27	0.19	0.21	0.27	0.12	0.27	0.31	0.29	0.27	0.04	0.31	0.19	0.19	1.00	
x	0.18	0.07	0.27	0.11	0.15	0.25	0.12	0.27	0.20	0.22	0.09	0.10	0.19	0.20	0.18	0.22	0.24	0.23	0.22	0.28	0.17	0.10	0.15	1.00

Table 7.2 *Unidimensionality, reliability and commonalities of 24 items (combined samples)*

Item	Item-to-total correlation	Alpha if item delated
a	0.55	0.873
b	0.40	0.876
c	0.54	0.873
d	0.53	0.873
e	0.48	0.874
f	0.44	0.876
g	0.50	0.874
h	0.54	0.873
i	0.50	0.874
j	0.59	0.871
k	0.52	0.873
l	0.43	0.876
m	0.63	0.870
n	0.50	0.874
o	0.53	0.873
p	0.57	0.872
q	0.65	0.869
r	0.54	0.873
s	0.49	0.875
t	0.55	0.872
u	0.49	0.874
v	0.54	0.873
w	0.45	0.875
x	0.42	0.876

Alpha for all items = 0.878.

Cronbach's Alpha

The third procedure, the use of *Cronbach's alpha*, is probably the most commonly used test for scale reliability. Reliability refers to the capacity of a measure to produce consistent results. A measure will be unreliable if all or at least some of its items are unreliable. The classical way to test for reliability is to apply a measure to the same individuals on two different occasions, the test–retest method. However, unless the interval between the two applications is long enough for the respondents to have forgotten how they responded on the first occasion, the estimate of reliability might be inflated. Another method is to select two sets of items that are as alike as possible, known as the parallel or split-half method. Both parts are administered at the same time and the mean scores for each half compared. However, it is challenging enough to construct one good scale without having to create another that does exactly the same thing. These disadvantages have led to the use of other methods that use internal statistical procedures, particularly Cronbach's alpha.[4]

This coefficient ranges between 0 and 1, with a high value indicating a high level of consistency among the items. However, it is important to note that the value of alpha is influenced by the number of items in a scale; it increases as the number of items increases.

Apart from being able to calculate alpha with software packages such as SPSS, it is also possible to see whether removing any of the items individually will improve its value, thus indicating which of the items are unreliable, if any. Table 7.2 shows the item-to-total correlation coefficients, the alpha coefficient and the alpha coefficient if any particular item was deleted.

According to the criteria being adopted here, the item-to-total coefficients suggest that items 'b', 'e', 'f', 'l', 's', 'u', 'w' and 'x' are candidates for exclusion. However, the reliability test indicates that the alpha coefficient would not be increased by the removal of any of the items, that is, the total alpha of 0.878 would be lowered if any item were deleted. Therefore, it is not clear what decisions should be made. Further analysis is required.

Factor Analysis

We can now turn to the fourth procedure, factor analysis, for further assistance in deciding whether to exclude any items from the scale. *Factor analysis* is designed to identify underlying factors or *latent variables* present in the patterns of correlations among a set of measures, in this case, responses to a set of attitude statements. It is possible that in a matrix of correlation coefficients between a set of measures there are clusters of high correlation coefficients between subsets of the measures. Factor analysis identifies these clusters; it establishes how much variance they have in common and the extent to which each measure contributes to this common variance. Hence, a large set of measures can be reduced to a small set of factors, or even just one factor, that can explain the maximum amount of common variance in the bivariate correlations between them.

In the context of a set of related attitude statements, factor analysis can establish whether a common factor is present, that is, whether all the items are highly correlated and can be regarded as making up a common factor or a single scale. It also establishes the extent to which each item contributes to such a common factor. Alternatively, and perhaps more commonly in a large set of items, factor analysis can establish whether there is more than one factor or scale present in the responses to the items, that is, whether subsets of items form separate scales, or whether there are subscales within a general scale.

Correlation Matrix

Before applying factor analysis, it is a good idea to inspect the matrix of correlation coefficients. The first thing to do is to see if any item has very low coefficients with all or most of the other items. Such items are not going to find their way into any factor and would be best excluded. The second thing is to look for items that correlate very highly (0.90 or above) with any of the others. While common sense would suggest that scales should consist of highly correlated items, high correlation coefficients can also upset the analysis. We need not go into the mathematics of this here. However, the researcher is faced with the choice of eliminating all but one of such items. The correlation coefficients in the matrix of the 24 items have a range from 0.52 ('d' with 'v') to 0.00 ('b' with 'f'); the majority are between 0.20 and 0.35 (see Table 7.1). Hence, the second problem is absent and no item has consistently low coefficients with the other items.

Sampling Adequacy

The first step in factor analysis is to establish whether the set of items is a suitable selection. The commonly used statistic for this is the Kaiser–Meyer–Olkin (KMO) measure of *sampling adequacy* of the items. Its values range from 0 to 1. A value of 0.70 or more is generally considered sufficiently high, while a value below 0.50 is unsatisfactory and one over 0.90 is outstanding. The KMO for this set of items, with the two samples combined, is 0.92!

A related consideration is whether the sample of respondents is sufficiently large to run factor analysis reliably. A general rule of thumb is that a sample of at least 300 will usually provide reliable results.[5] Our sample of 867 is more than adequate.

Commonality

The total variance present in the responses to any item is made up of three components: some variance is specific and consistently related to the item (unique variance); some may be shared with other variables or items (common variance); and there may be some variance that is specific to but not consistently related to the item (error or random variance). The proportion of common variance is known as an item's *commonality*. Factor analysis begins by establishing the commonality for each item, that is, the proportion of its variance that is explained by the factors that are present. It is produced by squaring each item's contribution to or loading on the number of factors present, and then summing the products. However, these values are dependent on the number of factors that are included in the analysis. The greater the number of factors being considered, the higher the commonalities are likely to be. Methods for determining how many factors should be considered will be discussed shortly.

Table 7.3 includes a list of the commonalities. The highest values are for items 'd' (0.63), 'a' (0.60), 'v' (0.60), 's' (0.60) and 'x' (0.58), while the lowest values are for items 'k' (0.47), 'j' (0.43), 'g' (0.43), and 'w' (0.38). This means that the items in the first set make a high level of total contribution to the variance of the factors to which they contribute, and the items in the second set make the lowest level of total contribution. However, for the moment, all values can be regarded as satisfactory, although we will return to them to assist with later decisions.

Factor Loadings

The relationship of any item to a factor is indicated by its *factor loading*. This is a measure of the contribution an item makes to a particular factor. Ideally, an item should have a 'high' loading on only one factor. As in other aspects of factor analysis, experts differ on what constitutes a 'high' loading. However, when a sample is being used, its size is important in determining whether a loading is statistically significant, that is, whether it can also be expected to exist in the population from which the sample was drawn. For a level of significance of 0.01 (two-tailed), the minimum loading for a sample of 50 is 0.72, for 100 is 0.51, for 200 is 0.36, for 300 is 0.30, for 600 is 0.21 and for 1000 is 0.16 (Stevens,

Table 7.3 *Commonalities and unrotated factors with 24 items (combined samples)*

Item	Commonalities	Factor 1	Factor 2	Factor 3	Factor 4	Factor 5	Factor 6
a	0.60	0.53		-0.38	0.33		
b	0.57	0.41	-0.38		-0.42		-0.21
c	0.54	0.54	0.21				-0.38
d	0.63	0.51		-0.59			
e	0.51	0.49	-0.23		0.39		-0.22
f	0.54	0.41	0.59				
g	0.43	0.53	-0.23			0.25	
h	0.52	0.53				-0.43	
i	0.50	0.47	0.34	0.25			-0.20
j	0.43	0.60					
k	0.47	0.52		-0.43			
l	0.52	0.43		0.21	0.31	0.23	0.33
m	0.58	0.64			-0.25		-0.32
n	0.58	0.48	0.40			0.29	0.29
o	0.51	0.55			-0.29	0.29	
p	0.52	0.61	-0.32				
q	0.50	0.66					
r	0.50	0.55	-0.25			-0.28	
s	0.60	0.45	0.58				
t	0.58	0.57	-0.28	0.28			0.25
u	0.66	0.49			0.48		-0.36
v	0.60	0.53		-0.55			
w	0.38	0.47	-0.36				
x	0.58	0.40		0.31		-0.53	
Eigenvalue		6.49	1.77	1.47	1.12	1.04	0.94
Variance (%)		27.1	7.4	6.1	4.7	4.3	3.9

1992). However, Stevens also recommends that only loadings of 0.40 and above should be taken seriously, although another common recommendation is 0.30 and above. In effect, a loading of 0.40 means that 16 per cent of the item's variance contributes to the factor (arrived at by squaring the loading and multiplying by 100). A loading of 0.30 only accounts for 9 per cent of an item's variance. To include such an item in a scale is to take on board 91 per cent of unrelated variance, thus producing very 'muddy' and imprecise scales. I will be using a number of criteria, all of which are higher than these.

Unidimensionality

We can now go through the steps involved in establishing whether or not this set of 24 items is *unidimensional*, that is, whether they all measure the same thing. However, in doing so, it is not possible to provide a detailed review of factor analysis itself. I recommend de Vaus (1995) for a very readable outline, Hair et al. (1998) and Field (2000) for more detailed reviews and Lewis-Beck (1994) for a collection of more technical discussions.[6]

As we have seen, the aim in establishing a scale is to reduce a number of measures, such as these 24 attitude items, to a single variable. Factor analysis establishes unidimensionality by showing which measures or items have a high loading on only one factor. If one common factor is not possible, then perhaps

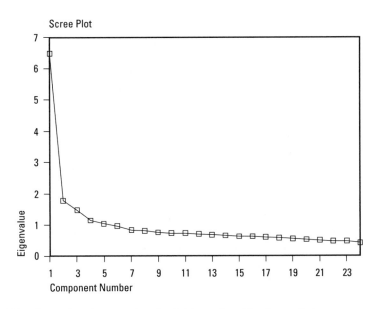

Figure 7.1 *Scree plot of eigenvalues for 24 items (combined samples)*

more than one factor can be located, each of which would need to be shown to be unidimensional.

Unrotated Solution

When an exploratory[7] factor analysis[8] is run on a set on attitude items, it produces an initial solution on the number of factors that might be present in the responses to the items. This is usually referred to as the *unrotated solution*. It is the first attempt to identify factors. Subsequent solutions involve some method of rotation, in our case varimax. This rotation attempts to find a small number of items that have high loadings on any factor. It is a useful approach that makes for a relatively easy interpretation of factors.

If a number of factors emerge from a large set of items, a decision has to be made about how many should be considered. The normal procedure is to use a statistic called the *eigenvalue*. It measures the amount of the total variance for which each factor accounts. The higher the eigenvalue, the greater the variance explained by that factor. A common rule of thumb is to consider only factors with eigenvalues greater than 1.0, although values as low as 0.7 are also recommended. However, another method can also be used, known as a *scree plot*.[9] It involves creating a graph in which the eigenvalues (*Y* axis) are plotted against each factor (*X* axis). A scree plot makes it possible to quickly discover a change of gradient in the magnitude of the eigenvalues. Normally the first factor or two have relatively high eigenvalues, then the magnitude decreases and later factors usually show little change.

Figure 7.1 shows the plot of eigenvalues for the 24 items in the combined sample. It is a typical plot in which the first factor (component) is high (6.49) and there is the same number of factors as there are items. Five factors have an eigenvalue of 1.0 or more, and there are 11 with values of 0.7 or more. A carefully inspection of the plot shows three critical changes in the gradient of the line, although they are rather subtle in the second and third cases. The first is at the second factor where there is a major change; the second is at the fourth factor; and the third at the seventh. In view of the first big change in gradient, we could decide to use only two factors, but this would only account for 34.4 per cent of the total variance. Alternatively, we could use the first four factors (45.2 per cent of the total variance), or we could go as far as the seventh factor (56.9 per cent). As already noted, using a minimum eigenvalue of 1.0, five factors would be included. Hence, our choice would seem to lie somewhere between four and six factors. Initially, six will be requested in the factor analysis.

Table 7.3 shows the factor loadings of at least 0.20 on these six factors. A major aim in this analysis is to explain as much of the variance as possible in the responses to a set of items. While this can be done by including more factors, as we shall see, this is not a good strategy as the value of the analysis seems to decline with each additional factor. Some of the weaker factors may have only one item contributing to them to any degree; hence they hardly constitute a useful scale. In other words, factor analysis extracts the 'strong' factors first and then proceeds to extract further factors of declining strength. It is better to eliminate items that do not contribute to a limited set of factors, or which contribute to more than one factor. The latter tend to pull the analysis in two or more different directions. By eliminating such items, we sharpen up the factors so that they account for more of the variance.

From Table 7.3 we can also see that the unrotated solution has all the items with substantial loadings on factor 1, thus suggesting the presence of a common factor. The loadings range from 0.40 to 0.66. If the criterion for inclusion in a factor were set as at least 0.40, factor 1 would include all 24 items. Four other factors have eigenvalues of at least 1.0 and item loadings of at least 0.40:

factor 2   'f' (0.59), 'n' (0.40), 's' (0.58);
factor 3   'd' (−0.59), 'k' (−0.43),'v' (−0.55);
factor 4   'b' (−0.42),'u' (0.48);
factor 5   'h' (−0.43),'x' (−0.53).

As factor 6 has no loadings of at least 0.40, it will be excluded from the subsequent analysis. (It has four of at least 0.30; 'c' (−0.38), 'u' (−0.36), 'l' (0.33) and 'm' (−0.32).) This decision is supported by the criterion of including only those factors with an eigenvalue of at least 1.0.

We need to note that some items, namely, 'a', 'b' and 'x', have loadings of at least 0.30 on two factors, apart from the general one, and 'e', 'g', 'i', 'l', 'n', 'o', 'r' and 't' also have multiple but weaker loadings. Such items are contenders for exclusion as the dual loadings suggest that they are contributing to more than one factor.

Rotated Solution

In order to try to sort this out, it is necessary to try a *rotated solution*. The method used here is principal components with varimax rotation.[10] Table 7.4 records all loadings of at least 0.30, given that five factors with eigenvalues of

Table 7.4   *Rotated solution for five factors with 24 items (combined samples)*

Item	Commonalities	Factor 1	Factor 2	Factor 3	Factor 4	Factor 5
a	0.59			0.64		
b	0.52	0.70				
c	0.39		0.47			
d	0.63			0.77		
e	0.46				0.62	
f	0.53		0.67			
g	0.42	0.39		0.33	0.39	
h	0.49					0.57
i	0.46		0.57		0.36	
j	0.41	0.43	0.34			
k	0.47			0.60		
l	0.41				0.59	
m	0.47	0.46	0.38			
n	0.49		0.66			
o	0.51	0.58	0.38			
p	0.50	0.54				0.34
q	0.48	0.45				0.36
r	0.50				0.42	0.48
s	0.57		0.70			
t	0.51	0.38			0.43	0.43
u	0.52				0.66	
v	0.59			0.71		
w		0.38	0.53			
x	0.58					0.71
Eigenvalue		2.74	2.62	2.44	2.21	1.86
Variance (%)		11.4	10.9	10.2	9.2	7.8

at least 1.0 are extracted. The general factor does not appear this time as the method of rotation tries to produce higher loadings on a smaller number of items on each factor. It is worth noting that a number of items have loadings on more than one factor, in particular, 'g', 'i', 'j', 'm', 'o', 'p', 'q', 'r' and 't'. This list has considerable overlap with the multiple loaded items in the unrotated solution. This time, the criterion for inclusion in a factor is set at 0.50, although a stricter criterion could also be considered and will be used as the analysis is refined. The following five factors account for 49.5 per cent of the variance:

> factor 1   'b' (0.70), 'o' (0.58), 'p' (0.54), 'w' (0.53);
> factor 2   'f' (0.67), 'i' (0.57), 'n' (0.66), 's' (0.70);
> factor 3   'a' (0.64), 'd' (0.77), 'k' (0.60), 'v' (0.71);
> factor 4   'e' (0.62), 'l' (0.59), 'u' (0.66);
> factor 5   'h' (0.58), 'x' (0.71).

There is some similarity with the unrotated factors. The first factor ('bopw') appears to be about the need for intervention, mostly by governments, in order to conserve resources, although 'p' is about pollution. The second factor ('fins') is about the role of science and technology in solving environmental problems. The third factor ('adkv') is concerned with the relationship between humans and nature. The other two factors are rather mixed bags. In the fourth factor (elu), 'e' and 'u' are about humans upsetting the balance of nature, while 'l' is

Table 7.5   *Rotated solution for six factors with 24 items (combined samples)*

Item	Factor 1	Factor 2	Factor 3	Factor 4	Factor 5	Factor 6
a		0.64			0.30	
b				0.71		
c			0.31	0.43	0.39	0.32
d		0.77				
e	0.36				0.57	
f			0.65			
g	0.43	0.34				
h						0.60
i			0.46		0.51	
j	0.42		0.35	0.31		
k		0.60				
l	0.65					
m					0.56	
n			0.71			
o	0.30		0.35	0.54		
p	0.54			0.37		
q	0.45			0.33		
r	0.52					0.38
s			0.72			
t	0.67					0.30
u					0.77	
v		0.72				
w	0.37			0.45		
x						0.69
Eigenvalue	2.60	2.48	2.28	2.17	1.67	1.62
Variance (%)	10.8	10.3	9.5	9.0	7.0	6.8

about conservation of resources, and the fifth factor ('hx') combines the need to control pollution with controls on economic growth.[11]

In order to illustrate that great care must be taken in drawing conclusions from factor analysis, I have also produced a rotated solution with six factors. This is suggested by the scree plot presented in Figure 7.1. The loadings of at least 0.30 are shown in Table 7.5. Again, using 0.50 as the criterion for inclusion, some of the factors are the same or very similar to the five-factor solution; 'adkv' and 'hx' appear again, and 'fins' becomes 'fns', although 'i' almost makes it in. In addition, 'elu' becomes 'eiu', 'bopw' now becomes 'bmo', although 'w' is not far away. What is surprising is that a new factor is extracted first consisting of 'lprt', with a number of other items having quite high loadings on it. Hence, an apparently innocent decision to add another factor can change the results.

Analysis with Some Items Excluded

We can conclude from the analysis thus far that, while a common factor may be present among all 24 items, a number of subscales also appear to exist within it. We could leave the analysis at this point, making a decision to go with either the five-factor or six-factor solution and perhaps strengthening the criterion for inclusion in the subscales to 0.55 or even 0.60. However, the mix of items in some of these factors, and the fact that a few of the items have multiple loadings, suggest that further investigation is necessary. In addition, the existence of

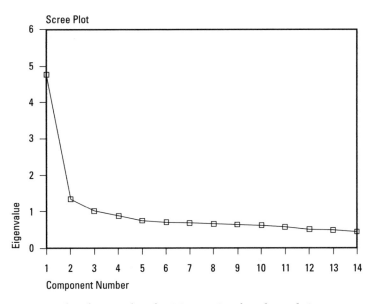

Figure 7.2   *Scree plot of eigenvalues for 14 items (combined samples)*

the common factor is dependent on using quite a low criterion, that is, 0.40. Therefore, we also have to decide whether to accept this criterion and go with the common factor, or to exclude some items with lower loadings on it. I am going to adopt the criterion that to be in the common factor an item must have a loading of at least 0.50. This is a rather strict requirement, but I hope it will become clear why its use is justified.

We now end up with only 14 items, having removed 'b', 'e', 'f', 'i', 'l', 'n', 's', 'u', 'w' and 'x'. This list is very similar to the one produced by the criteria set for the item-to-total correlation coefficients, 'i' and 'n' having been added here. It includes only 8 of the 17 items in the five-factor subscales, suggesting that there may be independent scales rather than just subscales here. Factor analysis can now be run on these 14 items. This time the KMO is 0.90, still very high. On the unrotated analysis, only three factors have eigenvalues of at least 1.0. However, the scree plot suggests that up to five factors could be considered, although the fourth has an eigenvalue of only 0.87 and the fifth, only 0.75 (see Figure 7.2). All three of these possibilities were run, but I came to the conclusion that three factors provided the best solution.

Table 7.6 shows the loadings of at least 0.30 on the unrotated factors. Again, factor 1 is a common factor on which all items load between 0.53 and 0.69, considerably higher than for all 24 items. Again, setting a loading of at least 0.40 as the criterion, factor 2 includes 'a' (0.45), 'd' (0.57) and 'v' (0.45), and factor 3 'c' (0.53), 'm' (0.42) and 't' (−0.40).

We can now try a rotated solution on these 14 items. Table 7.6 shows the loadings of at least 0.40 on the three factors. As these factors will be regarded as subscales within the general factor, I am setting a very strict criterion of at least 0.60 for inclusion. They are:

Table 7.6 *Unrotated and rotated solutions with 14 retained items (combined samples)*

Item	Unrotated solution			Rotated solution		
	Factor 1	Factor 2	Factor 3	Factor 1	Factor 2	Factor 3
a	0.54	0.45			0.67	
c	0.53		0.53			0.76
d	0.56	0.57			0.79	
g	0.54			0.49		
h	0.54					0.50
j	0.60					0.51
k	0.56	0.37			0.61	
m	0.65		0.42			0.71
o	0.55	−0.31				0.53
p	0.64			0.67		
q	0.69			0.53		0.41
r	0.57		−0.32	0.65		
t	0.58	−0.38	−0.40	0.78		
v	0.59	0.45			0.72	
Eigenvalue	4.76	1.34	1.01	2.45	2.38	2.28
Variance (%)	34.0	9.6	7.2	17.5	17.0	16.3

Table 7.7 *Unidimensionality and reliability of 10 rejected items (combined samples)*

Item	Item-to-total correlation	Alpha if item delated
b	0.36	0.700
e	0.50	0.677
f	0.56	0.668
i	0.61	0.660
l	0.47	0.684
n	0.61	0.659
s	0.58	0.665
u	0.56	0.667
w	0.43	0.686
x	0.48	0.682

Alpha for all items = 0.698.

factor 1 'p' (0.67), 'r' (0.65) and 't' (0.78);
factor 2 'a' (0.67), 'd' (0.79), 'k' (0.61) and 'v' (0.72);
factor 3 'c' (0.76) and 'm' (0.71).

While 'adkv' appeared in the earlier rotated solutions, 'cm' rather than 'hm' has turned up here. Factor 1, 'prt', was signalled in the previous six-factor rotated solution. The items in this factor refer to the need for controls on industry and the need to conserve forests. The third factor ('cm') is concerned with the benefits and problems of economic growth, and makes more sense than 'hm'.

Analysis of Excluded Items

It is also possible to run factor analysis on the excluded items. Before doing this, however, we need to do some preliminary analysis. First, the alpha coefficient is 0.698, just below the minimum criterion of 0.70. Second, the item-to-total correlation coefficients, and the alpha coefficients if items are removed, are shown

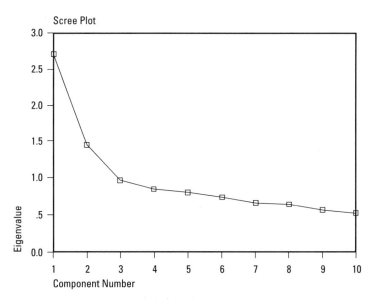

Figure 7.3 *Scree plot of eigenvalues for nine items (combined samples)*

in Table 7.7. Four items, 'b', 'l', 'w' and 'x', have correlation coefficients of less than 0.50, the minimal criterion. In addition, the removal of 'b' would raise the value of alpha. All this suggests that this set of items is not unidimensional.

Factor analysis was run on these excluded items to see if more than one factor is present. If there are multiple factors, they can be regarded as independent of the scale and subscales already established. In this case, the KMO is lower (0.77), but still satisfactory. The scree plot (Figure 7.3) suggests that three factors should be extracted, with the third having an eigenvalue of 0.98, and all three including 51.6 per cent of the variance. The commonalities range from 0.29 to 0.67, the former ('x') being much lower than the others. Rotated solutions have been tried with and without 'x' and a decision made to exclude this item.

Table 7.8 shows all loadings of at least 0.30 on the unrotated solution, without 'x', and of at least 0.40 on the rotated solution. Again, using the loading criterion of 0.60, the following factors were extracted:

    factor 1   'f' (0.75), 'n' (0.70), 's' (0.79);
    factor 2   'e' (0.72), 'l' (0.60), 'u' (0.73);
    factor 3   'b' (0.81), 'w' (0.72).

Factor 1 appeared in both the earlier solutions on the 24 items. Factor 2 appeared earlier in the five-factor solution on the 24 items (see Table 7.4), but 'bw' is new. The latter two items deal with alternative sources of energy.

Incidentally, if the minimum eigenvalue had been set at 1.0, two factors would have been extracted with loadings as follows:

    factor 1   'f' (0.74), 'n', (0.68) and 's' (0.74);
    factor 2   'b' (0.61), 'e' (0.67) and 'w' (0.66).

Table 7.8   *Unrotated and rotated solutions with nine rejected items (combined samples)*

Item	Unrotated solution			Rotated solution		
	Factor 1	Factor 2	Factor 3	Factor 1	Factor 2	Factor 3
b	0.32	0.52	0.58			0.84
e	0.51	0.45	−0.32		0.72	
f	0.56	−0.48		0.75		
i	0.63			0.52		
l	0.47	0.31			0.59	
n	0.63	−0.33		0.70		
s	0.59	−0.47		0.79		
u	0.60		−0.44		0.73	
w	0.41	0.52	0.38			0.72
Eigenvalue	2.56	1.46	0.97	1.99	1.68	1.32
Variance (%)	28.4	16.2	10.8	22.1	18.7	14.6

Four items, 'i', 'l', 'w' and 'x', would have been left out, although 'i' (0.59) could have been considered for inclusion in factor 1.

It is important to note that while factor analysis seeks to identify items on which responses either do or do not follow a consistent pattern, the presence of inconsistent items can 'upset' the analysis. This is why it is important to identify and exclude such items, and then try the analysis without them. Clearly, the inclusion or exclusion of items is a matter of judgement based mainly on recognized rules of thumb and this trial-and-error process. For example, I have considered including 'l' in the second independent factor, even though it does not meet the very strict criterion, mainly because its content is consistent with items 'b' and 'w'. At the same time, 'e' could have been excluded, even with its high loading, because its content is different.

Orthogonal and Oblique Rotations

The extraction of factors thus far has used varimax rotation. This is described technically as an orthogonal rotation and has the effect of keeping the factors independent as they are rotated. An alternative is oblique rotation, which allows the factors to correlate. This can be done using the direct oblimin rotation, but other methods are also available. The choice of method has to be made on theoretical grounds.[12] I have opted for the varimax rotation in order to see whether independent factors exist. The oblimin rotation was also run, using the same steps (initially with the 24 items, then with 14, and finally with the rejected 10), and the same criteria, to see how robust the factors are. The following factors and loadings were produced. For ease of comparison, the varimax loadings are shown second and in italics.

sub-factor 1   'p' (0.67/*0.67*), 'r' (0.66/*0.65*), 't' (0.84/*0.78*);
sub-factor 2   'a' (0.68/*0.67*), 'd' (0.82/*0.79*), 'k' (0.60/*0.61*), 'v' (0.73/*0.72*);
sub-factor 3   'c' (0.82/*0.76*), 'm' (0.72/*0.71*);
       factor 2   'f' (0.76/*0.75*) 'n' (0.70/*0.70*), 's' (0.81/*0.79*);
       factor 3   'e' (0.74/*0.72*), 'l' (0.60/*0.60*), 'u' (0.75/*0.73*);
       factor 4   'b' (0.86/*0.81*), 'w' (0.71/*0.72*).

Table 7.9 *Distributions on the 24 items (combined samples)*

Item	Minimum	Maximum	Mean	Standard deviation	Skewness
a	1	5	3.13	1.11	0.131
b	1	5	4.27	0.82	−1.311
c	1	5	3.79	0.89	−0.659
d	1	5	3.87	1.11	−0.820
e	1	5	4.22	0.83	−1.286
f	1	5	2.28	0.94	0.995
g	1	5	4.41	0.66	−1.079
h	1	5	3.39	1.08	−0.211
i	1	5	3.24	1.04	−0.191
j	1	5	3.99	0.93	−0.914
k	1	5	3.97	0.89	−0.860
l	1	5	3.91	0.89	−0.983
m	1	5	3.56	0.97	−0.399
n	1	5	3.52	1.05	−0.582
o	1	5	4.21	0.74	−1.217
p	1	5	4.19	0.74	−1.033
q	1	5	3.87	0.99	−0.903
r	1	5	4.12	0.93	−0.939
s	1	5	2.95	1.03	0.193
t	1	5	3.99	0.81	−0.846
u	1	5	3.90	0.88	−0.675
v	1	5	4.04	0.96	−0.989
w	1	5	4.17	0.73	−0.840
x	1	5	2.56	0.89	0.410

The factors are identical and the loadings are almost the same. The decision not to include item 'i' in 'fns' is also confirmed as its loading is now only 0.46.

Using Ordinal-level Data

Before leaving this analysis, I want to return to the issue of whether it is legitimate to do factor analysis on data that are, strictly speaking, only ordinal. Factor analysis uses correlation coefficients (in this case Pearson's r) as its foundation, and such coefficients are only appropriate for interval-level and ratio-level data. Further, the distributions on variables used in such analysis should be approximately normal. In short, the data should meet the requirements of parametric measurement. On the first point, I have already indicated that it has become common practice to assume that Likert-type categories constitute interval-level rather than ordinal-level measurement. As soon as the responses to a set of items are summed, this assumption applies. However, on the second point, the distributions on the 24 items from the two samples are, in many cases, badly skewed, mostly negatively, and have varying dispersions (see Table 7.9).

It is always a good idea to examine such distributions before proceeding to undertake correlations and factor analysis. One solution to this problem of skewed distributions is to transform skewed distributions into normal distributions. A further refinement to the analysis could have included such transformations. Without it, some of the correlation coefficients will be more conservative (lower) than if the transformations had been done (see p. 87).

Table 7.10 *Distributions on scales and subscales (combined samples)*

Scale	Mean	Standard deviation	Skewness
EWVGSC	3.89	0.53	−0.294
HUSENV	3.75	0.76	−0.385
GOVCONT	4.10	0.64	−0.757
ECGROW	3.67	0.79	−0.485
SCITEK	2.92	0.77	0.237
IMPACT	4.01	0.62	−0.747
ALTENGY	4.22	0.62	−0.721

Scales and Subscales

I have gone through the process of establishing these scales and subscales in considerable detail to illustrate that arriving at a final set of factors, and hence a set of new variables, involves experimenting with different possibilities and making defendable decisions. We could have gone through this process in other ways, such as discovering which are the 'troublesome' items early on and eliminating them. However, to discover troublesome items requires considerable experimentation with different combinations of items. It is an interesting process if numbers fascinate you. Fortunately, the calculations are done almost instantaneously.

Having established one general scale, which includes three subscales, and three independent scales, the next step is to name each one. This entails finding a short title that captures the content of that particular set of items. What we hope to find is consistency in the content of the items in each of the scales. The following titles and abbreviations will be used:

1 Environmental Worldview general scale (acdghjkmopqrtv) – EWVGSC
1a Human use of the environment (adkv) – HUSENV
1b Government controls (prt) – GOVCONT
1c Economic growth (cm) – ECGROW
2 Faith in science and technology (fns) – SCITEK
3 Human impact on the environment (elu) – IMPACT
4 Alternative energy (bw) – ALTENGY

The scale based on the original set of 24 items will be referred to as:

Environmental Worldview total scale – EWVTSC.

While the 24-item scale was used in the examples in Chapters 3–6, it will not be used in the analysis related to the research questions in the next chapter.

Finding consistency in the content of the items in the various scales confirms that they are not just artefacts of the method of analysis. However, it is possible to find items that have not been included having similar content to those in a particular scale (e.g. 'i' in SCITEK and 'x' in ECGROW), and to find items with manifestly different content included in a scale (e.g. 'l' in IMPACT).[13]

To test whether the decisions made about the scales and subscales were appropriate, we can now go back and run item-to-total correlations, and the

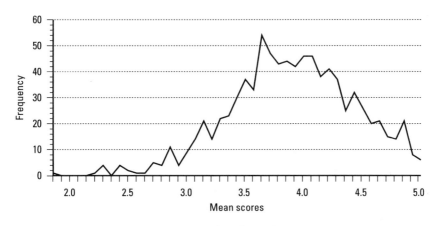

Figure 7.4   *EWVGSC mean scores (combined samples)*

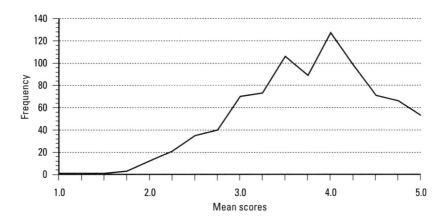

Figure 7.5   *HUSENV mean scores (combined samples)*

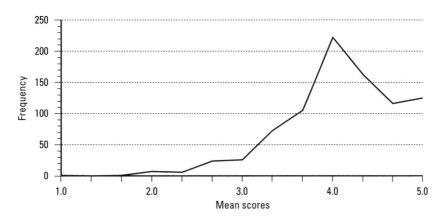

Figure 7.6   *GOVCONT mean scores (combined samples)*

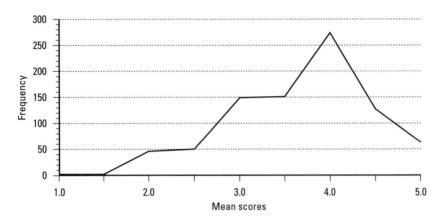

Figure 7.7   *ECGROW mean scores (combined samples)*

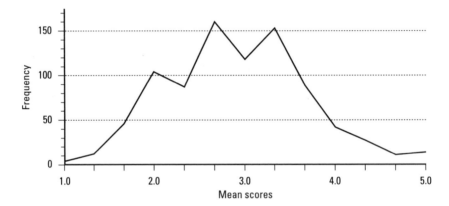

Figure 7.8   *SCITEK mean scores (combined samples)*

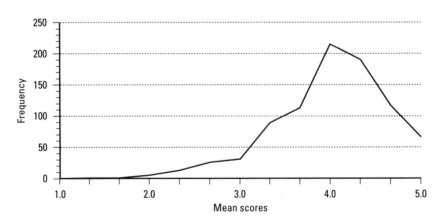

Figure 7.9   *IMPACT mean scores (combined samples)*

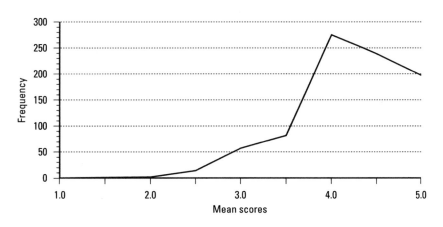

Figure 7.10 *ALTENGY mean scores (combined samples)*

reliability test (Cronbach's alpha). However, before doing this, we should examine their distributions (see Table 7.10 and Figures 7.4–7.10). With the exception of SCITEK, which is almost normally distributed with only a slight positive skewness (0.237), all scales and subscales are negatively skewed. However, the only really 'deviant' distributions are for GOVCONT (–0.757), IMPACT (–0.747) and ALTENGY (–0.721).

Table 7.11 indicates that EWVGSC has a high alpha but that the item-to-total correlation coefficients are generally weaker than for all the other scales and subscales. The others have consistently good item-to-total correlations coefficients and weaker alpha coefficients. However, we must expect that the correlations coefficients will be higher for scales with few items as each item plays a more significant role in the scale itself. In other words, each item is being correlated with itself as well as the other items. This is very evident in two-item scales, such as ECGROW and ALTENGY. Allowance must be made for this in assessing these coefficients. Hence, they can only be used as a guide rather than a precise measurement of unidimensionality. They simply confirm what has already been established by factor analysis.

It might even be argued that factor analysis and these tests are not appropriate for two-item scales, and that all that is needed is to examine the correlation co-efficients to see if the items are sufficiently related. For the two items in ECGROW the coefficient is 0.43, and for ALTENGY 0.30. Hence, the former would appear to be more reliable than the latter. However, given that factor analysis has thrown up these two scales, they need to be given serious consideration.

If we were to apply the reliability test very strictly (see Table 7.11), we might conclude that EWVGSC is the only scale or subscale that can be used as it is the only one with an alpha value of at least 0.80, and only HUSENV passes the lower criterion of 0.70. Should we discard the rest? I think not. For a start, we have used very strict criteria for the factor loadings; secondly, HUSENV and SCITEK keep falling out of the analysis at every turn; and, thirdly, we can expect the alpha coefficient to be lower in scales with a limited number of

Table 7.11   *Reliability of scales and subscales (combined samples)*

Scale	Item	Item-to-total correlation	Alpha if item deleted	Alpha
EWVGSC	a	0.58	0.838	
	c	0.53	0.839	
	d	0.60	0.837	
	g	0.52	0.839	
	h	0.57	0.839	
	j	0.59	0.835	
	k	0.57	0.837	0.846
	m	0.65	0.831	
	o	0.52	0.839	
	p	0.60	0.834	
	q	0.68	0.829	
	r	0.57	0.837	
	t	0.55	0.837	
	v	0.61	0.835	
HUSENV	a	0.74	0.678	
	d	0.79	0.622	0.723
	k	0.67	0.696	
	v	0.75	0.643	
GOVCONT	p	0.75	0.575	
	r	0.79	0.638	0.666
	t	0.80	0.501	
ECGROW	c	0.83	–	0.603
	m	0.86	–	
SCITEK	f	0.74	0.579	
	n	0.76	0.599	0.653
	s	0.80	0.487	
IMPACT	e	0.74	0.344	
	l	0.70	0.506	0.531
	u	0.72	0.437	
ALTENGY	b	0.83	–	0.464
	w	0.78	–	

items. However, we may want to give less importance to ECGROW and IMPACT and, particularly, to ALTENGY. An interesting issue here is whether it would be better to rely on single-item measurement, rather than scales of two or three items that have relatively low alpha values. I would opt for scales with a few items as long as they have been established by rigorous procedures and the inter-item correlation (as against item-to-total) coefficients are within the same range of those for scales with higher alpha coefficients.

It is important to reiterate that these tests for unidimensionality and reliability can only be interpreted in relation to the sample or population from which the data were collected. It is the pattern of responses to these items with a particular sample or population that is being examined. If a scale is used in other contexts, this same analysis must be repeated on each occasion, and adjustments may have to be made to the scales. This is particularly relevant when an established scale is borrowed for use in a different context. The fact that I have used this same set of items with four different samples, and over a five-year period,

Table 7.12   *Correlation matrix of EWV scales and subscales (combined samples)*

	EWVGSC	HUSENV	GOVCONT	ECGROW	SCITEK	IMPACT	ALTENGY
EWVGSC	1.00						
HUSENV	0.79	1.00					
GOVCONT	0.74	0.39	1.00				
ECGROW	0.70	0.40	0.41	1.00			
SCITEK	0.46	0.37	0.24	0.40	1.00		
IMPACT	0.53	0.35	0.48	0.37	0.26	1.00	
ALTENGY	0.48	0.30	0.42	0.34	0.11	0.30	1.00

provides an illustration of this. The tests have produced some differences between the two 1994 samples and the two earlier ones. There is no item that really had to be excluded from the total scale in all four samples. Hence, we are confronted with a dilemma. On the one hand, leaving the weaker items in with each application of a scale creates some lack of precision in the measurement of the variable. On the other hand, leaving different items out on different applications means that the results are not strictly comparable across different studies. In spite of having used the total scale in the 1989/90 studies, I am going to concentrate on the general scale (EWVGSC) and the other five scales here.

One final piece of analysis is appropriate before leaving these scales. Having separated the items into different scales and subscales, we can now examine the relationships between them by creating a correlation matrix. This involves calculating correlation coefficients for all combination of pairs of scales (see Table 7.12).

First, while not shown in the table, the total scale (EWVTSC) and the general scale (EWVGSC) are very highly correlated (0.96). This is not surprising as the latter is made up of a large part of the former. It does suggest, however, that the scales could be used interchangeably. Second, EWVGSC is more closely related to the three subscales (HUSENV, 0.79; GOVCONT, 0.74; ECGROW, 0.70) than it is to the other three scales (SCITEK, 0.46; IMPACT, 0.53; ALTENGY, 0.48). Again, this is not surprising as the subscales are all components of the general scale. However, it also confirms that the three independent scales should be treated as such. Third, among the subscales and the independent scales, the highest coefficient is between SCITEK and ECGROW (0.40) and the lowest between SCITEK and ALTENGY (0.11); most of the others are between 0.30 and 0.40. Hence, perhaps with one main exception (SCITEK with ALTENGY), these scales and subscales are related. However, the fact that they have been separated by factor analysis, allows for more detailed analysis.

It is clear that faith in the ability of science and technology to solve problems is not really related to the other components of environmental attitudes, particularly ALTENGY. This would suggest that environmentalists are divided about the role of science and technology, some having faith and others not, the former marginally outnumbering the latter. Likewise, it would appear that those with more negative environmental attitudes are also divided. We will explore this in the next chapter.

Table 7.13   *Unrotated and rotated solutions with Willingness*
                to Act itmes (combined samples)

Item	Unrotated solution	Rotated solution
1	0.76	0.77
2	0.72	0.71
3	0.78	0.72
4	0.69	0.73
5	0.61	0.65
6	0.78	0.73
Eigenvalue	3.30	3.14
Variance (%)	41.2	39.2

Willingness to Act Scale

In addition to the 24 EWV items, six additional attitude statements were used
with the two samples to measure Willingness to Act. The items are listed in
Chapter 2. When factor analysis was run on these six items, one factor was
extracted. Because of the manifest content of the items, the preliminary analysis
has been omitted. The rotated factor loadings are as follows:

'1' (0.77), '2' (0.71), '3' (0.72), '4' (0.73), '5' (0.65), '6' (0.73).

Table 7.13 shows the loadings on both the unrotated (at least 0.30) and the
rotated (at least 0.40) solutions. All of the latter are above the 0.60 minimum
criterion. The resulting scale is labelled ACTION.

Before leaving this analysis, we need to apply the two additional tests,
Cronbach's alpha and item-to-total correlations (see Table 7.14). The alpha
coefficient for the ACTION scale is very satisfactory (0.821). The item-to-total
correlations coefficients are also all adequate, although it is clear that item '5'
is the weakest. This is confirmed by the fact that eliminating it would reduce
the alpha coefficient by very little, to 0.816. This is not surprising as the content
of the item is different from the others, not only in expressing a negative action
towards the environment, but it is also a rather different kind of action. Hence,
consideration needs to be given to excluding it from the scale.

The analysis of the first factor with item '5' deleted is also shown in Table 7.14
as WILLACT. There are minor improvements in the item-to-total correlation
coefficients and, as anticipated, a slight reduction in the alpha coefficient. Eliminating any further items would reduce the alpha coefficient more than previously. However, the elimination of '5' can also be justified on the grounds that
it had the lowest loading on the factor, although still above the minimum criterion of 0.60. What this example is intended to illustrate is that there can be marginal
items about which a choice has to be made as to whether they should be
included in the scale. A number of indicators can be used and, in the end, it is
a matter of judgement. In this case, I am erring on the side of producing a
robust scale, even if it means sacrificing one item. Hopefully, the subsequent
analysis will be more useful because of this decision. Hence, only WILLACT

Table 7.14   *Reliability of behavioural scales (combined samples)*

Scale	Item	Item-to-total correlation	Alpha if item deleted	Alpha
ACTION	1	0.76	0.784	
	2	0.75	0.794	
	3	0.76	0.782	0.821
	4	0.71	0.800	
	5	0.64	0.816	
	6	0.76	0.782	
WILLACT	1	0.78	0.771	
	2	0.76	0.794	
	3	0.77	0.772	0.816
	4	0.73	0.796	
	6	0.78	0.768	

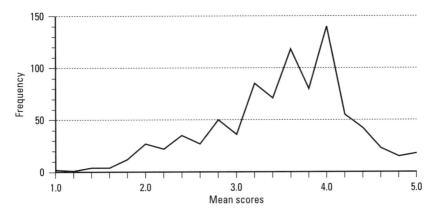

Figure 7.11   *WILLACT mean scores (combined samples)*

will be used to answer the research questions in Chapter 8. The distribution on the WILLACT scale is shown in Figure 7.11.

Indexes

An *index* represents a particular phenomenon or concept by measuring something that is related to it. For example, an index of social class position might be a person's occupational status.[14] Many measures in the social sciences can be regarded as indexes; a measure of one thing (e.g. occupational status) is used to represent another thing (e.g. social class). For example, an index of 'social class' could consist of the combination of measures of occupational status, level of income and educational attainment; these three measures can be justified theoretically. A second kind of index is created to estimate the level of intensity of some activity by counting the number of instances of it. For example, it would be possible to construct an index of how much a student reads by counting the number of books they borrow from the library.

Clearly in this last example there is room for error in that students may not read all that they borrow, they may read books in the library without borrowing them, they may read books from other sources and they may read other things as well. It is a characteristic of most indexes that they only estimate the phenomenon under investigation by counting readily available information. The challenge is to find a reliable estimator or index.

In contrast to a scale, in this research I am using the notion of an index as a combination of measures that has not been subjected to a test for unidimensionality. The justification for any particular combination of measures will normally be based simply on the face validity of the components. The rationale for constructing an index is that it should result in a more robust measure of the phenomenon.

Avoiding Environmentally Damaging Products

A number of indexes have been constructed to measure key variables in this research, namely, three measures of Environmentally Responsible Behaviour. For the first, respondents were asked to indicate the extent to which they avoided purchasing or using environmentally damaging products, in three response categories, 'Regularly', 'Occasionally' and 'Never'. In addition to asking about the extent to which they did this, respondents were also asked to list the products that they avoid. An index of the level of avoidance was constructed from the number of relevant products mentioned. The score is assumed to indicate the level of Environmentally Responsible Behaviour. Further, it was assumed that all products were of equal importance, and that the number of products listed indicates both knowledge of what products are damaging to the environment and the level of commitment to this form of behaviour.

Support for Environmental Groups

A second index of Environmentally Responsible Behaviour was concerned with support given to environmental groups. It was measured by two questions: the degree of support given ('Regularly', 'Occasionally' and 'Never'); and, for those who responded in the first two categories, the types of support. For the latter, seven response categories were offered ('Financial', 'Voluntary work', 'Attend meetings', 'On committees', 'Participate in demonstrations', 'Moral support only' and 'Other'). An index of support was created by scoring '1' for every category to which a response was made. It was assumed that each of these activities is of equal value. However they could have been weighted differently in terms of a scoring system arrived at by, say, a set of independent judges.

Recycling Behaviour

The third index of the practice of Environmentally Responsible Behaviour was concerned with recycling. Respondents were asked to indicate how regularly they recycled four types of waste products: glass containers, plastic containers, aluminium cans and paper. The response categories were: 'Regularly', 'Occasionally' and 'Never'. They were also given the opportunity to indicate whether they avoided using any of these products ('Do not use'). These four categories were then weighted: 'Regularly', 2; 'Occasionally', 1; 'Never', 0; and 'Do not use', 3. In the case of this latter category, it was assumed that deliberately avoiding the use of these products indicates a greater commitment to conserving resources than using and then recycling. Each respondent received a total score based on the sum of their responses to the four types of products. This was used as an index of recycling behaviour. A number of other assumptions are involved in this procedure: that these activities are motivated by environmental concerns; and, if they are, that they are all of equal importance from the respondent's point of view. As we shall see in the next chapter, the former assumption was probably incorrect.

Out of these processes of data reduction, three indexes have been produced:

- Avoiding Environmentally Damaging Products;
- Support for Environmental Groups;
- Recycling of waste products.

However, the Recycling index will not be used in the analysis in Chapter 8, and the other two types of behaviour will be measured by answers to single questions, the first in terms of regularity of avoidance (the three categories above), and the third in terms of level of support (also the three categories shown above). Some analysis (not presented here) indicates that, in both cases, the single question and the index are highly correlated. They have been presented here as examples of alternative ways of measuring this type of behaviour.

The purpose in creating such indexes is to produce simple measures based on what can sometimes be a complex phenomenon. It may just be impossible or impractical to try do deal with all the available information on a particular issue. Such procedures make the analysis more manageable. However, a great deal of information can be lost in the process, and many assumptions may need to be made. This is a common practice in quantitative research. In the end, it is a matter of judgement as to whether an index is meaningful, reliable and useful.

Recoding to Different Levels of Measurement

For the most part, *recoding* is undertaken to facilitate data analysis and data presentation. This includes the transformation of metric variables into categorical variables. It is this type of recoding that will be the focus of attention here. However, before proceeding to demonstrate how this is done, let us discuss briefly another three uses of recoding.

Before serious analysis commences, it is useful to examine the distributions on categorical variables. When response categories are established to facilitate the answering of a question in a questionnaire or interview schedule, it may not be possible to anticipate the distribution of responses. Some categories may end up with very few responses, or the distribution may be badly skewed. Some forms of analysis, such as cross-tabulations, require a minimum number in the cells to satisfy chi-square requirements. Combining categories is one way of achieving this, and this requires recoding.

A second use of recoding is to change the order of nominal categories. For example, categories of religious affiliation may have been listed in alphabetical order in a questionnaire or interview schedule. At the analysis stage, it may be useful to reorder the categories, say, from the one with the most responses to the one with the fewest responses. An example of combining and reordering categories occurred in the case of Political Party Preference. The original categories, in order, were: 'Labor', 'Liberal', 'National', 'Democrats', 'Undecided' and 'Other'. These were recoded into 'Liberal', 'Undecided' and 'Conservative'.

Recoding can also be used to deal with non-responses. Again, in analysis such as cross-tabulation, non-responses on either variable drop out of the analysis completely. When a set of categories forms an ordinal-level measurement, such as the five Likert-type response categories (ranging from 'Strongly agree' to Strongly disagree'), a conservative way of including non-responses in the analysis is to code them either in the middle category, or as near the middle as possible, or in the category in which the median falls. The non-response could be coded in the 'Neither agree nor disagree' category, or in the category on either side of this if the median is off-centre. It is a conservative method because in this position the assumed response has the minimum influence on measures of central tendency and dispersion, and also on measures of association.

The major use of recoding to be discussed here is to transform metric data into a set of categories. For example, in addition to calculating the mean Age of a sample of respondents, we might also want both to see their distribution in, say, ten-year intervals, and to be able to cross-tabulate such Age categories with the categories of another variable, such as Gender.

Three examples of recoding that are required for subsequent analysis will serve to illustrate common procedures. The first is the recoding of the EWV scales and subscales (assumed to be interval-level measurement) into four approximately equal categories (ordinal-level measurement). The second is the recoding of the Recycling index into four categories, and the third is the recoding of Age in years into a set of six categories.

Environmental Worldview Scales and Subscales

Having used factor analysis to determine which items are to be included in the seven scales and subscales, it is possible to calculate mean scores for each respondent on each one. This was done by summing each person's responses to each set of items and dividing by the number of items in the set. The distribution of the means has been used to establish the four categories for each scale and subscale. The aim was to have approximately the same number of respondents in each category, thus creating a rectangular distribution. The advantage of a rectangular distribution, compared with a normal distribution, is that cross-tabulations based on the recoded variables are less likely to have low frequencies in some cells, thus avoiding one of the major problems in using chi-square analysis.

In order to establish four ordinal categories for each scale and subscale, the data from both samples were combined. Once established, the categories were then applied to the distributions in each sample. The scales and subscales were recoded as follows. The range of mean scores is shown for each category and the percentage in each category is shown in brackets. This is as close as it is possible to achieve rectangular distributions across the four categories, given the range of possible mean scores.

ENVGSC   1.86–3.50 (24.0); 3.57–3.86 (25.5); 3.93–4.21 (24.6); 4.29–5.00 (26.0)

HUSENV   1.00–3.00 (21.2); 3.25–3.75 (30.9); 4.00–4.25 (26.0); 4.50–5.00 (21.9)

ECGROW   1.00–2.50 (11.9); 3.00–3.50 (34.6); 4.00 (31.6); 4.50–5.00 (21.9)

GOVCONT   1.00–3.33 (15.8); 3.67–4.00 (37.7); 4.33 (18.7); 4.67–5.00 (27.8)

SCITEK   1.00–2.00 (19.1); 2.33–2.67 (28.5); 3.00–3.33 (31.3); 3.67–5.00 (21.1)

IMPACT   1.00–3.33 (19.1); 3.67–4.00 (37.8); 4.33 (21.9); 4.67 (21.1)

ALTENGY   1.50–3.50 (18.0); 4.00 (31.7); 4.50 (27.6); 5.00 (22.7)

WILLACT   1.00–3.00 (25.4); 3.20–3.60 (31.6); 3.80–4.00 (25.4); 4.20–5.00 (17.6)

The four categories have been given the labels 'Low', 'Moderate', 'High' and 'Very high'.[15]

Recycling Index

The second example of recoding is to take the Recycling index scores and create four categories. While the scores range from 0 to 12, the distribution is rather uneven. Slightly more than half of the combined sample received a score of 8, and 84 per cent have score of 6–9. Hence, it is not possible to create a rectangular distribution. Instead, it is more like a slightly skewed normal distribution. The categories are as follows: 0–5 (15.1 per cent), 6 and 7 (25.6 per cent), 8 (50.9 per cent) and 9–12 (8.4 per cent).

Age

The third recoding example comes from the Age distributions of both samples. While it is possible to use the same coding categories for both samples, because of their very different Age distributions, for some types of analysis different categories are more useful. This recoding has already been done in Chapter 3 (see Table 3.9).

The examples discussed in this section of the chapter indicate that recoding can be used to:

- change the order of a set of response categories, such as Religion, perhaps from an alphabetical listing to a decreasing order of size;
- combine categories, such as putting those with very low responses into an 'other' category, or consolidating adjoining categories with low responses;
- eliminate non-responses, such as locating them in the median category of a distribution, or in or as near as possible to the middle category; and
- transform a distribution of numbers or scores (discrete or continuous variables) into a set of categories, such as Age or scores from an attitude scale.

There are no fixed rules about how and when recoding should be done; it depends on the nature of the variables and their distributions, and the requirements of the analysis. Judicious recoding can enhance and clarify data analysis.

Characteristics of the Samples

Before we proceed to undertake the analysis required to answer the six research questions, it will be helpful to prepare a description of the basic characteristics of the two samples. This is fairly standard practice as it provides a background for the analysis that follows. Only a limited set of characteristics will be discussed here. They include:

- Gender;
- Age;
- Education;
- Religion;
- Religiosity;
- Environmental Worldview (ENVGSC); and
- Willingness to Act (WILLACT).

These characteristics will be described briefly by comparing the two samples (see Table 7.15).

The Student sample has an overrepresentation of females (55 per cent), reflecting a trend in university education in many countries. There is a Gender balance in the Resident sample, confirming that the sampling procedure used to achieve this was successful (see Table 3.10). As expected, the Age distribution of the two samples is very different. A majority of Students are under 25 years of age (87 per cent), while the distribution of Residents covers the full range. For more details of the Age distributions, see particularly Table 3.9 and also Tables 3.4, 3.5, 3.6, 3.11 and 3.13.

As with Age, the level of Education achieved in the two samples is very different. Clearly, all Students are university educated, although they have still to complete their degrees. The Age distribution of Residents reflects the changing

Table 7.15   *Characteristics of both samples*

		Students (n = 465)	Residents (n = 402)
Gender:	Females	55%	50%
Age:	Mean (std. dev.)	21.2 (4.0)	46.1 (18.0)
	Under 25	87%	12%
	25–44	12%	40%
	45–64	ᵃ%	29%
	65 and over	0%	20%
Education	Primary/some secondary	0%	19%
	Technical certificate	0%	15%
	Completed secondary	0%	24%
	University education	100%	42%
Religion:	Catholic	31%	21%
	Anglican	13%	23%
	Uniting	7%	14%
	Other	17%	18%
	No religion	33%	25%
Religiosity:	Very religions	15%	24%
	Not at all religions	25%	13%
ENVGSC:	Mean (std. dev.)	3.97 (0.54)	3.81 (0.52)
	Low	19%	30%
	Very high	31%	20%
WILLACT:	Mean (std. dev.)	3.59 (0.75)	3.38 (0.73)
	Low	22%	30%
	Very high	24%	10%

ᵃThe percentage is less than 0.5.

patterns of education over at least three generations. This is illustrated in Table 4.8 and the accompanying discussion in Chapter 4. What is somewhat surprising is the high percentage of university-educated people in this sample (42 per cent).

The distributions of Religion on the two samples provide some interesting differences, as does Religiosity. The Student sample is nearly one-third 'Catholic' (31 per cent) compared with about a fifth (21 per cent) of the Resident sample. The figures are reversed for the major Protestant denominations; 20 per cent of the Students are either 'Anglican' or 'Uniting' church, compared with 37 per cent of the Residents. While 25 per cent of the Residents profess to have 'No religion', this is the case for 33 per cent of Students. The percentage of 'Catholics' in the student sample is closer to that of the Melbourne metropolitan area (MMA) than is the Resident sample. The underrepresentation of 'Catholics' in the latter reflects the history of the dominance of a Protestant middle class in this part of the MMA. It is clear that the Resident sample has a higher level of Religiosity than does the Student sample. Nearly a quarter (24 per cent) of the former say they are 'Very religious', compared with 15 per cent of the latter. The reverse is the case for 'Not at all religious': 13 per cent compared with 25 per cent.

The Student sample has a higher mean score on the Environmental World-view scale (EWVGSC) than the sample of Residents. The same difference is evident in the mean scores on the Willingness to Act scale (WILLACT). This comparison, and those on related scales and subscales, will be dealt with in more detail in the next chapter.

When samples are being described in a 'real' research project, if possible, it would be appropriate to compare the distributions (such as Gender, Age, Education and Religion)[16] with that from a relevant census or other data on the population from which the sample was drawn, or with related populations. The distributions in the Resident sample could be compared with those produced in the chronologically closest census for the city from which the sample was drawn. This would provide a check on the representativeness of the sample. Comparisons could also be made with census data from the MMA, and even state and national data. The comparisons are more limited between the Student sample and the census, although comparing the distribution on Religion with the MMA etc. would be useful. It may also be possible to get data about students from the university itself (for example, on Gender, Age and Religion), or from state and national sources. The point is that such comparisons are useful when interpreting the results or making judgements about their generality.

Summary

- Data reduction procedures prepare data for analysis by reorganizing or combining response categories, by transforming metric variables (both discrete and continuous) into ordinal categories and, more particularly, by reducing a number of items of data, or responses to a number of questions, to one or more new variables.
- Data in categories are reordered, or the number of categories are reduced, to meet the requirements of appropriate analysis, and to simplify the analysis and the presentation of results.
- Metric variables are transformed into ordinal categories to allow for alternative methods of analysis and to provide different ways of understanding the forms of association.
- Responses to a set of questions are reduced to scales and indexes to discover latent variables, to measure variables more reliably and to simplify analysis.
- Typically, a scale is produced from responses to a set of attitude items by demonstrating that the items all measure the same thing, that is, that they are unidimensional. These procedures can also establish subscales within a general scale, or separate scales within a set of items.
- An index measures a concept indirectly by assuming that what is measured is related to that concept. For example, income, occupation and education, either separately or together, have been used as an index of social class position. However, as the indirect character of an index is typical of a great deal of social scientific measurement, in this book the notion of an index is confined to the measurement of a concept by a combination of responses or items of information, the unidimensionality of which has not been demonstrated.
- The construction of attitude or similar scales, such as Environmental Worldview, can include the following procedures.

1. Create or borrow a set of items (say, at least 10 and possibly more than 20) whose content is related to the phenomenon to be measured.
2. Pre-test the items on a sample (say, about 50) that is similar to the one that is to be investigated, and then apply item analysis to the responses. Discard items for which the pattern of responses is seriously inconsistent.
3. Administer the remaining items in the study. Examine the item-to-item and item-to-total correlation coefficients. Look for low coefficients on both methods of analysis and consider discarding any weak items.
4. Apply Cronbach's alpha as a further test of the reliability of the set of items. If the value of alpha is below 0.70, the set of items may be an unreliable measure of the concept. It may be possible to improve the value of alpha by eliminating one or more items.
5. Conduct an exploratory factor analysis on the remaining items.

    (a) Run a check on the sampling adequacy of the items; a KMO of at least 0.70 is satisfactory.
    (b) Examine the commonality for each item to see what proportion of its variance contributes to all the factors extracted.
    (c) Try an unrotated solution to see if a common factor is present or whether there may be more than one factor. Factor loadings of at least 0.40 are desirable for an item to be included in a possible scale.
    (d) Use the eigenvalues to establish the number of factors to be extracted. The number is normally determined by those with a value of at least 1.0. A scree plot of the values can assist this decision.
    (e) Rerun the unrotated solution with this number of factors specified and examine the results.
    (f) Try a rotated solution to see if there are subscales within a general scale that may be present, and to confirm the existence of other scales that may be suggested by the unrotated solution. Use loadings of at least 0.40, and possibly higher, to determine whether an item should be included in a scale or subscale.
    (g) Items that do not have at least a 0.40 loading on any factor, or which load on more than one factor, should be considered for exclusion.
    (h) If items are excluded at this stage, the analysis should be rerun to confirm any scales and/or subscales, and to see if the loadings have been improved.
    (i) If there are sufficient of them, consider running a factor analysis on the excluded items. This may not be worthwhile if there are less than four or five items.
    (j) Apply Cronbach's alpha to all scales and subscales to confirm their reliability.
    (k) Create and label the scales and subscales that have survived.
    (l) If multiple scales and/or subscales have been produced, prepare a correlation matrix and examine the values of the coefficients.

Notes

[1] The more correct procedure would be to calculate median scores as the response categories only form ordinal-level measurement. However, to do this precisely enough is very cumbersome (see pp. 69–71 for the procedure). The mean is a useful approximation for this purpose.

[2] While this method is rather crude, it is useful for small samples in which the analysis can be done manually. The basis of the procedure can be readily understood, and the outcome may be as effective as more complex and less readily grasped procedures.

[3] A common rule of thumb is to reject any item with a coefficient of less than 0.30, but I wish to set a stricter criterion.

[4] Two other methods are also available, *theta* and *omega*, but they will not be considered here. See Maxim (1999) for a brief discussion.

[5] See Field (2000: 443) for a brief review of more detailed considerations.

[6] Factor analysis is a useful tool. However, it has many features that cannot be understood intuitively. It requires careful study to understand how to use it sensibly. As the mathematics on which it is based is beyond many social researchers, it may be wise to seek the advice of a sympathetic expert if what follows is unclear or is of insufficient mathematical sophistication for you.

[7] Factor analysis has two main uses: to explore the underlying factors present in responses to a set of measures, and to confirm whether a set of measures are related in the form specified in a model of their relationships. *Exploratory* factor analysis sets out with the assumption that everything is related to everything, while a *confirmatory* factory analysis specifies how the variables might be related and then sets out to show whether this is the case. We are using only the former here.

[8] There are in fact a number of versions of factor analysis. The version used here is 'principle component analysis', which appears to be the most commonly used. An explanation of the differences between the versions is beyond the scope of this discussion. For technical details, see the two contributions by Kim and Mueller (1978a, 1978b) that are also included in Lewis-Beck (1994).

[9] This concept comes from geomorphology and refers to a steep slope of rubble that is formed as the result of natural erosion of a large rock formation. When such a slope meets a plain or valley below, there is a sudden change in the gradient from steep to flat.

[10] This is a bit of a mouthful, and just happens to be a very common method.

[11] It is worth noting that 'fins' and 'adkv' also appeared as strong factors in the analysis of the 1989/90 samples.

[12] See Hair et al. (1998) and Field (2000: 438–40) for discussions of the methods of rotation, and various sections in Lewis-Beck (1994) for greater detail.

[13] In fact, in the 1989/90 studies, 'fins' rather than 'fns', 'adv' rather than 'adkv', 'cx' rather than 'cm', and some other combinations, formed subscales (see Blaikie, 1992). This illustrates how scales can change with different samples.

[14] As the literature on the meaning and measurement of social class is vast, this is not the place to engage in a debate about the merits of such an index.

[15] This procedure is easily achieved with the facilities in programs such as SPSS.

[16] Other variables, such as income and country of birth, could also be used if they were available.

8

Real Data Analysis: Answering Research Questions

Introduction

The time has come to apply the methods of data analysis discussed in Chapters 3–6 to answering the six research questions that were stated in Chapter 2. After all, it is by answering research questions that we advance knowledge of social phenomena and, to get our answers, we need to use appropriate methods of data analysis. It is important to note that what follows in this chapter is not intended to be a model of how analysis should be presented in a research report. Rather, the aim is to explore various ways in which the data from the two samples could be analyzed to answer the research questions. In the process, some comparisons are made between alternative methods associated with different levels of measurement. This is achieved by working with a set of variables in both their categorical and metric forms, where this is possible. In real research, the aim would be to work at the highest level of measurement in order to obtain the benefits of more sophisticated procedures. However, by making these comparisons, I hope to show that the procedures appropriate for lower levels of measurement can frequently add to our understanding of the data.

The approach taken in the analysis is pragmatic rather than following statistical theory slavishly. It should also be noted that only limited interpretations are made of the results. Serious theoretical discussion is beyond the scope of this book.

Some of the research questions to be examined require univariate descriptive analysis, some bivariate descriptive analysis and others explanatory analysis. They will all involve the use of inferential analysis as the two samples were selected by probability methods. Hence, this chapter is structured around the first three methods of analysis, with inferential analysis being undertaken where appropriate.

Univariate Descriptive Analysis

In addition to the examples used in Chapter 3, at the end of the previous chapter some preliminary descriptive analysis was undertaken in order to establish

Table 8.1 *Sample comparisons of Environmental Worldview metric variables*

Metric variables	Students ($n = 465$)		Residents ($n = 402$)		$\bar{x}_1 - \bar{x}_2$	p
	$\bar{x}_1$	s	$\bar{x}_2$	s		
EWVGSC	3.97	0.54	3.81	0.52	+0.16	<0.001
HUSENV	3.83	0.75	3.66	0.75	+0.17	<0.001
ECGROW	3.70	0.79	3.64	0.78	+0.06	n.s.
GOVCONT	4.17	0.68	4.02	0.59	+0.15	<0.001
SCITEK	2.97	0.84	2.86	0.69	+0.11	<0.05
IMPACT	4.01	0.64	4.00	0.60	+0.01	n.s.
ALTENGY	4.30	0.61	4.13	0.63	+0.17	<0.001

the characteristics of the samples. However, in this section of the chapter, we will attempt to answer the first two research questions, both of which are 'what' questions. While they are not the only 'what' questions in the list, they are the only two that require univariate analysis. They are:

1. To what extent do students and urban residents hold different environmental worldviews?
2. To what extent do they practise environmentally responsible behaviour?

It would be possible to ask these questions with reference to only one sample at a time: 'What environmental worldviews are held by students?', and the same for residents. The fact that these research questions require comparative analysis between the characteristics of students and residents just means that a more elaborate form of description is necessary.

Environmental Worldview

To answer research question 1, all the Environmental Worldview scales and subscales are used, with both the metric and categorical forms of the variables. While this makes the analysis more complex, it provides a comprehensive picture and may raise some further questions for consideration. Table 8.1 presents the relevant data.

The answer to research question 1 is, of course, dependent on how EWV is measured. In Chapter 7, factor analysis was used to demonstrate that the set of 24 items can be regarded as consisting of four scales, with one scale (the general scale) having three subscales. Hence, there are various aspects of EWV that can be examined and used to compare the Student and Resident samples. The first thing to note is that in both samples the mean scores on all except one of the seven scales and subscales are above the midpoint (3.0) of the distributions, that is, they are skewed in a pro-environmental direction. The variable with the highest mean scores is ALTENGY, which indicates that respondents have more positive views on this issue than on any of the others. The exception to the positive trend in the pattern is for SCITEK. The items in this scale were coded to indicate that being in favour of scientific or technological solutions indicated a negative attitude to the environment. This is based on the assumption that it is not necessary to conserve forests or fossil fuels because science will find alternatives to forest products and existing sources of energy. Clearly, this coding assumption is debatable, as finding economically viable alternatives to, say, fossil fuels in wind, wave and solar power requires technological innovations. However, even if the coding had been reversed, the mean score would be 3.03 (Students) and 3.14 (Residents), both of which are still considerably lower than any of the other means. Therefore, there appears to be something different about the responses to the SCITEK items, perhaps because it is not really an environmental worldview variable. This scale is measuring something different. Just how we make sense of the differences in responses to these EWV scales and subscales requires an explanatory account that is beyond the scope of the present discussion. Perhaps you can find or develop a theory that could be tested to explain these patterns.

An examination of the differences in EWV between Students and Residents shows that, in every case, Student mean scores are higher than those of Residents (see Table 8.1). The largest differences are for EWVGSC (0.16), HUSENV (0.17), GOVCONT (0.15) and ALTENGY (0.17), while the smallest differences are for ECGROW (0.06), SCITEK (0.11) and IMPACT (0.01). However, all of these are rather small.

Now the question arises as to whether the differences that have been found between the samples could also be expected to exist between the populations from which the samples were drawn. To establish this, we have to apply an appropriate method of inferential analysis. To test the difference between the Student and Resident means, we need to use the group t test (see pp. 193–7). First, the pooled estimate of the standard deviation must be calculated using equation (6.7), which applies to the situation where the two standard deviations are similar but the sample sizes are different. Then this value is entered into equation (6.9) to calculate the standard error of the difference, for samples of different sizes. Finally, this value is entered into equation (6.6) to arrive at a value for t. Knowing the degrees of freedom, this is then checked against the t distribution to see if it exceeds that required for the test as defined in terms of level of confidence and whether it is one-tailed or two-tailed (see Table 3 in Appendix D). The levels of significance for the EWV variables are shown in Table 8.1 for a two-tailed test and for the highest level of significance.[1]

All except three of the differences between the means are very significant (being beyond the 0.001 level), SCITEK being 0.05 and ECGROW and IMPACT both not significant. The level of significance for the latter two is not surprising because the differences are very small, 0.06 and 0.01. What is surprising is that the others are highly significant even though their differences are also quite small. However, the test of significance does not tell us how we should interpret such differences or what we should do with them, only that we can be very confident that they also exist between the two populations.

A major disadvantage in comparing means is that the means themselves tell us very little about the distributions; the mean is *only* a measure of central tendency. To get a better idea about the distributions, we can examine the

Table 8.2 *Sample comparisons of Environmental Worldview categorical variables (percentages)*

Categorical variables		Students	Residents	Difference
EWVGSC	Low	18.9	29.9	−11.0
	Moderate	23.4	27.9	−4.5
	High	26.7	22.1	+4.6
	Very high	31.0	20.1	+10.9
HUSENV	Low	18.1	24.9	−6.8
	Moderate	30.8	31.1	−0.3
	High	25.4	26.6	−1.2
	Very high	25.8	17.4	+8.4
ECGROW	Low	5.6	13.7	−8.1
	Moderate	41.9	31.6	+10.3
	High	28.6	35.1	−6.5
	Very high	23.9	19.7	+4.2
GOVCONT	Low	14.2	17.7	−3.5
	Moderate	33.1	43.0	−9.9
	High	17.4	20.1	−2.7
	Very high	35.3	19.2	+16.1
SCITEK	Low	18.9	19.4	−0.5
	Moderate	23.9	33.8	−9.9
	High	32.9	29.4	+3.5
	Very high	24.3	17.4	+6.9
IMPACT	Low	19.4	18.9	+0.5
	Moderate	37.0	38.8	−1.8
	High	20.2	23.9	−3.7
	Very high	23.4	18.4	+5.0
ALTENGY	Low	17.6	18.4	−0.8
	Moderate	23.7	41.0	−17.3
	High	32.0	22.4	+9.6
	Very high	26.7	18.2	+8.5

percentage differences across the categorical versions of the variables (see Table 8.2). What we find is that the percentages in the 'Very high' categories, and sometimes in the 'High' category, are consistently higher for Students than for Residents. For example, on the EWVGSC scale, the difference is 10.9 per cent in the 'Very high' category. Similarly, the percentages for Students are generally lower in the 'Moderate' and 'Low' categories, and certainly when these two categories are combined. Again, on the EWVGSC scale, the difference in the 'Low' category is 11.0 per cent. In order to make these differences clearer, we can create some pictorial representation of the distributions, such as bar charts. This can be illustrated with the EWVSGC scale (see Figure 8.1). There are clearly differences in the distributions that the mean scores do not reveal. The patterns are similar for the other scales and subscales.

Environmentally Responsible Behaviour

To answer research question 2, the WILLACT scale and the three metric measures of Environmentally Responsible Behaviour (ERB) are used: Support

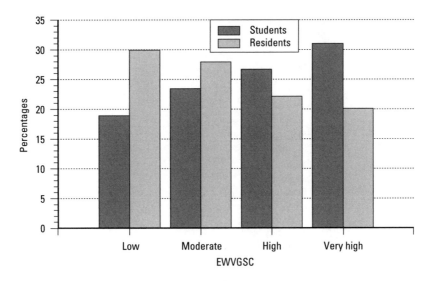

Figure 8.1   *EWVGSC categories (both samples)*

Table 8.3   *Sample comparison of Environmentally Responsible Behaviour metric variables*

Metric variables	Students ($n = 465$)		Residents ($n = 402$)		$\bar{x}_1 - \bar{x}_2$	p
	$\bar{x}_1$	s	$\bar{x}_2$	s		
WILLACT	3.59	0.75	3.38	0.73	+ 0.21	<0.001
Support Groups	0.56	0.50	0.39	0.49	+ 0.17	<0.001
Avoid Products	1.38	1.05	1.41	1.05	− 0.03	n. s.
Recycling	6.51	2.08	7.62	1.26	− 1.11	<0.001

for Environmental Groups (Support Groups), Avoiding Environmentally Damaging Products index (Avoid Products) and the Recycling index. Support Groups is an ordinal-level variable with three response categories, 'Regularly', 'Occasionally' and 'Never'. If this is recoded into two categories, 'Yes' (1) and 'No' (0), it becomes a dummy variable. The relevant data are presented in Table 8.3.

While the means produced for the WILLACT scale can be interpreted in a similar way to the EWV scales and subscales, the other three metric variables have to be interpreted differently. The mean for Support Groups must lie somewhere between 0 and 1, the means for the Avoid Products index summarize the number of products mentioned and, in the case of the Recycling index, the magnitude of the means is determined by weights used for the four response categories of the four types of materials recycled.

In terms of respondents' willingness to take some positive actions on environmental issues (WILLACT scale), we find similar mean scores to those for the EWV variables, and a relatively small difference between the samples. The mean for Students is 0.21 higher than for Residents (see Table 8.3). A similar pattern can be found for Support Groups; the Student mean on the

Table 8.4 *Sample comparison of Environmentally Responsible Behaviour categorical variables (percentages)*

Categorical variables		Students	Residents	Difference
WILLACT	Low	21.5	29.9	−8.4
	Moderate	30.1	33.3	−3.2
	High	24.5	26.4	−1.9
	Very high	23.9	10.4	+13.5
Support Groups	Never	43.9	60.7	−16.8
	Occasionally	42.2	26.6	+15.6
	Regularly	13.9	12.7	+1.2
Type of Support	No support	42.5	60.7	−18.2
	Moral support	10.6	6.7	+3.9
	Donations	23.9	14.2	+9.7
	Financial member	7.2	11.2	−4.0
	Attend meetings	3.5	1.7	+1.8
	Voluntary work	9.5	2.7	+6.8
	Demonstrate	0.7	1.2	−0.5
	On committees	2.2	1.5	+0.7
Avoid Products	Yes	77.5	77.4	+0.1
	None	25.5	25.1	+0.4
	One	28.6	26.6	+2.0
	Two	27.9	30.6	−2.7
	Three or more	17.9	17.7	+0.2
Recycling	Low	22.3	6.7	+15.6
	Moderate	33.5	16.5	+17.0
	High	39.4	64.1	−24.7
	Very high	4.8	12.7	−7.9

dichotomized variable is 0.17 higher than for the Residents. When the results are examined for the Avoid Products index we find only a minor and negative difference (−0.03) between the two samples, meaning Residents have higher means. In the case of Recycling, the difference is also negative (−1.11).

Again, we need to know whether these differences exist between the two populations. The group *t* test is the appropriate statistic, using the same procedure as just outlined for testing the significance of the difference between the means on the EWV scales and subscales (see Table 8.3). All but one of the ERB variables is significant at beyond the 0.001 level, the exception being Avoid Products, which is not significant (how could it be when the difference is only 0.03!). Therefore, with this exception, we can also expect these differences in sample means to exist between the populations, and with great confidence. However, the differences are again relatively small.

Table 8.4 presents the categorical versions of these variables, plus Type of Support for environmental groups.[2] In the case of WILLACT, we find that in the 'Very high' category the Student percentage is 13.5 higher than for the Residents, and the reverse is the case for the 'Low' category (8.4 per cent). The differences in Willingness to Act are clearly evident in Figure 8.2.

In both samples, there is a small core of respondents (13.9 per cent of Students and 12.7 per cent of Residents) who 'Regularly' support environmental groups (see Table 8.4). However, the Students are more likely to provide

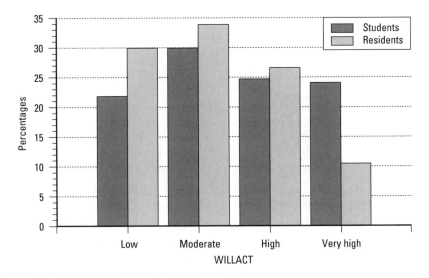

Figure 8.2 *WILLACT categories (both samples)*

'Occasional' support (42.2 per cent compared with 26.6 per cent) and the Residents are more likely to provide 'No support' (43.9 per cent and 60.7 per cent, respectively).

Support for Environmental Groups was also measured in terms of the kind of support offered. Seven categories were provided in a random order and respondents were asked to tick as many as were relevant to them. Later, the categories were recoded to form a hierarchy from low to high, the first being added to include those who did not tick any category: 'No support', 'Moral support only', 'Donations', 'Financial member', 'Attend meetings', 'Voluntary work', 'Demonstrate' and 'On committees'. The highest-level category ticked was then coded as the response. This measurement also shows Students as being more active supporters than Residents, perhaps because they have more opportunities with the existence of campus-based environmental groups, and may have stronger peer support for such activities. However, the data do not support the view that participating in demonstrations on environmentally related issues is a common student activity (see Table 8.4).[3]

When the results are examined for Avoid Products, both the 'Yes/No' response and the number of products mentioned, we find only minor differences between the samples. The 'Yes' response differs by only 0.1 per cent, and the percentages for the four categories covering the number of products mentioned are very similar.

When we come to the Recycling index, the ordinal categories confirm the reversed pattern found in the difference between the means. In the 'Very high' Recycling category, the Resident percentage is 7.9 per cent higher than for the Students, and the difference is 15.6 per cent in the reverse direction in the 'Low' category. The sample differences on these three ERB variables are clearly evident in Figures 8.3–8.5.

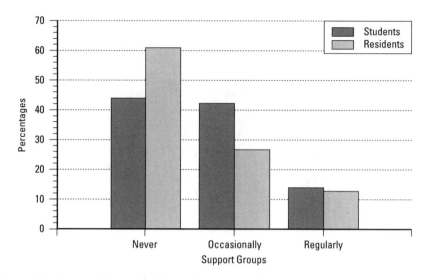

Figure 8.3   *Support Groups (both samples)*

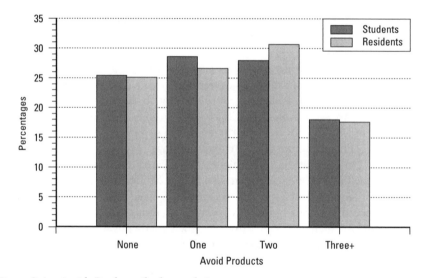

Figure 8.4   *Avoid Products (both samples)*

What we seem to have found are relatively small but consistent differences between the samples in their EWV, in their Willingness to Act in support of environmental causes, and in their Support for Environmental Groups. A greater proportion of Students than Residents are environmentalists. However, when it comes to Avoiding Environmentally Damaging Products, the differences largely disappear and for Recycling behaviour the situation is reversed; Residents are more regular recyclers than Students.

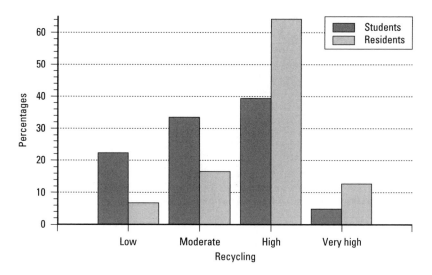

Figure 8.5   *Recycling index (both samples)*

We will come back to the differences between the samples on these variables later in the chapter. At this point, it is worth exploring why there are differences in the patterns. On the issue of Avoiding Products, it is possible that media campaigns that were mounted in the late 1980s and early 1990s, particularly on the connection between aerosol sprays and the developing hole in the ozone layer, caught most people's attention. This is supported by the fact that by far the most commonly mentioned product to be avoided was spray cans; almost everyone in the two samples knew about CFCs. Southern hemisphere residents are now all too familiar with the consequences of ozone depletion. Other products, such as household chemicals, also got caught up in this campaign. On the issue of recycling, there may be some practical explanations. For a start, students are likely to have fewer household responsibilities and are therefore less likely to have to be concerned about recycling household waste. In addition, the introduction of convenient systems for the separation and collection of household garbage has meant that most householders do this fairly automatically. They do not have to be avid environmentalists to be motivated to undertake this form of environmentally responsible behaviour.

Bivariate Descriptive Analysis

Three of our research questions, 3, 4 and 5, require some form of associational analysis. As we saw in Chapter 4, associational analysis is a search for patterns in the data, within a sample or population rather than between them. While such analysis is just an elaborate form of description, it serves two purposes.

Table 8.5 *Correlation matrix for EWV and ERB variables (Pearson's r; Students)*

EWV & ERB	1	1a	1b	1c	2	3	4	5	6	7	8
1 EWVGSC	1.00										
1a HUSENV	0.78	1.00									
1b ECGROW	0.69	0.35	1.00								
1c GOVCONT	0.75	0.42	0.40	1.00							
2 SCITEK	0.48	0.36	0.43	0.22	1.00						
3 IMPACT	0.54	0.36	0.36	0.49	0.33	1.00					
4 ALTENGY	0.46	0.26	0.34	0.39	0.08***	0.28	1.00				
5 WILLACT	0.73	0.52	0.49	0.57	0.40	0.43	0.41	1.00			
6 Support Gps	0.40	0.32	0.28	0.25	0.32	0.21	0.19	0.50	1.00		
7 Avoid Prods	0.43	0.34	0.25	0.28	0.30	0.19	0.19	0.49	0.39	1.00	
8 Recycling	0.20	0.12**	0.14*	0.19	0.11**	0.09**	0.13*	0.24	0.23	0.18	1.00

***Not significant. **$p < 0.05$. *$p < 0.01$. For all other coefficients, $p < 0.001$.

From one point of view, it is necessary to establish associations before we can begin to undertake explanatory analysis. From another point of view, patterns of association among variables can provide some understanding, even possible explanations, of a social phenomenon and may facilitate making predictions about it. For the present, we will be concerned with using the most appropriate method for establishing the associations that are called for in the following research questions.

3. In what ways and to what extent is environmentally responsible behaviour related to environmental worldviews?
4. In what ways and to what extent is age related to environmental worldviews and environmentally responsible behaviour?
5. In what ways and to what extent is gender related to environmental worldviews and environmentally responsible behaviour?

Environmental Worldview and Environmentally Responsible Behaviour

Given the range of variables used to measure both EWV and ERB, including both metric and categorical forms, a variety of measures of association can be used to answer question 3.

Metric Variables

Let us start with the metric variables. The associations between the EWV scales and subscales, for the combined samples, were examined in Table 7.12. It is now possible to provide the coefficients for the two samples separately, and to include the metric versions of the ERB variables. The appropriate statistic for this is Pearson's r (see Tables 8.5 and 8.6).[4]

Focusing for the moment on the EWV scales and subscales, it is evident that there are some differences between the samples in the correlation coefficients, but the overall pattern in both is consistent with those for the combined

Table 8.6   *Correlation matrix for EWV and ERB variables (Pearson's r; Residents)*

EWV & ERB	1	1a	1b	1c	2	3	4	5	6	7	8
1 EWVGSC	1.00										
1a HUSENV	0.80	1.00									
1b ECGROW	0.72	0.46	1.00								
1c GOVCONT	0.72	0.33	0.42	1.00							
2 SCITEK	0.42	0.37	0.36	0.24	1.00						
3 IMPACT	0.53	0.33	0.38	0.47	0.15**	1.00					
4 ALTENGY	0.49	0.33	0.33	0.44	0.13**	0.33	1.00				
5 WILLACT	0.62	0.35	0.43	0.56	0.24	0.42	0.44	1.00			
6 Support Gps	0.41	0.29	0.34	0.30	0.23	0.19	0.28	0.44	1.00		
7 Avoid Prods	0.43	0.33	0.34	0.30	0.22	0.19	0.26	0.44	0.35	1.00	
8 Recycling	0.04***	0.03***	0.08***	–0.01***	0.02***	0.02***	–0.06***	0.09***	0.14	0.16	1.00

***Not significant. **$p < 0.05$. *$p < 0.01$. For all other coefficients, $p < 0.001$.

samples. However, there is a tendency for the coefficients in the Resident sample to be higher than in the Student sample. Most of the differences are around 0.05, and only two exceed 0.10, between HUSENV and ECGROW (0.11) and SCITEK and IMPACT (0.18). With one exception in the Student sample (SCITEK and ALTENGY), and two exceptions in the Resident sample (SCITEK with both IMPACT and ALTENGY), all coefficients are significant at the 0.001 level. The exception in the Student sample is not significant, while the two in the Resident sample are at the 0.01 level.

When we examine the associations between the four ERB variables, we find that the strongest ones in both samples are WILLACT with Support Groups (Students, $r = 0.50$; Residents, $r = 0.44$)[5] and WILLACT with the Avoid Products index (Students, $r = 0.49$; Residents, $r = 0.44$). The weakest associations in both samples are all between the Recycling index and the three other variables. For Recycling with WILLACT, $r = 0.24$ in the Student sample and $r = 0.09$ in the Resident sample; with Support Groups, 0.23 and 0.14, and with Avoid Products, 0.18 and 0.16, respectively. The coefficients are all significant at the 0.001 level in the Student sample, but the levels are mostly lower in the Resident sample, with the association between WILLACT and Recycling being not significant (see Tables 8.5 and 8.6).

Now we come to the associations between EWV and ERB (research question 3). As there are 28 possible combinations here, we will not discuss them all. The central Environmental Worldview variable, EWVGSC, shows a strong association with WILLACT (Student $r = 0.73$; Resident $r = 0.62$), and moderate associations with both Support Groups (0.40 and 0.41) and Avoid Products (both 0.43). As might be expected, the coefficients with Recycling are weaker (Student $r = 0.20$; Resident $r = 0.04$). All the associations are significant at the 0.001 level, except that with Recycling for Residents, which is not significant. You may like to explore the differences on the other EWV scales and subscales (see Tables 8.5 and 8.6).

Just a few comments here about these patterns. It is interesting to note that the associations between WILLACT and the other three ERB variables are generally stronger than between the EWV scales and subscales and the ERB variables. Hence, WILLACT turns out to be a better predictor of ERB than

Table 8.7 *Cross-tabulations between EWVGSC and WILLACT, Support Groups, Avoid Products and Recycling (percentages; both samples)*

	EWVGSC									
	Students					Residents				
WILLACT	Low	Mod.	High	V. high	Total	Low	Mod.	High	V. high	Total
Low	**64**	27	9	2	22	**64**	21	16	6	30
Moderate	26	**41**	38	17	30	23	**49**	39	21	33
High	10	26	**33**	25	24	12	27	**34**	38	26
Very high	0	6	20	**56**	24	1	3	**11**	35	10
	Gamma = 0.70; *p* < 0.001					Gamma = 0.62; *p*<0.001				
Support Groups										
Never	**69**	55	45	20	44	**85**	63	56	26	61
Occasionally	28	39	**50**	47	42	12	30	28	**41**	27
Regularly	3	6	6	**33**	14	3	6	16	**33**	13
	Gamma = 0.52; *p* < 0.001					Gamma = 0.57; *p*<0.001				
Avoid Products										
None	**52**	29	20	11	25	**51**	22	11	6	25
One	30	28	**35**	22	29	27	**28**	25	27	27
Two	12	**31**	30	34	28	18	**33**	39	36	31
Three+	6	12	15	**32**	18	4	17	25	**31**	18
	Gamma = 0.42; *p* < 0.001					Gamma = 0.47; *p* < 0.001				
Recycling										
Low	**35**	22	23	13	22	9	6	2	9	7
Moderate	23	34	**40**	35	34	**20**	15	15	15	16
High	**40**	39	34	44	39	58	64	**72**	65	64
Very high	2	5	3	8	5	13	**14**	11	11	13
	Gamma = 0.16; *p* < 0.01					Gamma = 0.05; not significant				
Total	100	100	100	100	100	100	100	100	100	100
n		88	109	124	144	465	120	112	89	81
402										

EWVGSC, and certainly much better than the other EWV scales and subscales. It is perhaps not surprising that GOVCONT has comparatively strong associations with the ERB variables. They are all concerned with interventions on behalf of the environment, one by governments and the other by individuals.

Categorical Variables

Establishing associations between the categorical forms of the variables is rather more cumbersome than for the metric forms. It is necessary to prepare cross-tabulations for each pair of variables. Apart from the 28 combinations between the seven EWV scales and subscales and the four ERB variables, there are 21 between the EWV scales and subscales themselves and another 6 between the ERB variables. And then there are two samples, making a total of 110 cross-tabulations! This is how many correlation coefficients there are altogether in Tables 8.5 and 8.6.

Table 8.8 *Correlation matrix for EWV and ERB variables (gamma; Students)*

EWV & ERB	1	1a	1b	1c	2	3	4	5	6	7	8
1 EWVGSC	1.00										
1a HUSENV	0.83	1.00									
1b ECGROW	0.72	0.42	1.00								
1c GOVCONT	0.75	0.46	0.42	1.00							
2 SCITEK	0.49	0.39	0.46	0.20	1.00						
3 IMPACT	0.59	0.45	0.41	0.53	0.35	1.00					
4 ALTENGY	0.48	0.27	0.43	0.47	0.11**	0.37	1.00				
5 WILLACT	0.70	0.52	0.45	0.56	0.40	0.45	0.47	1.00			
6 Support Gps	0.52	0.41	0.42	0.38	0.43	0.34	0.34	0.71	1.00		
7 Avoid Prods	0.42	0.35	0.26	0.28	0.35	0.22	0.21	0.53	0.53	1.00	
8 Recycling	0.16*	0.12**	0.13**	0.17*	0.10***	0.05***	0.13**	0.21	0.23	0.25	1.00

***Not significant. **$p < 0.05$. *$p < 0.01$. For all other coefficients, $p < 0.001$.

Therefore, we will need to be selective. I will concentrate on four cross-tabulations, between EWVGSC and the four ERB variables (see Table 8.7).

With the exception of Recycling, the forms of the relationships in both samples are generally linear and very similar. The associations between EWVGSC and WILLACT are strong in both samples (Student gamma = 0.70; Resident gamma = 0.62). Similar patterns can be found with Support Groups; the associations are moderate in both samples (0.52 and 0.57, respectively). However, in the Student sample, there is a tendency for the relationship to be slightly curved. The relationship in the Resident sample is definitely linear.

There is a moderate, linear relationship between EWVGSC and Avoid Products in the Student sample (gamma = 0.42). The relationship is slightly stronger for Residents (gamma = 0.47), but there is a slight curve due mainly to both the '2' and '3+' Avoid Products categories having overrepresentation in both the 'High' and 'Very high' EWV categories. However, this degree of curve should have little bearing on the calculation of both Pearson's r and gamma.

The situation with the Recycling categories is very different. The coefficient is very weak in the Student sample and close to zero, and not significant in the Resident sample. An inspection of the cells with overrepresentation will indicate why this is so.

These contingency tables can help us to understand the nature of the associations – in particular, to spot any deviations from the linear form. Pearson's r can mask such deviations, with the result that its coefficients may be conservative at best, and close to zero at worst. I believe it is good practice to recode metric-level variables into categories and then examine the contingency tables for evidence of the form of the relationship. The same thing can be achieved by plotting graphs of one variable on the other.

To compensate for not examining all 110 contingency tables, two matrices of the gamma coefficients from all the cross-tabulations are presented in Tables 8.8 and 8.9.[6] As software packages such as SPSS do not generate such matrices, they have been constructed from the coefficients produced from individual contingency tables. They provide a comparison with the Pearson's r coefficients that appear in Tables 8.5 and 8.6.

Table 8.9 *Correlation matrix for EWV and ERB variables (gamma; Residents)*

EWV & ERB	1	1a	1b	1c	2	3	4	5	6	7	8
1 EWVGSC	1.00										
1a HUSENV	0.83	1.00									
1b ECGROW	0.76	0.52	1.00								
1c GOVCONT	0.72	0.37	0.48	1.00							
2 SCITEK	0.41	0.36	0.40	0.28	1.00						
3 IMPACT	0.62	0.41	0.48	0.58	0.23	1.00					
4 ALTENGY	0.53	0.40	0.37	0.49	0.17*	0.39	1.00				
5 WILLACT	0.62	0.37	0.43	0.55	0.26	0.41	0.50	1.00			
6 Support Gps	0.57	0.43	0.49	0.46	0.36	0.37	0.47	0.63	1.00		
7 Avoid Prods	0.47	0.36	0.35	0.31	0.26	0.20*	0.30	0.42	0.49	1.00	
8 Recycling	0.05***	0.01***	0.04***	–0.05***	–0.04***	0.03***	–0.03***	0.12***	0.22*	0.17**	1.00

***Not significant. **$p < 0.05$ level. *$p < 0.01$ level. For all other coefficients $p < 0.001$ level.

Comparing Metric and Categorical Variables

There is a high level of agreement between the metric (r) and categorical (gamma) coefficients. In both samples, the differences are almost all in the second decimal place, and most are no greater than 0.05. However, one variable, Support Groups, is a major exception. In the Student sample, all but two of the gamma coefficients with the other variables are at least 0.10 higher, and one is 0.21 higher than the corresponding r coefficients (see Tables 8.5 and 8.8). The differences between the two coefficients in the Resident sample are negligible, again with Support Groups being the exception – here the differences are even greater than in the Student sample (see Tables 8.6 and 8.9).

How can we explain the fact that the gamma coefficients are higher than r for the Support Groups variable in association with all the others? One possibility is that the relationship is curvilinear, which leads to r being an underestimate of the overall level of association. Another is that the distribution is badly skewed, and that this has affected the values for r. The first possibility can be dismissed as the variable is dichotomized, with the result that a curve cannot be detected. However, the fact that the variable has been dichotomized to allow the use of Pearson's r may partly account for the lower r values. When the three ordinal-level categories for Support Groups are assumed to be interval-level, and r is calculated on this basis, the values are, on average, about 0.05 higher in the Student sample and 0.03 higher in the Resident sample. In the Student sample, the differences are more in line with those for the other variables, mostly around 0.07, although still 0.16 with WILLACT. However, the differences remain higher in the Resident sample, ranging from 0.10 to 0.18.

To explore this further, let us examine two cross-tabulations for Support Groups with EWVGSC (Table 8.7) and WILLACT (Table 8.10). In the Student sample, the dichotomized version of Support Groups is distributed reasonable evenly (44 per cent for 'No' and 56 per cent for 'Yes'). However, when the three-category version is used the distribution is skewed. There is also a definite curve in the relationships with EWVGSC and, to a lesser extent, with

Table 8.10   *Cross-tabulations of Support Groups with WILLACT (percentages; both samples)*

	WILLACT									
	Students						Residents			
Support Groups	Low	Mod.	High	V. High	Total		Low	Mod.	High	V. High	Total
Never	79	59	31	8	44		87	60	49	14	61
Occasionally	16	40	61	49	42		13	33	31	36	27
Regularly	5	1	8	43	14		0	7	20	50	13
Total	100	100	100	100	100		100	100	100	100	100
n	98	140	113	111	462		120	134	106	42	402
	Gamma = 0.71; $p <0.001$						Gamma = 0.63; $p < 0.001$				

WILLACT. In the Resident sample, the distribution on the dichotomized version of Support Groups is badly skewed (61 per cent 'No' and 39 per cent 'Yes'), and this makes the three-category version even more skewed. However, with both EWVGSC and WILLACT, the relationships are essentially linear. Therefore, the explanations for the 'deviant' differences in the measures of association for Support Groups might be different for each sample. Nevertheless, neither explanation seems to provide a satisfactory answer.

Conclusion

The overall answer to research question 3, concerning the associations between EWV and ERB is as follows:

1. With one exception, the relationships are positive, generally linear and very significant in both samples.
2. The strengths of the associations vary depending on which variables are considered.
3. Of all the Environmental Worldview scales and subscales, EWVGSC has the strongest associations with each of the ERB variables.
4. All the EWV scales and subscales have stronger associations with WILLACT than the other ERB variables.
5. The strengths of the associations between the EWV scales and subscales on the one hand, and Support Groups and Avoid Products on the other, are very similar.
6. The Recycling variable has the weakest associations with the EWV scales and subscales, all of which are not significant in the Resident sample.
7. With the latter exception, the patterns of the associations in the two samples are very similar.

This analysis cannot be interpreted as suggesting any causal relationships between these variables. However, on theoretical grounds, it could be argued that Environmental Worldview influences Willingness to Act on environmental issues and that this willingness can lead to Environmentally Responsible Behaviour of various kinds. This possibility will be taken up later in the chapter.

Age, Environmental Worldview and Environmental Responsible Behaviour

Research question 4 is concerned with the associations between Age and the EWV and ERB variables. The reason for asking this question is that previous research has shown some consistent patterns as well as some alternatives. For the most part, environmentalism seems to be of more concern to the young than to the elderly, that is, there is generally a linear, negative association between Age and environmentalism. However, the two 1989/90 samples showed a curvilinear relationship in which respondents between 30 and 40 had the most positive EWV, followed by the younger respondents and then the elderly. An explanation for this was suggested in terms of both an 'ageing' and a 'cohort' influence (see Blaikie, 1992). The latter refers to the fact that the early middle-aged cohort (in 1989) was, in the late 1960s and early 1970s, part of the youth cohort. At that time, there was a high level of environmental awareness and concern, and it was the youth who were heavily involved in environmental issues. It was suggested that this age cohort has maintained its environmental commitment and has responded more favourably than the other age cohorts to the 'second wave' of environmentalism that commenced in the late 1980s. If this theory is correct, then the peak in environmentalism should now appear in a later age category than was found in 1989/90.

Metric Variables

In order to explore this idea, a number of types of analysis can be undertaken. However, because of the very skewed Age distribution in the Student sample, the analysis will only be done with the Resident sample. The simplest analysis is to correlate Age (in years) with the metric versions of the EWV and ERB variables. Of course, this will be based on the assumption that the relationships are linear. We can explore deviations from linearity with the categorical versions of the variables.

Table 8.11 reports Pearson's r for Age with the metric versions of the EWV and ERB variables. With one exception, all the coefficients are negative, which indicates that as Age increases EWV and ERB decrease; the young are stronger environmentalists than the elderly. The strongest associations are with EWVGSC (−0.34), HUSENV (−0.31) and WILLACT (−0.31), followed closely by ECGROW (−0.27), Support Groups (−0.26) and Avoid Products (−0.25). The other EWV variables have rather weak coefficients, and for Recycling it is almost zero. All the coefficients above 0.25 are significant at the 0.001 level, and two, both those below 0.10, are not significant.

Another way to examine these associations is to calculate the mean scores for each of the Age categories, six in this case (see Table 8.12). What we are looking for are changes in the means across the Age categories, for each of the variables. With the exception of Recycling, there is a consistent pattern. The highest mean scores are for either the '18–24' or the '35–44' Age categories. There is a dip in the means in the '25–34' Age category and then the scores tail off in the older Age categories. Take the EWVGSC for example (variable 1 in the table). The highest mean score is for the '18–24' category (4.03), followed

Table 8.11 *EWV and ERB by Age (Pearson's r and gamma; Residents)*

												EWV and ERB[a]
Age	1	1a	1b	1c	2	3	4	5	6	7	8	n
r	−0.34	−0.31	−0.27	−0.15	−0.14	−0.09	−0.13	−0.31	−0.26	−0.25	0.04	401
p	<0.001	<0.001	<0.001	<0.01	<0.01	n.s.	<0.01	<0.001	<0.001	<0.001	n.s.	
G	−0.35	−0.31	−0.25	−0.19	−0.17	−0.17	−0.16	−0.28	−0.31	−0.23	0.11	401
p	<0.001	<0.001	<0.001	<0.001	<0.01	<0.01	<0.01	<0.001	<0.001	<0.001	n.s.	

[a] See Table 8.5 for key to variable names.

Table 8.12 *EWV and ERB means and standard deviations by Age (Residents)*

						EWV and ERB[a]						
Age		1	1a	1b	1c	2	3	4	5	6	7	8	n
18–24	$\bar{x}$	4.03	3.92	3.83	4.16	3.04	4.19	4.21	3.61	0.57	1.55	7.28	47
	s	0.52	0.84	0.69	0.54	0.81	0.57	0.75	0.64	0.50	1.02	1.62	
25–34	$\bar{x}$	3.89	3.84	3.66	4.00	2.81	3.90	4.11	3.47	0.38	1.46	7.60	81
	s	0.57	0.79	0.83	0.65	0.73	0.68	0.61	0.76	0.49	1.11	1.19	
35–44	$\bar{x}$	3.99	3.84	3.94	4.14	3.03	4.09	4.28	3.67	0.59	1.81	7.76	79
	s	0.43	0.61	0.70	0.53	0.70	0.59	0.68	0.58	0.49	0.98	1.13	
45–54	$\bar{x}$	3.85	3.66	3.79	4.10	2.89	4.06	4.21	3.43	0.46	1.58	7.63	59
	s	0.45	0.69	0.67	0.43	0.61	0.58	0.60	0.65	0.50	0.89	1.26	
55–64	$\bar{x}$	3.71	3.56	3.62	3.97	2.82	3.99	4.00	3.11	0.23	1.41	7.63	56
	s	0.48	0.74	0.70	0.68	0.58	0.55	0.55	0.77	0.43	1.06	1.21	
65+	$\bar{x}$	3.46	3.23	3.15	3.81	2.65	3.88	3.99	3.02	0.16	0.76	7.72	79
	s	0.44	0.67	0.72	0.58	0.67	0.54	0.55	0.71	0.37	0.89	1.22	
Total	$\bar{x}$	3.81	3.66	3.65	4.02	2.56	4.00	4.13	3.38	0.39	1.41	7.63	401
	s	0.52	0.75	0.77	0.59	0.69	0.60	0.63	0.73	0.49	1.05	1.26	

[a] See Table 8.5 for key to variable names.

closely by the '35–44' category (3.99), then, in order, the '25–34' (3.89), '45–54' (3.85), '55–64' (3.71) and '65+' (3.46) categories. For some of the other variables, the mean scores for the '35–44' category are higher than for the '18–24' category, and the '45–54' category are sometimes higher than the '25–34' category. This is the case for ECGROW (variable 1b) and ALTENGY (variable 4) but, more particularly, for Support Groups (variable 6) and Avoid Products (variable 7). It is in the area of ERB that the bimodal distribution in the mean scores is the most obvious, with the '35–44' Age category having the highest mean scores.[7]

This pattern has some similarities to and some differences from that in the 1989/90 data. It is clear that the peak in these earlier studies has moved on about five years, precisely the difference between the dates of the two studies. However, the other peak in the youngest Age category is new. Perhaps this age cohort has been most influenced by the 'second wave' of environmentalism. They may either represent a second peak to pass through the age cohorts, or they may represent a more lasting plateau in the level of environmentalism. Such an interpretation of these data goes against the idea that level of environ-mentalism simply declines with age and suggests, rather, that the level is more dependent on the influence of high-priority issues in different periods on 'susceptible' youth. These periods seem to have less influence on older cohorts, except to possibly reinforce the views and behaviour of those who developed a high level of commitment in their youth, that is, in the '35–44' Age category in this case.

It is interesting to note that the behaviour scores for the '35–44' Age category are comparatively higher than for the '18–24' cohort for the ERB compared with the EWV variables. This would suggest that it is ERB rather more than EWV that has been reinforced by the 'second wave' in the '35–44' Age category. Clearly, there are some interesting issues to be explored here, but this is beyond the scope of this book.

Categorical Variables

The size of the differences between the mean scores in the analysis just completed might suggest that the patterns are not worth taking very seriously. To some extent this contention is supported by the size of the r coefficients, although six of them are certainly high enough to warrant attention. Table 8.11 also reports the gamma coefficients for Age with the EWV and ERB variables. Most of the values are very similar to those for r, the majority being within 0.05. The major exceptions are IMPACT and Recycling, the former having a non-significant r value and the latter being not significant for both coefficients.

To explore these relationships further, we can turn to the cross-tabulations between Age and the EWV and ERB variables. Just as for the analysis between the EWV and ERB variables themselves, we cannot examine all the cross-tabulations here, although in this case there are only 11.

Let us begin with the associations between Age and the two EWV variables with the highest and lowest gamma coefficients, EWVGSC and IMPACT (see Table 8.13). The cross-tabulation between Age and EWVGSC is generally linear and negative. However, some of the cells with overrepresentation deviate from this pattern. For example, respondents in the '25–34' Age category are fairly evenly distributed across the EWVGSC categories, and this accounts for the 'dip' in the means scores at this category (see Table 8.12). It is not difficult to see why the association between Age and IMPACT is so weak. There is a hint of a curvilinear relationship, but the distribution for the '25–34' and '35–44' categories, in particular, works against this.

Now we can turn to a comparison of the association of Age with the four ERB variables. The pattern of association between Age and WILLACT is very clearly linear and negative (gamma = −0.28). However, we find a reasonably even distribution across the WILLACT categories for both the '25–34' and '45–54' Age categories and, to a lesser extent, across the '35–44' Age category. Therefore, while the pattern of the relationship is clear, its strength is reduced by the distributions in the '25–54' Age categories. It is also these distributions that have given the double peak in the patterns for the mean scores. Hence, while the relationship has a linear appearance, there is an S-curve lurking in there.

It should be fairly obvious why there is a weak association between Age and Recycling (gamma = 0.11). The cells in which there is overrepresentation are scattered across the table and are mostly small. However, there is a trend

Table 8.13 *Cross-tabulation for Age with EWVGSC, IMPACT, WILLACT, Recycling, support Groups and Avoid Products (percentages; Residents)*

				Age					
EWVGSC	18–24	25–34	35–44	45–54	55–64	65+	Total	Gamma	p
Low	13	18	19	15	21	38	20		
Moderate	25	41	34	32	50	47	39		
High	30	20	35	41	21	13	26		
Very high	32	21	22	12	7	2	15	−0.35	< 0.001
IMPACT									
Low	9	21	20	14	18	27	19		
Moderate	34	38	30	37	41	49	39		
High	25	25	24	34	27	13	24		
Very high	32	16	25	15	14	11	18	−0.17	< 0.01
WILLACT									
Low	23	27	10	29	39	49	30		
Moderate	32	31	35	32	36	34	33		
High	21	27	43	29	20	15	26		
Very high	23	15	11	10	5	1	11	−0.28	< 0.001
Recycling									
Low	9	6	5	10	4	6	6		
Moderate	32	17	10	8	20	17	17		
High	51	65	71	70	68	58	64		
Very high	9	11	14	12	9	19	13	0.11	n.s.
Support Groups									
Never	43	62	40	54	77	83	61		
Occasionally	38	31	32	29	20	14	27		
Regularly	19	7	28	17	4	3	13	−0.31	< 0.001
Avoid Products									
0		19	27	11	8	27	51	25	
1		26	21	24	44	21	27	27	
2		36	31	37	29	36	19	31	
3+		19	21	28	19	16	4	18	−0.23
< 0.001									
Total		100	100	100	100	100	100	100	
n		47	81	79	59	56	79	401	

towards a positive but a rather curved (possibly S-shaped) relationship. Both r and gamma have picked up the positive trend, although both are unable to handle the curve ($r = 0.04$). Certainly, the young appear not to be involved in recycling, and most of the other Age categories are rather mixed. The question arises as to whether there might be a gender difference here; we will come back to this shortly.

Given the particular pattern in the means scores across the six Age categories for Support Groups and Avoid Products, it is worth examining both their cross-tabulations with Age (see Table 8.13). With Support Groups, the pattern of cells with overrepresentation is clearly S-shaped, thus confirming the pattern for the mean scores (gamma $= -0.31$). There is a very definite peak in the '35–44' Age category, supported, to some extent, by the '45–54' category, and then followed by the '18–24' category, and a clear 'dip' in the '25–34' category.

The relationship between Age and Avoid Products shows something of the same pattern, except in the '25–34' Age category (gamma = –0.23). Unlike with Support Groups, this Age category is very divided with Avoid Products, having a slight overrepresentation at each extreme but a relatively even distribution across all four categories. The '55–64' Age category is similarly dispersed.

Coming back to research question 4, we can conclude the following:

- There are moderate and very significant associations between Age and the key EWV variable (EWVGSC), two of the subscales (HUSENV and ECGROW), WILLACT and two of the ERB variables, Support Groups and Avoid Products.
- The remaining variables have either weak and less significant associations (GOVCONT, SCITEK, ALTENGY), or negligible and not significant associations (IMPACT and Recycling).
- While all but IMPACT and Recycling have negative linear associations, there is evidence that the distributions across the six Age categories are bimodal, with peaks in the '18–24' and '35–44' categories, and a tail extending into old age.

Gender, Environmental Worldview and Environmentally Responsible Behaviour

Research question 5 is concerned with the associations between Gender and the EWV and ERB variables. In spite of the fact that Gender is a nominal-level variable, its dichotomous nature means that it can be regarded as a dummy variable; men are coded '0' and women '1'. Hence, the analysis required is very similar to that for Age with these variables, except that Gender is a less complex variable, and it can be analyzed in both samples.

Table 8.14 provides the *r* coefficients for the associations between Gender and the EWV and ERB variables. In the Student sample, three of the EWV variables, EWVGSC (variable 1), HUSENV (variable 1a) and SCITEK (variable 2), have weak to moderate and highly significant associations (0.26, 0.25 and 0.30, respectively). The same is the case for three of the ERB variables, WILLACT (variable 5; 0.25), Support Groups (variable 6; 0.24) and Avoid Products

Table 8.14 *EWV and ERB by Gender (Pearson's r and G; both samples)*

	EWV and ERB[a]											
	1	1a	1b	1c	2	3	4	5	6	7	8	*n*
Students												
r	0.26	0.25	0.12	0.15	0.30	0.16	0.00	0.25	0.24	0.30	0.13	464
p	*<0.001*	*<0.001*	*<0.01*	*<0.001*	*<0.001*	*<0.001*	*n.s.*	*<0.001*	*<0.001*	*<0.001*	*<0.01*	
G	0.36	0.33	0.17	0.21	0.42	0.24	0.00	0.36	0.39	0.45	0.12	464
p	*<0.001*	*<0.001*	*<0.05*	*<0.01*	*<0.001*	*<0.001*	*n.s.*	*<0.001*	*<0.001*	*<0.001*	*n.s.*	
Residents												
r	0.13	0.14	0.07	0.08	0.12	0.14	–0.04	0.04	–0.03	0.17	0.13	402
p	*<0.01*	*<0.01*	*n.s.*	*n.s.*	*<0.05*	*<0.01*	*n.s.*	*n.s.*	*n.s.*	*<0.001*	*<0.01*	
G	0.18	0.15	0.08	0.10	0.17	0.15	0.05	0.07	0.01	0.25	0.18	399
p	*<0.05*	*<0.05*	*n.s.*	*n.s.*	*<0.05*	*<0.05*	*n.s.*	*n.s.*	*n.s.*	*<0.001*	*<0.05*	

[a] See Table 8.5 for key to variable names.

(variable 7; 0.30). While ALTENGY (variable 4) has no association and is therefore not significant, the other variables all have weak but still significant associations. What this means is that women have higher mean scores than men on all these variables except ALTENGY.

The situation in the Resident sample, however, is rather different; the coefficients are generally much lower. While Avoid Products is the highest (0.17), as it also is in the Student sample (joint top with SCITEK), it is much lower. Five other variables have weak associations – EWVGSC (0.13), HUSENV (0.14), SCITEK (0.12), IMPACT (0.14) and Recycling (0.13) – all of which are significant at the 0.05 level. However, the remaining five variables have negligible associations that are not significant. This means that Gender differentiates EWV and ERB much less in the Resident sample than it does in the Student sample. This probably also means that female Students have higher scores than female Residents on all the variables, and the same may be the case for male respondents from the two samples. We can now explore this possibility.

Table 8.15 reports the means and standard deviations, for males and females in both samples, on each of the EWV and ERB variables. The patterns in these data confirm what was concluded from the r coefficients. Except for ALTENGY in both samples, and Support Groups in the Resident sample, females have higher mean scores than males on all variables in both samples. In addition, except for Recycling, Student females have higher mean scores than Resident females. However, the situation is rather mixed between Student and Resident males. Resident females have higher means than Student males, except for ALTENGY and Support Groups (where they are lower) and GOVCONT (where they are the same). Given that the mean age of Students (21.2) is much lower than the mean age for Residents (46.1), these differences support the earlier analysis on Age and EWV and ERB variables in the Resident sample. However, Gender differences complicate this.

Now the question is whether the differences between these means, both within each sample and between them, are significant. To establish this, we

Table 8.15   *EWV and ERB means and standard deviations by Gender (both samples)*

Gender		1	1a	1b	1c	2	3	4	5	6	7	8	n
						EWV and ERB[a]							
Students													
Male	$\bar{x}$	3.82	3.63	3.59	4.06	2.70	3.90	4.30	3.38	0.43	1.03	6.21	210
	s	0.55	0.78	0.83	0.72	0.80	0.65	0.63	0.79	0.50	1.03	2.31	
Female	$\bar{x}$	4.09	4.00	3.79	4.26	3.20	4.10	4.30	3.77	0.67	1.67	6.76	254
	s	0.49	0.68	0.76	0.63	0.80	0.62	0.60	0.67	0.47	0.98	1.83	
Total	$\bar{x}$	3.97	3.83	3.70	4.17	2.97	4.01	4.30	3.59	0.56	1.38	6.51	464
	s	0.54	0.75	0.80	0.68	0.84	0.64	0.61	0.75	0.50	1.05	2.08	
Residents													
Male	$\bar{x}$	3.74	3.56	3.59	3.97	2.78	3.92	4.15	3.35	0.41	1.23	7.46	200
	s	0.56	0.81	0.83	0.62	0.71	0.67	0.61	0.77	0.49	1.07	1.42	
Female	$\bar{x}$	3.88	3.77	3.70	4.06	2.94	4.09	4.11	3.41	0.38	1.59	7.79	199
	s	0.47	0.68	0.71	0.55	0.66	0.52	0.65	0.68	0.49	0.99	1.04	
Total	$\bar{x}$	3.81	3.66	3.65	4.02	2.86	4.00	4.13	3.38	0.39	1.41	7.62	399
	s	0.52	0.75	0.77	0.59	0.69	0.60	0.63	0.72	0.49	1.05	1.26	

a See Table 8.5 for key to variable names.

would need to do group *t* tests for both the within-sample and between-sample comparisons, 66 of them! You might like to try doing some of these.

Just as for the analysis between Age and EWV and ERB, we can also do cross-tabulations between Gender and some of these variables (see Table 8.16). SCITEK was chosen rather than IMPACT here because it differentiates males and females in the Student sample more than any of the other variables. In the Student sample, there are moderate linear associations between Gender and both EWVGSC (G = 0.36) and SCITEK (G = 0.42), with females being over-represented in the higher categories and males in the lower categories. What this means is that female Students have a more favourable EWV than male Students, and they also have less faith in the ability of science and technology to solve problems.[8] The associations in the Resident sample are much weaker (G = 0.18 for EWVGSC and G = 0.17 for SCITEK). This is due to a more even distribution across the four categories and, perhaps, to the fact that both associations in this sample show evidence of being curved; females are overrepresented across three categories, from 'Very high' to 'Moderate'.

The associations between Gender and the four ERB variables are rather mixed and are generally weaker than for the two EWV variables just examined. Again, they are stronger in the Student sample than in the Resident sample. The strongest association of all six variables in Table 8.16 is Avoid Products in the Student sample; the association is linear, with female Students scoring higher then male Students (G = 0.45). This association is only weak in the Resident sample (G = 0.18). The associations of Gender with WILLACT (G = 0.36) and Support Groups (G = 0.39) are both moderate in the Student sample, but negligible and not significant in the Resident sample (G = 0.07 and 0.01, respectively). The curve in the association with WILLACT no doubt contributes to the low value of gamma. Gender and Recycling show weak associations in both samples, with females being more regular recyclers than males. However, in the Student sample, the association is not significant. The complete set of gamma coefficients, and levels of significance, for all EWV and ERB variables, are shown in Table 8.14.

The conclusion to be drawn from this analysis with Gender is that, overall, females have a more favourable EWV than males and practice higher levels of ERB. However, the Gender differences are much more striking in the Student sample. Perhaps the most interesting aspect of the Resident sample is the fact that Willingness to Act and Support Groups are largely undifferentiated by Gender. The cross-tabulations not only confirm the analysis of the metric versions of the variables, but also indicate more clearly the forms of the relationships.

Explanatory Analysis

Explanatory analysis takes us on to the last stage of our journey through the examples of methods of data analysis. As we discovered in Chapter 5, it is by

Table 8.16 Cross-tabulation of Gender with EWVGSC, SCITEK, WILLACT, Recycling, Support Groups and Avoid Products (percentages; both samples)

	Students					Residents				
EWVGSC	Male	Female	Total	Gamma	p	Male	Female	Total	Gamma	p
Low	**26**	13	19			**37**	23	30		
Moderate	**28**	19	23			25	**31**	28		
High	25	**28**	27			19	**26**	22		
Very high	21	**39**	31	0.36	<0.001	19	**21**	20	0.18	<0.05
SCITEK										
Low	**27**	12	19			**26**	13	19		
Moderate	**31**	19	24			31	**36**	34		
High	28	**37**	33			27	**32**	30		
Very high	14	**32**	24	0.42	<0.001	16	**19**	17	0.17	<0.05
WILLACT										
Low	**31**	13	21			**33**	26	30		
Moderate	**31**	29	30			31	**37**	34		
High	22	**26**	25			25	**28**	26		
Very high	15	**31**	24	0.36	<0.001	**11**	9	10	0.07	n.s.
Recycling										
Low	**25**	20	22			**9**	3	6		
Moderate	34	33	34			**18**	15	17		
High	38	**41**	39			61	**68**	64		
Very high	3	6	5	0.12	n.s	12	**14**	13	0.18	<0.05
Support Groups										
Never	**57**	33	44			59	**62**	61		
Occasionally	33	**50**	42			**32**	22	27		
Regularly	10	**17**	14	0.39	<0.001	9	**16**	12	0.01	n.s.
Avoid Products										
0	**38**	15	25			**33**	16	25		
1	**33**	25	29			25	**29**	27		
2	16	**38**	28			27	**34**	31		
3	13	**22**	18	0.45	<0.001	15	**21**	18	0.18	<0.05
Total	100	100	100			100	100	100		
n	210	254	464			200	199	399		

far the most complex in terms of the methods themselves, the principles behind them, and the theoretical background that is required to inform what should be done. It is for this reason that 'why' research questions are much more difficult to answer than 'what' questions. Whereas the kind of analysis required to answer 'what' questions is usually obvious, 'why' questions themselves give us no clues as to where to look for the answers. We have a number of ways of solving this, depending on the research strategy that is adopted – see Blaikie (1993a, 2000) and the discussion in Chapter 1.

Only one research question in the list requires explanatory analysis:

6. Why are there variations in the levels of environmentally responsible behaviour?

In other words, what accounts for the fact that some people behave very responsibly towards the environment, others exhibit only moderate behaviour, and some seem to be indifferent? It would also be possible to ask the same kind of question about EWV: why some people have favourable worldviews and others not. However, this second question will not be attempted here. Some analysis related to it was done in Chapter 5 as an example of regression analysis. Here we will concentrate on explaining differences in ERB, such as avoiding the use of environmentally damaging products and providing support for environmental groups. Because Recycling has already been shown to have no meaningful association with the EWV variables and the other ERB variables, it will not be considered in the remainder of the analysis. Either the method used to measure it is not valid, or the explanation for recycling behaviour has to be found elsewhere.

The analysis to be undertaken here is based on the well-established idea that attitudes influence behaviour, that the beliefs and views that a person has about a particular object or issue are likely to influence the way they act towards it. In one area of research, the strength of a person's religious beliefs might be expected to influence the level of their religious practices; a highly committed believer would be expected to engage in religious practices at a much higher level than a moderate believer, and certainly more than a weak believer or non-believer. The same model has been applied to the role of various types of attitudes and related behaviour.

As EWV has been operationalized here, it can be regarded as including environmental attitudes. In some of the analysis in Chapter 5, the influence of EWV on ERB was explored. The model behind this is very simple:

EWVGSC ⟶ ERB   Model A

Until now in this analysis, WILLACT has been regarded as an ERB variable. However, it differs from the other three ERB variables in that it measures willingness to act rather than actions themselves. This raises the theoretical possibility that WILLACT could also have an influence on the two ERB variables, Support Groups and Avoid Products. Again, the model is a simple one:

WILLACT ─────────► ERB   Model B

It is possible that EWVGSC and WILLACT operate in tandem to influence ERB. This model suggests that individuals have both attitudes towards the environment and a propensity to behave in an environmentally responsible way. While these two variables have a somewhat independent influence on ERB, they are also related. In this case, the model would be represented thus:[9]

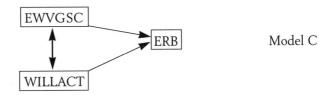

Model C

It is also possible to postulate a sequence of influence between these three variables – that EWVGSC influences WILLACT, which in turn influences ERB:

EWVGSC ─────────► WILLACT ─────────► ERB   Model D

This model assumes that EWVGSC has no direct influence on ERB; that WILLACT is an intervening variable. However, it is possible to modify this model to include both direct and indirect influence:

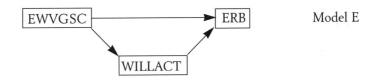

Model E

Now the effect of EWVGSC on ERB operates both directly and also through WILLACT. Models such as these were discussed and interpreted in Chapter 5 and outlined in Table 5.7. They will now be explored with this set of variables.

Bivariate Analysis

Simple bivariate analysis uses models A and B. This is the most elementary form of explanatory analysis available. It uses asymmetrical coefficients that indicate the degree of statistical influence of one variable on another. This method of analysis only goes a small step beyond associational analysis based on symmetrical coefficients. While a convincing explanation requires much more than this, it is a useful first step. We will examine models A and B with both categorical and metric versions of the variables.

Categorical Variables

As the categorical versions of all three variables are at the ordinal level, the appropriate coefficient is Somer's d, with Avoid Products and Support Groups as the outcome variables.[10] Data from both samples are analyzed (see Table 8.17).

The influence of the two explanatory variables, EWVGSC and WILLACT, on Avoid Products is linear and positive in both samples. The relationships are similar with Support Groups, but there is evidence of slight curves in the Student sample. The values for Somer's d for both samples are: EWVGSC on Support Groups, 0.33 (both samples);[11] EWVGSC on Avoid Products, 0.32 (Students) and 0.35 (Residents);[12] WILLACT on Support Groups, 0.46 and 0.37;[13] and WILLACT on Avoid Products, 0.41 and 0.32.[14] All these values are significant at the 0.001 level. There is clearly a similar degree of influence of EWVGSC on both outcome variables, and in both samples. The influence of WILLACT is similar to EWVGSC in the Resident sample, but is stronger in the Student sample. We can conclude from this analysis that EWV does have a moderate influence on ERB for both Students and Residents and that the higher level of support for environmental groups among Students is due to their greater Willingness to Act on behalf of the environment.

In addition to EWV and Willingness to Act, other variables could also be expected to influence ERB. We have already had good theoretical reasons for exploring the association of Age and Gender with all three variables. Let us examine the influence of Age (Resident sample only) and Gender (both samples) on the two ERB variables. If we use the categorical version of Age, Somer's d is the appropriate coefficient, while for Gender (regarded as two nominal categories) it is lambda. We find that the influence of Age on Support Groups and Avoid Products in the Resident sample is rather weak but highly significant ($d = -0.17$ and $p < 0.001$ in both cases). The influence of Gender is weak in the Student sample (lambda is 0.17 with $p < 0.05$ for Support Groups, and 0.14 with $p < 0.05$ for Avoid Products) and is even weaker in the Resident sample (lambda is 0.00 and 0.05, respectively, and both are not significant). This analysis confirms the patterns of associations established earlier (see Tables 8.13 and 8.16).

One other variable, Religion, is examined briefly. There are good theoretical reasons for doing so. Extensive research has shown that religion has an influence on behaviour, although in complex ways. Some religions also include beliefs about the need for humans to act as stewards of the environment, particularly flora and fauna. While religion may also influence environmental attitudes, it is only the influence of religious affiliation on ERB that will be discussed here; religious beliefs were not measured in this research. It turns out that the influence of Religion (in seven categories) is negligible in the Student sample (lambda is 0.05 and 0.03, respectively, and both are not significant) and in the Resident sample (lambda is 0.01 and 0.04, respectively, and both are not significant).

We need to note that as it is not appropriate to compare the values of Somer's d and lambda. Hence, we cannot draw any definite conclusions about the relative influence of these ordinal-level and nominal-level variables. In any case, the values for the coefficients are so low that there is nothing to say. However, other

Table 8.17 Influence of EWVGSC and WILLACT on Support Groups and Avoid Products (percentages; both samples)

Students

	EWVGSC					WILLACT				
Support Groups	Low	Mod.	High	Very high	Total	Low	Mod.	High	Very high	Total
Never	**69**	**55**	**45**	20	44	**79**	**59**	31	8	44
Occasionally	28	39	**50**	**47**	42	16	40	**61**	**49**	42
Regularly	3	6	6	**33**	14	5	1	8	**43**	14
	Somer's d = 0.33; $p<0.001$					Somer's d = 0.46; $p<0.001$				
Avoid Products										
0	**52**	**29**	20	11	25	**57**	**27**	14	7	25
1	**30**	28	**35**	22	29	**31**	**33**	27	23	29
2	12	**31**	**30**	**34**	28	8	**31**	**40**	**30**	28
3+	6	12	15	**32**	18	4	9	**19**	**40**	18
	Somer's d = 0.32; $p<0.001$					Somer's d = 0.41; $p<0.001$				
Total	100	100	100	100	100	100	100	100	100	100
n	87	108	123	144	462	98	140	113	111	462

Residents

	EWVGSC					WILLACT				
Support Groups	Low	Mod.	High	Very high	Total	Low	Mod.	High	Very high	Total
Never	**85**	**63**	**56**	26	61	**87**	**60**	**49**	14	61
Occasionally	13	**30**	28	**41**	27	13	**33**	**31**	**36**	26
Regularly	2	6	**16**	**33**	13	0	7	**20**	**50**	13
	Somer's d = 0.33; $p<0.001$					Somer's d = 0.37; $p<0.001$				
Avoid Products										
0	**51**	22	11	6	25	**49**	21	12	2	25
1	27	**28**	25	27	27	28	22	**34**	19	27
2	18	**33**	**39**	**36**	30	18	**34**	**31**	**53**	30
3+	4	17	**25**	**31**	18	4	**23**	**23**	**26**	18
	Somer's d = 0.35; $p<0.001$					Somer's d = 0.32; $p<0.001$				
Total	100	100	100	100	100	100	100	100	100	100
n	120	112	89	81	402	120	134	106	42	402

Table 8.18 *Means analysis of Gender and Religion (Students), and Age, Gender and Religion (Residents), with Support Groups and Avoid Products*

		Students							
		Support Groups				Avoid Products			
		$\bar{x}$	s	n	Eta/p	$\bar{x}$	s	n	Eta/p
Gender	Male	0.43	0.50	210	0.24	1.03	1.03	209	0.30
	Female	0.67	0.47	252	<0.001	1.67	0.98	249	<0.001
Religion	Catholic	0.48	0.50	138		1.22	1.02	136	
	Anglican	0.59	0.50	56		1.18	0.95	57	
	Uniting	0.62	0.49	29		1.39	1.03	28	
	Greek Orth.	0.47	0.51	17		1.19	0.91	16	
	Baptist	0.20	0.42	10		0.80	0.79	10	
	Other	0.57	0.50	46	0.17	1.52	1.03	46	0.17
	No religion	0.61	0.49	146	n.s.	1.53	1.10	146	<0.05
		Residents							
Age	18–24	0.57	0.50	47		1.55	1.02	47	
	25–34	0.38	0.49	81		1.46	1.11	81	
	35–44	0.59	0.49	79		1.81	0.98	79	
	45–54	0.46	0.50	59		1.58	0.89	59	
	55–64	0.23	0.43	56	0.33	1.41	1.06	56	0.33
	65+	0.16	0.37	79	<0.001	0.76	0.89	79	<0.001
Gender	Male	0.41	0.49	200	0.03	1.23	1.07	200	0.17
	Female	0.38	0.49	199	n.s.	1.59	0.99	199	<0.001
Religion	Catholic	0.36	0.48	85		1.24	1.03	85	
	Anglican	0.27	0.45	91		1.41	1.04	91	
	Uniting	0.40	0.49	55		1.33	1.06	55	
	Greek Orth.	0.22	0.44	9		1.44	1.13	9	
	Other	0.27	0.47	11	0.23	1.36	1.12	11	0.13
	No religion	0.57	0.50	100	<0.01	1.61	1.01	100	n.s.

methods of analysis using the metric versions of the variables, and some other tricks, may reveal a different picture.

Categorical and Metric Variables: Means Analysis

When the outcome variable is metric it is possible to compare the means on this variable between the categories of the predictor variable. This involves the use of eta (η). Age, Gender and Religion can be analyzed by this method, although only Gender and Religion can be usefully analyzed in the Student sample. For the purpose of this analysis, Support Groups is regarded as a dummy variable with 'Yes' coded 1 and 'No' coded 0.

Table 8.18 shows the means for Support Groups and Avoid Products on the categories of each variable, as well as the eta values and levels of significance for each combination. In the Student sample, Gender has a moderate influence on both ERB variables (eta is 0.24 for Support Groups and 0.30 for Avoid Products, with $p < 0.001$ in each case). The influence of Religion is rather weak (eta is 0.17 for both Support Groups and Avoid Products, with the former not significant and for the latter $p < 0.05$). In the Resident sample, Gender has virtually no influence on Support Groups (eta is 0.03 and not significant) and only a weak influence on Avoid Products (eta is 0.17 with $p < 0.001$). Age turns out to have the greatest influence (eta is 0.33, with $p < 0.001$, for both variables), followed by Religion (eta is 0.23 and 0.13, with $p < 0.01$ and not significant, respectively). Leaving aside categories with small numbers, the highest means are to be found in the '35–44' Age category and among those with 'No religion'. The lowest means are amongst those 65 years and over.

Metric Variables

The obvious candidate for measuring the influence between two metric variables is simple regression. Again, we will examine the two models to see what influence both EWVGSC and WILLACT have on the same two ERB variables, but this time using the metric versions of the variables. Table 8.19 provides the results of the regression calculations. We can compare the ability of the two predictor variables to explain the two outcome variables within and between the two samples. The relevant coefficients are *beta*, the standardized coefficient for the slope (b) of the regression line, and R^2, the coefficient of determination or the measure of how well the line fits the data. In the Student sample, the beta values suggest that WILLACT is a slightly better predictor of both Support Groups and Avoid Products than is EWVGSC, ranging from 0.55 for WILLACT and Support Groups, down to 0.43 for EWVGSC and Avoid Products. In the Resident sample, both predictor variables are about as equally powerful (*beta* ranges from 0.48 to 0.43) with WILLACT on Support Groups being slightly ahead. WILLACT accounts for more of the variance in Support Groups (23.0 per cent) compared with around 19 per cent in the other three. This analysis produces a very similar picture to that obtained from the categorical versions of the variables (see Table 8.17).

Table 8.19 *Regression of ERB variables on WILLACT and EWVGSC (both samples)*

Predictor	Outcome	Intercept	Slope	Std. Error	Beta	p	R	R^2	se_{est}
				Students[a]					
WILLACT	Support Gps	−1.12	0.51	0.04	0.55	<0.001	0.55	0.298	0.59
	Avoid Prods	−1.06	0.68	0.06	0.49	<0.001	0.49	0.238	0.92
EWVGSC	Support Gps	−1.68	0.60	0.05	0.46	<0.001	0.46	0.211	0.62
	Avoid Prods	−1.93	0.83	0.08	0.43	<0.001	0.43	0.181	0.95
				Residents				($n = 401$)	
WILLACT	Support Gps	−1.06	0.47	0.04	0.48	<0.001	0.48	0.230	0.62
	Avoid Prods	−0.72	0.63	0.07	0.44	<0.001	0.44	0.192	0.94
EWVGSC	Support Gps	−1.77	0.60	0.06	0.44	<0.001	0.44	0.195	0.64
	Avoid Prods	−1.89	0.87	0.09	0.43	<0.001	0.43	0.185	0.95

[a]$n = 457$ for Avoid Products and 461 for Support Groups.

Multivariate Analysis

As a first step in the direction of multivariate analysis, model C will be explored (see p. 273). This model links models A and B by introducing an association between the two explanatory variables. If it turns out that there is little or no association between EWVGSC and WILLACT, it can be concluded that they influence ERB independently. However, if they are highly associated, their influence can be seen as combined in some way. This would need to be explored. Initially, this can be done by examining the extent to which WILLACT influences the ERB variables when the influence of EWVGSC is removed, and the extent to which EWGSC influences the ERB variables when the influence of WILLACT is removed.

The second step is to explore models D and E to establish whether WILLACT is an intervening variable between EWVGSC and the ERB variables. As we saw in Chapter 5, it is the interpretation of the differences in the magnitudes of the coefficients of association and influence that allows conclusions to be drawn.

These analyses are done using both the categorical and metric versions of the variables. Other variables will be added at certain points.

Categorical Variables

The first step is to examine the associations between categorical versions of EWVGSC and WILLACT in light of their separate influences on the categorical versions of the ERB variables (model C). We know from earlier analysis that gamma for the association between the two explanatory variables is 0.70 for Students and 0.62 for Residents (Table 8.7). We know from Table 8.17 that WILLACT has a greater influence on Support Groups ($d = 0.46$ and 0.37) and Avoid Products ($d = 0.41$ and 0.32) than EWVGSC has on both (for Support Groups, $d = 0.33$ for both Students and Residents; for Avoid Products, $d = 0.32$ and 0.35, respectively). We also know that the associations between WILLACT and the two ERB variables are strong (with Support Groups, $G = 0.71$ for Students and 0.63 for Residents; with Avoid Products, $G = 0.53$ and 0.42, respectively). The associations between EWVGSC and the ERB variables are generally a bit weaker than these (with Support Groups, $G = 0.52$ and 0.57, respectively; with Avoid Products, $G = 0.42$ and 0.47, respectively).

A conclusion that can be drawn from all these data is that the strongest associations are between EWVGSC and WILLACT and between WILLACT and Support Groups, with the coefficients being marginally higher for Students than Residents. In addition, we know that WILLACT has more influence on Support Groups and Avoid Products than does EWVGSC. What happens when we control one of these predictor variables by the other? Does WILLACT continue to influence the two ERB variables when the influence of EWVGSC is controlled, and vice versa? This analysis tells us the extent to which WILLACT and EWVGSC influence the ERB variables independently. If WILLACT continues to influence the ERB variables when EWVGSC is controlled, but EWVGSC does not influence the ERB variables when WILLACT is controlled, then this would indicate that WILLACT is an intervening variable between EWVGSC and ERB (see model E).

In order to sort this out with categorical variables we can turn to three-way contingency tables. Such tables allow us to introduce a control variable and to see to what extent a bivariate relationship still exists when the influence of a third variable is controlled – in effect, removed. This allows us to gauge the extent to which two predictor variables, which are related to some extent, independently influence the outcome variable.

We already know that in order to be able to claim that some form of influence is involved between combinations of two variables, it is necessary to use asymmetrical measures such as lambda when at least one of the variables is nominal, and Somer's d when they are both ordinal. When a third categorical variable is applied as a control, it does not matter whether it is nominal or ordinal. The decision about the appropriate coefficient must be based on the level of measurement of the two variables between which influence is assumed. However, in three-way analysis of categorical variables, it is also useful to use measures of association, such as Cramér's V and the standardized contingency coefficient (when at least one variable is nominal) and gamma (when both are ordinal). In three-way analysis, we are looking for the degree of change in the coefficients as the result of introducing a control variable. While this can be done by using either symmetric or asymmetric coefficients, the latter are more appropriate when the model indicates influence rather than association.

EWVGSC and WILLACT with ERB

To save space, only the tables for the Student sample will be examined. Tables 8.20 and 8.21 present conditional contingency tables when both versions of the controls are introduced. Table 8.20 presents EWVGSC controlled for WILLACT with both of the ERB variables. Compared with the values for Somer's d in the uncontrolled table ($d = 0.33$ for Support Groups and 0.32 for Avoid Products; see Table 8.17), all but one of the values for d are lower. The exception is in the 'Very high' WILLACT category with Avoid Products ($d = 0.39$). The same EWVGSC category with Support Groups has a d similar to the uncontrolled table (0.32), and the d values in these two conditional tables are the only ones that are significant. These patterns are confirmed by the values for gamma, shown in brackets below the d values. Hence, introducing this control essentially eliminates the influence of EWVGSC on the two ERB variables in all but the 'Very high' WILLACT conditional tables. It is only respondents in this category whose ERB is also influenced by their EWV.

The situation is quite different in Table 8.21, although the conclusion is similar. When WILLACT is controlled for EWVGSC, the values of Somer's d for the 'Very high' EWVGSC category are higher than for the uncontrolled table (see Table 8.17), 0.52 compared to 0.46 for Support Groups and 0.43 compared to 0.41 for Avoid Products. For the other three EWVGSC categories, the values for d are lower but still significant. This would suggest that WILLACT continues to have an influence on the ERB variables, regardless of EWV. Again, these patterns are confirmed by the values for gamma.

What can we conclude from these two tables? They suggest that the influence of EWVGSC on ERB only occurs in the highest WILLACT category, while

Table 8.20 Influence of EWVGSC on Support Groups and Avoid Products controlled for WILLACT (percentages; Students)

Control	Predictor	Support Groups						Avoid Products					
WILLACT	EWVGSC	Never	Occ.	Reg.	Total	n	d (G)	0	1	2	3+	Total	d (G)
Low	Low	82	13	5	100	55	0.05***	60	31	5	4	100	0.09***
	Moderate	72	24	3	100	29	(0.15)***	55	31	10	3	100	(0.15)***
	High	82	18	0	100	11		55	27	9	9	100	
	Very high	67	0	33	100	3		33	33	33	0	100	
	Total	79	16	5	100	98		57	31	8	4	100	
Moderate	Low	56	44	0	100	23	−0.03***	50	23	18	9	100	0.01***
	Moderate	53	44	2	100	45	(−0.06)***	16	33	42	9	100	(0.01)***
	High	66	34	0	100	47		24	35	28	13	100	
	Very high	56	40	4	100	25		32	36	28	4	100	
	Total	59	40	1	100	140		27	33	31	9	100	
High	Low	22	78	0	100	9	0.09***	11	44	33	11	100	0.05***
	Moderate	43	50	7	100	28	(0.18)***	21	14	39	25	100	(0.06)***
	High	32	58	10	100	40		12	34	42	12	100	
	Very high	22	69	8	100	36		11	26	40	23	100	
	Total	31	61	8	100	113		14	27	40	19	100	
Very high	Low	0	0	0	0	0	0.32*	0	0	0	0	0	0.39
	Moderate	33	17	50	100	6	(0.51)*	40	40	0	20	100	(0.52)
	High	8	80	12	100	25		12	42	21	25	100	
	Very high	6	41	53	100	80		4	16	34	46	100	
	Total	8	49	43	100	111		7	23	29	40	100	
Total						462	0.33/(0. 52)						0.32/(0.42)
												($n = 458$)	

***Not significant. **$p < 0.05$ level. *$p < 0.01$ level. For all other coefficients, $p < 0.001$ level.

Table 8.21 Influence of WILLACT on Support Groups and Avoid Products controlled for EWVGSC (percentages; Students)

Control EWVGSC	Predictor WILLACT	Support Groups						Avoid Products					
		Never	Occ.	Reg.	Total	n	d (G)	0	1	2	3+	Total	d (G)
Low	Low	82	13	5	100	55	0.32	60	31	5	4	100	0.29*
	Moderate	56	44	0	100	23	(0.59)	50	23	18	9	100	(0.43)*
	High	22	78	0	100	9		11	44	33	11	100	
	Very high	0	0	0	0	0		0	0	0	0	0	
	Total	69	28	3	100	87		52	30	12	6	100	
Moderate	Low	72	24	3	100	29	0.22	55	31	10	3	100	0.31
	Moderate	53	44	2	100	45	(0.40)	16	33	42	9	100	(0.41)
	High	43	50	7	100	28		21	14	39	25	100	
	Very high	33	17	50	100	6		40	40	0	20	100	
	Total	55	39	6	100	108		29	28	31	12	100	
High	Low	82	18	0	100	11	0.41	55	27	9	9	100	0.18**
	Moderate	66	34	0	100	47	(0.70)	24	35	28	13	100	(0.25)**
	High	32	58	10	100	40		12	34	42	12	100	
	Very high	8	80	12	100	25		12	42	21	25	100	
	Total	45	50	6	100	123		20	35	30	15	100	
Very high	Low	67	0	33	100	3	0.52	33	33	33	0	100	0.43
	Moderate	56	40	4	100	25	(0.75)	32	36	28	4	100	(0.57)
	High	22	69	8	100	36		11	26	40	23	100	
	Very high	6	41	53	100	80		4	16	34	46	100	
	Total	20	47	33	100	144		11	22	34	32	100	
Total 0.41/(0.53)		20	47	33	100	462	0.46/(0.71)	11	22	34	32	100	(n = 458)

**p < 0.05 level. *p < 0.01 level. For all other coefficients, p < 0.001 level.

the influence of WILLACT on ERB occurs in spite of EWVGSC. Therefore, the relatively strong association that we have found between EWVGSC and WILLACT (gamma = 0.70), and between both of these variables and the two ERB variables (gamma = 0.52 and 0.42 for EWVGSC with Support Groups and Avoid Products respectively, and 0.71 and 0.53 for WILLACT and these two variables) only reveals part of the picture. This analysis provides support for model D, although it only partially applies to those respondents with 'Very high' scores on both WILLACT and EWVGSC.

A rather different picture emerges when this analysis is undertaken in the Resident sample. Table 8.22 shows the values for Somer's d and gamma. No clear pattern emerges. The only conclusion that can be drawn is that both predictor variables have an influence on the outcome variables. This varies across the categories of the predictor variables, such that when one predictor has some influence the other seems to have less. While the 'Very high' category of both predictor variables with Support Groups shows a pattern similar to that for the Student sample, that is, this category has a higher d value than the other categories, and similar to the uncontrolled table, the complete reverse occurs with Avoid Products. In general, these reversed patterns for the two ERB variables in the Resident sample suggest that both predictor variables have a direct influence on the outcome variable, even if there are some differences across the categories. However, the interpretation of the Resident sample data is not straightforward. What we can conclude is that the relationships between EWVGSC, WILLACT and the ERB variables are different in the two samples.

Table 8.22 *Influence of EWVGSC and WILLACT on Support Groups and Avoid Products with controls for WILLACT and EWVGSC (Residents)*

Control	Predictor		Support Groups			Avoid Products		
			d	G	p	d	G	p
WILLACT	EWVGSC	Low	0.11	0.41	n.s.	0.25	0.36	<0.01
		Moderate	0.25	0.46	<0.001	0.26	0.35	<0.001
		High	0.15	0.24	n.s.	0.28	0.38	<0.001
		Very high	0.32	0.49	<0.05	−0.02	−0.03	n.s.
		Total	0.33	0.57	<0.001	0.35	0.47	<0.001
EWVGSC	WILLACT	Low	0.23	0.66	<0.01	0.21	0.31	<0.05
		Moderate	0.13	0.26	n.s.	0.18	0.24	<0.05
		High	0.25	0.43	<0.01	0.17	0.23	<0.05
		Very high	0.38	0.55	<0.001	0.10	0.14	n.s.
		Total	0.37	0.63	<0.001	0.32	0.42	

WILLACT, Age and Gender with ERB

Further three-way analysis can be done with other variables. In light of research questions 3 and 4, we will examine the extent to which the influence of WILLACT on ERB varies according to Age and Gender. In other words, what happens to the influence of WILLACT when Age and Gender are controlled separately? Only the analysis with Gender can be done with the Student sample.

Table 8.23 Influence of WILLACT on Support Groups and Avoid Products controlled for Gender (percentages; both samples)

	Males						Females					
	WILLACT						WILLACT					
Students	Low	Mod.	High	V. high	Total	d (G)	Low	Mod.	High	V. high	Total	d (G)
Support Groups												
Never	85	67	36	12	57	0.43	67	51	27	6	33	0.44
Occasionally	11	33	57	41	33	(0.70)	27	46	64	52	50	(0.68)
Regularly	5	0	6	47	10		6	3	9	42	17	
Total	100	100	100	100	100		100	100	100	100	100	
n	65	66	47	32	210		33	74	66	79	252	
Avoid Products												
No products	63	33	26	16	38	0.34	46	21	6	4	15	0.40
One product	29	35	35	34	33	(0.47)	33	31	22	18	25	(0.53)
Two products	3	23	24	16	16		18	39	51	35	38	
Three or more	5	9	15	34	13		3	10	21	43	22	
Total	100	100	100	100	100		100	100	100	100	100	
n	65	66	46	32	209		33	72	67	77	249	
Residents												
Support Groups												
Never	87	57	43	17	59	0.39	88	63	55	11	62	0.34
Occasionally	13	39	41	44	32	(0.66)	12	27	23	26	22	(0.60)
Regularly	0	3	16	39	9		0	10	21	63	16	
Total	100	100	100	100	100		100	100	100	100	100	
n	67	61	49	23	200		51	73	56	19	199	
Avoid Products												
No products	57	31	18	4	33	0.33	37	12	7	0	16	0.29
One product	19	25	33	22	25	(0.44)	41	19	36	16	29	(0.38)
Two products	21	26	27	48	27		16	41	34	58	34	
Three or more	3	18	22	26	15		6	27	23	26	21	
Total	100	100	100	100	100		100	100	100	100	100	
n	67	61	49	23	200		51	73	56	19	199	

For all coefficients, p<0.001 level. Tests are two-tailed.

Table 8.24   *Influence of WILLACT on Support Groups and Avoid Products* controlled
for Age (Residents)

Predictor	Control		Support Groups			Avoid Products		
			Somers' d	Gamma	p	Somers' d	Gamma	p
WILLACT	**Age**	18–24	0.34	0.51	<0.001	0.31	0.41	<0.001
		25–34	0.32	0.59	<0.001	0.42	0.54	<0.001
		35–44	0.32	0.48	<0.001	0.13	0.17	n.s.
		45–54	0.36	0.58	<0.001	0.12	0.17	n.s.
		55–64	0.25	0.61	<0.05	0.27	0.36	<0.05
		65+	0.26	0.75	<0.01	0.23	0.34	<0.05
		Total	0.37	0.63	<0.001	0.32	0.42	<0.001

In both samples, it is clear that the influence of WILLACT on Support Groups and Avoid Products is not really affected by Gender (see Table 8.23). With one exception, the values for *d* in the two conditional tables for each of the ERB variables, and in both samples, differ from the values of *d* in the uncontrolled tables by no more than 0.03. The exception is in the Student sample for males with Avoid Products, but even here the difference is only 0.07. This suggests that male Avoidance of Environmentally Damaging Products is slightly less dependent on their Willingness to Act than it is for females.

The conditional tables have not been presented for the control by Age on the influence of WILLACT on the two ERB variables. Instead, Table 8.24 provides the values for Somer's *d* and gamma for the six Age categories in the Resident sample. We know that the level of Support for Environmental Groups, and the Avoidance of Environmentally Damaging Products, is much lower for older respondents (55+) than for younger respondents (see Tables 8.13 and 8.18). We also know that the Willingness to Act is much lower among older respondents (see Table 8.13). What we now know is that the influence of WILLACT on Support Groups shows very limited differentiation in terms of Age; the influence is only marginally lower among older respondents. However, for Avoid Products, it is respondents in the '35–44' and '45–54' Age categories who show the least influence from their Willingness to Act. The values of *d* are about 0.20 lower than for all uncontrolled influences and are about 0.30 lower than for the '25–34' Age category. Again, the gamma coefficients confirm the patterns, although the value of 0.75 for the '65+' Age category, compared with 0.63 for the uncontrolled association, is 'deviant'. Hence, Avoiding Environmentally Damaging Products is not as easily explained by these variables, as is Support for Enviromental Groups.

An extension of these three-way analyses would involve controlling Age by Gender to see to what extent these two variables have independent influences, that is, whether Age is somehow 'contaminated' by Gender. For example, are differences between Age categories in the way the predictor variable (WILLACT) influences the outcome variables (Support Groups and Avoid Products) due just to Age or, to some extent, to different Gender compositions in the Age categories? We could test this by doing a four-way analysis. However, this would stretch the Resident sample beyond the capabilities of its size. As other methods are available when the metric versions of the variables are used, this will be explored later.

Table 8.25   *Means analysis of EWVGSC on Support Groups and Avoid Products controlled for WILLACT (Students)*

Control	Predictor	Support Groups			Avoid Products		
WILLACT	**EWVGSC**	$\bar{x}$	s	n	$\bar{x}$	s	n
Low	Low	0.18	0.39	55	0.53	0.77	55
	Moderate	0.28	0.45	29	0.62	0.82	29
	High	0.18	0.40	11	0.73	1.01	11
	Very high	0.33	0.58	3	1.00	1.00	3
	Total	0.21	0.41	98	0.59	0.81	98
Mod.	Low	0.43	0.51	23	0.86	1.04	22
	Moderate	0.47	0.50	45	1.44	0.87	45
	High	0.34	0.48	47	1.30	0.99	46
	Very high	0.44	0.51	25	1.04	0.89	25
	Total	0.41	0.49	140	1.23	0.95	138
High	Low	0.78	0.44	9	1.44	0.88	9
	Moderate	0.57	0.50	28	1.68	1.09	28
	High	0.68	0.47	40	1.54	0.87	41
	Very high	0.78	0.42	36	1.74	0.95	35
	Total	0.69	0.46	113	1.63	0.95	113
V. High	Low	0.00	0.00	0	0.00	0.00	0
	Moderate	0.67	0.52	6	1.00	1.22	5
	High	0.92	0.28	25	1.58	1.02	24
	Very high	0.94	0.24	80	2.23	0.86	80
	Total	0.92	0.27	111	2.03	0.97	109
	Low	0.31	0.47	87	0.71	0.89	86
	Moderate	0.45	0.50	108	1.26	1.01	107
	High	0.55	0.50	123	1.39	0.97	122
	Very high	0.80	0.40	144	1.87	0.99	143
Total		0.56	0.50	462	1.38	1.05	458
Eta			0.36				0.39

Categorical and Metric Variables: Means Analysis

Earlier, in Table 8.18, we undertook a comparison of means for the two ERB variables across a number of categorical variables. It is also possible to introduce a third variable into this type of analysis, with a similar logic to that used in three-way contingency tables. For example, we can calculate means instead of distributions across the categories of the ERB variables, for categories of WILLACT controlled for EWVGSC, and vice versa. The only real difference between a means analysis on these variables and the use of conditional contingency tables is the way the data are utilized. In the latter, the outcome variable is categorical, while in the former it is metric. Again, the two versions of the two ERB variables are used here just to illustrate the different types of analysis. For this purpose, the Avoid Products categories can be regarded as either categorical or metric, while the Support Groups categories need to be dichotomized into a dummy variable to make them the equivalent of a metric variable.

EWVGSC and WILLACT with ERB

Table 8.25 presents the analysis with EWVGSC as the predictor variable, controlled for WILLACT, and Table 8.26 reverses the role of these two variables. The patterns in the results confirm those found in Tables 8.20 and 8.21. In Table 8.25, the overall mean for Support Groups is 0.56, which ranges across the EWVGSC categories from 0.31 ('Low') to 0.80 ('Very high'), with an eta of 0.36 (see the section at the foot of the table). When WILLACT is introduced as a control variable, this pattern changes in all the conditional tables; the influence of EWVGSC tends to disappear. This is evident from the similar values for the means across the EWVGSC categories in each conditional table, thus indicating that WILLACT influences Support Groups regardless of EWV. To put this into non-statistical language, the level of a person's Willingness to Act to protect the environment influences their level of Support for Environmental Groups, regardless of their Environmental Worldview.

When the roles of predictor and control variables are reversed, the results are very different (see Table 8.26). This time the Support Groups mean ranges from 0.21 ('Low') to 0.92 ('Very high') across the WILLACT categories, with an eta of 0.52 (see the section at the foot of the table). The linear relationship between WILLACT and Support Groups is maintained across all the conditional tables. However, this pattern simply reinforces what was found in Table 8.25; it is WILLACT rather than EWVGSC that influences Support Groups.

To conclude this analysis, we need to discuss the influence of EWVGSC and WILLACT on Avoid Products (see Tables 8.25 and 8.26). Again, the relationships are linear. In Table 8.25, the overall mean for Avoid Products is 1.38, ranging from 0.71 ('Low') to 1.87 ('Very high') across the EWVGSC categories, with an eta of 0.39 (see the section at the foot of the table). When WILLACT is introduced as a control, the same pattern appears in the partial tables for the extreme WILLACT categories, but not for the two middle categories. This would suggest that both EWV and Willingness to Act influence the level of Avoiding Environmentally Damaging Products of respondents with extreme WILLACT scores, but this is not the case for the other respondents. The latter are not particularly influenced by either their EWV or their Willingness to Act. This confirms the findings of the analysis in the three-way contingency tables (see Tables 8.20 and 8.21).

Now, returning to Table 8.26, we find that the Avoid Products mean ranges from 0.59 ('Low') to 2.03 ('Very high') across the WILLACT categories, with an eta of 0.48 (see the section at the foot of the table). While we know that WILLACT influences Avoid Products (see Table 8.17), there is some evidence in Table 8.26 that EWVGSC may have an influence on Avoid Products alongside WILLACT. This is certainly the case for those in the extreme EWVGSC categories, but not in the two middle categories. Therefore, we have further evidence to support the conclusion drawn from the control of WILLACT on EWVGSC (see Table 8.25). The patterns for both the ERB variables, with both methods of control, could be further supported if eta coefficients were calculated for each of the partial tables, as Somer's d was in Tables 8.20 and 8.21. Unfortunately, SPSS does not do this, although it could be done with a calculator. You might like to try this.

Table 8.26 *Means analysis of WILLACT on Support Groups and Avoid Products controlled for EWVGSC (Students)*

Control	Predictor	Support Groups			Avoid Products		
EWVGSC	*WILLACT*	$\bar{x}$	s	n	$\bar{x}$	s	n
Low	Low	0.18	0.39	55	0.53	0.77	55
	Moderate	0.43	0.51	23	0.86	1.04	22
	High	0.78	0.44	9	1.44	0.88	9
	Very high	0.00	0.00	0	0.00	0.00	0
	Total	0.31	0.47	87	0.71	0.89	86
Mod.	Low	0.28	0.45	29	0.62	0.82	29
	Moderate	0.47	0.50	45	1.44	0.87	45
	High	0.57	0.50	28	1.68	1.09	28
	Very high	0.67	0.52	6	1.00	1.22	5
	Total	0.45	0.50	108	1.26	1.01	107
High	Low	0.18	0.40	11	0.73	1.01	11
	Moderate	0.34	0.48	47	1.30	0.99	46
	High	0.68	0.47	40	1.54	0.87	41
	Very high	0.92	0.28	25	1.58	1.02	24
	Total	0.55	0.50	123	1.39	0.97	122
V. high	Low	0.33	0.58	3	1.00	1.00	3
	Moderate	0.44	0.51	25	1.04	0.89	25
	High	0.78	0.42	36	1.74	0.95	35
	Very high	0.94	0.24	80	2.23	0.86	80
	Total	0.80	0.40	144	1.87	0.99	143
	Low	0.21	0.41	98	0.59	0.81	98
	Moderate	0.41	0.49	140	1.23	0.95	138
	High	0.69	0.46	113	1.63	0.95	113
	Very high	0.92	0.27	111	2.03	0.97	109
Total		0.56	0.50	462	1.38	1.05	458
Eta			0.52			0.48	

WILLACT and Gender with ERB

To complete this means analysis, we can now turn to the combinations that we explored previously with the categorical forms of the variables in Table 8.23. Table 8.27 shows the effects of controlling for Gender on the association between WILLACT and both Support Groups and Avoid Products in Student sample (see also Figures 8.6 and 8.7). The mean scores for each conditional table indicate a strong linear relationship for both males and females, with a range between the 'Low' and 'Very high' WILLACT categories of 0.73 for males and 0.61 for females for Support Groups, and of 1.20 for males and 1.38 for females for Avoid Products. In addition, females have higher means than males across all the WILLACT categories, particularly for Avoid Products. We can conclude that while females have higher mean scores than males on both the ERB variables, WILLACT differentiates both males and females.

The same strong linear relationships between WILLACT and the two ERB variables are evident in the Resident sample for both males and females (see

Table 8.27   *Means analysis of WILLACT on Support Groups and Avoid Products controlled for Gender (Students)*

Control	Predictor	Support Groups			Avoid Products		
Gender	*WILLACT*	$\bar{x}$	s	n	$\bar{x}$	s	n
Males	Low	0.15	0.36	65	0.49	0.77	65
	Moderate	0.33	0.48	66	1.08	0.97	66
	High	0.64	0.49	47	1.28	1.03	46
	Very high	0.88	0.34	32	1.69	1.12	32
	Total	0.43	0.50	210	1.03	1.03	209
Females	Low	0.33	0.48	33	0.79	0.86	33
	Moderate	0.49	0.50	74	1.38	0.93	72
	High	0.73	0.45	66	1.87	0.81	67
	Very high	0.94	0.25	79	2.17	0.86	77
	Total	0.67	0.47	252	1.67	0.98	249
	Low	0.21	0.41	98	0.59	0.81	98
	Moderate	0.41	0.49	140	1.23	0.95	138
	High	0.69	0.46	113	1.63	0.95	113
	Very high	0.92	0.27	111	2.03	0.97	109
Total		0.56	0.50	462	1.38	1.05	458
Eta			0.52			0.48	
Difference	Low	0.18			0.30		
(F – M)	Moderate	0.16			0.30		
	High	0.09			0.59		
	Very high	0.06			0.48		
	Total	0.24			0.64		

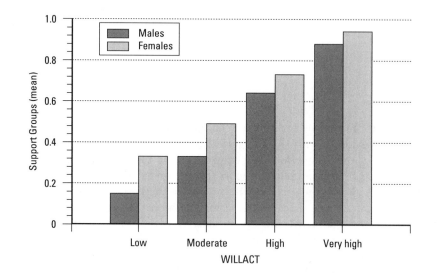

Figure 8.6   *Support Groups by WILLACT controlled for Gender (Students)*

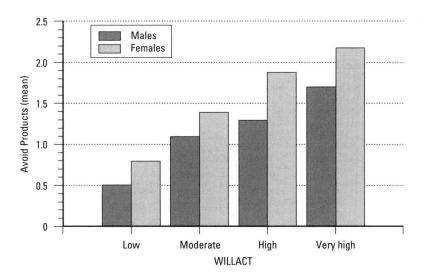

Figure 8.7   *Avoid Products by WILLACT controlled for Gender (Students)*

Table 8.28   *Means analysis of WILLACT on Support Groups and Avoid Products controlled for Gender (Residents)*

Control Gender	Predictor WILLACT	Support Groups			Avoid Products		
		$\bar{x}$	s	n	$\bar{x}$	s	n
Males	Low	0.13	0.34	67	0.70	0.90	67
	Moderate	0.43	0.50	61	1.31	1.10	61
	High	0.57	0.50	49	1.53	1.04	49
	Very high	0.83	0.39	23	1.96	0.82	23
	Total	0.41	0.49	200	1.23	1.07	200
Females	Low	0.12	0.33	51	0.90	0.88	51
	Moderate	0.37	0.49	73	1.84	0.97	73
	High	0.45	0.50	56	1.73	0.90	56
	Very high	0.89	0.32	19	2.11	0.66	19
	Total	0.38	0.49	199	1.59	0.99	199
	Low	0.13	0.33	118	0.79	0.89	118
	Moderate	0.40	0.49	134	1.60	1.06	134
	High	0.50	0.50	105	1.64	0.97	105
	Very high	0.86	0.35	42	2.02	0.75	42
Total		0.39	0.49	399	1.41	1.05	399
Eta			0.45			0.41	
Difference (F – M)	Low	−0.01			0.20		
	Moderate	−0.06			0.53		
	High	−0.12			0.20		
	Very high	0.06			0.15		
	Total	−0.03			0.36		

Table 8.28). The range between the 'Low' and 'Very high' WILLACT categories is 0.70 for males and 0.77 for females with Support Groups and is 1.26 for males and 1.21 for females with Avoid Products (see also Figures 8.8 and 8.9).

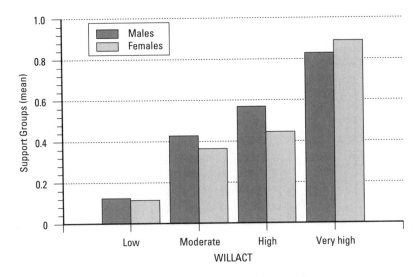

Figure 8.8   *Support Groups by WILLACT controlled for Gender
(Residents)*

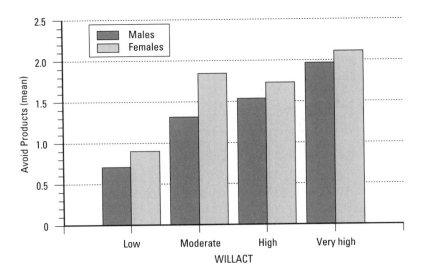

Figure 8.9   *Avoid Products by WILLACT controlled for Gender
(Residents)*

However, in this sample, there are very small differences between males and females across the WILLACT categories for Support Groups (males are actually higher in all except the 'Very high' category). However, females do have higher means than males for Avoid Products across all the WILLACT categories, ranging from 0.20 ('Low' and 'High') to 0.53 ('Moderate').[15] Nevertheless, both males and females are differentiated in their ERB in terms of their Willingness to Act.

Table 8.29   *Means analysis of WILLACT on Support Groups and Avoid Products controlled for Age (Residents)*

Control Age	Predictor WILLACT	Support Groups			Avoid Products		
		$\bar{x}$	s	n	$\bar{x}$	s	n
18–24	Low	0.27	0.47	11	1.00	0.89	11
	Moderate	0.67	0.49	15	1.53	1.13	15
	High	0.50	0.53	10	1.50	1.08	10
	Very high	0.82	0.40	11	2.18	0.60	11
	Total	0.57	0.50	47	1.55	1.02	47
25–34	Low	0.18	0.39	22	0.68	0.95	22
	Moderate	0.32	0.48	25	1.44	1.19	25
	High	0.41	0.50	22	1.77	0.92	22
	Very high	0.83	0.39	12	2.33	0.49	12
	Total	0.38	0.49	81	1.46	1.11	81
35–44	Low	0.25	0.46	8	0.88	0.99	8
	Moderate	0.57	0.50	28	1.96	0.92	28
	High	0.62	0.49	34	1.85	0.96	34
	Very high	0.89	0.33	9	2.00	0.87	9
	Total	0.59	0.49	79	1.81	0.98	79
45–54	Low	0.12	0.33	17	1.06	0.75	17
	Moderate	0.53	0.51	19	2.11	0.81	19
	High	0.59	0.51	17	1.47	0.87	17
	Very high	0.83	0.41	6	1.67	0.82	6
	Total	0.46	0.50	59	1.58	0.89	59
55–64	Low	0.09	0.29	22	1.05	1.09	22
	Moderate	0.25	0.44	20	1.50	1.05	20
	High	0.27	0.47	11	1.91	0.94	11
	Very high	1.00	0.00	3	1.67	0.58	3
	Total	0.23	0.43	56	1.41	1.06	56
65+	Low	0.05	0.22	39	0.49	0.72	39
	Moderate	0.15	0.36	27	1.11	1.01	27
	High	0.50	0.52	12	0.92	0.90	12
	Very high	1.00		1	0.00		1
	Total	0.16	0.37	79	0.76	0.89	79
	Low	0.13	0.33	119	0.78	0.89	119
	Moderate	0.40	0.49	134	1.60	1.06	134
	High	0.51	0.50	106	1.64	0.97	106
	Very high	0.86	0.35	42	2.02	0.75	42
Total		0.39	0.49	401	1.41	1.05	401
Eta			0.45			0.41	

It is also possible to use Age as a control instead of Gender in the Resident sample (see Table 8.29).[16] On the basis of the difference in the mean scores for the two extreme WILLACT categories, for each of the six Age categories, we can conclude that Willingness to Act is less important in determining the level of Support for Environmental Groups among those in the '18–24' Age category than in any other Age category. The difference in means in the youngest age category is 0.55 while the others range between 0.64 and 0.95 (overall the difference is 0.73).[17] The reverse is the case for the Avoid Products; the differences in the means are higher in the three youngest age categories, particularly in the '25–34' category (1.65, compared with 0.61 for the '45–54' category and 1.24 overall). Again, the conclusion is that while WILLACT differentiates all Age categories on both ERB variables, it has more influence in some Age categories than others.

The results from the two samples would suggest that young females are the most likely category to have their ERB influenced by their Willingness to Act. However, to be confident about this conclusion we would need to control for both Age and Gender together, and, to draw any conclusions about influence, we would need to calculate eta coefficients and tests of significance for all the conditional tables in such an analysis. On the latter point, the three-way means analysis just reported, on its own, only produces differences between categories that suggest but do not establish influence. Unfortunately, such a four-way analysis is beyond the scope of the Resident sample.

Metric Variables

Before proceeding to the most important method of multivariate analysis to be discussed here, I want to explore the use of *partial correlation*.

Partial correlation

This method goes beyond three-way cross-tabulations and means analysis in that it produces two coefficients, one for the two-way (zero-order) analysis and another for the three-way analysis. In the latter, the effect of the control variable is partialled out statistically. In multivariate analysis using categorical variables, the effects of introducing a control variable were assessed by comparing the coefficients, say Somer's *d* for each partial table, with each other and with the uncontrolled relationship (see, for example, Tables 8.22 and 8.24). In partial correlation, there is only one coefficient when the control variable is introduced. It represents what is left in an association once the influence of the controlling variable has been removed (see discussion in Chapter 5).

Let us begin with the three-way association between EWVGSC, WILLACT and the ERB variables. We have already examined this with the categorical versions of these variables (see Tables 8.20–8.22). Now we can explore a method of analysis appropriate for the metric versions in order to answer the research question, using both samples (see the first part of Table 8.30). It is clear that when EWVGSC is introduced as a control on the associations between WILLACT and both Support Groups and Avoid Products, the size of all coefficients is reduced. For Support Groups, this is by 0.17 (34 per cent) in the Student sample and by 0.19 (43 per cent) in the Resident sample. For Avoid Products it is reduced by 0.20 in both samples (41 per cent for Students and 45 per cent for Residents). What this means is that while WILLACT accounts for about 25 per cent of the variance in the two ERB variables in the Student sample, when the control for EWVGSC is applied, WILLACT continues to account for only between 8 per cent (Avoid Products) and 11 per cent (Support Groups). In the Resident sample, WILLACT on its own accounts for 19 per cent

Table 8.30 *WILLACT by Support Groups and Avoid Products controlled for EWVGSC (Pearson's r; both samples)*

WILLACT		Students			Residents		
		EWVGSC	Support Groups	Avoid Products	EWVGSC	Support Groups	Avoid Products
Zero order	r	0.73	0.50	0.49	0.62	0.44	0.44
	p	<0.001	<0.001	<0.001	<0.001	<0.001	<0.001
Controlled for EWVGSC	r		0.33	0.29		0.25	0.24
	p		<0.001	<0.001		<0.001	<0.001
EWVGSC							
Zero order	r	0.73	0.40	0.43	0.62	0.41	0.43
	p	<0.001	<0.001	<0.001	<0.001	<0.001	<0.001
Controlled for WILLACT	r		0.06	0.12		0.20	0.22
	p		n.s.	<0.05		<0.001	<0.001

of the variance in both ERB variables, but the control variable reduces this to 6 per cent in both cases.

This result is not surprising as there is a strong association between EWVGSC and WILLACT in both samples ($r = 0.73$ for Students and 0.62 for Residents). What we now know is that EWVGSC is playing some part here. However, we cannot conclude from this analysis what is the percentage of the variance. This requires reversing the role of EWVGSC and WILLACT, that is, using the latter as a control on the relationships of the ERB variables with the former (see the second part of Table 8.30). What this reveals is that while EWVGSC accounts for 16–17 per cent of the variance in Support Groups and 18 per cent of Avoid Products in both samples, the application of WILLACT as a control reduces this to almost nothing in the Student sample, and to 4 per cent for Support Groups and 5 per cent for Avoid Products in Resident sample. What we can conclude from this is that WILLACT appears to play a greater role in predicting the two ERB variables than does EWVGSC, but more particularly for Students where the latter plays no part. This conclusion is consistent but more precise than that arrived at by the other methods of analysis.

Multiple regression

The use of three-way contingency tables, means analysis and partial correlation can provide elementary explanatory analysis. Certainly, the relative influence of two explanatory variables on an outcome variable can be revealed, including identifying intervening or moderating variables. Models C, D and E can be explored, and this can be done with either symmetrical or asymmetrical coefficients. We can now take these methods of analysis another step forward by applying multiple regression to establish the influence of a number of predictor variables on an outcome variable.

Multiple regression allows us to establish the independent influence of a set of predictor variables on an outcome variable. In determining the influence of a particular predictor variable, the influence of all the other predictors is held constant, that is, their influence is controlled. The basic model on which multiple regression is based is as follows:

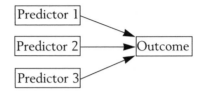

Further predictor variables can be added to the model. However, a major limitation of this type of analysis is that it is not useful for identify intervening and moderating variables. All predictor variables are regarded as having the same role, that is, of possibly contributing to an explanation of the outcome variable.

In order to pursue an answer to research question 6, about variations in ERB, multiple regression is first applied to the variables that have been the core of the explanatory analysis so far: EWVGSC, WILLACT, Age (Resident sample only), Gender and the two ERB variables, Support Groups and Avoid Products. The aim is to sort out the level of influence of the predictor variables on the two outcome variables. To illustrate how the analysis works with these variables, bivariate regression will be used first with each of the outcome variables. Then combinations of the predictors will be dealt with in turn (see Table 8.31 for Students and Table 8.32 for Residents).

When Support Groups is the outcome variable, WILLACT explains 25 per cent of the variance, EWVGSC explains 16 per cent and Gender only 6 per cent (see R^2 values), all of which are significant at the 0.001 level (see Table 8.31). There is clearly a hierarchy in terms of the capacity of these variable to predict the outcome variable.

When WILLACT and EWVGSC are used together as predictors, there is only a marginal improvement in the percentage of the variance explained (26 per cent). Their individual contributions, with the effects of the other predictors controlled, are indicated by the beta coefficients; the former is now 0.45 and the latter is 0.07. In addition, the latter is not significant. This would suggest that EWVGSC adds nothing to our capacity to predict the outcome; WILLACT is fine on its own. However, we need to be cautious. You will recall from Chapter 5 that when predictor variables are themselves highly correlated, the regression procedure is unable to sort out the contributions of each one. This is the problem of *collinearity*, or multiple collinearity. In order to determine whether this is the case, two diagnostics can be used, *tolerance* and the *variance inflation factor* (VIF). A tolerance value of 1 indicates that the variable is not correlated with the other(s) and a value of 0 that it is perfectly correlated. Likewise, a VIF value of more than 2 indicates a close correlation and a value approaching 1 as little or no association. These diagnostics confirm the collinearity between WILLACT and EWVGSC. Of course, examining Pearson's r for the bivariate associations adds further confirmation.

When WILLACT and Gender are used as predictor variables there is a slight improvement in the percentage of the variance explained (now 27 per cent). The

Table 8.31 *Regression of ERB variables on EWVGSC, WILLACT and Gender (Students)*

Outcome	Predictor	R	R²	Intercept	Slope	Std error	Beta	p	Tolerance	VIF
Support	WILLACT	0.50	0.25	−0.63	0.33	0.03	0.50	<0.001		
Groups	EWVGSC	0.40	0.16	−0.91	0.37	0.04	0.40	<0.001		
	Gender	0.24	0.06	0.43	0.24	0.05	0.24	<0.001		
	WILLACT	0.50	0.26	−0.77	0.30	0.04	0.45	<0.001	0.47	2.12
	EWVGSC				0.06	0.05	0.07	n.s.	0.47	2.12
	WILLACT	0.52	0.27	−0.62	0.31	0.03	0.47	<0.001	0.94	1.07
	Gender				0.12	0.04	0.12	<0.01	0.94	1.07
	WILLACT	0.52	0.27	−0.72	0.29	0.04	0.44	<0.001	0.94	1.07
	Gender				0.12	0.04	0.12	<0.01	0.94	1.07
	EWVGSC				0.05	0.05	0.05	n.s.	0.47	2.15
Avoid	WILLACT	0.49	0.24	−1.06	0.68	0.06	0.49	<0.001		
Products	EWVGSC	0.43	0.18	−1.93	0.83	0.08	0.43	<0.001		
	Gender	0.30	0.09	1.03	0.64	0.09	0.30	<0.001		
	WILLACT	0.50	0.25	−1.67	0.53	0.08	0.38	<0.001	0.47	2.14
	EWVGSC				0.29	0.12	0.15	<0.05	0.47	2.14
	WILLACT	0.52	0.27	−1.03	0.61	0.06	0.44	<0.001	0.94	1.07
	Gender				0.38	0.09	0.18	<0.001	0.94	1.07
	WILLACT	0.53	0.28	−1.52	0.50	0.08	0.36	<0.001	0.46	2.15
	Gender				0.38	0.09	0.18	<0.001	0.92	1.09
	EWVGSC				0.23	0.12	0.12	<0.05	0.46	2.17

beta coefficients are 0.47 for the former and 0.12 for the latter (see Table 8.31). In this case, there are absolutely no problems with collinearity, as is indicated by the two diagnostics. When all three predictor variables are used together, there is no further improvement in the percentage of variance explained. Again, there is collinearity between EWVGSC and WILLACT. Hence, only one of these variables should be included, and this should be WILLACT because it makes a higher individual contribution. Including Gender with it is also worthwhile.

Staying with the Student sample, and turning to the other outcome variable, Avoid Products, we find a very similar picture (see Table 8.31). The percentages of variance explained by the various predictor variables, individually and in the various combinations, are almost identical. The only difference worth noting is that EWVGSC plays a marginally more important role, as is evidenced by the various beta values and the fact that it is significant in combinations with the other two variables. However, the collinearity problem is also present here. WILLACT with Gender accounts for 27 per cent of the variance, compared with 24 per cent for WILLACT on its own.

When this same analysis is done with the Resident sample, with Age now included, the results are similar. The R and *beta* coefficients are generally a little lower than in the Student sample, for WILLACT and EWVGSC and their combination, with both of the ERB variables (see Table 8.32). However, both of these predictors make almost equal contributions to the two outcome variables and the collinearity issue is less pronounced. On its own, and in combination with WILLACT, Gender is a weaker predictor of both variables in this sample.

Table 8.32 Regression of ERB variables on EWVGSC, WILLACT and Gender (Residents)

Outcome	Predictor	R	R²	Intercept	Slope	Std error	Beta	p	Tolerance	VIF
Support Groups	WILLACT	0.44	0.19	-0.60	0.29	0.03	0.44	<0.001		
	EWVGSC	0.41	0.17	-1.08	0.39	0.04	0.41	<0.001		
	Age	-0.26	0.07	0.72	-0.01	0.00	-0.26	<0.001		
	Gender	0.03	0.00	0.41	0.00	0.05	-0.03	n.s.		
	WILLACT	0.47	0.22	-1.09	0.20	0.04	0.29	<0.001	0.61	1.64
	EWVGSC				0.21	0.05	0.23	<0.001	0.61	1.64
	WILLACT	0.45	0.21	-0.31	0.26	0.03	0.39	<0.001	0.91	1.10
	Age				0.00	0.00	-0.14	<0.01	0.91	1.10
	WILLACT	0.44	0.19	-0.57	0.29	0.03	0.43	<0.001	1.00	1.00
	Gender				-0.01	0.04	-0.05	n.s.	1.00	1.00
	WILLACT	0.46	0.21	-0.29	0.26	0.03	0.39	<0.001	0.91	1.10
	Age				-0.03	0.00	-0.15	<0.01	0.91	1.10
	Gender				-0.06	0.04	-0.06	n.s.	1.00	1.00
	WILLACT	0.48	0.23	-0.80	0.18	0.04	0.27	<0.001	0.60	1.66
	EWVGSC				0.20	0.06	0.21	<0.001	0.58	1.72
	Age				0.00	0.00	-0.11	<0.05	0.87	1.15
	Gender				0.08	0.04	-0.08	n.s.	0.98	1.02
Avoid Products	WILLACT	0.44	0.19	-0.72	0.63	0.07	0.44	<0.001		
	EWVGSC	0.43	0.19	-1.89	0.87	0.09	0.43	<0.001		
	Age	-0.25	0.07	2.09	-0.01	0.00	-0.25	<0.001		
	Gender	0.17	0.03	1.24	0.36	0.10	0.17	<0.001		
	WILLACT	0.48	0.23	-1.91	0.40	0.08	0.28	<0.001	0.61	1.64
	EWVGSC				0.52	0.11	0.26	<0.001	0.61	1.64
	WILLACT	0.45	0.21	-0.15	0.57	0.07	0.40	<0.001	0.91	1.10
	Age				-0.01	0.00	-0.13	<0.01	0.91	1.10
	WILLACT	0.46	0.21	-0.82	0.61	0.07	0.43	<0.001	1.00	1.00
	Gender				0.32	0.09	0.15	<0.001	1.00	1.00
	WILLACT	0.47	0.22	-0.29	0.56	0.07	0.39	<0.001	0.91	1.10
	Age				-0.07	0.00	-0.13	<0.01	0.91	1.10
	Gender				0.31	0.09	0.15	<0.01	1.00	1.00
	WILLACT	0.50	0.25	-1.41	0.38	0.08	0.26	<0.001	0.60	1.66
	EWVGSC				0.43	0.12	0.22	<0.001	0.58	1.73
	Age				-0.01	0.00	-0.09	<0.05	0.87	1.15
	Gender				0.27	0.09	0.13	<0.01	0.98	1.02

Age makes some contribution and, in the end, about the same as Gender. Hence, while there are some minor differences in the two samples in the way these variables combine, WILLACT remains the best predictor. On its own, WILLACT accounts for 19 per cent of the variance on both ERB variables in combination with Age it accounts for 21 per cent on both ERB variables and; in combination with Gender, 19 per cent on Support Groups and 21 per cent on Avoid Products. Perhaps, the most useful combinations are WILLACT with Age on Support Groups and WILLACT with Age and Gender on Avoid Products.

To complete the examination of research question 6, we can do a more extensive multiple regression in which a wider range of variables is included. In practice, the inclusion of such variables needs to be justified theoretically rather than being a trial and error process. Such justification could be provided for all the variables to be discussed here, but space neither permits it nor is it required by the purpose of illustrating this method of analysis.

Given what we have discovered thus far, research question 6 could have some subsidiary questions added to it. For example:

Why are younger people and women more inclined than older people and men to practice environmentally responsible behaviour?

The analysis already undertaken in this chapter should have provided a clear picture of the Age and Gender patterns, and their combinations, with ERB. We also know that there are Age and Gender differences in EWV; that middle-aged people and women are more inclined than older people and men to hold a favourable EWV. There are other variables, such as Religion, Religiosity, Education, Occupation, Political Party Preference and Number of Children, which have yet to be explored. Each of these variables could be justified theoretically, although this would involve postulating links between some of these variables. This leads us to a further question:

What is the relative contribution of these variables to the prediction of a person's level of environmentally responsible behaviour?

One way of answering this question, as well as research question 6, is to use multiple regression. However, some words of caution are in order before we do this. First, this analysis will be cumbersome because a number of these predictor variables are categorical and will each need to be converted into a set of dummy variables. Second, as some of these variables, such as Education, Occupation, Marital Status and Number of Children, are not useful in the Student sample, this analysis can only be conducted with the Resident sample. Third, there are bound to be associations between some of these variables and this will require us to be alert to problems of collinearity.

One way to be clearer about this third issue is to do a correlation matrix of all the predictor variables. This requires the use of sets of dummy variables for all the strictly categorical variables (Gender, Marital Status, Education, Occupation, Religion, Religiosity and Political Party Preference). To simplify the analysis, three variables have been dichotomized; Marital Status (0 = 'No partner', 1 = 'Has

Table 8.33   Correlation matrix of potential predictor variables (Pearson's r, Residents)

Variables	1	2	3	4	5	6	7	8	9	10	11	12	13	14	15	16	17	18	19
1 Support Gps	1.00																		
2 Avoid Prods	0.35***	1.00																	
3 Age	-0.26***	-0.25***	1.00																
4 Gender	-0.03	0.17***	-0.06	1.00															
5 Partnered	-0.04	0.08	0.19***	0.09	1.00														
6 Children	-0.14**	-0.05	0.55***	0.13*	0.52***	1.00													
7 Univ. Edn.	0.25***	0.20***	-0.13*	-0.01	-0.16**	-0.01	1.00												
8 Manage Prof	-0.20***	-0.14**	-0.05	0.01	-0.15**	-0.09	-0.55***	1.00											
9 White collar	0.07	-0.01	-0.01	-0.04	-0.03	-0.02	0.15**	-0.48***	1.00										
10 Manual	0.06	0.11*	-0.03	0.26***	0.10*	0.08	0.30***	-0.35***	-0.32***	1.00									
11 Unemployed	0.12*	0.09	0.11*	-0.23***	0.12*	0.06	0.21***	-0.32***	-0.30***	-0.21***	1.00								
12 Protestant	-0.13**	-0.03	0.27***	0.04	0.12*	0.24***	-0.04	-0.08	-0.06	0.09	0.07	1.00							
13 Catholic	-0.03	-0.09	0.05	0.11*	0.01	0.02	-0.07	0.09	0.03	-0.02	-0.13*	-0.40***	1.00						
14 Other	-0.04	0.00	-0.06	0.06	-0.01	-0.04	-0.02	0.05	-0.02	-0.04	0.00	-0.34***	-0.23***	1.00					
15 No Religion	0.21***	0.11*	-0.30***	-0.20***	-0.13**	-0.25***	0.12*	-0.04	0.06	-0.05	0.04	-0.45***	-0.30***	-0.26***	1.00				
16 Religiosity	0.02	0.09	0.15**	0.10*	0.01	0.08	0.00	-0.09	0.02	0.11*	-0.03	0.05	0.12*	0.14**	-0.29***	1.00			
17 Liberal	0.25***	0.18***	-0.12*	-0.07	-0.04	-0.07	0.07	-0.03	-0.05	0.00	0.09	-0.24***	0.01	0.06	0.21***	0.02	1.00		
18 Conservative	-0.28***	-0.18***	0.26***	0.05	0.11*	0.20***	-0.06	-0.01	0.01	0.01	-0.01	0.21***	-0.02	0.01	-0.23***	0.12*	-0.52***	1.00	
19 Undecided	0.02	-0.01	-0.13**	0.02	-0.07	-0.12*	-0.01	0.04	0.05	-0.01	-0.09	0.04	0.01	-0.07	0.01	-0.14**	-0.52***	-0.46***	1.00

*$p < 0.05$. **$p < 0.01$. ***$p < 0.001$. All other coefficients are not significant.

partner'); Number of Children (0 = 'No children', 1 = 'Some children'); and Education (0 = 'Not university educated', 1 = 'University educated').

Table 8.33 presents a matrix of correlation coefficients for the two ERB variables and possible predictors of these. The first thing to note is the threshold at which the coefficients reach the three levels of significance. A coefficient is significant at the 0.05 level as long as it is at least 0.10, at the 0.01 level if it is at least 0.13,[18] and at the 0.001 level if it is at least 0.17. These values are all very low and are very much related to the size of the sample; they would be even lower with a larger sample. Hence, level of significance is not a useful criterion on which to decide whether a variable should be included in the multiple regression. The absolute value of the coefficient must be used. However, there are no rules of thumb for deciding this; it must be a matter of judgement.

At first glance, it is clear that the variables that have at least a reasonable association with Support Groups and Avoid Products are Age (negative for both), Gender (positive for Avoiding Products), Have Children (negative for Support Groups), University Education (positive for both), being in a Managerial/ Professional occupation (negative for both), being Protestant (negative for Support Groups), having No Religion (positive for Support Groups) and Political Party Preference (positive for Liberal and negative for Conservative). They are all worth considering. In fact, the only variable in the correlation matrix that is left out of this list is Marital Status, shown as the Partnered dummy variable.

We also need to note whether there are associations between these variables that could create collinearity problems. Age is associated with Have Children, with being Protestant, with having No Religion, and with supporting a Conservative political party. Have children is also related to being Protestant, professing No Religion and supporting a Conservative political party. Education is associated with all the occupational categories in the expected directions. Being Protestant is associated with not supporting a Liberal political party and with supporting a Conservative one. Having No Religion is also associated with support of these two types of political parties, but in the opposite direction. Hence, there are a number of interrelationships of which we need to be aware.

We can now proceed with the multiple regression with some expectations about what is likely to happen. However, what we want to find out is what the contributions of these variables are to predicting ERB when, for each one, the influence of all other predictors is controlled. You will recall that in the case of the sets of dummy variables, one category needs to be left out. All the variables listed above, plus EWVGSC and WILLACT, were entered into the regression analysis. In the case of Occupation, 'White collar' was left out; for Religion, 'Other'; and for PPP, 'Undecided'.

Table 8.34 presents four different combinations of predictor variables with Support Groups. Before your eyes glaze over at the sight of all these figures, let me explain the steps that were taken in the analysis. In the first section of the table, all predictor variables are included. While together they account for 29 per cent of the outcome variance (R^2), it is clear that many of them make very little contribution (see the *beta* values). I then decided to limit the analysis to those that did seem to be making a contribution, persisting with both Age and Gender because of the earlier analysis. The second section of the table reports

Table 8.34 Regression of Support Groups on selected predictor variables (Residents)

Outcome	Predictors	R	R^2	Intercept	Slope	Std error	Beta	p	Tolerance	VIF
Support Groups	WILLACT	0.54	0.29	−0.54	0.14	0.04	0.21	<0.01	0.54	1.87
	EWVGSC				0.17	0.06	0.18	<0.01	0.53	1.90
	Age				−0.002	0.002	−0.09	n.s.	0.57	1.74
	Gender				−0.05	0.05	−0.05	n.s.	0.83	1.21
	Children				−0.01	0.06	−0.01	n.s.	0.67	1.50
	Univ. Edn				0.08	0.06	0.08	n.s.	0.63	1.59
	Man/Prof				−0.15	0.06	−0.14	<0.05	0.57	1.76
	Manual				−0.02	0.07	−0.01	n.s.	0.70	1.43
	Unemployed				0.04	0.07	0.03	n.s.	0.71	1.40
	Protestant				−0.01	0.07	−0.01	n.s.	0.44	2.26
	Catholic				0.06	0.07	0.05	n.s.	0.54	1.85
	No Religion				0.05	0.07	0.05	n.s.	0.49	2.06
	Liberal				0.04	0.06	0.04	n.s.	0.65	1.54
	Conservative				−0.11	0.06	−0.10	n.s.	0.66	1.52
	WILLACT	0.53	0.28	−0.46	0.51	0.04	0.22	<0.001	0.56	1.78
	EWVGSC				0.16	0.05	0.17	<0.01	0.57	1.77
	Age				−0.003	0.001	−0.10	<0.05	0.83	1.20
	Gender				−0.06	0.04	−0.07	n.s.	0.98	1.03
	Education				0.08	0.05	0.08	n.s.	0.65	1.53
	Man/Prof				−0.15	0.06	−0.14	<0.01	0.67	1.50
	Conservative				−0.13	0.05	−0.13	0.01	0.83	1.21
	WILLACT	0.52	0.27	−0.02	0.21	0.03	0.32	<0.001	0.80	1.26
	Age				−0.004	0.001	−0.13	<0.01	0.87	1.16
	Gender				−0.05	0.04	−0.05	n.s.	0.99	1.01
	Education				0.08	0.05	0.08	n.s.	0.65	1.53
	Man/Prof				−0.16	0.06	−0.16	<0.01	0.67	1.49
	Conservative				−0.15	0.05	−0.14	<0.01	0.83	1.20
	WILLACT	0.51	0.26	0.02	0.22	0.03	0.32	<0.001	0.81	1.24
	Man/Prof				−0.21	0.05	−0.20	<0.001	0.99	1.01
	Age				−0.004	0.001	−0.14	<0.01	0.88	1.14
	Conservative				−0.15	0.05	−0.14	<0.01	0.84	1.19

this analysis. There is only a 1 per cent reduction in the percentage of the variance accounted for. At the same time, we have eliminated some of the collinearity problems.

The next step was to remove EWVGSC because of its close association with WILLACT. The latter was preferred in this choice, as we have already demonstrated that it has a more direct influence on the ERB variables (see the third section of the table). Again the reduction in the explanatory power is only a further 1 per cent. Finally, the regression analysis was run with these remaining variables being entered in the *forward* mode (see the discussion of this procedure in Chapter 5). The last section of the table reports the variables that this procedure included, and the order in which they were entered. While there has been a further reduction of 1 per cent in the variance accounted for, we now have sets of relatively powerful predictors, all of which are significant, and without any collinearity problems. Only four variables were included: in addition to WILLACT and Age, Managerial/Professional occupations and Conservative PPP (both negative). In other words, there is a decided lack of Support for Environmental Groups in the highest-status Occupational category, compared to all other occupations, as well as among the elderly and those who prefer Conservative political parties.

Table 8.35 presents the same analysis with Avoid Products as the outcome variable. The full set of predictor variables accounts for 28 per cent of the variance, although this declines to 24 per cent in the third section of the table and to 23 per cent in the fourth section. The same variables (as in Table 8.34) were retained in the second and third sections. However, when a forward analysis was undertaken, in addition to WILLACT and Age, Gender and Education were included, both with positive contributions. Hence, we can conclude that Avoiding of Environmentally Damaging Products is more common among women, the better-educated and younger people.

Even though we have ended up with only four variables to explain these two forms of ERB, the explanations are parsimonious. This means that we can achieve almost as powerful an explanation, and a more satisfactory one, with four variables as was achieved with many more. It is important to note, however, that different decisions about which variables to include in the analysis may produce different conclusions. What is important in this process is to be able to justify the decisions and, preferably, have theoretical as well as statistical reasons for making them.

Finally, let us summarize the results of the use of multiple regression to answer the research question. Focusing on the Resident sample, we have found that Willingness to Act is the best predictor of a person's ERB, although EWV comes a close second. Age makes some contribution to predicting both of the ERB variables. Occupation and Political Party Preferences also contribute to predicting the support offered to environmental groups, and Gender and Education to avoiding environmentally damaging products. As the student sample is homogeneous with respect to Age and Education, and the majority do not have an occupation[19] or children, we are left with Gender as the major additional predictor. Religion, which was not included in the analysis, may also play some role. While these conclusions are consistent with the limited analysis that

Table 8.35 Regression of Avoid Products on selected predictor variables (Residents)

Outcome	Predictors	R	R^2	Intercept	Slope	Std error	Beta	p	Tolerance	VIF
Avoid Products	WILLACT	0.53	0.28	−1.26	0.35	0.09	0.24	<0.001	0.54	1.87
	EWVGSC				0.40	0.12	0.20	<0.01	0.53	1.90
	Age				−0.007	0.003	−0.13	<0.05	0.57	1.74
	Gender				0.28	0.10	0.13	<0.01	0.83	1.21
	Children				0.12	0.12	0.05	n.s.	0.67	1.50
	Univ. Edn				0.15	0.12	0.07	n.s.	0.63	1.59
	Man/Prof				−0.13	0.13	−0.06	n.s.	0.57	1.76
	Manual				−0.001	0.15	0.00	n.s.	0.70	1.43
	Unemployed				0.16	0.15	0.06	n.s.	0.71	1.40
	Portestant				0.02	0.14	0.01	n.s.	0.44	2.26
	Catholic				−0.09	0.15	−0.03	n.s.	0.54	1.85
	No Religion				−0.09	0.15	−0.04	n.s.	0.49	2.06
	Liberal				0.03	0.12	0.02	n.s.	0.65	1.54
	Conservative				−0.05	0.12	−0.02	n.s.	0.66	1.52
	WILLACT	0.51	0.26	−1.30	0.37	0.09	0.26	<0.001	0.56	1.78
	EWVGSC				0.42	0.12	0.21	<0.001	0.57	1.77
	Age				−0.004	0.003	−0.07	n.s.	0.83	1.20
	Gender				0.26	0.09	0.13	<0.01	0.98	1.03
	Education				0.15	0.12	0.07	n.s.	0.65	1.53
	Man/Prof				−0.17	0.12	−0.08	n.s.	0.67	1.50
	Conservative				−0.03	0.11	−0.01	n.s.	0.83	1.21
	WILLACT	0.49	0.24	−0.16	0.53	0.07	0.37	<0.001	0.80	1.26
	Age				−0.006	0.003	−0.10	<0.05	0.87	1.16
	Gender				0.31	0.09	0.15	<0.01	0.99	1.01
	Education				0.15	0.12	0.07	n.s.	0.65	1.53
	Man/Prof				−0.21	0.12	−0.10	n.s.	0.67	1.49
	Conservative				−0.05	0.11	−0.02	n.s.	<0.83	1.20
	WILLACT	0.48	0.23	−0.42	0.54	0.07	0.38	<0.001	0.89	1.23
	Gender				0.31	0.09	0.15	<0.01	1.00	1.00
	Education				0.27	0.10	0.13	<0.01	0.97	1.03
	Age				−0.006	0.003	−0.10	<0.05	0.90	1.11

was done using the other methods, the major advantages of multiple regression over them are that it can handle a large number of predictor variables at once, and that it can provide a measure of the relative contributions of all of these variables.

Conclusion

Two important conclusions need to be drawn from the analysis conducted in this chapter. The first is that while metric data are generally preferred to categorical data, because the procedures appropriate for the former are regarded as being more powerful and usually less cumbersome than those appropriate for latter, there are many situations in which using categorical data, or categorical versions of metric data, will tell you more about what is going on than will the statistically more sophisticated procedures. Patterns in data can invariably be understood better using cross-tabulations and comparison of means across categories. Hence, the pressure to use the most advanced level of analysis needs to be at least complemented by lower-level analysis. While some analysis must remain at a lower level because of the restrictions that result from the level of measurement used, for example, nominal-level data, recoding metric data into categories and using lower-level analysis can help a researcher get a better feel for what is happening.

There are, of course, many limitations associated with the use of categorical data. One that is obvious from this analysis is the limited scope these data have for undertaking multivariate analysis. It is clear that multiple regression, and other more advanced methods that have not been discussed here, are more adept at this kind of analysis. Given the use of dummy variables, it is possible to include variables covering the full range of measurement. However, there is a price to be paid for this. Dichotomizing categorical variables inevitably means the loss of information. For example, converting an extensive range of religions into a simple dichotomy must mask important variations across such categories. While doing trials using various possible dichotomies can help to highlight the more important differences, there is a bluntness about such procedures. This is an interesting paradox because the advantage of metric variables over categorical ones is that the former can handle greater detail, for example, Age in years compared with categories.

This brings me to the second main conclusion. I hope that this excursion through the various types of analysis applied in these two samples to the set of research questions has produced a reasonably detailed picture of environmental attitudes and behaviour, and their interconnection. There are many more research questions that could have been explored and other types of analysis that could have been undertaken. Nevertheless, when it comes to the most challenging aspect of any research, providing satisfactory answers to 'why' questions, quantitative analysis can leave us rather dissatisfied.

Quantitative data analysis is absolutely essential for answering many types of research questions. Sometimes, there are no alternatives. It is useful for describing characteristics of and patterns between relatively 'simple' variables. However, the problem is that variables used in quantitative analysis inevitably entail assumptions about the nature of social life and, in particular, about how it is understood by the social actors. At the same time, the process of converting the characteristics of people and social processes into variables keeps the researcher at arm's length (or further) from social reality, that is, reality as it is constructed and maintained by social actors.

There is a temptation to push quantitative data analysis beyond its practical and theoretical limits, just because it is easy to do this. In the end, the social world can end up being represented by a network of variables that may have little relationship to the social process experienced by the participants. Of course, if you work with ontological assumptions that social reality exists independently of people, then this may not seem to be a problem. On the other hand, if you work with the ontological assumptions of interpretivism or similar philosophical or theoretical positions, in which social reality is seen to be socially constructed and maintained by social actors, then the capacity of quantitative analysis to misrepresent or distort social reality is a serious problem.

The solution is to turn to other methods of analysis and different kinds of data that are compatible with these latter ontological assumptions, namely, qualitative methods. While these methods may lack the statistical rigour that is desired by many social researchers, in the right hands they have the advantage of getting much closer to people and their social situations and, in the end, can provide more satisfying answers to research questions.[20]

Notes

[1] I have reiterated this procedure here in order to suggest that you might like to calculate some of these tests by hand, as I have had to do! Note that with the high value for degrees of freedom (865), we can also use the values in the z distribution.

[2] The latter could also be dichotomized, but would produce essentially the same result as for Support Groups dichotomized.

[3] Note that the percentages for the categories 'Never' and 'No support' are the same for the Residents (60.7) but differ slightly for the Students (43.9 and 42.5). It is possible that the first question, 'Do you support any environmental groups?' was interpreted narrowly as active support, while the second question ('In what ways do you support these groups?') allowed for something as weak as moral support.

[4] The ns for the correlation coefficients in the Student sample range from 458 to 465, indicating that for some of the variables (mostly Avoid Products) data are missing for some respondents. However, in the Resident sample, the ns are either 401 or 402.

[5] An alternative to this dichotomized version of Support Groups would be to treat the three response categories, 'Regularly', 'Sometimes' and 'Never' as interval-level measurement. This would be another example of adopting the controversial assumption that ordinal-level measurement can, for all practical purposes, be treated as interval. When this is done, these two coefficients become 0.55 and 0.48, respectively. Generally, they would be between 0.02 and 0.05 higher than the other variables in the matrix. The reason for this is that more information is being used with three rather than two categories.

[6] Depending on the level of measurement being used, other coefficients, such as Cramér's V for nominal-level data, could be used in such a matrix. However, it would be inadvisable to

include a mixture of coefficients as each one has it own particular characteristics, and they are not really comparable.

[7]It would be possible to do a multiple analysis of variance (MANOVA) to test the significance of the differences between the means across the Age categories.

[8]As indicated earlier, the items in the SCITEK scale were weighted such that a high score represented less faith in science and technology.

[9]In models of this kind, a double-headed arrow indicates an association while a single-headed arrow indicates an influence in the direction of the arrow.

[10]While they are not strictly appropriate for the purpose at hand, the values for Cramér's V, the standardized contingency coefficient (C_s) and gamma are also reported just to show how these values for symmetric measures differ from asymmetric values. Gamma, of course, would be the most appropriate measure of association for linear relationships, but the other two are useful for other types of relationship.

[11]$V = 0.32$, $C_s = 0.49$ and $G = 0.52$ for Students; $V = 0.33$, $C_s = 0.50$ and $G = 0.57$ for Residents.

[12]$V = 0.24$, $C_s = 0.44$ and $G = 0.42$ for Students; $V = 0.26$, $C_s = 0.48$ and $G = 0.47$ for Residents.

[13]$V = 0.45$, $C_s = 0.64$ and $G = 0.71$ for Students; $V = 0.38$, $C_s = 0.56$ and $G = 0.63$ for Residents.

[14]$V = 0.30$, $C_s = 0.54$ and $G = 0.53$ for Students; $V = 0.26$, $C_s = 0.47$ and $G = 0.42$ for Residents.

[15]It would be possible to do a MANOVA on the comparison of the means on each variable to establish whether the differences are significant.

[16]There are rather too many distributions here to be represented pictorially.

[17]However, note that in the two oldest Age categories the numbers are too small to draw any definite conclusions.

[18]One coefficient of 0.13, Education with Partnered, is only significant at the 0.05 level. In fact, this coefficient is only 0.126 but rounding up shows it as 0.13.

[19]It is not possible to be precise about how many students were currently employed at the time of the study, or who might have had previous occupational experiences, as this was not addressed. However, we can assume that their future employment is most likely to be in higher-status occupations.

[20]For a discussion of the range of ontological positions in the social sciences, see Blaikie (1993a), and for some suggestions on alternative ways to answer research question 6, see the fourth sample research design in Chapter 8 of Blaikie (2000).

Glossary

The number in parentheses at the end of each entry is the page number on which the term first appears and/or receives considerable attention.

abductive logic A strategy for advancing social science knowledge, derived from social actors' meanings and interpretations. (34)

alternative hypothesis (H_1) A statement specifying that a relationship exists between two variables in a population, different from that specified in the null hypothesis. (179)

analysis of variance (ANOVA) Tests the significance of the differences between more than two means, either within a sample (between categories of one predictor variable) or between samples (the same predictor variable in different samples). (154, 201)

applied research Deals with social or practical problems and is concerned with practical outcomes, with trying to solve some practical problem, with helping practitioners accomplish tasks, and with the development and implementation of policy. (12)

arithematic mean See **mean**. (71)

association Two variables are said to be associated if the values of one variable vary or change together with the values of the other variable; the variables are said to be co-related. (89)

asymmetrical measure of association A measure of the directional influence of one variable on another. (96, 120)

bar chart A graphical representation of a frequency distribution across the categories of a categorical variable, represented by a set of vertical or horizontal bars. (63, 101)

basic research Deals with theoretical problems and is concerned with advancing fundamental knowledge about the social world, in particular with the development and testing of theories. (12)

bell curve See **normal distribution**. (67)

beta (β) Standardized regression coefficient. (130, 149)

between-sample comparisons   A procedure for establishing whether differences between the means of two or more samples also exist between the populations from which the samples were drawn. (184)

between-sample variance   The extent of the differences between means, of either categories of a variable or different samples. (202)

biased sample   See **sampling bias**. (162)

bivariate descriptive analysis   Analysis concerned with establishing either associations between two variables. (29, 47, 89)

bivariate explanatory analysis   Analysis concerned with establishing influence between two variables. (120)

bivariate regression   A procedure for predicting the values of one variable from those of another variable by establishing a straight line that best represents the relationship between the two variables. (125)

categorical measurement   The classification of objects, events or people into a set of nominal-level or ordinal-level categories. Any numbering of such categories is only for identification, and cannot be used for mathematical manipulation. However, it is possible to analyze the frequencies within categories and compare these across the categories. (23)

causality   The distribution on one variable is said to produce the distribution on another variable if it can be established that the two variables are associated, that the second variable follows the first in a time sequence, and that other possible causes can be eliminated. (117)

census   A count of all elements in a population. (160)

central limit theorem   The theorem states that when many probability samples are drawn from a population, increasing the sample size will increase the possibility of the distribution of sample means approaching the normal distribution and the overall mean of the sample means approaching the population mean. This is true regardless of the shape of the distribution of the population values. (165)

chi-square   A test of significance for association between nominal-level variables. (97)

cluster sampling   A method of sampling that involves combining population elements into groups or clusters and then selecting a number of the groups rather than individual population elements. (169)

coefficient of multiple determination (R^2)   A measure of the total amount of variance explained by all the predictor variables in regression analysis. (130)

collinearity (multiple collinearity)   A problem encountered in multiple regression when two or more predictor variables are closely associated. (150, 294)

commonality   The proportion of the total variance an item contributes to all the factors produced by factor analysis. (221)

conditional associations   See **interacting variables** and **moderating variables.** (139)

concordant pairs   Two objects, events or individuals that are ranked similarly on two variables. (102, 124)

conditional tables   Three-way contingency tables used to establish the form of the relationships between three categorical variables. (138, 141)

confidence interval   The range of values around the sample value within which the population value is expected to lie. (172)

confidence level   In inferential analysis, it is the degree to which we are confident that the null hypothesis can be rejected in favour of the alternative hypothesis, that values or differences found in a sample can be expected to be present in the population from which the sample was drawn. Confidence levels are commonly set at 95 per cent, 99 per cent and 99.9 per cent. See also **significance level.** (172)

confidence limits   The two extreme values of a confidence interval. (172)

contingency coefficient   A measure of association, appropriate for relationships between nominal-level variables, based on the sum of the chi-square values for all cells in a contingency table. (97)

contingency table   A table of two or more variables cross-tabulated into cells that show the frequencies in the combination of categories of the variables. (91)

continuous scale   Measurement that can have an unlimited number of intermediate values (e.g. fractions or decimal points) between the whole numbers. (26, 53)

correlation   See **association.** (89)

correlation coefficient   A measure of the extent to which two continuous (interval-level or ratio-level) variables are related. (108)

covariance   The extent to which two continuous variables vary together, that is, the variance on one variable coincides with the variance on another variable. (107, 159)

Cramér's V A measure of association, based on chi-square, that is appropriate for two categorical variables, particularly at the nominal level, both of which have more than two categories. (101)

critical rationalism The philosophy of science, based on the work of Karl Popper, which rejects the inductive logic of positivism in favour of deductive logic for theory testing. (17)

Cronbach's alpha A measure of the reliability of a scale produced by factor analysis. (219)

cross-sectional design Research in which all variables are measured at the same time. (118)

cross-tabulation See **contingency table**. (91)

curvilinear relationship An association between two variables that can be represented by a curved line. (96)

data In quantitative research, data are regarded as being the products of the measurement of concepts according to agreed and replicable procedures. (15)

data analysis An essential step in the process of answering research questions about characteristics, relationships, patterns or influences in social phenomena. (28)

data reduction Procedures for reorganizing or combining response categories, or combining a number of items of data into a single variable. (45, 214)

deductive logic A set of steps for advancing knowledge that starts with a theory or possible explanation and then proceeds to test the theory by deducing from it one or more hypotheses that are then matched against appropriate data. (34)

degrees of freedom The number of values that are free to vary when certain restrictions are placed on the data. (190)

dependent samples A traditional method for classifying samples used in experimental research where they are drawn from the same population. They can be separate samples in which the members of one are matched against the members of the other, perhaps to form an experimental and a control group, or they can be produced by collecting data from one sample at two points in time, usually before and after some treatment or intervention. They are also known as related samples. (183)

dependence techniques Methods of explanatory analysis that examine the influence of predictor variables on outcome variables. (153)

dependent variable   See **outcome variable**. (31, 119)

descriptive analysis   Procedures used to summarize the characteristics of some phenomenon in terms of distributions on variables (univariate), or patterns of association between two variables (bivariate). (48)

discrete scale   Measurement that involves units in whole numbers and, usually, equal intervals between the numbers. (26, 53)

discordant pairs   Two objects, events or individuals that are ranked differently on two variables. (102, 124)

distribution-free tests   See **non-parametric tests**. (171)

dummy variable   A dichotomous variable of two categories created from a categorical (nominal-level or ordinal-level) variable with three or more categories. When converted into a set of dummy variables, such categorical variables can be used in regression analysis. (135)

eigenvalue   A measure of the amount of the variance accounted for by each factor. (223)

empirical evidence   Data collected on the assumption that unprejudiced 'observation', through the use of the human senses, produces reliable 'evidence' about the 'empirical' world. (15)

epistemological assumptions   Assumptions about how social reality can be known. (16)

error of estimation   See **sampling error**. (162)

eta (η)   A measure of influence in means analysis. (134)

experiment   Procedure used to control the influence between variables and to eliminate the influence of other variables in order to satisfy the criteria for inferring causation. (117)

explanatory analysis   Procedures for establishing the direction and strength of influence between variables. (30, 47, 116)

explanatory variable   See **predictor variable**. (119)

F statistic   A procedure used in analysis of variance to establish whether or not differences between means are significant. (201)

factor analysis   A procedure for identifying underlying factors or latent variables present in the patterns of correlations among a set of measures. (220)

factor loading A measure of the contribution an item makes to a particular factor. (221)

first-order relationships Relationships between three variables with one as a control. (141)

frequency counts The numbers in the categories of categorical data and discrete and grouped metric data. (53)

frequency distribution A table or graphical representation of frequencies in the categories of categorical data and discrete and grouped metric data. (53, 59)

gamma (γ or G) An appropriate measure of association for use with contingency tables that have two ordinal-level variables. (102)

generative view of causation The view of causality based on the idea that events must be regarded as networks or systems and cannot be seen as discrete and isolatable. (31)

group _t_ test A procedure for establishing whether a sample characteristic or pattern lies in the extreme tails of the normal curve of all possible samples, that is, that the sample characteristic or pattern is not significant. The distribution of values of _t_ represents a theoretical symmetrical distribution with a mean of zero but with a standard deviation that becomes smaller as the degrees of freedom increase. When the degrees of freedom exceed 100, the _t_ distribution approximates the normal distribution. (193)

heteroscedasticity The clustering of points towards one end of the length of the line of best fit in the scatter plot of two associated variables. (134)

histogram A form of bar chart used mainly with interval-level or ratio-level distributions that are based on whole numbers or grouped data. (64)

homoscedasticity A uniform spread of points on both sides of the length of the line of best fit in the scatter plot of two associated variables. (134)

hypotheses Possible answers to 'why' questions. (13)

independent samples A traditional method for classifying samples used in experimental research where they are drawn from different populations, or from different groups or categories in the same population. They are also known as unrelated samples. (183)

independent variable See **predictor variable**. (31, 119)

index A combination of measures that is not tested for unidimensionality. (239)

inductive logic A set of steps used to advance knowledge by generalizing from accumulated data to produce patterns or connections between events or variables. (33)

inferential analysis Procedures used to generalize sample statistics to population parameters. Such procedures involve estimating whether the characteristics or relationships found in a sample, or differences between samples, could be expected to exist in the population or populations from which the sample or samples were randomly drawn. (32, 47, 159)

inferential statistics Measures for estimating population parameters from sample statistics. (161)

interacting variables Interaction occurs when the influence of one variable on another is contingent on the presence of a third variable. (137)

interdependence techniques Methods that do a simultaneous analysis of all the variables in the set with no assumptions about direction of influence. (153)

interquartile range A measure of the dispersion of distributions of ordinal-level data, and discrete and grouped interval-level and ratio-level data, by subtracting the value for the first quartile from that of third quartile. It is used in association with the median. (78)

interpretivism The philosophy of social science based on the ontological assumption that social reality consists of intersubjectively shared, socially constructed meaning and knowledge that is produced and reproduced by social actors in the course of their everyday lives. It is assumed that knowledge of social reality can only be achieved by collecting social actors' accounts of *their* reality and then redescribing these accounts in social scientific language, using abductive logic. Also known as social constructionism. (17)

interval-level measurement Metric-level measurement that uses a scale with known and usually equal intervals between the categories or scores. The zero point is arbitrary. (25)

intervening variable A variable that links two other in a causal chain: a predictor variable influences an intervening variable which, in turn, influences an outcome variable. (137)

Kendall's rank correlation coefficient (τ) A symmetric measure of association used with a small number of objects, events or individuals that are given unique rankings on two variables. (105)

Kendall's tau-*b* A symmetric measure of association for ordinal-level variables, particularly in tables with the same number of rows and columns. It allows for ties on both variables and is an alternative to gamma. (104)

lambda (λ)   A symmetric measure of association and an asymmetric measure of the influence between two nominal-level variables in any size of contingency table. (120)

latent variable   An unmeasured variable that lies behind a set of measurements. (220)

levels of measurement   Different ways of assigning numbers to objects, events or people, or of assigning objects, events or people to a numerical scale, according to sets of predetermined but arbitrary rules. The former is referred to as categorical measurement and the latter as metric measurement. Within each of these two types of measurement are two further levels: categorical measurements may be at the nominal or ordinal level, and metric measurements interval or ratio. (22)

line graph   An area graph or a frequency polygon produced by joining with straight lines the midpoints of equal-width bars in a histogram. (66)

linear relationship   An association between two variables that can be represented by a straight line. (96)

Mann–Whitney U test   A distribution-free test that is appropriate either when the parametric requirements of the t test cannot be met, or with ordinal-level variables. (197)

marginal   The total of cell values of rows and columns in a contingency table. (91)

mathematical adjective   The modification of a mathematical noun by attaching a subscript to it to identify the values of a variable to which it refers. (48)

mathematical adverb   The modification of a mathematical verb by specifying very precisely the values on which the operations are to be applied. (49)

mathematical noun   Letter used as shorthand to refer to values on a variable or the total of such values. (48)

mathematical verb   Operator used to indicate actions to be taken on the values of variables, such as summing, taking the root of or raising to a power. (49)

mean   A measure of central tendency in which the sum of a set of values is divided by the number of the values in the set. It is the point in a distribution of values about which the sum of the deviations is equal to zero. (71)

mean absolute deviation   The mean of the deviations of all values from the mean. (80)

mean deviation method   A method for calculating Pearson's r (110) and the slope of a regression line (128).

mean weighted percentage   The overall mean of sample means when the samples are of different sizes. (75)

measurement   The assignment of numbers to objects, events or people, or the assignment of objects, events or people to a numerical scale, according to sets of predetermined but arbitrary rules. (22)

measures of association   Measures designed to indicate the strength of the relationship between two variables. (89, 96)

measures of central tendency   Measures designed to indicate the 'middle' or 'most typical' point (e.g. category or score) in a distribution. (68)

measures of dispersion   Measures of the characteristics of a distribution in terms of how widely it is spread. (78)

median   A measure of central tendency that is the position in a distribution above and below which one half of the frequencies fall. (69)

metric measurement   The assignment to objects, events or people of a number from a scale of numbers with equal intervals between the positions on the scale. Adding equal or measurable intervals between positions on a continuum transforms categorical measurement into metric measurement. (24)

mode   A measure of central tendency that is the value for the category in a distribution with the highest frequency. The most basic of the three measures of central tendency. (68)

moderating variable   A third variable that affects the relationship between two other variables, depending on its value. (137)

multiple correlation coefficient (R)   A measure of association between predictor variables and an outcome variable. (130)

multiple regression   A procedure for analyzing the relationship between a single metric outcome variable and two or more predictor variables with, for each predictor variable, the effects of all the other predictor variables held constant. (146)

multi-stage sampling   The selection of a sample in stages, using different methods at each stage. (169)

multivariate analysis   Procedures for examining the associations or influences between three or more variables. (48)

multivariate analysis of variance (MANOVA) A test of the significance of the differences between the means of one or more predictor variables with several dependent variables. (154, 202)

necessary condition A condition that needs to be present in order for an event or relationship to occur. (30)

negative relationship An association between two variables in which an increase in the values for one variable is accompanied by a decrease in the values for the other variable. (90, 95)

negatively skewed distribution A distribution that tends to 'lean' towards the end with the higher values and tail off at the end with the lower values. (67)

no relationship An association in which a position or score on one variable is not associated with a position or score on the other variable. (90, 95)

non-parametric tests Tests of significance that are appropriate for categorical variables (nominal-level and ordinal-level) and metric variables with non-normal distributions. Also known as distribution-free tests. (171)

non-probability sample A sample that is drawn in such a way as not to give every population element a chance of selection. (161)

nominal-level measurement Categorical-level measurement in which categories identify different types of objects, events or people that share the same characteristics. Assignment to a category is in terms of some criterion and the categories have no intrinsic order to them. Analysis is limited to frequency counts in each category and a comparison of these. (23, 53)

normal distribution A frequency distribution in a symmetrical bell-shaped form. (67)

null hypothesis (H_0) A statement specifying that no relationship exists between two variables in a population. Occasionally, a null hypothesis may specify a specific value for a population parameter. (179)

observation The use of the human senses to produce 'evidence' about the 'empirical' world. (15)

one-sample tests Tests used to establish whether the value for a particular variable in a sample is different from some known or assumed population value, that is, whether or not the sample comes from a population with a particular mean. (184)

one-tailed test A test of the significance of a directional alternative hypothesis. (182)

one-way analysis of variance A test of the significance of the difference between the means of several categories of one predictor variable or the means for the same variable in two different samples. (201)

ontological assumptions Assumptions about the nature of social reality. (16)

operationalize To specify the procedures used to classify or measure the phenomenon being investigated. (22)

ordinal-level measurement Categorical-level measurement in which categories identify different types of objects, events or people that share the same characteristics. Assignment to a category is in terms of some criterion and, unlike nominal-level measurement, the categories are ordered along some continuum. (23, 53)

outcome variable A variable whose values are influenced or predicted by one or more predictor variables. (31, 119)

outliers The points that are very deviant from the dominant pattern in two variables that are associated. (133)

parametric tests Test of significance appropriate for metric variables with normal distributions. (171)

partial correlation A procedure for examining the effect of one variable, the control, on the relationship between two other variables. It is possible to discover whether the relationship is spurious, and whether the control variable is intervening in or moderating the relationship. (146)

Pearson's product moment correlation coefficient (r) The measure of association appropriate for two metric variables. It indicates the extent to which objects, events or individuals occupy the same relative position on two variables. (108)

percentage A proportion expressed to the base of 100. It is arrived at by dividing a frequency by the total of all frequencies and multiplying the product by 100. (59)

percentiles The set of divisions of a distribution into 100 equal parts. (79)

phi (ϕ) The measure of association appropriate for two dichotomous, nominal-level variables expressed in the form of a 2 by 2 contingency table, or for one dichotomous variable and one multi-category variable. (101)

pie chart The pictorial representation of a categorical distribution in the form of segments of a circle such that the area of a segment corresponds to the frequency in that category. (63)

pooled estimate A procedure used to estimate the standard error of the difference between two means when the standard deviations of the two groups are approximately equal; the two standard deviations are pooled together. (194)

population An aggregate of all units or cases that conform to some designated set of criteria, also called the target population, universe or sampling frame. (160)

population element A member or unit of a population, such as people, social actions, events, places, times or things. (160)

population parameter The characteristic of some aspect of a population. (161)

positive relationship An association between two variables in which an increase in the values for one variable is accompanied by an increase in the values for the other variable. (90, 95)

positively skewed distribution A distribution that tends to 'lean' towards the end with the lower values and tail off at the end with the higher values. (67)

positivism The philosophy of science based on the assumptions that social reality is external to the people involved and that knowledge of this reality can be obtained by the unprejudiced use of the human senses. The measurement of concepts is regarded as establishing a bridge between social reality and the observer, and inductive logic is used to advance knowledge. (17)

post hoc fallacy The inappropriate use of correlations to establish causation. (116)

predictor variable A variable that is involved in influencing or predicting the values of an outcome variable. (31, 119)

primary data Data that are generated by a researcher who is responsible for the design of the study and their collection, analysis and reporting. (18)

probability sample A sample in which every population element has a known (usually equal) and non-zero chance of being selected. (161)

probability theory Uses the fact that the distribution of the means from all possible samples drawn from a population approximates the normal curve to estimate population parameters from sample statistics. It is based on the theoretical chances of not drawing a representative sample. One important principle of probability theory is the central limit theorem. (163)

proportion A measure of the contribution the frequency in a particular category makes to the total of the frequencies in all categories of a distribution;

calculated by dividing the frequency in that category by the total of the frequencies in all categories. (59)

proportional reduction in error   A measure of influence based on the ratio of the prediction errors without information about the predictor variable to the prediction errors having information about the outcome variable. (121)

quantitative data   Data that are transformed into numbers immediately after they are collected or prior to the analysis, that remain in numbers during the analysis, and the findings from which are reported in numbers. (20)

qualitative data   Data that are recorded in words, that remain in words throughout the analysis, and the findings from which are reported in words. (20)

quartile   The set of divisions of a distribution into four equal parts. (78)

random sample   See **probability sample**. (161)

range   A measure of dispersion based on the interval between the highest and lowest scores or frequencies. (79)

rate   A comparative measure of the frequency of events occurring in a population or category over time, or between different populations or categories. (62)

ratio   A method of comparing the relative size of the frequencies in two categories; calculated by dividing the frequency in the larger category by the frequency in smaller one. (61)

ratio-level measurement   Metric-level measurement that uses a scale with known and usually equal intervals between the categories or scores and has an absolute or true zero. (25)

raw score method   A method for calculating Pearson's r (110) and the slope of a regression line (129).

recoding   A procedure for reordering categories, combining categories or transforming metric variables into categorical variables. (241)

reference category   The category of a multi-category dummy variable that is excluded from multiple regression analysis, and against which the coefficients of the other categories are compared. (150)

regression line   A straight line that best represents the linear relationship between two variables. (126)

relationships   See **association**. (89)

research objective   The scientific purpose of social research: to explore, describe, understand, explain, predict, change, evaluate or assess aspects of social phenomena. (11)

research problem   The social or theoretical issue, the solution of which the research is designed to contribute. It provides the starting point in any research. (11)

research questions   Questions that a research project endeavours to answer. They define its nature and scope and are the vital step between a research problem and the choice of strategies and methods for its investigation. (13)

residual   The deviation of a measurement's value from its position had it fallen on the regression line. (131)

response rate   The percentage of usable responses from a sample survey. (167)

retroductive logic   A method for advancing knowledge that involves the building of models of structures and mechanisms that might produce observed effects. (34)

rotated solution   A factor analytic method that rotates the factors to give items maximum loading on only one factor. (224)

rules for rounding   Conventions for eliminating the last digit in a number, particularly the last decimal place. (53)

sample   A selection of elements (members or units) from a population. (161)

sample statistic   The characteristic of some aspect of a sample. (161)

sampling adequacy   Measured by the Kaiser–Meyer–Olkin index that establishes whether a set of scale items are a suitable selection. (221)

sampling bias   The extent to which the characteristics of a sample do not represent those in the population from which it was drawn. (162)

sampling error   The extent to which a sample statistic does not accurately represent the parameters of the population from which it was drawn. (162)

sampling fraction   See **sampling ratio**. (161)

sampling ratio   A measure of the relationship between the size of a sample and the size of the population from which it was drawn. (161)

second-order relationships   The relationships between four variables with two as controls. (141)

secondary data   Raw data that have been collected by someone other than the researcher in question, either for some general information purpose, such as a government census, or for a specific research project. (18)

scale   A combination of measures, into a single score, and tasted for uni-dimensionality. (215)

scatter diagram   A graph in which all points of intersection between two variables are plotted. (107)

scientific realism   The philosophy of science that rejects both positivism and critical rationalism in favour of the view that reality consist of layers or domains, the most important of which is an underlying 'real' layer consisting of the structures and mechanisms that produce the regularities that can be observed at the surface layer. Knowledge of this 'real' layer can only be gained by constructing imaginary models of how these structures and mechanisms might operate. (17)

scree plot   A graph of the magnitude of the eigenvalues in factor analysis. (223)

significance level   The probability of wrongly accepting the alternative hypothesis when the null hypothesis is true, that is, making a type I error. It is based on the theoretical probability of the occurrence of rare sample values that could have been produced using probability procedures. If the level set is equalled or exceeded in the analysis, the sample value or difference is said to be significant, that is to say, this value or difference is expected to be present in the population from which the sample was drawn. Common significance levels are 0.05, 0.01 and 0.001. See also **confidence level**. (172)

simple random sampling   A method of sampling that gives every possible sample of a particular size the same chance of selection. Tables of random numbers are normally used to make the selections. (168)

simple regression   See **bivariate regression**.

skewed distribution   A distribution that deviates from the symmetrical by 'leaning' somewhat to one end and tailing off at the other end. (66)

skewness   See **skewed distribution**. (76)

Somer's *d*   A measure of influence (or association) between ordinal-level variables. (124)

Spearman's rank correlation coefficient (r_s)   A measure of association used with a small number of objects, events or individuals that are given unique rankings on two variables. (105)

spurious association   A relationship between two variables that is the result of their association with a third variable. (136)

standard deviation   A measure of the dispersion of distributions of interval-level and ratio-level data. The square root of the sum of the squared deviations of all values from the mean, divided by the number of values. (80)

standard error of the difference   An estimate of the standard deviation of the distribution of the differences between all the means for two subsamples. (194)

standard error of the estimate   In regression analysis, it is the standard deviation of the distribution of errors between the predicted and actual values of the outcome variable. (131)

standard error of the mean   A theoretical standard deviation of the means of a sample of a given size, drawn from a specified population. (165, 175)

standard error of the proportion   An estimate of the standard deviation of the sampling distribution of proportions. (173)

standard error of the slope   An estimate of the standard deviation of the sampling distribution of the slope of a regression line. (208)

standard normal distribution   See **normal distribution**. (85)

standard score (z-score) A score, expressed in standard deviation units, that represents the deviation of a specific score from the mean. (84)

standardized contingency coefficient (cs)   The contingency coefficient corrected for its upper limit.

statistical hypothesis   A statement claiming that a relationship between two variables in a probability sample also exists in the population from which the sample was drawn. (178)

stratified sampling   A method of sampling in which the population is first divided into a number of strata, based on a specified criterion, and selections made within each stratum. (169)

successionist view of causation   The view of causality based on the idea that events in the world can be explained if they follow a regular sequence. (30)

sufficient condition   A condition that on its own, or perhaps in combination with one or two other conditions, will lead to the occurrence of an event. (30)

symmetrical distribution   A distribution in which the two halves will coincide when folded vertically along the middle. (66)

symmetrical measure of association   A measure of the mutual association between two variables. It assumes a relationship can be examined from the point of view of either of the variables; no direction of influence is inferred. (96, 120)

systematic sampling   A method of sampling in which the list of the population elements is divided into equal-sized zones and selections made from the same position within each zone. (168)

tertiary data   Data that have been analyzed either by the researcher who generated them or by an analyst of secondary data. The original raw data may not be available, only the results of this analysis. (18)

test of significance   A procedure used to establish whether a relationship found in a sample could also be expected to exist in the population from which the sample was drawn. (33, 177)

theoretical hypothesis   A tentative answer to a 'why' question. (178)

three-way contingency table   Cross-tabulation with three categorical variables. (141)

tolerance   A test for collinearity in multiple regression. (150, 294)

trimmed mean   A mean in which both the upper and lower 5 per cent of values have been excluded. (74)

trivariate analysis   Analysis between three variables. (136)

truncated range   A distribution that is skewed, that is, restricted across its categories, positions or scores. (90)

two-sample test   A test of significance used to establish either whether the values for the same variable measured in two samples are different in the populations from which they were drawn, or whether, in terms of the same variable, two categories of the same sample could have been drawn from different 'populations'. (184)

two-tailed test   A test of significance used for a non-directional alternative hypothesis. (182)

two-way analysis of variance A method for testing the significance of the difference between the means of a combination of categories from two predictor variables. (202)

type I error The rejection of the null hypothesis when it is actually true, which means claiming that an association exists in a population when it does not. (180)

type II error The rejection of the null hypothesis when it is actually false, which means claiming that an association does not exist when it does. (180)

unidimensional The property of a scale in which all the items measure the same thing. (222)

univariate descriptive analysis The analysis of one variable at a time. (29, 47)

unrotated solution The initial factor analytic solution of the number of factors present in the associations between a set of variables. (223)

variable Any characteristic of objects, events or people that can vary. (22)

variance The sum of the squared deviances of all values from the mean, divided by the number of values. (80, 83)

variance inflation factor (VIF) A test for collinearity in multiple regression. (150, 294)

weighted mean A method for calculating the mean of means that are based on different-sized samples or populations. (74)

Wilcoxon test See **Mann–Whitney *U* test**. (198)

within-sample comparisons A procedure for establishing whether differences between categories of a variable within a sample can be expected to exist within the population from which it was drawn. (184)

within-sample variance The dispersion around the mean for each category or sample being compared. (202)

z-scores See **standard scores**. (84)

zero-order correlation coefficient See **Pearson's product moment correlation coefficient**. (111)

zero-order relationship A bivariate relationship. (141)

Appendix A

SYMBOLS

Symbol	Description	Page
a	Intercept of a regression line on the Y axis	127
b	Slope of a regression line	127
β	Regression coefficient (beta)	130
c	Number of columns in a contingency table	100
C	Concordant pairs	102
C	Contingency coefficient of association	99
C_s	Standardized contingency coefficient of association	100
χ^2	Chi-square statistic	97
CI	Confidence interval	173
Cov	Covariance	108
d	Somer's coefficient of influence	124
df	Degrees of freedom	190
D	Discordant pairs	102
η	Eta measure of influence	134
E	Expected frequency	97
ε	Error value in a regression equation	132
f	Frequency	53
F	Fisher's test of significance	201
G or γ	Gamma; Goodman and Kruskal's coefficient of association	102
λ	Lambda; Goodman and Kruskal's coefficient of influence	120
L	Upper limit of the contingency coefficient	100
μ	Mean of population values (see also $\bar{X}$ and $\bar{Y}$)	72
n	Sample size	48
n_t	Total of sample totals	203
N	Population size	72
O	Observed frequency	97
$\%$	Percentage	60
$\overline{\%}_w$	Mean weighted percentage	75
ϕ	Phi coefficient of association for 2 by 2 contingency tables	101
p	Proportion	59
p	Significance level	172
r	Pearson's correlation coefficient (sample)	108
r	Number of rows in a contingency table	100
r^2	Total variance explained	111
ρ	Pearson's correlation coefficient (population)	205
r_S	Spearman's rank correlation coefficient for ordinal-level data	105

R	Multiple correlation coefficient	130
R^2	Coefficient of multiple determination	130
R_1	The sum of the ranks for one category in calculating U	199
R_E	The sum of the ranks if there was no difference between the categories in the U test	199
SK	Coefficient of skewness	76
$\sqrt{}$	Square root	49
s	Standard deviation (sample)	83
σ	Standard deviation (population)	83
s^2	Variance (sample)	83
σ^2	Variance (population)	83
$se_{est\ y}$	Standard error of the estimate (sample)	131
se_m	Standard error of a sample mean	175
se_p	Standard error of a sample proportion	173
se_s	Standard error of the slope of a regression line (sample)	209
se_U	Standard error of the value of U	199
s_o	Standard deviation of the outcome variable (sample)	130
s_p	Standard deviation of the predictor variable (sample)	130
s_p	Pooled estimate of the standard deviation (sample)	195
Σ	Summmation	49
t	t-test of significance	193
τ (tau)	Kendall's rank order coefficient of association for ordinal-level data (small samples with unique ranks)	105
τ_b (tau-b)	Kendall's rank order coefficient of association for ordinal-level data (larger samples with grouped data)	104
T_d	Tied pairs on the outcome (dependent) variable	124
T_x	The number of ties on the x variable	104
T_y	The number of ties on the y variable	104
U	Mann–Whitney coefficient of significance	198
V	Cramér's coefficient of association for nominal-level data	101
x	Individual sample values (x_1, x_2, x_3, etc.)	48
x_m	Midpoint of a category	72
X	Individual population values (X_1, X_2, X_3, etc.)	
x^2	Square of the value for x	49
$\bar{x}$	Mean of all sample values for x	72
$\bar{x}_w$	Weighted mean of sample values	74
$\bar{X}$	Mean of all population values for X	72
y	Individual sample values (y_1, y_2, y_3, etc.)	110
y^2	Square of the value for y	110
$\bar{y}$	Mean of all sample values for y	108
$\bar{Y}$	Mean of all population values for Y	
z	Standard score (values in a standardized normal distribution)	85
$<$	Less than	205
$>$	Greater than	

EQUATIONS

To calculate:	Use equation:	Number	Page
Beta coefficient (multiple regression)	$\beta = b \times \dfrac{s_p}{s_o}$	(5.9)	130
Chi-square	$\chi^2 = \text{sum} \dfrac{(\text{observed } f - \text{expected } f)^2}{\text{expected } f}$ $= \sum \dfrac{(O - E)^2}{E}$	(4.1)	97
Chi-square (2 by 2)	$\chi^2 = \dfrac{n([a \times d] - [b \times c] - n/2)^2}{(a + b)(c + d)(a + c)(b + d)}$	(4.2)	98
Confidence interval of the proportion	$CI = p \pm (z \times se_p)$	(6.2)	173
Confidence interval of the mean	$CI = \bar{x} \pm (z \times se_m)$	(6.4)	175
Confidence interval of slope of the regression line	$CI = b \pm (z \times se_s)$	(6.26)	209
Contingency coefficient	$C = \sqrt{\dfrac{\chi^2}{n + \chi^2}}$	(4.3)	99

Covariance	$$Cov_{xy} = \frac{\Sigma(x - \bar{x})(y - \bar{y})}{n - 1}$$	(4.10)	108
Cramér's V	$$V = \sqrt{\frac{\chi^2}{n \times (\text{smaller of } r - 1 \text{ and } c - 1)}}$$	(4.7)	101
Fisher's test	$$F = \frac{\text{between-sample variability}}{\text{within-sample variability}}$$	(6.16)	202
Gamma	$$G = \frac{C - D}{C + D}$$	(4.8)	102
Kendall's tau-b	$$\tau_b = \frac{C - D}{\sqrt{(C + D + T_x)(C + D + T_y)}}$$	(4.9)	104
Lambda	$$\lambda = \frac{(\text{errors using Rule I}) - (\text{errors using Rule II})}{\text{errors using Rule I}}$$	(5.1)	121

$$= \frac{\begin{array}{c}\text{sum of the within-} \quad \text{modal frequency of}\\ \text{category modes of } - \text{ the outcome}\\ \text{the predictor} \quad \text{variable}\\ \text{variable}\end{array}}{\text{sample size} - \begin{array}{c}\text{modal frequency of}\\ \text{the outcome variable}\end{array}} \qquad (5.2) \quad 123$$

Mann–Whitney test	$$U = n_1 n_2 + \frac{n_1(n_1 + 1)}{2} - R_1 \quad \text{(for small } ns\text{)}$$	(6.11)	198

$$z = \frac{R_1 - R_E}{se_u} \qquad \begin{array}{l}\text{(when both } ns\\ \text{are greater than 20)}\end{array} \qquad (6.12) \quad 199$$

where

$$R_E = \frac{n_1(n_1 + n_2 + 1)}{2} \qquad (6.13) \quad 199$$

$$se_U = \sqrt{\frac{n_1 n_2(n_1 + n_2 + 1)}{12}} \qquad (6.14) \quad 199$$

$$se_U = \sqrt{\frac{n_1 n_2}{n(n - 1)}\left(\frac{n^3 - n}{12} - \Sigma T\right)} \qquad (6.15) \quad 199$$

| Mean (population) | $\mu = \dfrac{\Sigma x}{n}$ | (3.8) | 72 |

Mean (sample) $\bar{x} = \dfrac{\text{sum of the values}}{\text{number of values}}$

$$= \frac{x_1 + x_2 + x_3 + \ldots + x_n}{n} \qquad (3.7) \quad 72$$

$$= \frac{\Sigma x}{n}$$

| Mean (ungrouped frequencies) | $\bar{x} = \dfrac{\Sigma fx}{n}$ | (3.9) | 72 |

| Mean (weighted) | $\bar{x}_w = \dfrac{\Sigma f\bar{x}}{\Sigma f}$ | (3.11) | 74 |

$$\text{or} = \frac{n_1\bar{x}_1 + n_2\bar{x}_2 + n_3\bar{x}_3 + \ldots}{n_t} \qquad (6.17) \quad 203$$

| Mean (weighted %) | $\overline{\%}_w = \dfrac{\Sigma \%n}{\Sigma n}$ | (3.12) | 75 |

| Mean (grouped frequencies) | $\bar{x} = \dfrac{\Sigma fx_m}{n}$ | (3.10) | 74 |

| Mean absolute deviation | $= \dfrac{\Sigma f|x - \bar{x}|}{n}$ | (3.15) | 80 |

| Median position | $= \dfrac{n + 1}{2}$ | (3.6) | 69 |

Pearson's r	$r = \dfrac{Cov_{xy}}{s_x s_y}$	(4.11)	108
	$= \dfrac{\Sigma(x - \bar{x})(y - \bar{y})}{(n-1)s_x s_y}$	(4.12)	108
	$= \dfrac{\Sigma(x - \bar{x})(y - \bar{y})}{\sqrt{[\Sigma(x_i - \bar{x})^2 \Sigma(y_i - \bar{y})^2]}}$	(4.13)	108
	$= \dfrac{n(\Sigma xy) - (\Sigma x)(\Sigma y)}{\sqrt{[n(\Sigma x^2) - (\Sigma x)^2][n(\Sigma y^2) - (\Sigma y)^2]}}$	(4.14)	110
	$= \dfrac{\Sigma(z_x z_y)}{n}$	(4.15)	111
Percentage	$\% = \dfrac{f}{n} \times 100$	(3.2)	60
Percentage change	$= \dfrac{\text{(quantity at time 2)} - \text{(quantity at time 1)}}{\text{(quantity at time 1)}} \times 100$	(3.3)	60
Phi	$\phi = \sqrt{\dfrac{\chi^2}{n}}$	(4.6)	101
Proportion	$p = \dfrac{f}{n}$	(3.1)	59
Rate	$= \dfrac{\text{number of events}}{\text{total population of events}} \times 1000$	(3.5)	62
Ratio	$= \dfrac{\text{number in the largest category}}{\text{number in the smallest category}}$	(3.4)	61
Regression line (bivariate)	$y = \text{intercept} + (\text{slope} \times x) = a + bx$	(5.5)	127
	or $= a + bx + \varepsilon$	(5.11)	132

| Regression intercept (mean deviation method) | $a = \bar{y} - b\bar{x}$ | (5.6) | 129 |

where

$$b = \frac{\Sigma(x - \bar{x})(y - \bar{y})}{\Sigma(x - \bar{x})^2}$$ (5.7) 129

| (raw score method) | $b = \dfrac{n(\Sigma xy) - (\Sigma x)(\Sigma y)}{n(\Sigma x^2) - (\Sigma x)^2}$ | (5.8) | 129 |

| Regression line (multiple) | $y = a + b_1 x_1 + b_2 x_2 + \ldots$ | (5.12) | 147 |

| Sample variability (between sample) | $= \dfrac{n_1(\bar{x}_1 - \bar{x}_w)^2 + n_2(\bar{x}_2 - \bar{x}_w)^2 + n_3(\bar{x}_3 - \bar{x}_w)^2 + \ldots}{c - 1}$ | (6.18) | 203 |

| Sample variability (within-sample) | $= \dfrac{(n_1 - 1)s_1^{\,2} + (n_2 - 1)s_2^{\,2} + (n_3 - 1)s_2^{\,3}\,\text{etc.}}{n_t - c}$ | (6.19) | 203 |

| Skewness | $SK = \dfrac{3(\text{mean} - \text{median})}{\text{standard deviation}}$ | (3.14) | 76 |

| Somer's d | $d = \dfrac{C - D}{C + D + T_d}$ | (5.3) | 124 |

$$= \frac{2(C - D)}{n^2 - \text{sum of the squares of the marginals for the outcome variable}}$$ (5.4) 125

| Standard deviation | $s = \sqrt{\dfrac{\Sigma f(x - \bar{x})^2}{n}}$ | (3.16) | 83 |

| Standard deviation (grouped data) | $s = \sqrt{\dfrac{\Sigma f x^2}{n} - \bar{x}^2}$ | (3.18) | 84 |

Standard deviation (pooled estimate)

$$S_p = \sqrt{\frac{n_1 s_1^2 + n_2 s_2^2}{n_1 + n_2}} \quad \text{(s of groups approx. equal)} \quad (6.7) \quad 195$$

$$= \sqrt{\frac{s_1^2 + s_2^2}{2}} \quad \text{(size of categories approx. equal)} \quad (6.8) \quad 195$$

Standard error of the difference

$$se_d = s_p \sqrt{\frac{1}{n_1} + \frac{1}{n_2}} \qquad (6.9) \quad 195$$

where

$$S_p = \sqrt{\frac{s_1^2}{n_1} + \frac{s_2^2}{n_2}} \quad \text{(s of groups approx. equal)} \quad (6.10) \quad 195$$

Standard error of the estimate

$$se_{\text{est } y} = \sqrt{\frac{\Sigma(y - y')^2}{n - 2}} \qquad (5.10) \quad 131$$

Standard error of the mean (estimated)

$$se_m = \frac{s}{\sqrt{n}} \qquad (6.3) \quad 175$$

Standard error of the proportion (estimated)

$$se_p = \sqrt{\frac{p(1 - p)}{n}} \qquad (6.1) \quad 173$$

Standard score

$$z = \frac{\text{score} - \text{mean}}{\text{standard deviation}} = \frac{x - \bar{x}}{s} \qquad (3.20) \quad 85$$

t test (group)

$$t = \frac{\text{difference between the means}}{\text{estimated standard error of the difference}}$$

$$= \frac{\bar{x}_1 - \bar{x}_2}{se_d} \qquad (6.6) \quad 194$$

t test (Pearson's r)	$t = r\sqrt{\dfrac{n-2}{1-r^2}}$	(6.20)	204

Upper limit of χ^2 (square table) $\quad L = \sqrt{\dfrac{r-1}{r}}$ (4.4) 100

Upper limit of χ^2 (other tables) $\quad L = \sqrt[4]{\dfrac{r-1}{r} \times \dfrac{c-1}{c}}$ (4.5) 100

Variance $\quad s^2 = \dfrac{\Sigma f(x-\bar{x})^2}{n}$ (3.17) 83

Variance (grouped data) $\quad s^2 = \dfrac{\Sigma fx^2}{n} - \bar{x}^2$ (3.19) 84

z test for gamma $\quad z = G\sqrt{\dfrac{C+D}{n(1-G^2)}}$ (6.5) 191

z test for lambda $\quad z = \dfrac{\lambda - \text{predicted value of } \lambda}{se_\lambda}$ (6.22) 205

where

$$se_\lambda = \sqrt{\dfrac{\left(n - \substack{\text{sum of within-category}\\ \text{modes of the predictor}}\right)\left(\substack{\text{sum of within-category}\\ \text{modes of the predictor}} + \substack{\text{modal } f \text{ of}\\ \text{the outcome}} - 2 \times \substack{\text{modal } f \text{ in the row with the}\\ \text{modal } f \text{ of the outcome}}\right)}{(n - \text{modal } f \text{ of the outcome})^3}}$$

(6.21) 205

z test for Somer's d $\quad z = \dfrac{d}{\sqrt{var_d}}$ (6.23) 206

where

$$var_d = \dfrac{4 \times \Sigma(\text{each cell multiplied by the sum of its diagonal cells squared})}{[\text{total squared} - \Sigma(\text{each column marginal squared})]^2}$$

(6.24) 207

or, if population distributions can be assumed to be uniform,

$$var_d = \dfrac{4(r^2-1)(c+1)}{9nr^2(c-1)}$$

(6.25) 207

Appendix C

SPSS PROCEDURES

This appendix sets out the steps in the SPSS software for undertaking elementary forms of the various types of analysis covered in Chapters 3–8. All analysis starts with a selection from one of the pull-down menus and is then followed by a choice from among the procedures offered. The selections to be made are shown in bold type, such as **Analyze**, and arrows (**➡**) are used as shorthand for 'then click on'. What follows can be used with SPSS versions 8 to 10, and possibly later versions.

Chapter 3   Descriptive Analysis: Univariate

Distribution, Central Tendency and Dispersion

From the **Analyze** menu, **➡ Descriptive Statistics ➡ Frequencies**.
Select the variables to be analyzed by double-clicking on them in the left-hand column.
Click on **Statistics** and then select the procedures desired for that level of measurement.
Click on **Continue**.
Click on **Charts** if required and select the type desired. Click on **Continue**.
Click on **OK**.

Chapter 4   Descriptive Analysis: Bivariate

Cross-tabulations (nominal-level and ordinal-level variables)

From the **Analyze** menu, **➡ Descriptive Statistics ➡ Crosstabs**.
Enter variables for analysis in **Row** and **Column**.
Click on **Statistics** and then select the procedures desired for the levels of measurement, **Contingency coefficient**, or **Phi** or **Cramér's *V*** for nominal-level variables and **Gamma** for ordinal-level variables.
Click on **Continue**.
Click on **Cells** and select **Counts** and **Percentages** to be included in the crosstabulations.
Click on **Continue**. Click on **OK**.

Correlation (interval-level and ratio-level variables)

From the **Analyze** menu, ➡ **Correlate** ➡ **Bivariate**.
Enter variables to be analyzed by double-clicking on them in the left-hand column.
Select **Correlation coefficient** (Pearson's r is already selected and would normally be used).
Click on **OK**.
If a scatter diagram is desired, from the **Graphs** menu, ➡ **Scatter**. Select **Simple**.
Click on **Define**. Enter variables for the X and Y axes by clicking on the variable name and then on the appropriate arrow.
Click on **OK**.

Chapter 5   Explanatory Analysis

Bivariate Analysis with Categorical Variables

From the **Analyze** menu, ➡ **Descriptive Statistics** ➡ **Crosstabs**.
Enter variables for analysis in **Row** and **Column**.
Click on **Statistics** and then select the procedures desired for the levels of measurement, **Lambda** for nominal-level variables and **Somer's d** for ordinal-level variables.
Click on **Continue**.
Click on **Cells** and select **Counts** and **Percentages** to be included in the crosstabulations.
Click on **Continue**. Click on **OK**.

Bivariate Analysis with Metric Variables

From the **Analyze** menu, ➡ **Regression** ➡ **Linear**.
Enter one variable in each of the **Independent** (Predictor) and **Dependent** (Outcome) spaces.
Select the **Method** of regression to be used.
Click on **Statistics** and select the coefficients desired.
Click on **Continue**. Click on **OK**.

Multivariate Analysis with Categorical Variables

From the **Analyze** menu, ➡ **Descriptive Statistics** ➡ **Crosstabs**.
Enter variables for the bivariate analysis in **Row** and **Column** and the control variable in **Layer 1 of 1**.
Click on **Statistics** and select the procedures desired for the levels of measurement, **Contingency coefficient**, **Phi** or **Cramér's V** for nominal-level variables and **Gamma** for ordinal-level variables.

Click on **Continue.**
Click on **Cells** and select **Counts** and **Percentages** to be included in the crosstabulations.
Click on **Continue.** Click on **OK.**

Multivariate Analysis with Metric Variables

Partial correlation

From the **Analyze** menu, ➡ **Correlate** ➡ **Partial.**
Enter the variables to be correlated in the **Variables** space and the control variable in the **Controlling for** space.
Click on **Options** and selected the **Statistics** to be shown.
Click on **Continue.** Click on **OK.**

Multiple regression

From the **Analyze** menu, ➡ **Regression** ➡ **Linear.**
Enter one variable in the **Dependent** (Outcome) space and the desired number of variables in the **Independent** (Predictor) space.
Select the **Method** of regression to be used.
Click on **Statistics** and select the coefficients desired.
Click on **Continue.** Click on **OK.**

Chapter 6   Inferential Analysis

Univariate Analysis with Categorical Variables

This is not available in SPSS and would need to be done manually.

Univariate Analysis with Metric Variables

From the **Analyze** menu, ➡ **Compare Means** ➡ **One-sample T test.**[1]
Select the **Test Variable.**
Click on **Options** and set the confidence level (shown as **Confidence Interval**).
The default level is 95%.
Click on **Continue.** Click on **OK.**
(The upper and lower confidence limits, as well as the level of significance, are shown.)

Bivariate Analysis with Categorical Variables

From the **Analyze** menu, ➡ **Descriptive Statistics** ➡ **Crosstabs.**
Enter variables for analysis in **Row** and **Column.**

Click on **Statistics** and then select the procedures desired for the levels of measurement.

Click on **Continue.** Click on **OK.**

The approximate levels of significance for the symmetric measures of association are shown.

(This procedure would normally be done in conjunction with cross-tabulation above.)

Bivariate Analysis with Metric Variables

From the **Analyze** menu, ➡ **Correlate** ➡ **Bivariate.**

Select the variables to be analyzed by double-clicking on them in the left-hand column.

Select the **Correlation Coefficient** desired (Pearson's *r* is already selected and would normally be used).

Select either **One-tailed** or **Two-tailed** test, as appropriate.

Click on **OK.**

(This procedure would normally be done in conjunction with correlation above.)

Inferential Analysis with Categorical Variables

Nominal-level variables

From the **Analyze** menu, ➡ **Descriptive Statistics** ➡ **Crosstabs.**

Enter variables for analysis in **Row** and **Column** following the convention for the position of independent (predictor) and dependent (outcome) variables.

Click on **Statistics** and then select **Lambda.**

Click on **Continue.** Click on **OK.**

The value for lambda and the approximate level of significance are shown for the designated dependent variable.[2]

(This procedure would normally be done in conjunction with cross-tabulation above.)

Ordinal-level variables

Follow the procedure for nominal-level variables but select **Somer's *d*** rather than lambda.[3]

Inferential Analysis with Metric Variables

Regression

In bivariate regression, the procedure for testing the significance of the regression line is the same as the test of significance for Pearson's *r* (see above).

In multiple regression, it is necessary to first test the significance of the multiple regression coefficient (R). If this turns out to be significant, then the significance of the individual *beta* coefficients can be tested.

From the **Analyze** menu, ➡ **Regression** ➡ **Linear.**

Enter one variable in the **Dependent** (Outcome) space and the desired number of variables in the **Independent** (Predictor) space.

Select the **Method** of regression to be used.

Click on **Statistics** and select **Confidence intervals** from the **Regression Coefficients** section. Click on **Continue.**

Click on **Options** and set the level of probabilities or values for F. (Unless there is some reason for doing otherwise, use the default values.)

Click on **Continue.** Click on **OK.**

The level of significance for R is shown in the table for ANOVA. Both the levels of significance and confidence limits are provided for the *beta* coefficients for each independent variable in the next table.

(This procedure would normally be done in conjunction with regression above.)

Comparing Means

From the **Analyze** menu, ➡ **Compare Means** ➡ **Independent-Samples T Test** or **Paired-Samples T Test,** as appropriate.[4]

Click on **Options** and set the confidence level (shown as **Confidence Interval**). The default level is 95%.

Click on **Continue.** Click on **OK.**

The upper and lower confidence limits, as well as the level of significance, are shown.

Chapter 7   Data Reduction

Cronbach's Alpha

From the **Analyze** menu, ➡ **Scale** ➡ **Reliability Analysis.**

Enter scale items to be analyzed by double-clicking on them in the left-hand column.

Select the **Model** of analysis to be used (**Alpha** would normally be used).

Click on **Statistics** and select those to be used (normally not required).

Click on **Continue.** Click on **OK.**

Factor analysis

From the **Analyze** menu, ➡ **Data Reduction** ➡ **Factor.**

Enter scale items to be analyzed by double-clicking on them in the left-hand column.

Click on **Descriptive** and select **Statistics** (normally **Initial solution**).
Click on **Continue**.
If a **Correlation Matrix** is required, select **Coefficients** and possibly **Significance levels**. In any case, **KMO and Bartlett's test of sphericity** should be selected.
Click on **Continue**.
Click on **Extraction** and select a **Method** (**Principle components** is commonly used), **Correlation matrix** (if required), **Unrotated factor solution**, **Scree plot** (can be useful) and **Eigenvalues over 1** (normally used). The maximum number of iterations can also be set (the default is 25).
Click on **Continue**.
Click on **Rotation** and select a **Method** (**Varimax** in commonly used).
Click on **Continue**. Click on **OK**.
This analysis may be done in stages, the unrotated solution first and a rotated solution after consideration of these results.

Recoding metric variables into categorical variables

From the **Transform** menu, ➡ **Recode** ➡ **Into Different Variables**.
Select from the **Input Variable** list by double-clicking in the left-hand column.
Name and **Label** the **Output Variable**. Click on **Change**.
Click on **Old and New Values** and enter **Old Values** (using **Range**) and the **Value** for the corresponding category (normally 1, 2 etc.). Click on **Add**.
Repeat the previous procedure to create the rest of the new categories.
Click on **Continue**. Click on **OK**.

Notes

[1] This procedure is normally used to test for the significance of a difference between the mean of a variable and a specified value. However, it can also be used to establish confidence limits about the sample mean.

[2] Note that lambda can be treated as both a symmetric and an asymmetric measure. Note also that the procedure used by SPSS is different from that discussed in Chapter 6 (pp. 205–6) but the outcome is the same.

[3] Note that the SPSS procedure is different from that discussed in Chapter 6 (pp. 206–8) but the outcome is the same.

[4] For a discussion of alternative ways of classifying types of *t* tests, see pp. 183–5.

Appendix D

STATISTICAL TABLES

Table 1   *Chi-square distribution*

df	One-tailed test			Two-tailed test		
	0.05	0.01	0.001	0.05	0.01	0.001
1	3.84	6.63	10.83	5.02	7.88	12.12
2	5.99	9.21	13.82	7.38	10.60	15.20
3	7.82	11.34	16.27	9.35	12.84	17.73
4	9.49	13.28	18.47	11.14	14.86	20.00
5	11.07	15.09	20.52	12.83	16.75	22.11
6	12.59	16.81	22.46	14.45	18.55	24.10
7	14.07	18.48	24.32	16.01	20.28	26.02
8	15.51	20.09	26.12	17.53	21.95	27.87
9	16.92	21.67	27.88	19.02	23.59	29.67
10	18.31	23.21	29.59	20.48	25.19	31.42
11	19.68	24.72	31.26	21.92	26.76	33.14
12	21.03	26.22	32.91	23.34	28.30	34.82
13	22.36	27.69	34.53	24.74	29.82	36.48
14	23.68	29.14	36.12	26.12	31.32	38.11
15	25.00	30.58	37.70	27.49	32.80	39.72
16	26.30	32.00	39.25	28.85	34.27	41.31
17	27.59	33.41	40.79	30.19	35.72	42.88
18	28.87	34.81	42.31	31.53	37.16	44.43
19	30.14	36.19	43.82	32.85	38.58	45.97
20	31.41	37.57	45.31	34.17	40.00	47.50
21	32.67	38.93	46.80	35.48	41.40	49.01
22	33.92	40.29	48.27	36.78	42.80	50.51
23	35.17	41.64	49.73	38.08	44.18	52.00
24	36.42	42.98	51.18	39.36	45.56	53.48
25	37.65	44.31	52.62	40.65	46.93	54.95
26	38.89	45.64	54.05	41.92	48.29	56.41
27	40.11	46.96	55.48	43.19	49.64	57.86
28	41.34	48.28	56.89	44.46	50.99	59.30
29	42.56	49.59	58.30	45.72	52.34	60.73
30	43.77	50.89	59.70	46.98	53.67	62.16
35	49.80	57.34	66.62	53.20	60.27	69.20
40	55.76	63.69	73.40	59.34	66.77	76.09
45	61.66	69.96	80.08	65.41	73.17	82.88
50	67.50	76.15	86.66	71.42	79.49	89.56
55	73.31	82.29	93.17	77.38	85.75	96.16
60	79.08	88.38	99.61	83.30	91.95	102.69
65	84.82	94.42	105.99	89.18	98.11	109.16
70	90.53	100.43	112.32	95.02	104.21	115.58
75	96.22	106.39	118.60	100.84	110.29	121.94
80	101.88	112.33	124.84	106.63	116.32	128.26
85	107.52	118.24	131.04	112.39	122.32	134.54
90	113.15	124.12	137.21	118.14	128.30	140.78
95	118.75	129.97	143.34	123.86	134.25	146.99
100	124.34	135.81	149.45	129.56	140.17	153.17

Table 2　*The normal (z) distribution*

z	0.00	0.01	0.02	0.03	0.04	0.05	0.06	0.07	0.08	0.09
				Second Decimal Place of z						
0.0	0.5000	0.4960	0.4920	0.4880	0.4840	0.4801	0.4761	0.4721	0.4681	0.4641
0.1	0.4602	0.4562	0.4522	0.4483	0.4443	0.4404	0.4364	0.4325	0.4286	0.4247
0.2	0.4207	0.4168	0.4129	0.4090	0.4052	0.4013	0.3974	0.3936	0.3897	0.3859
0.3	0.3821	0.3783	0.3745	0.3707	0.3669	0.3632	0.3594	0.3557	0.3520	0.3483
0.4	0.3446	0.3409	0.3372	0.3336	0.3300	0.3264	0.3228	0.3192	0.3156	0.3121
0.5	0.3085	0.3050	0.3015	0.2981	0.2946	0.2912	0.2877	0.2843	0.2810	0.2776
0.6	0.2743	0.2709	0.2676	0.2643	0.2611	0.2578	0.2546	0.2514	0.2483	0.2451
0.7	0.2420	0.2389	0.2358	0.2327	0.2296	0.2266	0.2236	0.2206	0.2177	0.2148
0.8	0.2119	0.2090	0.2061	0.2033	0.2005	0.1977	0.1949	0.1922	0.1894	0.1867
0.9	0.1841	0.1814	0.1788	0.1762	0.1736	0.1711	0.1685	0.1660	0.1635	0.1611
1.0	0.1587	0.1562	0.1539	0.1515	0.1492	0.1469	0.1446	0.1423	0.1401	0.1379
1.1	0.1357	0.1335	0.1314	0.1292	0.1271	0.1251	0.1230	0.1210	0.1190	0.1170
1.2	0.1151	0.1131	0.1112	0.1093	0.1075	0.1056	0.1038	0.1020	0.1003	0.0985
1.3	0.0968	0.0951	0.0934	0.0918	0.0901	0.0885	0.0869	0.0853	0.0838	0.0823
1.4	0.0808	0.0793	0.0778	0.0764	0.0749	0.0735	0.0721	0.0708	0.0694	0.0681
1.5	0.0668	0.0655	0.0643	0.0630	0.0618	0.0606	0.0594	0.0582	0.0571	0.0559
1.6	0.0548	0.0537	0.0526	0.0516	0.0505	0.0495	0.0485	0.0475	0.0465	0.0455
1.7	0.0446	0.0436	0.0427	0.0418	0.0409	0.0401	0.0392	0.0384	0.0375	0.0367
1.8	0.0359	0.0352	0.0344	0.0336	0.0329	0.0322	0.0314	0.0307	0.0301	0.0294
1.9	0.0287	0.0281	0.0274	0.0268	0.0262	0.0256	0.0250	0.0244	0.0239	0.0233
2.0	0.0228	0.0222	0.0217	0.0212	0.0207	0.0202	0.0197	0.0192	0.0188	0.0183
2.1	0.0179	0.0174	0.0170	0.0166	0.0162	0.0158	0.0154	0.0150	0.0146	0.0143
2.2	0.0139	0.0136	0.0132	0.0129	0.0125	0.0122	0.0119	0.0116	0.0113	0.0110
2.3	0.0107	0.0104	0.0102	0.0099	0.0096	0.0094	0.0091	0.0089	0.0087	0.0084
2.4	0.0082	0.0080	0.0078	0.0075	0.0073	0.0071	0.0069	0.0068	0.0066	0.0064
2.5	0.0062	0.0060	0.0059	0.0057	0.0055	0.0054	0.0052	0.0051	0.0049	0.0048
2.6	0.0047	0.0045	0.0044	0.0043	0.0041	0.0040	0.0039	0.0038	0.0037	0.0036
2.7	0.0035	0.0034	0.0033	0.0032	0.0031	0.0030	0.0029	0.0028	0.0027	0.0026
2.8	0.0026	0.0025	0.0024	0.0023	0.0023	0.0022	0.0021	0.0021	0.0020	0.0019
2.9	0.0019	0.0018	0.0018	0.0017	0.0016	0.0016	0.0015	0.0015	0.0014	0.0014
3.0	0.0013	0.0013	0.0013	0.0012	0.0012	0.0011	0.0011	0.0011	0.0010	0.0010
3.1	0.0010	0.0009	0.0009	0.0009	0.0008	0.0008	0.0008	0.0008	0.0007	0.0007
3.2	0.0007	0.0007	0.0006	0.0006	0.0006	0.0006	0.0006	0.0005	0.0005	0.0005
3.3	0.0005	0.0005	0.0005	0.0004	0.0004	0.0004	0.0004	0.0004	0.0004	0.0003
3.4	0.0003	0.0003	0.0003	0.0003	0.0003	0.0003	0.0003	0.0003	0.0003	0.0002
3.5	0.0002	0.0002	0.0002	0.0002	0.0002	0.0002	0.0002	0.0002	0.0002	0.0002
3.6	0.0002	0.0002	0.0001	0.0001	0.0001	0.0001	0.0001	0.0001	0.0001	0.0001
3.7	0.0001	0.0001	0.0001	0.0001	0.0001	0.0001	0.0001	0.0001	0.0001	0.0001

This table shows *p* values for one-tailed tests. The value for a two-tailed test is double that shown for a particular z score. For example, the two-tailed *p* value for a z of 2.12 is 0.0348.

Table 3   *Student's t distribution*

	One-tailed test			Two-tailed test		
df	0.05	0.01	0.001	0.05	0.01	0.001
1	6.314	31.821	318.309	12.706	63.657	636.619
2	2.920	6.965	22.327	4.303	9.925	31.599
3	2.353	4.541	10.215	3.182	5.841	12.924
4	2.132	3.747	7.173	2.776	4.604	8.610
5	2.015	3.365	5.893	2.571	4.032	6.869
6	1.943	3.143	5.208	2.447	3.707	5.959
7	1.895	2.998	4.785	2.365	3.499	5.408
8	1.860	2.896	4.501	2.306	3.355	5.041
9	1.833	2.821	4.297	2.262	3.250	4.781
10	1.812	2.764	4.144	2.228	3.169	4.587
11	1.796	2.718	4.025	2.201	3.106	4.437
12	1.782	2.681	3.930	2.179	3.055	4.318
13	1.771	2.650	3.852	2.160	3.012	4.221
14	1.761	2.624	3.787	2.145	2.977	4.140
15	1.753	2.602	3.733	2.131	2.947	4.073
16	1.746	2.583	3.686	2.120	2.921	4.015
17	1.740	2.567	3.646	2.110	2.898	3.965
18	1.734	2.552	3.610	2.101	2.878	3.922
19	1.729	2.539	3.579	2.093	2.861	3.883
20	1.725	2.528	3.552	2.086	2.845	3.850
21	1.721	2.518	3.527	2.080	2.831	3.819
22	1.717	2.508	3.505	2.074	2.819	3.792
23	1.714	2.500	3.485	2.069	2.807	3.768
24	1.711	2.492	3.467	2.064	2.797	3.745
25	1.708	2.485	3.450	2.060	2.787	3.725
26	1.706	2.479	3.435	2.056	2.779	3.707
27	1.703	2.473	3.421	2.052	2.771	3.690
28	1.701	2.467	3.408	2.048	2.763	3.674
29	1.699	2.462	3.396	2.045	2.756	3.659
30	1.697	2.457	3.385	2.042	2.750	3.646
40	1.684	2.423	3.307	2.021	2.704	3.551
50	1.676	2.403	3.261	2.009	2.678	3.496
60	1.671	2.390	3.232	2.000	2.660	3.460
70	1.667	2.381	3.211	1.994	2.648	3.435
80	1.664	2.374	3.195	1.990	2.639	3.416
90	1.662	2.368	3.183	1.987	2.632	3.402
100	1.660	2.363	3.174	1.984	2.626	3.390
120	1.658	2.358	3.160	1.980	2.617	3.373
∞*(z)*	1.645	2.326	3.090	1.960	2.576	3.291

Table 4 F distribution

Numerator df

Denominator df	1	2	3	4	5	6	7	8	9	10	20	50	100
1	161	199	216	225	230	234	237	239	241	242	248	252	253
	4052	*4999*	*5403*	*5625*	*5764*	*5859*	*5928*	*5981*	*6022*	*6056*	*6209*	*6303*	*6334*
2	18.51	19.00	19.16	19.25	19.30	19.33	19.35	19.37	19.38	19.40	19.45	19.48	19.49
	98.50	*99.00*	*99.17*	*99.25*	*99.30*	*99.33*	*99.36*	*99.37*	*99.39*	*99.40*	*99.45*	*99.48*	*99.49*
3	10.13	9.55	9.28	9.12	9.01	8.94	8.89	8.85	8.81	8.79	8.66	8.58	8.55
	34.12	*30.82*	*29.46*	*28.71*	*28.24*	*27.91*	*27.67*	*27.49*	*27.35*	*27.23*	*26.69*	*26.35*	*26.24*
4	7.71	6.94	6.59	6.39	6.26	6.16	6.09	6.04	6.00	5.96	5.80	5.70	5.66
	21.20	*18.00*	*16.69*	*15.98*	*15.52*	*15.21*	*14.98*	*14.80*	*14.66*	*14.55*	*14.02*	*13.69*	*13.58*
5	6.61	5.79	5.41	5.19	5.05	4.95	4.88	4.82	4.77	4.74	4.56	4.44	4.41
	16.26	*13.27*	*12.06*	*11.39*	*10.97*	*10.67*	*10.46*	*10.29*	*10.16*	*10.05*	*9.55*	*9.24*	*9.13*
6	5.99	5.14	4.76	4.53	4.39	4.28	4.21	4.15	4.10	4.06	3.87	3.75	3.71
	13.75	*10.92*	*9.78*	*9.15*	*8.75*	*8.47*	*8.26*	*8.10*	*7.98*	*7.87*	*7.40*	*7.09*	*6.99*
7	5.59	4.74	4.35	4.12	3.97	3.87	3.79	3.73	3.68	3.64	3.44	3.32	3.27
	12.25	*9.55*	*8.45*	*7.85*	*7.46*	*7.19*	*6.99*	*6.84*	*6.72*	*6.62*	*6.16*	*5.86*	*5.75*
8	5.32	4.46	4.07	3.84	3.69	3.58	3.50	3.44	3.39	3.35	3.15	3.02	2.97
	11.26	*8.65*	*7.59*	*7.01*	*6.63*	*6.37*	*6.18*	*6.03*	*5.91*	*5.81*	*5.36*	*5.07*	*4.96*
9	5.12	4.26	3.86	3.63	3.48	3.37	3.29	3.23	3.18	3.14	2.94	2.80	2.76
	10.56	*8.02*	*6.99*	*6.42*	*6.06*	*5.80*	*5.61*	*5.47*	*5.35*	*5.26*	*4.81*	*4.52*	*4.41*
10	4.96	4.10	3.71	3.48	3.33	3.22	3.14	3.07	3.02	2.98	2.77	2.64	2.59
	10.04	*7.56*	*6.55*	*5.99*	*5.64*	*5.39*	*5.20*	*5.06*	*4.94*	*4.85*	*4.41*	*4.12*	*4.01*
11	4.84	3.98	3.59	3.36	3.20	3.09	3.01	2.95	2.90	2.85	2.65	2.51	2.46
	9.65	*7.21*	*6.22*	*5.67*	*5.32*	*5.07*	*4.89*	*4.74*	*4.63*	*4.54*	*4.10*	*3.81*	*3.71*
12	4.75	3.89	3.49	3.26	3.11	3.00	2.91	2.85	2.80	2.75	2.54	2.40	2.35
	9.33	*6.93*	*5.95*	*5.41*	*5.06*	*4.82*	*4.64*	*4.50*	*4.39*	*4.30*	*3.86*	*3.57*	*3.47*
13	4.67	3.81	3.41	3.18	3.02	2.92	2.83	2.77	2.71	2.67	2.46	2.31	2.26
	9.07	*6.70*	*5.74*	*5.21*	*4.86*	*4.62*	*4.44*	*4.30*	*4.19*	*4.10*	*3.66*	*3.38*	*3.27*

Continued

Table 4 *Continued*

Denominator

df	Numerator df												
	1	2	3	4	5	6	7	8	9	10	20	50	100
14	4.60	3.74	3.34	3.11	2.96	2.85	2.76	2.70	2.65	2.60	2.39	2.24	2.19
	8.86	*6.51*	*5.56*	*5.03*	*4.69*	*4.46*	*4.28*	*4.14*	*4.03*	*3.94*	*3.51*	*3.22*	*3.11*
15	4.54	3.68	3.29	3.06	2.90	2.79	2.71	2.64	2.59	2.54	2.33	2.18	2.12
	8.68	*6.36*	*5.42*	*4.89*	*4.56*	*4.32*	*4.14*	*4.00*	*3.89*	*3.80*	*3.37*	*3.08*	*2.98*
16	4.49	3.63	3.24	3.01	2.85	2.74	2.66	2.59	2.54	2.49	2.28	2.12	2.07
	8.53	*6.23*	*5.29*	*4.77*	*4.44*	*4.20*	*4.03*	*3.89*	*3.78*	*3.69*	*3.26*	*2.97*	*2.86*
17	4.45	3.59	3.20	2.96	2.81	2.70	2.61	2.55	2.49	2.45	2.23	2.08	2.02
	8.40	*6.11*	*5.18*	*4.67*	*4.34*	*4.10*	*3.93*	*3.79*	*3.68*	*3.59*	*3.16*	*2.87*	*2.76*
18	4.41	3.55	3.16	2.93	2.77	2.66	2.58	2.51	2.46	2.41	2.19	2.04	1.98
	8.29	*6.01*	*5.09*	*4.58*	*4.25*	*4.01*	*3.84*	*3.71*	*3.60*	*3.51*	*3.08*	*2.78*	*2.68*
19	4.38	3.52	3.13	2.90	2.74	2.63	2.54	2.48	2.42	2.38	2.16	2.00	1.94
	8.18	*5.93*	*5.01*	*4.50*	*4.17*	*3.94*	*3.77*	*3.63*	*3.52*	*3.43*	*3.00*	*2.71*	*2.60*
20	4.35	3.49	3.10	2.87	2.71	2.60	2.51	2.45	2.39	2.35	2.12	1.97	1.91
	8.10	*5.85*	*4.94*	*4.43*	*4.10*	*3.87*	*3.70*	*3.56*	*3.46*	*3.37*	*2.94*	*2.64*	*2.54*
50	4.03	3.18	2.79	2.56	2.40	2.29	2.20	2.13	2.07	2.03	1.78	1.60	1.52
	7.17	*5.06*	*4.20*	*3.72*	*3.41*	*3.19*	*3.02*	*2.89*	*2.78*	*2.70*	*2.27*	*1.95*	*1.82*
100	3.94	3.09	2.70	2.46	2.31	2.19	2.10	2.03	1.97	1.93	1.68	1.48	1.39
	6.90	*4.82*	*3.98*	*3.51*	*3.21*	*2.99*	*2.82*	*2.69*	*2.59*	*2.50*	*2.07*	*1.74*	*1.60*
1000	3.85	3.00	2.61	2.38	2.22	2.11	2.02	1.95	1.89	1.84	1.58	1.36	1.26
	6.66	*4.63*	*3.80*	*3.34*	*3.04*	*2.82*	*2.66*	*2.53*	*2.43*	*2.34*	*1.90*	*1.54*	*1.38*

The first value in each row is the *F* required for a 0.05 level of significance.
The second value, in italics, is for a 0.01 level.

References

Agresti, A. and Finlay, B. (1997) *Statistical Methods for the Social Sciences* (3rd edn). Upper Saddle River, NJ: Prentice Hall.

Aldenderfer, M.S. and Blashfield, R.K. (1984) *Cluster Analysis*. Thousand Oaks, CA: Sage.

Allison, P.D. (1999) *Multiple Regression: A Primer*. London: Sage.

Asher, H.B. (1983) *Causal Modeling*. Beverly Hills, CA: Sage.

Babbie, E.R., Halley, F. and Zaino, J. (2000) *Adventures in Social Research*. Thousand Oaks, CA: Pine Forge Press.

Bacon, F. (1889) *Novum Organon*, trans. G.W. Kitchin. Oxford: Clarendon Press.

Balnaves, M. and Caputi, P. (2001) *Introduction to Quantitative Research Methods: An Investigative Approach*. London: Sage.

Berenson, M.L. and Levine, D.M. (1999) *Basic Business Statistics: Concepts and Applications* (7th edn). Upper Saddle River, NJ: Prentice Hall.

Bhaskar, R. (1979) *The Possibility of Naturalism: A Philosophical Critique of the Contemporary Human Sciences*. Brighton: Harvester.

Blaikie, N. (1968) 'An analysis of religious affiliation, activity and attitudes in St Albans, Christchurch'. MA thesis, University of Canterbury, New Zealand.

Blaikie, N. (1969) 'Religion, social status and community involvement: a study in Christchurch', *Australian and New Zealand Journal of Sociology*, 5: 14–31.

Blaikie, N. (1977) 'The meaning and measurement of occupational prestige', *Australian and New Zealand Journal of Sociology*, 13: 102–15.

Blaikie, N. (1978) 'Towards an alternative methodology for the study of occupational prestige: a reply to my reviewers', *Australian and New Zealand Journal of Sociology*, 14: 87–95.

Blaikie, N. (1979) *The Plight of the Australian Clergy: To Convert, Care or Challenge*. St Lucia, Qld: University of Queensland Press.

Blaikie, N. (1981) 'Occupational prestige and social reality', in P.C. Hiller (ed.), *Class and Inequality in Australia: Sociological Perspectives and Research*. Sydney: Harcourt Brace Jovanovich.

Blaikie, N. (1992) 'The nature and origins of ecological world views: an Australian study', *Social Science Quarterly*, 73: 144–65.

Blaikie, N. (1993a) *Approaches to Social Enquiry*. Cambridge: Polity Press.

Blaikie, N. (1993b) 'Education and environmentalism: ecological worldviews and environmentally responsible behaviour', *Australian Journal of Environmental Education*, 9: 1–20.

Blaikie, N. (2000) *Designing Social Research: The Logic of Anticipation*. Cambridge: Polity Press.

Blaikie, N. and Drysdale, M. (1994) 'Changes in ecological worldviews and environmentally responsible behaviour between 1989 and 1994: an Australian study'. Paper presented at the XIIIth World Congress of Sociology, Bielefeld, Germany, July.

Blaikie, N. and Ward, R. (1992) 'Ecological worldviews and environmentally responsible behaviour', *Sociale Wetenschappen*, 25: 40–63.

Blalock, H.M. (1964) *Causal Inference in Nonexperimental Research*. Chapel Hill, NC: University of North Carolina Press.

Bryman, A. and Cramer, D. (1997) *Quantitative Data Analysis with SPSS for Windows*. London: Routledge.

Campbell, D.T. and Stanley, J.C. (1963) *Experimental and Quasi-experimental Evaluations in Social Research*. Chicago: Rand-McNally.

Cohen, J. (1988) *Statistical Power Analysis for the Behavioral Sciences* (2nd edn). Hillsdale, NJ: Lawrence Erlbaum Associates.

Cook, T.D. and Campbell, D.T. (1979) *Quasi-experimentation: Design and Analysis Issues in Field Settings*. Chicago: Rand-McNally.

Cramer, D. (1994) *Introducing Statistics for Social Research*. London: Routledge.

de Vaus, D.A. (1995) *Surveys in Social Research* (4th edn). Sydney: Allen & Unwin.

Duncan, O.D. (1966) 'Path analysis: sociological examples', *American Journal of Sociology*, 72: 1–16.

Duncan, O.D. (1969) 'Contingencies in constructing causal models', in E.F. Borgatta (ed.), *Sociological Methodology 1969*. San Francisco: Jossey-Bass.

Dunlap, R.E. and van Liere, K.D. (1978) 'The "new environment paradigm": a proposed measuring instrument and preliminary results', *Journal of Environmental Education*, 9: 10–19.

Dunlap, R.E. and van Liere, K.D. (1984) 'Commitment to the dominant social paradigm and concern for environmental quality', *Social Science Quarterly*, 65: 1013–28.

Edwards, A.L. (1954) *Statistical Methods for the Behavioral Sciences*. New York: Holt, Rinehart and Winston.

Elifson, K., Runyon, R.P. and Haber, A (1998) *Fundamentals of Social Statistics* (3rd edn). Boston: McGraw-Hill.

Ester, P. and Seuren, B. (1992) 'Religion and environmental concern in Western Europe: a cross-cultural empirical analysis'. Paper presented at the International Conference on Current Developments in Environmental Sociology, Woudschoten, The Netherlands, July.

Field, A. (2000) *Discovering Statistics Using SPSS for Windows*. London: Sage.

Fielding, J.L. and Gilbert, G.N. (2000) *Understanding Social Statistics*. London: Sage.

Foddy, W.H. (1993) *Constructing Questions for Interviews and Questionnaires: Theory and Practice in Social Research*. Cambridge: Cambridge University Press.

Foster, J.J. (2001) *Data Analysis Using SPSS for Windows Versions 8–10: A Beginner's Guide*. London: Sage.

Freeman, L.C. (1965) *Elementary Applied Statistics*. New York: Wiley.

Freund, J.E. and Perles, B.M. (1999) *Statistics: A First Course* (7th edn). Upper Saddle River, NJ: Prentice Hall.

Gilbert, N. (1993) *Analyzing Tabular Data: Loglinear and Logistic Models for Social Researchers*. London: UCL Press.

Goldberger, A.S. and Duncan, O.D. (1973) *Structural Equation Modeling in the Social Sciences*. New York: Seminar Press.

Gorsuch, R.L. (1983) *Factor Analysis*. Hillsdale, NJ: Lawrence Erlbaum Associates.

Hair, J.F., Anderson, R.E., Tatham, R.L. and Black, W.C. (1998) *Multivariate Data Analysis* (5th edn). Upper Saddle River, NJ: Prentice Hall.

Harré, R. (1961) *Theories and Things*. London: Sheed & Ward.

Harré, R. (1970) *The Principles of Scientific Thinking*. London: Macmillan.

Harré, R. (1972) *The Philosophy of Science: An Introductory Survey*. London: Oxford University Press.

Harré, R. and Secord, P.F. (1972) *The Explanation of Social Behaviour*. Oxford: Blackwell.

Hayduk, L.A. (1996) LISREL: *Issues, Debates, and Strategies*. Baltimore, MD: Johns Hopkins University Press.

Hesse, D.R. (1969) 'Problems in path analysis and causal inference', in E.F. Borgatta (ed.), *Sociological Methodology 1969*. San Francisco: Jossey-Bass.

Huff, D. (1954) *How to Lie with Statistics*. New York: Norton.

Kaplan, D. (2000) *Structural Equation Modeling: Advanced Methods and Applications*. Thousand Oaks, CA: Sage.

Kelloway, E.K. (1998) *Using LISREL for Structural Equation Modeling*. Thousand Oaks, CA: Sage.

Kidder, L.H. and Judd, C.M. (1986) *Research Methods in Social Relations* (5th edn). New York: CBS Publishing.

Kim, J.-O. and Mueller, C.W. (1978a) *Introduction to Factor Analysis: What It Is and How to Do It*. Beverly Hills, CA: Sage.

Kim, J-O. and Mueller, C.W. (1978b) *Factor Analysis: Statistical Methods and Practical Issues*. Beverly Hills, CA: Sage.

Kish, L. (1965) *Survey Sampling*. New York: Wiley.

Labovitz, S. (1970) 'The nonutility of significance tests: the significance of tests of significance reconsidered', *Pacific Sociological Review*, 13: 141–48.

Land, K.C. (1969) 'Principles of path analysis,' in E.F. Borgatta (ed.), *Sociological Methodology 1969*. San Francisco: Jossey-Bass.

Lenski, G.E. (1961) *The Religious Factor*. Garden City, NY: Doubleday.

Lewis-Beck, M.S. (ed.) (1993) *Regression Analysis*. Thousand Oaks, CA: Sage.

Lewis-Beck, M.S. (ed.) (1994) *Factor Analysis and Related Techniques*. Thousand Oaks, CA: Sage.

Lind, D.A., Mason, R.D. and Marchal, W.G. (2000) *Basic Statistics for Business and Economics* (3rd edn). Boston: McGraw-Hill.

Maxim, P.S. (1999) *Quantitative Research Methods in the Social Sciences*. New York: Oxford University Press.

Merton, R.K. (1968) *Social Theory and Social Structure*. Glencoe, IL: Free Press.

Miles, J. and Shevlin, M. (2001) *Applying Regression and Correlation: A Guide for Students and Researchers*. London: Sage.

Mill, J.S. (1947) *A System of Logic*. London: Longmans, Green & Co.

Mills, C.W. (1959) *The Sociological Imagination*. New York: Oxford University Press.

Mol, J.J. (1971) *Religion in Australia*. Melbourne: Nelson.

Narayan, R.K. (1988) *A Writer's Nightmare: Selected Essays 1958–1988*. New Delhi: Penguin Books India.

Neuman, W.L. (2000) *Social Research Methods: Qualitative and Quantitative Approaches* (4th edn). Boston: Allyn & Bacon.

Pawson, R. (1989) *A Measure of Measures: A Manifesto for Empirical Sociology*. London: Routledge.

Pawson, R. (1995) 'Quality and quantity, agency and structure, mechanisms and contexts, dons and cons', *Bulletin de Méthodologie Sociologique*, 47: 5–48.

Pawson, R. (1996) 'Theorizing the interview', *British Journal of Sociology*, 47: 295–314.

Pawson, R. and Tilley, N. (1997) *Realistic Evaluation*. London: Sage.

Popper, K.R. (1959) *The Logic of Scientific Discovery*. London: Hutchinson.

Richmond, J.M. and Baumgart, N. (1981) 'A hierarchical analysis of environmental attitudes', *Journal of Environmental Education*, 13: 31–7.

Salkind, N.J. (2000) *Statistics for People Who (Think They) Hate Statistics*. Thousand Oaks, CA: Sage.

Scott, M. (1995) *Applied Logistic Regression Analysis*. Thousand Oaks, CA: Sage.

Selvin, H. (1957) 'A critique of tests of significance in survey research', *American Sociological Review*, 22: 519–27.

Siegel, A.F. (1994) *Practical Business Statistics* (2nd edn). Burr Ridge, IL: Irwin.

Siegel, S. (1956) *Nonparametric Statistics for the Behavioral Sciences*. New York: McGraw-Hill.

Siegel, S. and Castellan, N.J. (1988) *Nonparametric Statistics for the Behavioral Sciences*. Boston: McGraw-Hill.

Stern, P.C., Dietz, T. and Kalof, L. (1993) 'Value orientations, gender, and environmental concern', *Environment and Behavior*, 25: 322–48.

Stevens, J.P. (1992) *Applied Multivariate Statistics for the Social Sciences* (2nd edn). Hillsdale, NJ: Erlbaum.

Stewart, D.W. and Kamis, M.A. (1984) *Secondary Research Information Sources and Methods*. Beverly Hills, CA: Sage.

Weber, M. (1958) *The Protestant Ethic and the Spirit of Capitalism*. New York: Scribners.

Whewell, W. (1847) *The Philosophy of the Inductive Sciences*, 2 vols. London: Parker.

Wright, D.B. (1997) *Understanding Statistics: An Introduction for the Social Sciences*. London: Sage.

Index

Summary Chart of Methods

Measures of Central Tendency, Dispersion, Association, Influence and Tests of Significance

Type of analysis	Level of measurement		
	Nominal	Ordinal	Interval/ratio
Univariate descriptive	Central tendency: Mode Dispersion: Variation ratio	Central tendency: Median Dispersion: Interquartile range	Central tendency: Mean Dispersion: Standard deviation
Bivariate descriptive (association)	Contingency tables: (a) Three or more categories Cramér's *V* Contingency coefficient (C$_s$) (b) One or both dichotomous Phi	Contingency tables Gamma Kendall's *tau*-b Ordered items, small samples Spearman's *rho* Kendall's *tau*	Pearson's *r*
Explanatory (influence)	Contingency tables Lambda Three-way contingency tables Lambda Cramér's *V* or C$_s$ Means analysis Eta	Contingency tables Somer's *d* Three-way contingency tables Somer's *d* Gamma Means analysis Eta	Bivariate regression Partial correlation (trivariate) Multiple regression
Inferential (tests of significance)	Contingency tables Chi-square test *z* test for lambda Means analysis Two means: group *t* test More than two: *F* test	Contingency tables Chi-square test *z* test for gamma *z* test for Somer's *d*	*t* test for Pearson's *r* *t* test for R (regression)